Publishing in School Psychology and Related Fields

Publishing in School Psychology and Related Fields: An Insider's Guide aims to help students, early career professionals, and seasoned scholars alike better understand the process of peer review and publishing in journals, books, and other professional-oriented forums. Edited by a former editor of the *Journal of School Psychology* and containing chapters from insiders who have operated as productive authors, reviewers, and editors, this informative new resource contains practical and invaluable advice for anyone looking to increase their scholarly productivity and jump start their career.

Dr. Randy G. Floyd, PhD is a Professor of Psychology, Training Director for the School Psychology doctoral program, and Associate Chair in the Department of Psychology at the University of Memphis. He has contributed to more than 90 publications and is a former editor of the *Journal of School Psychology* (2010–2014).

Publishing in School Psychology and Related Fields
An Insider's Guide

Edited by
Randy G. Floyd

NEW YORK AND LONDON

First published 2018
by Routledge
711 Third Avenue, New York, NY 10017

and by Routledge
2 Park Square, Milton Park, Abingdon, Oxon, OX14 4RN

Routledge is an imprint of the Taylor & Francis Group, an informa business

©2018 Taylor & Francis

The right of Randy G. Floyd to be identified as the author of the editorial material, and of the authors for their individual chapters, has been asserted in accordance with sections 77 and 78 of the Copyright, Designs and Patents Act 1988.

All rights reserved. No part of this book may be reprinted or reproduced or utilized in any form or by any electronic, mechanical, or other means, now known or hereafter invented, including photocopying and recording, or in any information storage or retrieval system, without permission in writing from the publishers.

All references used were live at time of publication.

Trademark notice: Product or corporate names may be trademarks or registered trademarks, and are used only for identification and explanation without intent to infringe.

Library of Congress Cataloging-in-Publication Data
A catalog record for this book has been requested

ISBN: 978–1–138–64596–7 (hbk)
ISBN: 978–1–138–64599–8 (pbk)
ISBN: 978–1–315–62781–6 (ebk)

Typeset in Goudy
by Keystroke, Neville Lodge, Tettenhall, Wolverhampton

Dedications

To Kevin, for nurturing my emergent research and writing skills.

To Vinny and Bruce, for appointing me to serve on editorial boards early in my career.

To John H. and John K., for nurturing my emergent reviewing skills.

To Ed, for trusting in me to serve in important editorial positions.

Contents

List of Figures	xi
List of Tables	xiii
Acknowledgments	xv
List of Contributors	xvii

PART 1
Recommendations for Success in Writing and Publishing   1

1   Writing for Publication   3
RANDY G. FLOYD

2   Selecting the Optimal Journal Outlets   22
RANDY G. FLOYD

3   The Peer-Review Process and Responding to Reviewer
Feedback   45
RANDY G. FLOYD

4   Ethics in Manuscript Preparation, Publishing, and Dissemination   62
RANDY G. FLOYD

PART 2
Publishing in the School Psychology Generalist Journals   81

5   Publishing in the *Journal of School Psychology*   83
MICHELLE K. DEMARAY

6   Publishing in *Psychology in the Schools*   91
DAVID E. McINTOSH

viii *Contents*

7 Publishing in *School Psychology International* 97
AMITY L. NOLTEMEYER AND CAVEN S. McLOUGHLIN

8 Publishing in *School Psychology Quarterly* 105
SHANE R. JIMERSON AND RICHARD C. GILMAN

9 Publishing in *School Psychology Review* 113
AMY L. RESCHLY

10 Publishing in the *Canadian Journal of School Psychology* 119
DONALD H. SAKLOFSKE

11 Publishing in *Contemporary School Psychology* 127
MICHAEL R. HASS

12 Publishing in the *International Journal of School &
Educational Psychology* 133
RIK CARL D'AMATO AND YUAN YUAN WANG

13 Publishing in the *Journal of Applied School Psychology* 138
FRANK J. SANSOSTI

14 Publishing in *School Psychology Forum: Research in Practice* 145
OLIVER W. EDWARDS AND STEVEN R. SHAW

15 Publishing in *Trainers' Forum* 152
KELLY KENNEDY

PART 3
Publishing in Specialty Journals in School Psychology
and Related Fields 157

16 Publishing in Behavioral Research Journals 159
SCOTT P. ARDOIN AND KEVIN M. AYRES

17 Publishing in Assessment and Measurement Journals 169
MATTHEW R. REYNOLDS, CHRISTOPHER R. NIILEKSELA,
AND EMILY M. MEYER

18 Publishing in Educational Psychology and Education Journals 182
DANIEL H. ROBINSON

Contents ix

19 Publishing in Special Education and Literacy Journals 191
ELIZABETH B. MEISINGER AND MELISSA F. ROBINSON

20 Publishing in Clinical and Pediatric Journals 204
THOMAS J. POWER AND KATY E. TRESCO

21 Publishing in Developmental Psychology Journals 217
IBRAHIM H. ACAR AND KATHLEEN MORITZ RUDASILL

PART 4
Publishing in Other Outlets 227

22 Publishing in Professional Newsletters 229
ROSEMARY FLANAGAN, JOHN DESROCHERS, AND GREG MACHEK

23 Publishing Books 238
DAWN P. FLANAGAN AND MEGAN C. SY

24 Publishing Tests and Assessment Instruments 252
BRUCE A. BRACKEN

PART 5
Writing with Goals in Mind 263

25 Building Theory and Promoting Basic Science in School
Psychology Research 265
MATTHEW K. BURNS AND SHAWNA PETERSEN-BROWN

26 Writing for Research to Practice 276
SUSAN G. FORMAN AND CHRISTINA N. DIAZ

27 Engaging in Advocacy and Affecting Public Policy 289
FRANK C. WORRELL, RENA F. SUBOTNIK,
AND PAULA OLSZEWSKI-KUBILIUS

Index 303

Figures

2.1	Journal Impact Factor, 5-Year Impact Factor, and Immediacy Index for School Psychology Journals	38
2.2	CiteScore and Impact per Publication for School Psychology Journals	39
2.3	SCImago Journal Rank and Source Normalized Impact per Paper for School Psychology Journals	40
2.4	Eigenfactor Scores, Normalized Eigenfactor Scores, and Article Influence Score for School Psychology Journals	41
2.5	Articles Published in School Psychology Journals from 1996 to 2015	42

Tables

1.1	Prominent Books Focusing on Scholarly Writing and Their Content	4
1.2	A Checklist for Developing and Evaluating Research Manuscripts	10
1.3	Reference Management Software Programs and Their Costs and Features	12
2.1	Descriptive Information about the School Psychology Generalist Journals	23
2.2	Citation-Based Indices Indicating Journal Quality	33
3.1	An Example Journal Submission Letter Addressing Basic Features and Ethical Imperatives	47
3.2	The Initial Sections of an Example Letter Introducing Responses to Reviewers' Comments	55
3.3	Examples of Appropriate Responses to Reviewer Comments and Recommendations	57
4.1	Prominent Plagiarism Detection Programs and Their Costs and Features	68
4.2	Online Posting Policies of School Psychology Journals Obtained from the SHERPA/RoMEO Database	78
5.1	Journal Operations for the *Journal of School Psychology* in 2015	86
6.1	Editors of *Psychology in the Schools*	91
6.2	Journal Operations for Original Submissions to *Psychology in the Schools* in 2015	93
6.3	Journal Operations for All Submissions to *Psychology in the Schools* in 2015	94
7.1	Journal Operations for *School Psychology International* in 2015	99
7.2	Number and Percentage of Articles by Type for *School Psychology International* in 2015	99
7.3	Three Articles from 2015 that Represent *School Psychology International*'s Goals	100
8.1	Recent Special Topic Sections Featured in *School Psychology Quarterly*	108
8.2	Key Components of Special Topic Sections in *School Psychology Quarterly*	109

xiv *Tables*

8.3	Submission Status for 2015 Submissions to *School Psychology Quarterly*	109
9.1	Journal Operations for *School Psychology Review* in 2015	116
10.1	Journal Operations for *Canadian Journal of School Psychology* in 2015	122
11.1	Journal Operations for *Contemporary School Psychology* in 2015	129
12.1	Journal Operations for the *International Journal of School & Educational Psychology* in 2015	135
12.2	Articles Published in the *International Journal of School & Educational Psychology* in the First Issue of 2015	136
13.1	Journal Operations for the *Journal of Applied School Psychology* in 2015	141
14.1	Supplemental Materials: Opportunities for Innovative Formats and Presentation of Materials with *School Psychology Forum*	146
14.2	Journal Operations for *School Psychology Forum* in 2015	148
15.1	Journal Operations for *Trainers' Forum* in 2015	154
15.2	Decision Time in Days for Submissions to *Trainers' Forum* in 2015	154
16.1	Behavioral Research Journals that Publish Research Conducted by School Psychology Researchers and that Frequently Cite Work Published within School Psychology Journals	163
17.1	Specialty Journals Publishing Articles on Assessment	171
17.2	Specialty Journals Publishing Articles on Measurement	176
18.1	Impact Factor Values, Aims and Scope (Taken from Journal Websites), and Editor Email Addresses for the Top Ten Educational Psychology Journals (According to Me)	184
19.1	Journals Addressing Special Education	192
19.2	Journals Addressing Literacy	198
20.1	Clinical Journals	207
20.2	Pediatric Journals	210
20.3	Journals Targeting Specific Populations	213
21.1	Developmental Psychology Journals	219
23.1	Required Elements in a Book Proposal for Wiley and Routledge/Taylor & Francis Group	248
23.2	Required Elements in a Book Proposal for Guilford Press and Oxford University Press	249
26.1	Information Recommended for Inclusion in an Implications for Practice Subsection	281
27.1	Considerations When Writing to Advocate and Influence Policy	291
27.2	Non-Exhaustive List of Journals that Influence Policy in Education and Psychology	294

Acknowledgments

I am pleased to have been able to work with an amazing team of publishing insiders to develop this book. A total of 16 current journal and newsletter editors agreed to write about their publications, and another 26 scholars agreed to contribute chapters to enhance this book. All produced insightful chapters that were well beyond my expectations. I am grateful for them all.

I am appreciative of University of Memphis graduate students Patrick McNicholas and Jane Joyner for assistance in developing Chapters 1 and 3. Patrick assisted in the development of Table 1.3, which presented reference management programs, and Jane assisted in the development of Table 3.1, which presented plagiarism detection programs. In addition, Patrick reviewed Chapters 1 and 4 for me. In addition, my colleague in Memphis, Tom Fagan, allowed me to review his archives to obtain information about the history of school psychology journals and shared his vast knowledge with me. Finally, I appreciate Carmen McGuinness for assisting me in developing this book's index and coordinating review of page proofs by the authors.

I was fortunate to have eight generous scholars review preliminary versions of Chapters 2, 3, and 4. They included Michelle Demaray, Tanya Eckert, Ryan Farmer, Sally Grapin, Bryn Harris, Renee Hawkins, Amanda Sullivan, and Ethan Van Norman. I was able to improve those chapters based on their rich feedback, but I accept that misstatements in those chapters are fully my own.

My daughter, Sophie Floyd, aided me in designing the cover of this book. She told me, as only a teenager can, "Well thanks, Dad, for trying to engage me in working on your book." Thank you, Sophie.

I am also thankful for Chris Teja, an editor formerly of Routledge, for supporting my proposal to write this book. I am sorry that I was unable to work with him to produce it. In the same vein, I appreciated Elizabeth Graber's support during the final stages of editing the book before her departure as editor. Most notably, I appreciate Amanda Devin, who joined Routledge as editor in time to review and publish this book, and Emma Star who assisted in the process. At Keystroke, Rachel Carter exercised superb attention to detail in copyediting all of the book's chapters, tables, and figures, while

xvi *Acknowledgments*

Kelly-Jayne Winter and Maggie Lindsey-Jones monitored the copyediting, typesetting, and proofreading procedures to maintain a brisk pace toward publication. In addition, Geraldine Lyons completed the final proofreading of the penultimate version of this book. I appreciate them all. Finally, I thank Anna Moore, Senior Editor at Routledge, who was always available to answer my questions.

Contributors

Ibrahim H. Acar	Istanbul Medipol University
Scott P. Ardoin	University of Georgia
Kevin M. Ayres	University of Georgia
Bruce A. Bracken	College of William and Mary
Matthew K. Burns	University of Missouri
Rik Carl D'Amato	Chicago School of Professional Psychology
Michelle K. Demaray	Northern Illinois University
John Desrochers	William James College
Christina N. Diaz	Rutgers, The State University of New Jersey
Oliver W. Edwards	University of Central Florida
Dawn P. Flanagan	St. John's University
Rosemary Flanagan	Touro College
Randy G. Floyd	The University of Memphis
Susan G. Forman	Rutgers, The State University of New Jersey
Richard C. Gilman	Cincinnati Children's Hospital Medical Center, University of Cincinnati Medical School
Michael R. Hass	Chapman University
Shane R. Jimerson	University of California, Santa Barbara
Kelly Kennedy	Chapman University
Greg Machek	University of Montana
David E. McIntosh	Ball State University
Caven S. Mcloughlin	Kent State University
Elizabeth B. Meisinger	University of Memphis
Emily M. Meyer	University of Kansas
Christopher R. Niileksela	University of Kansas
Amity L. Noltemeyer	Miami University
Paula Olszewski-Kubilius	Northwestern University
Shawna Petersen-Brown	Minnesota State University, Mankato
Thomas J. Power	The Children's Hospital of Philadelphia, Perelman School of Medicine of University of Pennsylvania
Amy L. Reschly	University of Georgia
Matthew R. Reynolds	University of Kansas

xviii *Contributors*

Daniel H. Robinson	The University of Texas at Arlington
Melissa F. Robinson	University of Memphis
Kathleen Moritz Rudasill	University of Nebraska-Lincoln
Donald H. Saklofske	University of Western Ontario
Frank J. Sansosti	Kent State University
Steven R. Shaw	McGill University
Rena F. Subotnik	American Psychological Association
Megan C. Sy	St. John's University
Katy E. Tresco	Philadelphia College of Osteopathic Medicine
Yuan Yuan Wang	Wuhan University
Frank C. Worrell	University of California, Berkeley

Part 1

Recommendations for Success in Writing and Publishing

1 Writing for Publication

Randy G. Floyd

You are probably picking up this book as a student, an early career scholar, or a more seasoned professional who is looking for ways to improve your writing skills and motivation to write. Alternately, you might be a university professor who is seeking to enhance your ability to instruct and mentor students in building their writing skills. In both cases, it is clear to you that scholarly productivity is vital to your success. Like me, you might have found that being a productive writer was not addressed adequately during your undergraduate and graduate training experiences. In addition, you might have found that writing excellence was not modeled well by your advisors and mentors. Furthermore, you might have been unable to identify one go-to resource covering writing for publication. To address these common limitations, this chapter establishes a framework for success in publishing not only journal articles but also book chapters, books, newsletter articles, and tests that are addressed in other chapters in this book.

In 2015, I contributed a blog post to the School Psychology Early Career Forum, sponsored by the Society for the Study of School Psychology and coordinated by Dr. Amanda Sullivan, Dr. Bryn Harris, and Dr. Robert Volpe. In this blog post (https://ssspresearch.org/earlycareerforum/foundations-successful-scholarship-school-psychology), I outlined ten recommendations for successful scholarship. In this chapter, I have expanded upon those recommendations most closely addressing writing for publication. The bulk of the chapter features how to be a "student of the game" by consuming and relying on available resources. I also briefly emphasize other key strategies, including identifying and protecting when and where you write best, spending sufficient time engaged in writing, using your experiences as a foundation for your writing, and finding your publishing niche. Throughout this chapter (and into the next two chapters), I have referenced many compelling books focused on publishing in psychology and other fields, and I have highlighted some of the most useful ones in Table 1.1. Reading these books will amplify the content of this chapter.

Table 1.1 Prominent Books Focusing on Scholarly Writing and Their Content

Day and Gastel (2015). *How to Write and Publish a Scientific Paper.* Includes eight sections: "Some Preliminaries" addresses scientific writing, ethics, and manuscript submissions. "Preparing the Text" and "Preparing Tables and Figures" address titles, standard sections of research manuscripts, and tables and figures. "Publishing the Paper" addresses rights and permission, submission of manuscripts, and the review and publication process. "Doing Other Writing For Publication" addresses writing review papers, book chapters, and publications for broad audiences. "Conference Communications" addresses presenting orally, presenting posters, and writing conference reports. "Scientific Style" addresses grammar and word choice. "Other Topics" addresses writing a thesis, preparing curricula vitae, grant proposals, and recommendation letters; and engaging in peer review.

Henson (2016). *Writing for Publication: Road to Academic Advancement.* Addresses writing habits, identifying writing topics, writing style, conducting literature searches, communicating with journal editors, and developing book and grant proposals.

Jalongo and Saracho (2016). *Transitions and Tools that Support Scholars' Success.* Includes three sections: "Professional Roles and Publishing Writing" addresses challenges to writing productivity and strategies to overcome them. "Conference Proposals and Article Types" addresses professional presentations, transforming projects to publications, and publishing research articles. "Writing as Professional Development" addresses developing books, maximizing productivity, and developing expertise.

Johnson and Mullen (2007). *Write to the Top: How to Become a Prolific Academic.* Addresses establishing the habit of writing, being disciplined, promoting writing "flow," employing an adaptive mindset and motivational strategies, collaborating and engaging in mentor relationships, and planning and revising your writing. Includes 65 recommendations.

Nicol and Pexman (2010a). *Displaying Your Findings: A Practical Guide for Creating Figures, Posters, and Presentations.* Addresses formatting of 11 types of figures (e.g., histograms and pie graphs) and provides models of correctly formatted figures.

Nicol and Pexman (2010b). *Presenting Your Findings: A Practical Guide for Creating Tables.* Addresses formatting of tables of results from 20 statistical analyses (e.g., correlations, multiple regression) as well as word tables. Provides models of correctly formatted tables.

Silvia (2007). *How to Write a Lot: A Practical Guide to Productive Writing.* Addresses barriers to productive writing, motivational tools, writing with the support of others, writing style, and the development of journal articles and books.

Silvia (2015). *Write It Up: Practical Strategies for Writing and Publishing Journal Articles.* Includes three sections: "Planning and Prepping" addresses selecting journals, writing basics, and collaboration. "Writing the Article" addresses standard manuscript sections. "Publishing your Writing" addresses the publication process and career development.

R. Sternberg and K. Sternberg (2016). *The Psychologist's Companion.* Includes three sections: "Planning and Formulating Papers" addresses writing misconceptions about writing, writing to influence, writing literature reviews and research papers, and ethics. "Presenting Your Ideas in Writing" addresses writing basics. "Presenting Yourself to Others" addresses poster presentations, book and grant proposals, class lectures, and job talks.

Writing is Hard—and Complicated

I like this quote from Silvia (2007, p. 4) that highlights the challenges of writing by referencing other elements of the research enterprise:

> If you do research, you probably enjoy it. Research is oddly fun. Talking about ideas and finding ways to test your ideas is intellectually gratifying. Data collection is enjoyable, too, especially when other people do it for you. Even data analysis is fun—it's exciting to see if a study worked. But writing about research isn't fun: Writing is frustrating, complicated, and un-fun. "If you find that writing is hard," wrote William Zinsser (2001), "it's because it *is* hard" (p. 12, emphasis in original).

Silvia is undoubtedly correct about the challenge of writing, but it is my hope that this chapter, and the resources linked to it, make writing far less challenging than it would otherwise be.

When most people think about writing, they think about generating words on a page (or in a document), but this conception of the writing process is too narrow. Writing is far more complicated than that, and this complexity, in part, is why writing is so hard to do. Most prominent models of the writing process (e.g., Bereiter & Scardamalia, 1987; Hayes, 1996; Hayes & Flower, 1980; Kellogg, 1994) describe at least three general stages of writing. At their most basic, these stages can be defined as *pre-drafting*, *drafting*, and *post-drafting*. (Notice I am not referring to "writing" in describing each stage, as some models do. To me, describing a stage in the process of writing as "writing" seems imprecise. Referring to "drafting" instead also takes some of the pressure off me; my drafts—by definition—need not be perfect!) Pre-drafting includes collecting, reading, and interpreting source material; taking notes; planning what to write (including outlining); and completing other steps that enable the generation and organization of text. Drafting includes the production of words and sentences, which is sometimes called text generation. Finally, post-drafting includes reflecting on and revising preliminary text that was drafted as well as formatting and proofing the text.

Pre-Drafting

For maximal productivity, I encourage writers to think about the stages of writing as being independent yet part of an interactive and iterative process. What follows are some examples about what I mean regarding the interplay across these stages. During pre-drafting, my first steps might be to open a document; add a title page, standard section headings, and corresponding page breaks; and save the document using a pithy title and the current date. I might then find the institutional review board (IRB) proposal I wrote before collecting data for the study and paste in content (e.g., the study title and the description of the procedures). I might also add a header and page numbers to the document. I might then develop outlines of sections of the manuscript

6 *Randy G. Floyd*

using prominent reporting standard guidelines (see the Structure and Content section later in this chapter) or online instructions to authors offered by the journal to which I plan to submit the manuscript (see Chapter 3, Floyd). My document is messy, but the basic structure of the manuscript is there.

With this structure in place, I might then turn to specific sections of the manuscript to engage in additional pre-drafting strategies. For example, I might complete data analysis to obtain basic statistics addressing study participants, paste in the output table from the analysis program in the document, extract the specific information I need (e.g., frequency and percentage data) for each variable of interest, delete the output table, and then end my writing session for the day. With this content available to me when I return, I will be able to translate those data I previously included in the document into complete sentences describing the participants. Other pre-drafting strategies are less closely linked to text generation. For example, I might spend several days reading articles, taking notes, pasting quotes from articles into the document (with quotation marks and page numbers associated with them!) until I reach an information-saturation point. Then, I might use what I have created to organize my Introduction in subsections; thus, I would reorganize the notes that are in my document. Once subsections have been reasonably conceptualized, I can return to the information I have collected to guide my drafting of text. In terms of matching my alertness and mood to a stage of writing, I feel like I can engage in most pre-drafting strategies even when I am the most fatigued and my thinking is discombobulated. Thus, even when I am at my worse, I can still enable my drafting of text through application of pre-drafting strategies.

Drafting

During the drafting phase, text generation should be conceived as unbridled production of words and sentences—without concern for spelling, cohesion, or formatting. (You can fix all those problems during the post-drafting stage!) While drafting, I know that my goal is to express important themes, concepts, and relationships (even if my main points are—at best—half-baked). Sometimes, I need creative strategies to organize and motivate myself to generate text. For example, when developing a portion of my Introduction section, I imagine that I must lecture to a class or answer a question about a narrow topic in order to generate the groundwork for the text. I think, "What would I say if I had to summarize what I know at this very moment?" Strategies such as this one help remove the impossible standard of writing a perfect, scholarly paragraph addressing the body of evidence on a topic.

In the same vein, I tell myself to "get ideas down on paper," knowing I can provide more details—"science it up" or "scholarize it"—and edit it carefully at a later point. For example, when developing a Results section, I might review my analysis output and write, in general and layperson's terms, what the key findings are. After generating that text, I can, in the post-drafting phase, refine the text structure describing the findings and add the details to support the findings (e.g., statistics for F and p). Sometimes, these production strategies produce only bullet points, telegraphic speech, and text that is one level better than a word salad; however, I often find that when I encounter this poorly constructed text during my next writing session, it allows me to move forward with refining the text and generating additional text. (On some rare occasions, it really is garbage, though!) In contrast to pre-drafting, I feel like drafting requires me to be at a higher state of alertness and in a more positive emotional state. Although I have gotten better over the years at forcing myself to draft text even when I am nowhere near my best, I feel confident that my clearest, most insightful text (albeit still highly flawed) is drafted when I am closer to a peak emotional state. (Truth be told, this state is often positively correlated with caffeine consumption.)

Post-Drafting

Post-drafting is often neglected when we think about the writing process, and many emerging writers have the notion that the editing strategies used during this stage (e.g., revising, formatting, and proofing) are those that they cannot do—or do well. Rather, they hope that someone else will do it for them. Although graduate students and early career scholars, for example, might benefit greatly from having more experienced researchers review and edit their writing (another smart strategy), they should, with practice, be able to edit most of the time on their own. Overall, the goals of revising, formatting, and proofing are to polish your manuscript so that it is of the highest quality.

The best writers are not those who only draft text well. Instead, the best writers are those who revise their text again and again until their message is clear and consistent. Their clarity and consistency in conveying their message are evident both within sentences and across connected sentences (i.e., evidencing local cohesion) as well as across paragraphs within a section of the manuscript and across sections of the manuscript as a whole (i.e., evidencing global cohesion). Thus, the best writers strive to get into the heads of readers and revise their text so that readers will see the patterns they want to highlight through their text. Revising is an incredibly complex process, but it always involves careful rereading and reworking of the text previously generated. As such, revising requires a high state of alertness and a positive emotional state.

After all your text has been revised and is reasonably clear and cohesive, you are often at the point where formatting must be emphasized. If you have, all along, organized your manuscript according to recommended standards and drafted text while relying on formatting conventions (e.g., with at least rough in-text citations and page numbers for quotations), this emphasis on formatting should not be difficult. Now is the time, however, to review in-text citations, references, word usage, headings, and so forth. Although formatting should be reviewed while proofing, I recommend devoting time to it ahead of reading your manuscript for meaning.

8   *Randy G. Floyd*

Finally, proofing is tedious, as you evaluate your refined text for grammar, punctuation, clarity, and cohesion. On the other hand, proofing requires a different mindset and a different set of skills than revising and formatting. Again, I cannot proof well when I am not at my best. I will explicitly address proofing strategies later in this chapter.

Be a Student of the Game by Consuming and Relying on Helpful Resources

Our research in the late 2000s and early 2010s revealed the importance of manuscript construction to journal editors and reviewers contributing to the peer-review process. For example, when editors were asked why they rejected manuscripts without full review by peer reviewers (see Chapter 3, Floyd), about 40% said that it was because the manuscripts were poorly written and poorly formatted (Floyd et al., 2011). As a journal editor, I saw this pattern frequently; many manuscript submissions were not formatted according to the journal recommendations and failed to meet basic expectations for organizing information in a manuscript. Clearly, surface-level features of manuscripts are not ignored by editors. Our research also demonstrated that reviewers fully expected manuscript authors "to produce high-quality research reports that provide appropriate details about their studies, report all the components prescribed by recent manuscript preparation guidelines . . . and in general, write well" (Albers, Floyd, Fuhrmann, & Martinez, 2011, p. 683).

Authors should take the perspective that many elements of manuscript preparation are highly scripted, and this contention is consistent with what we learned from some of the most productive individuals in the field of school psychology. According to Martinez, Floyd, and Erichsen (2011, p. 704):

> Highly productive scholars approach writing in a very practical way and several disclosed that they have "discover[ed] the 'template' necessary for writing quality research-based articles." Indeed, one highly productive scholar has been successful in his research career by "looking for formulaic ways to construct a manuscript based on articles already published in [a particular] journal."

The sections that follow address some of these elements.

Structure and Content

It makes sense to build your manuscripts from the bottom up, to compartmentalize content, and to fill those sections with relevant details. As all undergraduate psychology majors and many others have been taught to write papers following the Introduction, Method, Results, and Discussion (IMRAD) format (Day & Gastel, 2015), the vast majority of journals in the field of psychology will require the same general format. Some journals might alter the names of the sections (referring to Materials and Methods) or add additional sections (including Conclusions), but the same structure is apparent across them. Thus, the IMRAD format is the foundation for the vast majority of research manuscripts you will develop; it is wise to employ this underlying structure during the pre-drafting stage.

The ubiquity of the IMRAD format means that there are numerous resources available that guide emerging scholars to develop the relevant sections and remind more experienced authors what they might be omitting to the detriment of their manuscripts. For example, the *Publication Manual of the American Psychological Association* (APA, 2010) devotes most of its second chapter to this structure and provides 19 pages of examples from a sample manuscript. Of the books included in Table 1.1, Day and Gastel (2015) and Silvia (2015) include entire chapters devoted to each manuscript section and its typical content.

Several checklists have been offered to guide writers in structuring and evaluating manuscripts (e.g., Henson, 2016; Joireman & Van Lange, 2015; Onwuegbuzie & Daniel, 2005). One of my favorites is from R. Sternberg and K. Sternberg (2016), which includes 20 items ranging from those addressing the adequacy of the sample size and appropriateness of statistical tests to items related to authorship order and proofing. During my time as editor of *Journal of School Psychology*, several of my colleagues (including Dr. Michelle Demaray and Dr. Craig Enders) discussed developing a checklist to aid evaluation of manuscripts submitted to the journal. Although this checklist was never implemented during the journal's review process, the content of Table 1.2 represents many of the key elements we discussed. Because the checklist should apply to a wide variety of research studies, I recommend referencing it during the pre-drafting and post-drafting stages of writing.

Seeing the need for improved reporting of information about randomized controlled trials, medical journal editors (Moher, Schulz, & Altman, 2001; Standards of Reporting Trials Group, 1994) developed the Consolidated Standards of Reporting Trials (CONSORT) statement (www.consort-statement.org/), which became the model for all subsequent reporting standards. Following its dissemination, the American Educational Research Association (AERA; 2006) offered standards for reporting research studies in education. Soon afterward, the APA's Working Group on Journal Article Reporting Standards (2008) published its own Journal Article Reporting Standards (JARS), and they have been widely propagated. These JARS were incorporated into the most recent *Publication Manual of the American Psychological Association* (APA, 2010) as an appendix, and a book by Cooper (2011) was published that delineated the content of the JARS in more detail. The subtitle of APA's JARS is "Information Recommended for Inclusion in Manuscripts That Report New Data Collections Regardless of Research Design" (APA, 2010, p. 247). As such, the JARS include descriptions of specific content that should be included on the manuscript title page and in the abstract and Introduction, Method, Results, and Discussion sections.

10 Randy G. Floyd

Table 1.2 A Checklist for Developing and Evaluating Research Manuscripts

INTRODUCTION
- Is there a compelling rationale for the study based on prior research and theory?
- Does the study have the potential to inform science, practice, or policy?
- Was prior relevant research accurately summarized?
- Were research questions or hypotheses offered?

METHOD
- Were participants described thoroughly?
- Was information reported about how participants (or schools) were recruited? Was participation rate reported?
- Was information about how data were collected—how, when, and where researchers interacted with participants to obtain data—reported?
- Were the measurement instruments used in the study described thoroughly?
- Were the measurement instruments supported by reliability and validity evidence from prior research or results from the current sample?
- If participants completed multiple instruments, was information about order of completion (or techniques designed to control for them, such as counterbalancing) reported?

RESULTS
- Was there mention of missing data or missing data handling? Do statistics that reveal information about sample sizes (e.g., df values) indicate that the sample size was constant?
- Is a multilevel data structure apparent? If so, how has it been handled?
- If statistical significance testing was used, was an a priori alpha level selected and interpreted correctly?
- Were results presented in a manner that was consistent with the purpose of the study and the research questions or hypotheses offered in the Introduction?
- Were results presented in text clearly aligned with the content of tables and figures?
- Were tables and figures (including titles and captions) sufficiently developed to stand alone?

DISCUSSION
- Were the results accurately summarized in a manner consistent with the purpose of the study, research questions, or hypotheses?
- Were new findings compared to and contrasted with prior research (cited in the Introduction)?
- Were study limitations addressed?
- Were implications for science, practice, or policy addressed?

Consistent with the pattern established by the CONSORT statement (Moher et al., 2001), additional reporting standards devoted to specific research methods have proliferated. The CONSORT statement has since been revised (Schulz, Altman, Moher, & the CONSORT Group, 2010), and APA's Working Group on Journal Article Reporting Standards (2008) offered additional elements of its JARS that address experimental or intervention studies. APA (2008) also produced the Meta-Analysis Reporting

Standards (MARS), and Liberati et al. (2009) offered the Preferred Reporting Items for Systematic Reviews and Meta-Analyses (PRISMA, www.prisma-statement.org/PRISMAStatement/Default.aspx). There are also reporting standards for diagnostic accuracy studies (Bossuyt et al., 2015, www.stard-statement.org/), single-case research studies (Tate et al., 2016), structural equation modeling studies (Hoyle & Isherwood, 2013), and qualitative research studies (O'Brien, Harris, Beckman, Reed, & Cook, 2014; Tong, Sainsbury, & Craig, 2007), among others. Most of these reporting standards are cataloged on the Enhancing the QUAlity and Transparency Of health Research (EQUATOR) network webpage (www.equator-network.org/). Copies of these standards are offered in multiple languages, including English, Spanish, and Portuguese.

In addition to the reporting standards focusing on specific research methods, lists of reporting standards addressing specific statistical analyses have been published. For example, Hancock and Mueller's (2010) *The Reviewer's Guide to Quantitative Methods in the Social Sciences* includes 31 chapters covering statistical analyses ranging from correlations and ANOVAs to latent class analysis and survival analysis. Each chapter includes an overview of the statistical analysis as well as a detailed list of the elements associated with the analysis that should be reported in research publications. I find this book, despite its title, more helpful to me as a researcher and author than as a reviewer. Not only can its lists guide the design of studies and analysis, but they also can assist writers in determining what information should be included in each section (i.e., IMRAD) of the manuscript. I understand that a second edition of this book will be published soon. In summary, researchers have truly never had better resources available to assist them in reporting sufficient details about their method and analysis in manuscripts.

Managing References

Many writers (like me) spend countless hours finagling with in-text citations and references appearing at the end of manuscripts. Authors who write in the same topic area are easily able to reuse references across their manuscripts, but it is far more challenging for beginning authors or when exploring a new research domain. This citing and referencing should not interfere with the drafting of text; in fact, it should be addressed in one of the final stages of the writing process.

Numerous well-developed reference management software programs are available to make handling of references much easier. Table 1.3 summarizes the characteristics of ten of these programs. Based on my discussions with others, I believe that Mendeley and EndNote might be the most widely used in psychology. I encourage emerging scholars to adopt one of these programs to reduce the burden of formatting in-text citations and references and increase writing productivity. More seasoned authors (like me) should write smarter and adopt one of these programs, too.

Table 1.3 Reference Management Software Programs and Their Costs and Features

Program and website	Cost	Platform	Features
Citavi www.citavi.com	Free for projects up to 100 references. $119–$949 across seven account options.	MS Windows, can be used in a virtual machine on Linux or Mac OS X.	Account required. Data saved locally or on intranet server. Search databases from interface. Create tasks to return to later.
Docear www.docear.org	Free.	Cross-platform	Utilizes "literature suite" concept for mind mapping, PDF annotation import, file management, and academic search engine.
EasyBib www.easybib. com	Free. Premium service available for ~$10/month.	Online	Provides citation, note-taking, and research tools via browser.
EndNote http://endnote. com	Free basic web version. ~$250–$299 for EndNote X8.	Microsoft Windows, Mac OS X	Account required. Search references and organize downloads. Annotate PDFs.
JabRef www.jabref.org	Free.	Cross-platform	Provides citation, note-taking, and research tools. Plug-ins and add-ons to integrate into web browser for searching and importing PDFs.
Mendeley https://www. mendeley.com	Free. Additional storage space available for $5–$15.	Cross-platform	Account required. Free online storage up to 2 GB. Desktop and web program available for sharing papers, discovering data, and collaborating online.
ReadCube www.readcube. com	Free desktop and mobile app. Cloud storage $5/ month or $55/ year.	MS Windows. MacOS & iOS.	Account required. Desktop (Mac/PC) and web components available. Provides personalized recommendations, private group sharing, integrated web search, and enhanced PDF reader.
RefWorks https://refworks. proquest.com	$100/year. Sometimes offered through universities.	Online	Account required. Online research management, writing, and collaboration tool. Gather, manage, store, and share information and generate citations and bibliographies.

Program and website	Cost	Platform	Features
Sorc'd http:// marketing.sorcd. com	Free. ~$15/ month, ~$125/ year for premium. $20/month for business.	Online	Account required. Public cloud sharing with availability online. Integrate with Microsoft Office and Google Docs using the appropriate add-in or add-on.
Zotero www.zotero.org	Free. Online storage free up to 300 MB; more storage space available for fee.	Cross-platform	Account required. Firefox extension or stand-alone with connectors for Chrome and Safari. Web-based access to reference library available.

During the past decade, journals have been increasingly requiring authors to include digital object identifiers (DOIs) at the end of their references. In fact, the *Publication Manual of the American Psychological Association, Sixth Edition* (APA, 2010) states that they are required. Although many journals in school psychology do not require DOIs, some do. On at least one occasion, I have been asked by an editor to add DOIs to all my references when I had included none. In that case, I turned to Crossref (https://doi.crossref.org/simpleTextQuery) to obtain them. Using Crossref, I pasted in my references (and many at a time), and it produced the DOIs for each reference. Crossref is a highly reliable method to obtain DOIs for older articles that do not have DOIs printed in their pages. Again, writers should not stress about these DOIs in the early stages of the writing process. They are relatively trivial and can be added after revising text and while focusing on manuscript formatting.

Writing Well

When we asked some of the most productive scholars in school psychology to provide us the titles of published resources that were most helpful to them in their research and writing, only two resources addressing manuscript construction were offered more than once. Five scholars cited the *Publication Manual of the American Psychological Association, Sixth Edition* (APA, 2010), and I agree that its content should be the foundation of your writing repertoire. It is possible that many writers naively believe that it should be consulted only to aid in referencing and formatting a manuscript, but it contains so much more. For example, its chapter titled "Writing Clearly and Concisely" addresses manuscript organization, writing style, grammar, word usage, and methods to reduce bias in writing. The chapter "The Mechanics of Style" drills down even deeper to address use of punctuation, preferred spelling, capitalization rules, fonts (including italics), abbreviations, and reporting quantitative results.

14 *Randy G. Floyd*

As a heads up, you should know that almost all of this content is accessible via a quick internet search. Most frequently, I Google by keywords (e.g., "while vs. whereas APA style"), which typically leads me to the APA style blog (http://blog.apastyle.org/apastyle/), the Purdue Online Writing Lab (https://owl.english.purdue.edu/owl/), and Grammar Girl's page (www.quickanddirtytips.com/education/grammar). Accessing this reliable information online saves me a ton of time.

The second book suggested by school psychology's highly productive scholars was Strunk and White's (1999) *The Elements of Style*, which was first published in 1920 and is now in its fourth edition. Its approximately 100 pages contain rules for word usage, principles of composition, and pithy reminders to writers. It remains an accessible and insightful read after almost 100 years in print. Recently, renowned psycholinguist and popular science writer, Steven Pinker, released *A Sense of Style: The Thinking Person's Guide to Writing in the 21st Century* (2014), which united traditional (but largely idiosyncratic) writing rules with research findings from cognitive science to produce what is the most evidence based of all writing style guides. It is lengthy (3.5 times the length of *Elements*), and the content is challenging, focusing on esoteric terms for parts of speech, syntax rules, and cohesion markers, but if you can digest its main points and follow its examples, you will see dramatic improvements in your writing clarity and develop an enhanced writing style.

To improve the clarity of their writing, writers should also be familiar with Plain Language guidelines and resources to support them (www.plainlanguage.gov/index.cfm). Following the Plain Writing Act of 2010, United States federal agencies must make government documents accessible to readers. To support this Act, a website was developed to provide resources, tools, and examples to improve writing clarity. For example, under Tips and Tools, the Word Suggestions page (www.plainlanguage.gov/howto/wordsuggestions/index.cfm) includes the following points:

- "Simple words help you express your message clearly. Too many complex words are like hurdles in a race, slowing readers down."
- "Replacing complex words with simpler words lets your readers concentrate on your content. Using simple and familiar words where possible doesn't insult your readers' intelligence but emphasizes clarity rather than formality. Save longer or complex words for when they are essential."
- "Foreign words, jargon, and abbreviations may detract from the clarity of your writing. Readers often skip over terms they don't understand, hoping to get their meaning from the rest of the sentence. Readers complain about jargon more than any other writing fault. Every profession, trade, and organization has its own specialized terms. While we all complain about jargon, everyone writes it. We hate everyone else's jargon, but we love our own."
- "Plain language does not ban jargon and other specialist terms. But you need to understand your readers and match your language to their needs."

Apparently, the clearest writers write simply. Thus, we can all benefit from applying the Natural Language guidelines in our professional writing.

I was first exposed to *The Psychologist's Companion* (R. Sternberg & K. Sternberg, 2016) as an undergraduate, and I have loved it ever since. In particular, I am fond of chapter 7, which addresses how to improve the clarity of your writing, apply APA style, and use proper grammar. Chapter 8 is even better, as it lists commonly misused words. It is the nontechnical words, such as *that* and *which*, *affect* and *effect*, and *data* and *datum* that warrant study by emerging writers and review by those more seasoned. Reviewing and internalizing rules presented in *The Psychologist's Companion* will improve the quality of text you draft as well as your editing skills.

Recently, I encountered two online resources that emerging authors should review (Day & Gastel, 2015). They include the Manchester Academic Phrasebank (www.phrasebank.manchester.ac.uk/), which is, in many ways, like a thesaurus for turns of phrase used in professional writing. In particular, this resource provides guidance and wording for text included in all the major sections of a professional research manuscript (i.e., IMRAD). Furthermore, it provides numerous other suggestions for comparing and contrasting, applying criticism, offering examples, and marking transitions. The second resource of this type, AuthorAID (www.authoraid.info/en/), is far more expansive. According to its website, "AuthorAID is a global network that provides support, mentoring, resources and training for researchers in developing countries." The website includes links to news, funding sources, training events, and resources. Resources related to writing skills include papers addressing writing review articles, preparing the IMRAD sections of a manuscript, language editing services, and publishing ethics. Resources are mostly written in English, but a substantial number of others are written in Chinese. To me, what is most impressive about AuthorAID is that it facilitates a mentoring and collaboration program that links emerging researchers with mentors and with peers.

Editing

Many authors fail to devote sufficient effort to manuscript review and proofing during the post-drafting stage. They often pay the price for not doing so. They might find that chapter 12 of *The Psychologist's Companion* (R. Sternberg & K. Sternberg, 2016), titled "How to Make Your Article Even Better: Proofreading, Revising, and Editing" will enhance their skills in editing. It includes recommendations for checking for typos and structural errors in text, distancing themselves from what they have written, and writing with referees and readers in mind.

As an editor, I often found substantial inconsistencies in reviewing manuscripts that were in their final stages of peer review. First, there were frequent discrepancies between text and tables. For example, a summary of findings from correlations between variables in a Results section would be

16   *Randy G. Floyd*

inconsistent with the actual results presented in the correlation matrix within a table. These errors are serious but challenging to identify considering the structure of a standard manuscript, which places tables (and figures) at the end of the manuscript—dissociated from the text that describes their content. Thus, I highly recommend that authors review tables and figures in print copy form (or on another screen) when writing and completing final edits to the Results and Discussion sections. Peer reviewers should do the same when evaluating manuscripts.

Second, across lengthy (35- to 40-page) manuscripts, with text authored by several co-authors, it was common to see numerous terms used for the same characteristic or idea. Such potential errors are manifold across sections of a manuscript (e.g., referring to participants by gender-related terms in the Method section and by sex-related terms in Results), and such errors jeopardize global cohesion. All writers experience such challenges as there are numerous alternate terms used for most phenomena. In my own writing, my colleagues and I often alternate between interchangeable terms, such as "intelligence test" and "IQ test" as well as "factors" and "latent variables," when we should be using only a single term in each pair. To address this problem, you must decide on which term is the optimal one and remove others. Using the Find and Replace functions in word processing programs such as Microsoft Word is highly useful in achieving this goal, but careful editing (as described next) should also be undertaken.

In preparing a chapter focusing on writing psychoeducational assessment reports (Kranzler & Floyd, 2013), we reviewed the literature on proofing strategies. Although psychoeducational reports are not held to the same standards of scholarship as research manuscripts, some of our recommendations for proofing are relevant to all authors as they move from electronic evaluation, to editing on the computer screen, and to reviewing a hard copy of the manuscript. First, you should

> take advantage of electronic text analysis functions in your word processing program. For example, first use the Spelling and Grammar functions in Microsoft Word or other word-processing programs. In particular, you should make sure that you select the box "Use contextual spelling" to identify potential errors associated with homophone use (e.g., using *there* vs. *their*) in Microsoft Word in Word Options. However, if you do not uncheck the boxes in Word Options to "Ignore words in UPPERCASE" and "Ignore words that contain numbers" when checking for spelling errors, you may overlook a spelling error involving an acronym or test abbreviation. You should definitely uncheck them.
>
> (Kranzler & Floyd, 2013, p. 142)

Second, you should read through the manuscript on the screen. At this time, you should "proofread both for content errors and for mechanical errors (moving your cursor below each word and reading text aloud as you do so).

After you make edits to the text, read the sentence before each edit, the sentence(s) containing the edit, and the sentence that follows to ensure that you have not introduced errors" (Kranzler & Floyd, 2013, p. 143). Third, based on some research indicating that authors identify more errors when reading hard copies than when reading from a screen (e.g., Wharton-Michael, 2008), you should print and proof hard copies.

I suspect that my attention to detail wanes over time when proofing manuscripts, so I sometimes read it section by section in reverse order (from Discussion to Introduction). Recently, I have begun using text-to-speech programs to enhance my attention to each word while proofing. My favorite one at present is NaturalReader Text to Speech by NaturalSoft Limited, but I am certain there are many others. I like NaturalReader because I can access the manuscript on my cloud-based server (Dropbox.com) through the app on my smartphone and "play" the reader while I am proofing the manuscript using a computer. Using this method, I am often amazed at what errors I identify that I had previously overlooked. Proofing is always tedious, but using these electronic supports makes it far easier and more effective.

Committing to How, When, and Where You Write Best

So many of the books I reviewed when writing this chapter (see Table 1.1) address how to be a more productive writer. Those by Johnson and Mullen (2007) and Silvia (2007) might be the best of the bunch. Chapters from Johnson and Mullen on disciplined writing and selecting the optimal times for writing, and chapters from Silvia on barriers to writing and motivational tools are superb. They alone are worth the price of these books.

My goal in this section is to introduce key strategies conveyed in such books and from our study of highly productive scholars (Martinez et al., 2011), but I will not cover them exhaustively. From my perspective, the gist of all these strategies is to schedule and protect time for writing activities. Based on our study, discussions with colleagues, anecdotes from other books, and my own experience, there are many paths to enact this general strategy. Some writers consolidate their writing into a full work day, others write early in the morning (e.g., before children wake or before colleagues and students arrive at work), others write during a scheduled period each day, others write with a partner or with a work group, others primarily "burst write" near deadlines, and still others hold themselves to producing a certain number of words or a certain number of pages of text during a day or week (whenever they can fit writing in). Most use combinations of these strategies to maximize their success.

An important element addressed across sources—and perhaps the most important one for me as a writer—is finding a place to write without distractions. Again, there is notably variation in specific strategies that productive writers employ. Some scholars hole up in their university offices (with a Do Not Disturb sign on the door), others write primarily in coffee shops, others find cubbies in their university libraries, and others write exclusively in their

18 *Randy G. Floyd*

home offices. In any setting, preventing distractions that interrupt "writing flow" is paramount. With email and social media access on the same computers at which we write and smartphones with auditory and visual notifications of text, emails, and posts, it takes a disciplined writer to avoid major distractions. However, it must be done. Close webpages, disable notifications, and otherwise keep you smartphone out of sight if at all possible.

Find Your Publishing Identity—In Terms of Format and Content

Varying Publication Formats

Although many writers demonstrate substantial versatility, some writers display a writing style that makes their text more accessible and practical, whereas others write more technically and abstractly. Thus, some writers might be more apt to write for newsletters and books, where clear writing, meaningful recommendations for practice, and public policy implications are emphasized. Others might be more suited to writing journal articles, technical manuals supporting tests, or highly theoretical articles, chapters, and books. I recommend that you consider the expectations of your employers (e.g., tenure track faculty in university settings), build on your strengths that align you with some outlets, and enhance your skills in other areas that will allow you to contribute to other less-well-fitting outlets.

There is no doubt that this book has a disproportionate emphasis on publishing in peer-reviewed journals. The second chapter highlights publishing journal articles, and the next 11 chapters are authored by journal editors. Thus, approximately half of this book has this emphasis. However, it is important to recognize other publication outlets through which to demonstrate scholarship and enhance the field. In particular, there are professional newsletters; Chapter 22 (R. Flanagan, Desrochers, & Machek) addresses these sources. I have a colleague who repeats that if you want to write so that the greatest number of practitioners in the field will read your article, publish it in a professional newsletter. Other chapters in this book highlight publishing books (Chapter 23, D. Flanagan & Sy) and tests (Chapter 24, Bracken). Your talents and style might also lead you to write to apply and expand theory (Chapter 25, Burns & Petersen-Brown), translate research into practice (Chapter 26, Forman & Diaz), and write and advocate to affect public policy (Chapter 27, Worrell, Subotnik, & Olszewski-Kubilius).

In the same vein, collaboration (see Johnson & Mullen, 2007, Chapter 5 and Silvia, 2015, Chapter 3) might also allow writers to express their preferred style while contributing their best scholarship to impactful sources. For example, in a successful research collaboration, one author can draft the Introduction and Discussion sections, and a co-author can draft the Method and Results sections. Although coordinating these efforts is not always easy, collaborating with others who have expertise that you do not, and who write in a style that you might not, can yield major dividends.

Alignment of Content

One of the key general recommendations from our study of highly productive scholars was to find one's passion (Martinez et al., 2011), and professional writing can be a key part of finding and sharing this passion and melding your experience and your scholarship. It makes sense to combine these elements. For example, if you have extensive training in conducting applied behavior analysis for behavior problems and evaluating interventions using single-case designs, you might gravitate toward publishing research in specialty journals where these key features are prominent (see Chapter 16, Ardoin and Ayres). In the same vein, if you have been assigned to teach a course on assessment or measurement, it makes sense to use that experience to generate ideas that could be tested through programmatic research and published in specialty journals (see Chapter 17, Reynolds, Niileksela, & Meyer).

My interest in understanding the peer-review and publishing process began, in part, when I joined the *Journal of School Psychology* in late 2006 as an associate editor. I do not recall, prior to this, much interest in this topic beyond my own interest in learning strategies that would make me a more productive and successful writer. After seeing such little research on the topic during my first couple of years in that editorial position, I felt the need to complete this research myself. When I become editor of the journal several years later, I saw so much talent and diligent effort across authors while processing so many poorly developed manuscripts, I wanted to address skills and insights into the publication process more thoroughly through a book like this one. I hope that readers also see, for themselves, such paths for following their passions and addressing perceived needs in the field. Motivation to write—and write well—will almost certainly be enhanced when you channel this passion to share your experiences and ideas.

Conclusion

Writing is the foundation of success for undergraduate and graduate students as well as many scholars who choose careers in academia and research. Writing, however, is complex and challenging. Writers at all stages of development can become clearer communicators and more productive by employing some of the strategies and consulting some of the resources referenced in this chapter.

References

Albers, C. A., Floyd, R. G., Fuhrmann, M. J., & Martinez, R. S. (2011). Publication criteria and recommended areas of improvement within school psychology journals as reported by editors, journal board members, and manuscript authors. *Journal of School Psychology, 49*, 669–689.

American Educational Research Association. (2006). Standards for reporting on empirical social research in AERA publications. *Educational Researcher, 35*(6), 33–40.

20   *Randy G. Floyd*

American Psychological Association. (2010). *Publication manual of the American Psychological Association* (6th ed.). Washington, DC: American Psychological Association.

American Psychological Association Publications and Communications Board Working Group on Journal Article Reporting Standards. (2008). Reporting standards for research in psychology: Why do we need them? What might they be? *American Psychologist, 63,* 848–849.

Bereiter, C., & Scardamalia, M. (1987). *The psychology of written composition.* Hillsdale, NJ: Erlbaum.

Bossuyt, P. M., Reitsma, J. B., Bruns, D. E., Gatsonis, C. A., Glasziou, P. P., Irwig L., et al., and the STARD Group. (2015). STARD 2015: An updated list of essential items for reporting diagnostic accuracy studies. *Radiology, 277,* 826–832. doi: 10.1148/radiol.2015151516

Cooper, H. (2011). *Reporting research in psychology: How to meet journal article reporting standards.* Washington, DC: American Psychological Association.

Day, R. A., & Gastel, B. (2015). *How to write and publish a scientific paper* (7th ed.). Santa Barbara, CA: Greenwood.

Floyd, R. G., Cooley, K. M., Arnett, J. E., Fagan, T. K., Mercer, S. H., & Hingle, C. (2011). An overview and analysis of journal operations, journal publication patterns, and journal impact in school psychology and related fields. *Journal of School Psychology, 49,* 617–647.

Hancock, G. R., & Mueller, R. O. (Eds.). (2010). *The reviewer's guide to quantitative methods in the social sciences.* New York, NY: Routledge.

Hayes, J. R. (1996). A new framework for understanding cognition and affect in writing. In C. M. Levy & S. Ransdell (Eds.), *The science of writing: Theories, methods, individual differences, and applications* (pp. 1–27). Mahwah, NJ: Erlbaum.

Hayes, J. R., & Flower, L. S. (1980). Identifying the organization of writing processes. In L. W. Gregg & E. R. Steinbert (Eds.), *Cognitive processes in writing* (pp. 3–30). Hillsdale, NJ: Erlbaum.

Henson, K. (2016). *Writing for publication: Road to academic advancement.* San Antonio, TX: Pearson.

Hoyle, R. H., & Isherwood, J. C. (2013). Reporting results from structural equation modeling analyses in Archives of Scientific Psychology. *Archives of Scientific Psychology, 1,* 14–22.

Jalongo, M. R., & Saracho, O. N. (2016). *Transitions and tools that support scholars' success.* New York, NY: Springer.

Johnson, W. B., & Mullen, C. A. (2007). *Write to the top! How to become a prolific academic.* New York, NY: Macmillan.

Joireman, J., & Van Lange, P. A. M. (2015). *How to publish high-quality research: Discovering, building, and sharing the contribution.* Washington, DC: American Psychological Association.

Kellogg, R. T. (1994). *The psychology of writing.* New York, NY: Oxford University Press.

Kranzler, J. H., & Floyd, R. G. (2013). *Assessing intelligence in children and adolescents: A practical guide.* New York, NY: Guilford Press.

Liberati, A., Altman, D. G., Tetzlaff, J., Mulrow, C., Gøtzsche, P., et al. and the PRISMA Group. (2009). The PRISMA statement for reporting systematic reviews and meta-analyses of studies that evaluate health care interventions: Explanation and elaboration. *PLoS Med, 6:* e1000100. doi:10.1371/journal.pmed.1000100

Martinez, R. S., Floyd, R. G., & Erichsen, L. (2011). Strategies and attributes of highly productive scholars and contributors to the school psychology literature: Recommendations for increasing scholarly productivity. *Journal of School Psychology, 49*, 691–720.

Moher, D., Schulz, K. F., Altman, D. G., for the CONSORT Group. (2001). The CONSORT statement: Revised recommendations for improving the quality of reports of parallel-group randomised trials. *Lancet, 357*(9263), 1191–1194.

Nicol, A. A. M., & Pexman, P. M. (2010a). *Displaying your findings: A practical guide for creating figures, posters, and presentations* (6th ed.). Washington, DC: American Psychological Association.

Nicol, A. A. M., & Pexman, P. M. (2010b). *Presenting your findings: A practical guide for creating tables* (6th ed.). Washington, DC: American Psychological Association.

O'Brien, B. C., Harris, I. B., Beckman, T. J., Reed, D. A., & Cook, D. A. (2014). Standards for reporting qualitative research: A synthesis of recommendations. *Academic Medicine, 89*(9), 1245–1251.

Onwuegbuzie, A. J., & Daniel, L. G. (2005). Editorial: Evidence-based guidelines for publishing articles in research in the schools and beyond. *Research in the Schools, 12*(2), 1–11.

Pinker, S. (2014). *A sense of style: The thinking person's guide to writing in the 21st century.* New York, NY: Viking Penguin.

Schulz, K. F., Altman, D. G., Moher, D., for the CONSORT Group. (2010). CONSORT 2010 statement: Updated guidelines for reporting parallel group randomised trials. *BMJ, 340*: c332. doi: https://doi.org/10.1136/bmj.c332

Silvia, P. (2007). *How to write a lot: A practical guide to productive writing.* Washington, DC: American Psychological Association.

Silvia, P. (2015). *Write it up: Practical strategies for writing and publishing journal articles.* Washington, DC: American Psychological Association.

Standards of Reporting Trials Group. (1994). A proposal for structured reporting of randomized controlled trials. *JAMA, 272*(24), 1926–1931.

Sternberg, R. J., & Sternberg, K. (2016). *The psychologist's companion* (6th ed.). New York, NY: Cambridge University Press.

Strunk, W., & White, E. B. (1999). *The elements of style* (4th ed.). New York, NY: Longman.

Tate, R. L., Perdices, M., Rosenkoetter, U., Shadish, W., Vohra, S., Barlow, D. H., . . . Wilson B. (2016). The single-case reporting guideline in behavioural interventions (SCRIBE) 2015 statement. *Journal of School Psychology, 56*, 133–142.

Tong, A., Sainsbury, P., & Craig, J. (2007). Consolidated criteria for reporting qualitative research (COREQ): A 32-item checklist for interviews and focus groups. *International Journal for Quality in Health Care, 19*, 349–357.

Wharton-Michael, P. (2008). Print vs. computer screen: Effects of medium on proof-reading accuracy. *Journalism and Mass Communication Educator, 63*(1), 28–41.

Zinsser, W. (2001). *On writing well* (rev. 6th ed.). New York, NY: HarperCollins.

2 Selecting the Optimal Journal Outlets

Randy G. Floyd

One study of productive scholars in school psychology (Martinez, Floyd, & Erichsen, 2011) found that prolific authors excelled in applying their knowledge about journals in the field, including their foci, citation-based metrics, and editorial board composition. The goal of this chapter is to offer "tricks of the trade" used by these authors that will assist in identifying and selecting journal outlets in which to publish, as well as tailoring manuscripts to match the aims and scope of these journals. As it focuses on publishing in journals, readers should turn to Chapter 22 (by R. Flanagan, Derochers, & Machek) for discussion of publishing in professional newsletters, Chapter 23 (by D. Flanagan & Sy) for discussion of publishing books, and Chapter 24 (by Bracken) for discussion of publishing tests.

In What Journals Should I Publish My Research and Scholarship?

A recent blog post offered by Dr. Amanda Sullivan through the Society for the Study of School Psychology Early Career Forum (https://ssspresearch.org/earlycareerforum/where-should-i-send-my-manuscript-journals-options-researchers-school-psychology) underscored the importance of having a deep understanding of journal features and practices. As raised in Sullivan's post, emerging scholars often struggle to identify the journals that best fit with the content and quality of their manuscripts. For example, they might aim too high in their early submissions and become discouraged by having their manuscripts returned to them without full review or by the extent of reviewer feedback following full review. Conversely, they might devote excessive time and effort to publishing high-quality research articles in journals that are not held in the highest esteem by those in the field, when their articles could have had more influence when published elsewhere. Many such barriers to success can be overcome with a more complete understanding of the similarities and differences across journals.

A Strong Core

Based on prior publications (Fagan & Wise, 2007; Floyd et al., 2011; Hulac, Johnson, Ushijima, & Schneider, 2016), there are 11 core journals in school psychology. Hulac et al. (2016) referred to them as *school psychology-specific journals*, but I think that *school psychology generalist journals* (as opposed to specialty journals) is more accurate. These journals are often associated with school psychology professional organizations, include variants of "school psychology" in the title, and have editors and editorial board members who identify as school psychologists. They also have a broad scope in addressing issues of practice, research, and policy. These 11 journals are featured in Table 2.1, and editors of each of these journals have contributed insider knowledge in Chapters 5 through 15 in this book. I requested that these editors (a) describe the history, aims, and scope of their journal; (b) present the types and length of journal articles they publish; (c) offer a summary of their recent journal operations; and (d) provide recommendations to potential authors

Table 2.1 Descriptive Information about the School Psychology Generalist Journals

Journal	Date initiated	Publisher	Editors
Journal of School Psychology	1963	Pergamon Press, Elsevier	Donald Smith, Jack Bardon, Beeman Phillips, Thomas Oakland, Raymond Dean, Joel Meyers, Robert Pianta, Edward Daly III, Randy Floyd, Michelle Demaray*
Psychology in the Schools	1964	Clinical Psychology Publishing, Wiley	William Hunt, B. Claude Mathis, Gerald Fuller, Jr., LeAdelle Phelps, David McIntosh*
School Psychology International	1979	SAGE Publishing	Ludwig Lowenstein, Caven Mcloughlin*, Robert Burden, Amity Noltemeyer*
School Psychology Review[a]	1980	NASP	John Guidubaldi, Liam Grimley, Daniel Reschly, George Hynd, Stephen Elliott, Edward Shapiro, Patti Harrison, Susan Sheridan, Thomas Power, Matthew Burns, Amy Reschly*
Trainers' Forum[b]	1980	TSP	Richard Winnick, Charles Paskewicz, William Flook, Douglas Schooler, MaryAnn (née Ford) Biller, John Kenny, Francis Culbertson, Jack Orbrut, Robert Harrinton, Gilbert Gredler, David Mealor, Susan Vess, Anthony Paolitto, David McIntosh, Mardis Dunham, Enedina Vazquez, Fred Krieg, Kelly Kennedy*

(continued)

24   Randy G. Floyd

Table 2.1 Descriptive Information about the School Psychology Generalist Journals
(*continued*)

Journal	Date initiated	Publisher	Editors
Canadian Journal of School Psychology	1985	SAGE Publishing	G. Gerald Koe, Henry Janzen, Donald Saklofske,* Jeffrey Derevensky, Marvin Simner, Joseph Snyder
School Psychology Quarterly[c]	1990	SAGE Publishing, Guilford Press, APA	Thomas Kratochwill, Joseph Witt, Terry Gutkin, Rik D'Amato, Randy Kamphaus, Shane Jimerson, Richard Gilman*
Journal of Applied School Psychology[d]	2002	Routledge-Haward, Taylor & Francis	Charles Maher, David Wodrich, Frank Sansosti*
School Psychology Forum	2006	NASP	Ray Christner, Steven Shaw, Oliver Edwards*
Contemporary School Psychology[e]	2011	Cal SP, Springer Verlag	Shane Jimerson, Marilyn Wilson, Michael Hass*
International Journal of School & Educational Psychology	2013	Taylor & Francis	Rik D'Amato*

Note. In the absence of other information regarding editors, those listed as *coordinators* and *secretaries* in the earliest days of their journals were also listed as editors. NASP = National Association of School Psychologists. APA = American Psychological Association. Cal SP = California Association of School Psychologists. TSP = Trainers of School Psychologists.

*   Current editor, May 2017.
a   Formerly *School Psychology Digest*, 1972.
b   Formerly *The School Psych Scoop*, 1972.
c   Formerly *Professional School Psychology*, 1986.
d   Formerly *Special Services in the Schools*, 1984.
e   Formerly *The California School Psychologist*, 1996.

submitting to their journals. They came through in every case and provided some of the most up-to-date descriptions of the opportunities and expectations associated with publishing in their journals. As a result, readers should be able to directly compare features across these core journals in the field.

I encourage school psychologists to consider starting at home by submitting their best manuscripts to one of the field's core journals. In particular, if you identify as a school psychologist or serve as faculty in a school psychology graduate preparation program, publishing in these journals could be critical for maintaining your professional identity. You might need to discover some method for achieving this goal—at least once in a while—even if that means stepping outside of your comfort zone and being creative with research questions and the stated purpose of your research. In addition, if you do not identify as a school psychologist but conduct relevant research, you might find that school psychology journals provide opportunities to publish high-quality research that has the potential to affect children, adolescents, their families, and their adult caregivers in schools and related settings in ways that other journals do not. Opportunities abound!

Surveys of journal editors (e.g., Floyd et al., 2011) have revealed that one common reason that editors reject manuscripts submitted to their journals is that the manuscripts do not match the aims and scope of the journal. Many of the manuscripts I rejected as editor of *Journal of School Psychology* were clearly not consistent with the aims and scope of the journal or aligned with the field as a whole. The two most egregious examples I recall receiving were a manuscript focusing on inpatient treatment of geriatric adults with schizophrenia and a manuscript about testicular examinations. Sometimes, it is very challenging to identify what features match a manuscript to a journal (as discussed later in this chapter), but in many cases, it is not. For well-developed fields like school psychology, it is clear that submissions should be intricately linked—via citations or terminology—to the key features of the field. When editors screen manuscripts submitted to them to determine fit, they review titles and abstracts and search the manuscripts' surface-level features. For example, they might search for key words and review the Reference section for indicators of fit. For manuscripts focusing on topics I thought were marginally relevant to school psychologists, I would search for "school psych" in text and in the references. If there was no mention of the field, its members, or its most prominent journals or books, it was clear to me that the fit was weak. In most cases, I would return the manuscript to authors without additional review.

Even if your research is somewhat peripheral to the professional practice of school psychology and to the research typically published in journals in the field, you will benefit from tailoring your manuscript to match the journal you have targeted. Many of these tailored elements are surface-level features, as noted previously. When submitting to school psychology generalist journals, you should integrate relevant terms (e.g., school psychology or school psychologists), reference professional organizations (like those listed in Table 2.1) or their publications (e.g., newsletters and position statements), and integrate key features of the field's practice and research. Authors should review the public description of school psychology as a specialty offered by the American Psychological Association (APA; www.apa.org/ed/graduate/specialize/school. aspx); it addresses both scientific and theoretical contributions and the parameters that define professional practice in school psychology and provides preliminary information about the field. It might also be helpful to peruse the National Association of School Psychologists' description of the identity and practices of school psychologists (www.nasponline.org/about-school-psychology/who-are-school-psychologists).

It is important that authors review prominent books covering key issues, practices, and innovations in school psychology. They include *Best Practices*

26 *Randy G. Floyd*

in School Psychology (Harrison & Thomas, 2014); *The Handbook of International School Psychology* (Jimerson, Oakland, & Farrell, 2007); *The Handbook of School Psychology* (Gutkin & Reynolds, 2009); *Introduction to School Psychology: Controversies and Current Practice* (Burns, in press); *The Oxford Handbook of School Psychology* (Bray & Kehle, 2011), *Practical Handbook of School Psychology* (Gimpel Peacock, Ervin, Daly, & Merrell, 2010); *School Psychology for the 21st Century* (Merrell, Ervin, & Gimple Peacock, 2012); *School Psychology: Past, Present, and Future* (Fagan & Wise, 2007); and *School Psychology: Professional Issues and Practices* (Grapin & Kranzler, 2018). Citing these sources when articulating the relevance of the research to school psychologists (in the Introduction section) and when discussing the implications of the study's findings for research, practice, or policy (in the Discussion section) will go a long way in linking your study to the field of school psychology.

Branching Out

Maybe you are a school psychologist who wants to publish highly specialized research or to reach a broader audience outside of school psychology. Based on at least three studies examining patterns of publications of school psychologists (Carper & Williams, 2004; Hulac et al., 2016; Kranzler, Grapin, & Daley, 2011), you are not alone. Although school psychologists publish articles frequently—but not predominantly—in the school psychology generalist journals, they are equally or more likely to publish in related specialty journals. It is clear that school psychologists are (and must be) aware of other journal outlets in which to publish.

It is good news that there are numerous specialty journals very closely aligned with school psychology research and practice, as prominent school psychologists serve or have served as their editors. Examples include *Journal of Psychoeducational Assessment, Journal of Educational and Psychological Consultation, Journal of Behavioral Education,* and *Assessment for Effective Intervention* (see Hulac et al., 2016; Kranzler et al., 2011). In order to identify journals that commonly cited school psychology journals as well as journals that were commonly cited within these journals, I reviewed citation data from articles published in five such journals between 2005 and 2015. I called on Clarivate Analytics' Journal Citation Reports database, which is well known for yielding the citation-based metrics known as impact factors (Garfield, 2006). It indexes only five school psychology generalist journals: *Journal of School Psychology, Psychology in the Schools, School Psychology International, School Psychology Quarterly,* and *School Psychology Review.* The journals most likely to cite articles in these school psychology journals were *Early Education and Development, Journal of Educational and Psychological Consultation, Child Development, Learning and Individual Differences, Early Childhood Research Quarterly, Education and Treatment of Children, Psychological Bulletin, Journal of Educational Psychology, Journal of Psychoeducational Assessment,* and *School Mental Health.* In contrast, articles from the five school psychology journals were most likely to cite articles from *Journal of Educational Psychology*, *Child Development*, *Developmental Psychology*, *American Psychologist*, *Journal of Applied Behavior Analysis*, *Journal of Personality and Social Psychology*, *Psychological Methods*, *Psychological Assessment*, *Structural Equation Modeling*, and *Personality and Individual Differences*. Based on these and related results, I asked six sets of authors to develop chapters for this book that focused on behavioral research journals (Chapter 16, Ardoin & Ayres), assessment and measurement journals (Chapter 17, Reynolds, Niileksela, & Meyer), educational psychology and education journals (Chapter 18, D. Robinson), reading and literacy journals (Chapter 19, Meisinger & M. Robinson), clinical and pediatric journals (Chapter 20, Power & Tresco), and developmental psychology journals (Chapter 21, Acar & Rudasill). Reviewing these chapters should prove highly useful to authors as they include rich details about more than 100 specialty journals and others related to school psychology.

In addition to reviewing these chapters, you can engage in other strategies to identify journals relevant to school psychology. One simple strategy is to review the references you have cited in your manuscripts (Silvia, 2015). If you have conducted research extending studies published primarily in a subset of journals in the field, it is likely that those same journals would be receptive to your manuscript. Another strategy to identify potential journals is to review the publication records of other researchers with similar research interests to your own. Where they have been successful in publishing, you are likely to be successful, too. You can obtain copies of their curricula vitae through online searches, review their publications through search of reference databases, or find websites that catalog their prior publications (e.g., Google Scholar).

Numerous online resources are available that summarize journal information and promote matching of manuscript content to journals. Cabell's Directory of Publishing Opportunities (www.cabells.com/) is a subscription-based service providing summaries of journal information. The directory is organized into groups of journals, and as of May 2017, the Educational Set costs $1,890 and the Psychology and Psychiatry Set costs $1,203. The directory offers details about journal aims, scope, and operations as well as citation-based and distribution information. Although cost-prohibitive for individuals, check your university library to see if it has a subscription. Also, consider the free alternatives that are addressed next.

The coverage lists from reference databases can also be useful in identifying potential journals. I frequently used—and during my time as editor, encouraged others to consult—the APA's PsycINFO coverage list including more than 2,400 journals (www.apa.org/pubs/databases/psycinfo/coverage.aspx). I have searched the online list for key words, such as "assessment" or "reading," to identify potential journal outlets, but there is also the option of downloading an Excel file that includes all of these journal titles to enable searches. There are additional web-based pages that allow for more focused searches and that provide additional information about journals beyond their titles. For example, Elsevier's database Scopus can be searched by keyword and journal

28 *Randy G. Floyd*

(www.scopus.com/sources and https://journalmetrics.scopus.com/), and it yields journal citation data (discussed later in this chapter) that enables comparisons to be made across journals. The SCImago Journal and Country Rank website (www.scimagojr.com/) is also searchable by keyword and journal, yields information about journal scope and publishing history, and plots citation-based metrics across time.

During this past academic year, a couple of my department colleagues introduced me to the Journal/Author Name Estimator (JANE; http://jane.biose mantics.org/), which is a website that identifies journals that are compatible with research projects following your entry of a title, an abstract, or keyword information into the system. JANE accesses the Medline database, so many psychology journals are not indexed. Across school psychology journals, only *Journal of School Psychology* and *School Psychology Quarterly* are included, but for those publishing in pediatric psychology journals (see Chapter 20, Power & Tresco), JANE could be a useful tool. There is also Journal Guide (www.journal guide.com/), which includes a Paper Match feature. After entering a title and abstract, it identifies compatible journals, their publishers, and citation-based metrics. It also allows up to three journals to be compared concurrently. Journal Guide includes a greater number of school psychology generalist journals and specialty journals than does JANE. In addition to JANE and Journal Guide, search engines from several major publishers identify relevant journals they publish. They include Elsevier's Journal Finder (http://journalfinder. elsevier.com/), Springer's Journal Suggester (https://journalsuggester.springer. com/), and Wiley's Find the Right Journal page (https://authorservices.wiley. com/author-resources/Journal-Authors/find-a-journal/index.html). With all these resources, authors should not struggle to find potential journals for their manuscripts.

What Should I Consider When Targeting a Journal?

When considering options across the school psychology journals, specialty journals aligned with school psychology, and journals from other disciplines, authors have a lot of variables to consider. They must consider how to maximize the probability of their manuscript being published while concurrently striving to (a) meet or exceed the publication expectations of their employers (e.g., securing tenure and being promoted); (b) influence the science, policy, and practice through publication; and (c) in general, improve their reputations in the field. In the past, when authors were considering journal outlets, they were likely to highly value the circulation of the journal in hard copy form and the length of the period between acceptance and publication (a.k.a., publication lags). Although distribution of journal issues to members of professional organizations (see Table 2.1) remains important, circulation cannot be easily quantified as in the past due to electronic distribution practices, including publishers selling bundles of journals to libraries (rather than subscriptions to each journal). Publication lags are rarely a consideration now due to journals posting in-press articles online ahead of print. Considering current practices, I believe that authors should consider at least five primary variables when selecting journals to which to submit: the aim and scope of the journal, the types and length of articles published in the journal, journal operations, the journal editorial board composition, and citation-based metrics.

Aim and Scope

Knowing the aims and scope of the journal to which you are submitting is important because these parameters tell you what topics would fit well into the pages of the journal. Whereas the journal titles and lists of journals like those in Table 2.1 are helpful in a broad sense, not all journals in a category are the same. For example, some school psychology journals do not publish survey research. Some consider post-secondary student populations, whereas others do not. Some journals highly value the breadth of contribution of manuscripts submitted, such that narrowly focused studies (e.g., those presenting reliability and validity evidence from a single test) would not be considered. Often, descriptions of aim and scope are nebulous, so reviewing articles published in recent issues of the journal, locating editorials written by the editor, or emailing the editor with a brief description of your study might yield better indicators of fit with an editor's vision for the journal than reviewing the descriptions of a journal's aim and scope.

Several journals, including most in school psychology, allow authors to propose and coordinate special issues (sometimes called themed issues), which often include both articles solicited to fill the issue as well as unsolicited articles submitted in response to calls for submissions and other announcements. I requested that editors contributing to this book specifically address developing special issue proposals in their chapters. Although it takes vigilance and connectedness to a journal (reading the back matter of each issue and monitoring its website) to identify calls for submissions that might be aligned with one's research interests, corresponding with guest editors of these issues and submitting manuscripts for considerations will maximize fit between manuscript content and journal aims.

Types and Length of Articles

It is important to consider the types of articles published in a journal. Most—but not all—journals will publish quantitative research studies in full-length articles. Some will publish brief reports, and others will publish test reviews and book reviews. In more and more cases, journals (at least in school psychology) will not publish narrative reviews of the literature; reviews must be systematic and meta-analytic. These options for article types also tend to change over time across editors (see Floyd et al., 2011), so be sure to review Chapters 5 through 15 carefully as well as study journal websites for details.

30   *Randy G. Floyd*

Manuscript length and word count have become increasingly varied and vital to consider when developing and editing manuscripts before submission. These variables are important even during the pre-drafting of your manuscript (see Chapter 1, Floyd). In the late 2000s, one journal apparently rejected up to half of manuscripts received, in part because they were too lengthy (Floyd et al., 2011). I personally have had several manuscripts returned to me over the past decade because they exceeded (even by as few as 200 words) the recommended word count limit. It is fair to say that the expectation that each manuscript should be 35 to 40 pages in length (or roughly 10,500 to 12,000 words) represents a vestige of days gone by. I believe, however, that many editors are flexible in allowing submissions that are slightly longer than their published recommendations; I encourage you to contact them prior to submission if you have greatly exceeded the maximum page length or word limit count.

Journal Operations

Journal operations reports typically include details about the number of manuscripts submitted to a journal as well as how often they are accepted for publication. The first such report I saw was issued at a journal editorial board meeting in the early 2000s; it was distributed freely to editorial board members (which I was not) and ad hoc reviewers (which I was) but not published in the pages of the journal, posted online, or otherwise widely distributed. It contained a lot of important information that seemed to be available to only a select few. To this day, only three school psychology journals (*Journal of School Psychology*, *Psychology in the Schools*, and *School Psychology Quarterly*) have routinely published such reports; they usually appear in the pages of the journal, or in the case of *School Psychology Quarterly*, they appear online with other APA journals. In this vein, beginning in 2004, the APA began publishing its annual journal operations reports online, but that website has not been updated since 2013 (www.apa.org/pubs/journals/statistics.aspx). Its reports provide details about APA mainstay journals (e.g., *American Psychologist*, *Psychological Bulletin*, and *Psychological Review*) as well as the APA division journals (e.g., *School Psychology Quarterly* and *Educational Psychologist*). I always find it striking to see the range of numbers of submissions totaling far less than 100 (e.g., a low of 45 in 2013) to almost 1,000 (a high of 988 in 2013). Readers who compare the manuscript submissions across journals featured in this book will also see a wide range, from 26 (*Trainers' Forum*) to 312 (*Journal of School Psychology*) in 2015. Submission rates have major effects on editors and their editor boards, as higher rates often indicate that authors will receive less nurturance throughout the peer-review process. Thus, early career scholars, international scholars struggling to convey their messages clearly in English, and others who are new to the peer-review process might benefit from submitting to smaller, less popular journals.

Journal operations reports also offer indications of the difficulty in publishing in a journal. Most report a rejection rate, which is typically calculated by dividing the number of submissions rejected by the total number of submissions. (Whether resubmitted manuscripts are included in both counts varies somewhat.) Some journals also break down the different types of rejected manuscripts—including those rejected without full review (a.k.a., *desk-reject* or *reject-out-of-hand*), those rejected after full review with encouragement to resubmit (a.k.a., *reject: revise and resubmit*), and those rejected after full review without encouragement to resubmit. Some journals also report additional divisions, including the percentage of manuscripts tentatively accepted. As reported in Floyd et al. (2011) and evident in Chapters 5 through 15, editors are increasingly rejecting manuscripts without full review. For example, approximately one-third of submissions to *Journal of School Psychology* have been rejected without full review during recent years (see Chapter 5, Demaray). Rejection rates are one measure of journal quality, as they reflect the difficulty in publishing in the journal. They also provide insights into decisions you are likely to experience when submitting manuscripts to a journal. In seeking balance, I would concurrently review rejection rates relative to the absolute number of accepted manuscripts and published articles, as some journals (e.g., *Psychology in the Schools*) have a relatively high rejection rate but still publish a large number of articles, as addressed later in this chapter.

Editorial Board Composition

When studying journals, it is extremely important to review the list of people who serve on their editorial boards. They are frequently listed on journal webpages and inside the covers of print copies of the journal. Editorial boards are typically structured in a hierarchy: There is one editor (a.k.a., editor-in-chief) who is selected by a professional organization or the journal publisher to lead the journal. The editor typically populates the editorial board. Although some journals have editorial assistants (typically graduate students) or a journal manager (an employee of the publisher) who handle the processing of new submissions, the editor is typically involved in manuscript screening and assignment of manuscripts to handling editors. Handling editor is a general term (synonymous with action editor) that includes associate editors, who are editorial board members selected to process peer reviews on a regular basis, as well as guest editors, who process manuscripts as part of special issues or on an ad hoc basis. For some journals, the editor also serves as handling editor. Usually, associate editors are paid a small stipend, and the editor is paid about ten times that. Guest editors and other editorial board members are typically not compensated for their service beyond receiving subscriptions to the journal, access to the publisher's journal database, and public recognition. All editorial board members are typically engaging in peer review for journals in addition to their full-time jobs. Almost everyone contributing is a volunteer, and even those spending many hours per week facilitating journal operations are compensated very little. You should keep both the editorial board hierarchy and the nature of this service in mind when engaging with journals.

32   *Randy G. Floyd*

Many journal editors assign manuscripts to handling editors based on the match between (a) the manuscript content and (b) the expertise and interest of the handling editor, so you can sometimes accurately guess who will be assigned your manuscript. In my opinion (and others, see Martinez et al., 2011), handling editors contribute substantially to the quality of the peer-review process and are the true arbiters of editorial decisions in many cases. They are the ones who are likely to select three or four editorial board members and ad hoc reviewers to evaluate your manuscript, write the decision letter, and issue the decision about the viability of your submission. These handling editors (especially in the role as associate editor) play a large role in your experience interacting with a journal. When considering potential journal outlets, you should ask peers and senior colleagues to determine how much associate editors serving journals typically participate in the peer-review process (completing independent reviews of manuscripts themselves versus passing on the comments of the reviewers) and how detailed and encouraging their feedback tends to be.

It is important to understand who the editorial board members are because their philosophies, expectations, and methodological and statistical expertise affect the evaluation of manuscript submissions. Handling editors might call on ad hoc reviewers (often either early career scholars or those with specific expertise not commonly needed at a journal), but they will usually call on reviewers from the editorial board first. If you do not recognize the names of at least a quarter of the editorial board members and have not cited a publication from anyone on the editorial board, it is likely that the journal is a poor match to your manuscript. If you have determined that your manuscript matches the aim and scope of the journal and recognize many of the members of the editorial board but have not read their recent research or cited them, you might benefit from returning to the literature, reviewing their research, and citing them (R. Sternberg & K. Sternberg, 2016).

Editorial boards are increasingly adding statistical and methodological advisors—who are often trained outside of the content area and are quantitative psychologists or otherwise statistical or methodological experts—to their editorial boards. For example, they are currently prominent on the *Psychological Science* editorial board, and they are increasingly evident on the editorial boards of school psychology journals, including *Journal of School Psychology* and *School Psychology International*. It is possible that you, as an author, could become frustrated by comments from these reviewers because (a) they do not have the same training and do not know the research and practice in your field as you do and (b) they have much more expertise and higher standards for statistical analyses than you probably do. I believe, however, that the presence of statistical and methodological advisors indicates that you will experience a higher quality peer review.

Impact Factors

Journal websites include references to citation-based metrics and other indicators of the influence of their journals. The logic supporting the interpretation

Selecting the Optimal Journal Outlets   33

of citation-based metrics (sometimes referred to generally as impact factors) is that the more other journals are citing articles included in a journal, the greater influence those articles (and thus the journal) has on the field. Table 2.2

Table 2.2 Citation-Based Indices Indicating Journal Quality

Index	Source	Description, formula, and typical range for school psychology journals	Journals indexed
Journal Impact Factor (2-year Impact Factor)	Clarivate Analytics' Journal Citation Reports	Average citations in select year based on "research articles" published during previous 2 years. Formula: Citations in select year/citable items in previous 2 years. Includes citations from the journal in question. Tends to range from 0.2 to 3.4 (M = 1.1).	JSP, PITS, SPI, SPQ, SPR
5-year Impact Factor	Clarivate Analytics' Journal Citation Reports	Average citations in select year based on "research articles" published during previous 5 years. Formula: Citations in select year/citable items in previous 5 years. Includes citations from the journal in question. Tends to range from 0.4 to 4.3 (M = 2.1).	JSP, PITS, SPI, SPQ, SPR
Immediacy Index	Clarivate Analytics' Journal Citation Reports	Average citations in select year based on "research articles" published during select year. Formula: Citations in select year/citable items in select year. Includes citations from the journal in question. Tends to range from 0 to 1.9 (M = 0.4).	JSP, PITS, SPI, SPQ, SPR
CiteScore	Elsevier's Scopus	Average citations in select year based on all articles published during previous 3 years. Formula: Citations in select year/articles in previous 3 years. Includes citations from the journal in question. Tends to range from 0.6 to 3.9 (M = 1.8).	CJSP, JASP, JSP, PITS, SPI, SPQ, SPR
Impact Per Publication	CWTS Journal Indicators and formerly Elsevier's Scopus	Average citations in select year based on "research articles" published during previous 3 years. Formula: Citations in select year/articles in previous 3 years. Includes citations from the journal in question. Tends to range from 0.07 to 3.6 (M = 1.2).	CJSP, JASP, JSP, PITS, SPI, SPQ, SPR

(continued)

Table 2.2 Citation-Based Indices Indicating Journal Quality (*continued*)

Index	Source	Description, formula, and typical range for school psychology journals	Journals indexed
SCImago Journal Rank	Elsevier's Scopus and SCImago Journal & Country Rank	Average citations in select year based on all articles published during previous 3 years, weighted by the quality and impact of the citing sources. Includes citations from the journal in question. Tends to range from 0.1 to 2.7 (M = 0.8).	CJSP, JASP, JSP, PITS, SPI, SPQ, SPR
Source Normalized Impact per Paper	Elsevier's Scopus, CWTS Journal Indicators	Average citations in select year based on all articles published during previous 3 years, weighted for frequency of citations in discipline (a.k.a., "Database Citation Potential"). Formula: Impact per Publication/Database Citation Potential. Includes citations from the journal in question. Tends to range from 0.1 to 2.6 (M = 1.0).	CJSP, JASP, JSP, PITS, SPI, SPQ, SPR
Eigenfactor Score	Clarivate Analytics' Journal Citation Reports	Number of citations in a select year to articles published in previous 5 years weighted by the impact of the citing source. Reflects the proportion of all citations in a select year attributable to a journal. Excludes citations from the journal in question. Tends to range from 0.0005 to 0.005 (M = 0.002).	JSP, PITS, SPI, SPQ, SPR
Normalized Eigenfactor Score	Clarivate Analytics' Journal Citation Reports	Number of citations in a select year to articles published in previous 5 years weighted by the impact of the citing sources and scaled so that the average journal (across the database) yields a value of 1.0. Formula: Eigenfactor Score * number of journals in database/100. Excludes citations from the journal in question. Tends to range from 0.1 to 0.5 (M = 0.3).	JSP, PITS, SPI, SPQ, SPR

Index	Source	Description, formula, and typical range for school psychology journals	Journals indexed
Article Influence Score	Clarivate Analytics' Journal Citation Reports	Average number of citations in a select year to articles published in previous 5 years weighted by the impact of the citing sources. Formula: Eigenfactor score * 0.01/percentage of all citable items in previous 5 years in the journal relative to all journals in the database. Excludes citations from the journal in question. Tends to range from 0.1 to 1.7 ($M = 0.8$).	JSP, PITS, SPI, SPQ, SPR
h-index	SCImago Journal & Country Rank	The number of articles published in the journal over time (X) cited at least X times. Tends to range from 17 to 72.	CJSP, JASP, JSP, PITS, SPI, SPQ, SPR
h5-index	Google Scholar	The number of articles published during the past five years (X) cited at least X times. Tends to range from 18 to 32.	CJSP, JSP, PITS, SPI, SPQ, SPR
h5-median	Google Scholar	The median number of citations for articles contributing to the h5-index. Tends to range from 28 to 53.	CJSP, JSP, PITS, SPI, SPQ, SPR

Note. Statistics reported in this table cover the range of indexes reported from 1997 to 2015, based on results available from March to July, 2017. CJSP = *Canadian Journal of School Psychology*, JASP = *Journal of Applied School Psychology*, JSP = *Journal of School Psychology*, PITS = *Psychology in the Schools*, SPI = *School Psychology International*, SPQ = *School Psychology Quarterly*, and SPR = *School Psychology Review*.

presents a variety of citation-based metrics that are reported across journals. In all cases, metric values that are higher in magnitude are more desirable.

The most prominent of the citation-based metrics is called the Journal Impact Factor (a.k.a., the *2-year Impact Factor* or simply, *impact factor*). It is produced solely by Clarivate Analytics' Journal Citation Reports,[1] which indexes only five school psychology generalist journals, as previously noted. An impact factor value reflects the number of citations across journals in the Journal Citation Reports database for a select year (e.g., 2015) that reference articles published in a select journal during the two previous years (2013 and 2014) divided by the total number of research articles published during the same period. For example, an impact factor of 3.35 means that articles published during the two previous years were cited an average of 3.35 times during the following year. Essentially, it reflects the average number of citations per article during a given period. In Psychology, values 1.0 and lower can be considered *low impact*, higher values up to 2.0 can be considered *moderate impact*, and values higher than 2.0 can be considered *high impact* (Anseel, Duyck, De Baene, & Brysbaert, 2004).

Two other metrics from Journal Citation Reports have been commonly reported (Floyd et al., 2011). The 5-year Impact Factor is essentially the same metric as the impact factor, but the article coverage is five years versus two years. Thus, a 5-year Impact Factor of 4.26 means that articles published during the five previous years were cited an average of 4.26 times during the following year. The Immediacy Index focuses on citations from a single year, but the year of journal coverage is the same year as the articles were published. Thus, the Immediacy Index for 2015 reflects citations in 2015 to articles published in 2015. An Immediacy Index of 1.88 means that articles published in a given year were cited an average of 1.88 times that same year. In school psychology journals, the size of the Immediacy Index is usually driven by the inclusion of special issue articles that include citations to other articles within the issue.

Recently, Journal Citation Reports has produced three new indices: the Eigenfactor Score; the Normalized Eigenfactor Score, which is an adjusted version of its namesake; and the Article Influence score (see Table 2.2). These three metrics reflect citations to articles published during a five-year span (like the 5-year Impact Factor) but omit self-citations from other articles from the journal in question (unlike all other citation-based metrics reviewed in this chapter). Both the Eigenfactor Score and Normalized Eigenfactor Score reflect total citations relative to all citations in a given year across the entire Journal Citation Reports database, and their calculation also includes consideration of the impact of the journals contributing these citations (so that high-impact journals contribute more weight than low-impact journals). For school psychology journals, their values are always less than 1.0 and extremely low in magnitude, which makes them seem incongruent with other metrics and difficult to interpret due to decimal fractions extending several places out. For example, an Eigenfactor Score of .005 roughly means that citations to a journal's articles published during the five previous years compose only five one-thousandths of a percent of all the citations listed in Journal Citation Reports during a given year. The Article Influence score is more similar to the traditional impact indices, but it reflects the average Eigenfactor Score relative to articles published across journals during the select year. Although these values are innovative and valuable to contrast with traditional citation-based metrics, they remain abstruse. Thus, I do not believe that they are often referenced by authors and editors in school psychology and related fields.

Elsevier's Scopus database includes seven school psychology generalist journals, including *Canadian Journal of School Psychology* and *Journal of Applied School Psychology*, and produces alternate citation-based metrics. One difference in the metrics produced by Scopus compared to those previously discussed is the focus on citations to articles published during a three-year period. The CiteScore, the Impact per Publication, the SCImago Journal

Rank, and the Source Normalized Impact per Paper metrics are described in detail in Table 2.2.

h-index values tend to be employed to evaluate the influence of an individual author's publications on a field (see Egghe, 2010; Watkins & Chan-Park, 2015), but SCImago Journal & Country Rank and Google Scholar produce h-index values to evaluate the influence of journals. The h-index is what I call a *citation-to-article convergence metric*. In general terms, these metrics reflect the number of articles (X) that have been cited at least X times since their publication. As described in more detail in Table 2.2, the h-index focuses on articles published during the history of the journal. Thus, an h-index of 72 means that 72 articles published during this history of publication of the journal were cited an average of 72 times. In contrast, Google Scholar's h5-index focuses on articles published during the past five years. Thus, an h5-index 32 means that 32 articles published during the previous five years were cited at least 32 times since publication. In calculating the h5-index, citation counts are not divided by the number of articles published in a journal. One effect of this lessened constraint is that journals that publish more articles each year tend to have higher h5-index values. In the same vein, the h5-median values reflect the median number of citations of articles contributing to the h5-index. Recall that the h5-index reflects the number of articles (X) that have been cited at least X times since their publication; as the h-5 index represents the lowest level of convergence of citations and number of articles, the h5-median values are invariably higher than the h5-index values.

Finally, there are also other indices, called *altmetrics*, that are being increasingly referenced by publishers and journal editors. They usually reflect the attention garnered by articles through online access and social media (Neylon & Wu, 2009; Priem, Taraborelli, Groth, & Neylon, 2010). As these metrics are only emerging in their influence, I will not discuss them further in this chapter. Learn more about them by visiting www.altmetric.com/.

Figures 2.1, 2.2, 2.3, and 2.4 display citation-based metrics by journal from 1997 to 2015. Most figures include five journals, but several others include seven. Metric values stem from both Journal Citation Reports and Scopus. When I analyzed the relations between these data, I found several noteworthy patterns that authors should consider. For example, there are moderate to strong correlations across them. The Impact Factor (covering two years of articles) and the 5-year Impact Factor were highly correlated, $r = .92$. Across databases, similarly derived metrics were highly correlated; the Impact Factor and Impact per Publication (covering three years of articles, produced formerly by Scopus and recently only by CWTS Journal Indicators) were correlated, $r = .87$, and the 5-year Impact Factor and the Impact per Publication were correlated, $r = .89$. In contrast, there was some divergence; the Impact Factor and the Immediacy Index (covering one year of articles) were weakly correlated, $r = .35$. The Impact Factor and the Eigenfactor (covering five years of articles) were also moderately correlated, $r = .52$. The correlation was far higher in

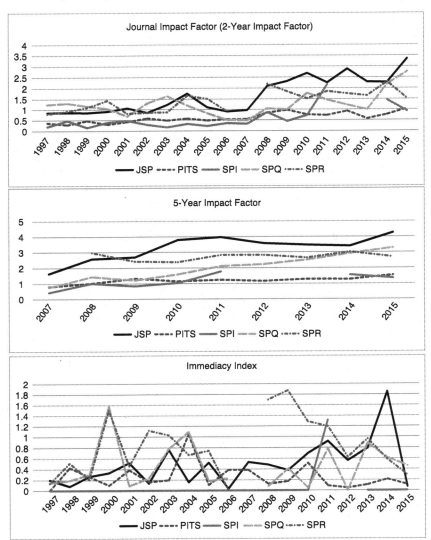

Figure 2.1 Journal Impact Factor, 5-year Impact Factor, and Immediacy Index for School Psychology Journals

Note. Values were obtained from the Journal Citation Reports database. JSP = *Journal of School Psychology*; PITS = *Psychology in the Schools*; SPI = *School Psychology International*; SPQ = *School Psychology Quarterly*; SPR = *School Psychology Review*.

magnitude when the same five years of articles were considered; the 5-year Impact Factor and the Eigenfactor were correlated, $r = .95$. As these values are all based on citations to "research articles," it is not surprising that they are at least moderately and often strongly positively correlated.

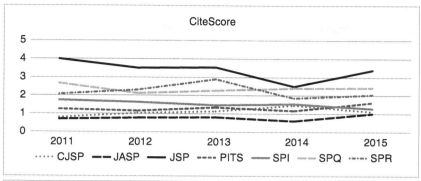
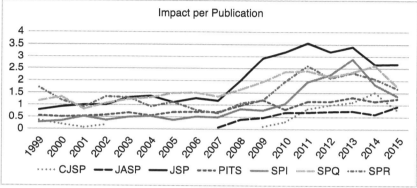

Figure 2.2 CiteScore and Impact per Publication for School Psychology Journals. Values were obtained from the Scopus database

Note. CJSP = *Canadian Journal of School Psychology*; JASP = *Journal of Applied School Psychology*; JSP = *Journal of School Psychology*; PITS = *Psychology in the Schools*; SPI = *School Psychology International*; SPQ = *School Psychology Quarterly*; SPR = *School Psychology Review*.

It is wise to review more than a single citation metric for a single year when selecting journals to which to submit your manuscripts. In terms of which metrics to consider, from my vantage point, the two primary citation-based metrics, the Impact Factor and the 5-year Impact Factor offer sufficient variation to evaluate the influence of a journal in the peer-reviewed literature. Although frequently referenced along with these two other impact factor values, the Immediacy Index is mercurial and varies most commonly across school psychology journals with the publication of special issues. CiteScore and Impact per Publication seem to be viable alternatives to the impact factor values for journals not listed in the Journal Citation Reports but included in other databases.

The patterns of correlations between the citation-based metrics are reflected in the patterns of highs and lows across Figures 2.1, 2.2, 2.3, and 2.4. For example, across the five journals listed in both Journal Citation

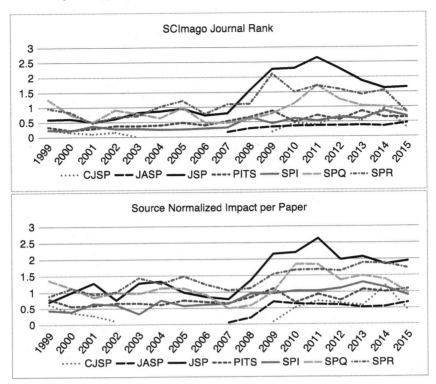

Figure 2.3 SCImago Journal Rank and Source Normalized Impact per Paper for School Psychology Journals. Values were obtained from the Scopus database

Note. CJSP = *Canadian Journal of School Psychology*; JASP = *Journal of Applied School Psychology*; JSP = *Journal of School Psychology*; PITS = *Psychology in the Schools*; SPI = *School Psychology International*; SPQ = *School Psychology Quarterly*; SPR = *School Psychology Review*.

Reports and Scopus, the Impact Factor, the 5-year Impact Factor, CiteScore, Impact per Publication, SCImago Journal Rank, and Source Normalized Impact per Paper, and Article Influence are highest for *Journal of School Psychology* and *School Psychology Review*. *Psychology in the Schools* and *School Psychology International* tend to have the lowest values across metrics. When *Canadian Journal of School Psychology* and *Journal of Applied School Psychology* are considered, their impact indices are the lowest of the seven journals. Exceptions to this pattern surface when the Eigenfactor Score and Normalized Eigenfactor Score values are considered, as these metrics (like the h- and h5-indices) do not adjust for the number of articles published in a journal and some journals publish many more articles each year than others. As evident in Figure 2.4, *Psychology in the Schools* demonstrates higher Eigenfactor Score and Normalized Eigenfactor Score values, relative to most other journals, than with other metrics as it publishes many more articles than all the other journals. Figure 2.5 makes it clear that *Psychology*

Selecting the Optimal Journal Outlets 41

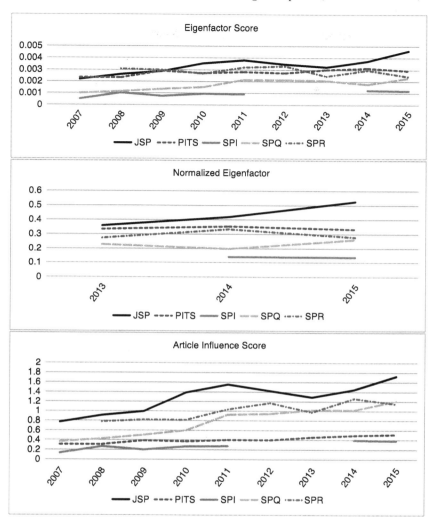

Figure 2.4 Eigenfactor Scores, Normalized Eigenfactor Scores, and Article Influence Score for School Psychology Journals

Note. Values were obtained from the Journal Citation Reports database. JSP = *Journal of School Psychology*; PITS = *Psychology in the Schools*; SPI = *School Psychology International*; SPQ = School Psychology Quarterly; SPR = *School Psychology Review*.

in the Schools publishes substantially more articles (M = 81.3, SD = 21.0) than other journals, which ranged from an average of 18 articles (*Journal of Applied School Psychology*) to 42 articles (*School Psychology International*).

The seven school psychology generalist journals indexed in Scopus are the most well-established and influential journals in the field. Although the patterns of influence of these journals might change over time and those not

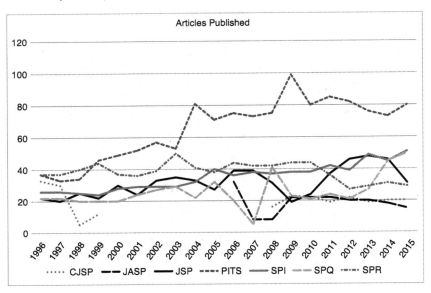

Figure 2.5 Articles Published in School Psychology Journals from 1996 to 2015

Note. Values were obtained from the Scopus database. CJSP = *Canadian Journal of School Psychology*; JASP = *Journal of Applied School Psychology*; JSP = *Journal of School Psychology*; PITS = *Psychology in the Schools*; SPI = *School Psychology International*; SPQ = *School Psychology Quarterly*; SPR = *School Psychology Review*. Scopus registered five articles published in *School Psychology Quarterly* during 2007, which is clearly an error; there may be other errors evident in the database that were not identified in preparing this figure.

indexed might have stronger influence in the near future, I suggest four tiers of generalist journals in school psychology based on recent patterns of citation-based metrics (see also Floyd et al., 2011). *Journal of School Psychology, School Psychology Quarterly,* and *School Psychology Review* are in the highest tier, *Psychology in the Schools* and *School Psychology International* are in a tier below, and *Canadian Journal of School Psychology* and *Journal of Applied School Psychology* are in a tier below that. Other journals listed in Table 2.1 not indexed in Journal Citation Reports, Scopus, or the like can be viewed as in the lowest tier.

The same general rules for determining tiers for journals in school psychology can be applied to specialty journals and journals from related fields. Those indexed by Clarivate Analytics' Journal Citation Reports, Elsevier's Scopus, and the like and receiving citation-based index values comparable to those of the top-tier journals in school psychology (with Impact Factor values of 2.0 or higher) should be considered desirable options. Those indexed but receiving lower values (e.g., Impact Factor values of around 1.0) and those indexed in only Elsevier's Scopus might be less desirable. Finally, those not indexed—such as many new online journals (including open-access journals; see Silvia, 2015)—should be considered least desirable. Alternately, ranking and percentile rank values associated with these values can be compared within fields. For example, values in the top 10% of journals in the Psychology-Educational category would be seen as having far higher impact than those in the bottom 10%.

Conclusion

In selecting journals to which to submit your manuscripts, you should aim high—striving to submit to the most well-known, high-impact journals. You want people to see your best work in the pages of those journals and to read, apply information from, and cite your articles. You must also balance payoffs and risks. Thus, you should be realistic in your expectations based on the quality of your research and writing as well as your other time commitments. Some of your manuscripts might be of the highest quality based on their key features (e.g., large sample size, methodological control, or statistical sophistication), but it is likely that many are not. Sometimes, you should go for the big payoffs, and other times you should settle for easy hits. As such, send your strongest manuscripts to the highest-tier journals and your weaker manuscripts to lower-tier journals (especially specialty journals). Do not forget to (a) seek out mentorship from more senior researchers when the decision point is not clear and (b) in cases of university professors, consider the expectations of your department, college, and university, as some are more concerned about publication numbers than the specific journals in which you publish and their impact factors.

Note

1 Clarivate Analytics' journal-based citation metrics are derived from the Journal Citation Reports database and not the Web of Science databases. These two databases are overlapping but distinct in their focus, as the former highlights features of journals and the latter highlights features of articles included within those journals.

References

American Psychological Association. (2010). *Publication manual of the American Psychological Association* (6th ed.). Washington, DC: American Psychological Association.

Anseel, F., Duyck, W., De Baene, W., & Brysbaert, M. (2004). Journal impact factors and self-citations: Implications for psychology journals. *American Psychologist, 59*, 49–51.

Bray, M. A., & Kehle, T. J. (Eds.). (2011). *Oxford handbook of school psychology.* New York, NY: Oxford University Press.

Burns, M. K. (Ed.). (in press). *Introduction to school psychology: Controversies and current practice.* New York, NY: Oxford University Press.

Cabell's International. (2015). *Electronic research database of academic journals* [data file]. Retrieved from www.cabells.com

Carper, R. M., & Williams, R. L. (2004). Article publications, journal outlets, and article themes for current faculty in APA-accredited school psychology programs: 1995–1999. *School Psychology Quarterly, 19*, 141–165.

44 Randy G. Floyd

Egghe, L. (2010). The Hirsch index and related impact measures. *Annual Review of Information Science and Technology, 44*, 65–114.

Fagan, T. K., &Wise, P. S. (2007). *School psychology: Past, present, and future*. Bethesda, MD: National Association of School Psychologists.

Floyd, R. G., Cooley, K. M., Arnett, J. E., Fagan, T. K., Mercer, S. H., & Hingle, C. (2011). An overview and analysis of journal operations, journal publication patterns, and journal impact in school psychology and related fields. *Journal of School Psychology, 49*, 617–647.

Harrison, P. L., & Thomas, A. (Eds.). (2014). *Best practices in school psychology* (6th ed.). Bethesda, MD: National Association of School Psychologists.

Hulac, D., Johnson, N. D., Ushijima, S. C., & Schneider, M. M. (2016). Publication outlets for school psychology faculty: 2010 to 2015. *Psychology in the Schools, 53*, 1085–1093.

Garfield, E. (2006). The history and meaning of the journal impact factor. *JAMA, 295*, 90–93.

Gimpel Peacock, G., Ervin, R. A., Daly, E. J., & Merrell, K. W. (Eds.). (2010). *Practical handbook of school psychology: Effective practices for the 21st century*. New York, NY: Guilford.

Grapin, S. L., & Kranzler, J. H. (Eds.). (2018). *School psychology: Professional issues and practices*. New York, NY: Springer.

Gutkin, T. B., & Reynolds, C. R. (Eds.). (2009). *The handbook of school psychology* (4th ed.). New York, NY: Wiley.

Jimerson, S. R., Oakland, T. D., & Farrell, P. T. (Eds.). (2007). *The handbook of international school psychology*. London, UK: SAGE.

Kranzler, J. H., Grapin, S. L., & Daley, M. L. (2011). Research productivity and scholarly impact of APA-accredited school psychology programs: 2005–2009. *Journal of School Psychology, 49*, 721–738.

Martinez, R. S., Floyd, R. G., & Erichsen, L. (2011). Strategies and attributes of highly productive scholars and contributors to the school psychology literature: Recommendations for increasing scholarly productivity. *Journal of School Psychology, 49*, 691–720.

Merrell, K. W., Ervin, R. A., & Gimpel Peacock, G. (2012). *School psychology for the 21st century: Foundations and practices* (2nd ed.). New York, NY: Guilford.

Neylon, C., & Wu, S. (2009). Article-level metrics and the evolution of scientific impact. *PLOS Biology*. https://doi.org/10.1371/journal.pbio.1000242

Priem, J., Taraborelli, D., Groth, P., & Neylon, C. (October, 26, 2010). Altmetrics: A manifesto. http://altmetrics.org/manifesto

Silvia, P. (2015). *Write it up: Practical strategies for writing and publishing journal articles*. Washington, DC: American Psychological Association.

Sternberg, R. J., & Sternberg, K. (2016). *The psychologist's companion* (6th ed.). New York, NY: Cambridge University Press.

Watkins, M. W., & Chan-Park, C. Y. (2015). The research impact of school psychology faculty. *Journal of School Psychology, 53*, 231–241.

3 The Peer-Review Process and Responding to Reviewer Feedback

Randy G. Floyd

The peer-review process seems daunting to many students, emerging scholars, and seasoned veterans. Even those scholars who routinely engage in this process as authors and as peer reviewers are frustrated with the tedium of manuscript preparation and submission, dejected by its slow pace, beaten down by its rigor, and infuriated by comments from reviewers. The goal of this chapter is to offer insights into submitting manuscripts for peer review, understanding the review process, and responding appropriately to reviewer feedback. These insights should greatly reduce the impact of these unpleasant experiences while also increasing the probability of having manuscripts accepted by journals in the field.

What Should I Know When Submitting Manuscripts to Journals?

If you have crafted a high-quality manuscript and selected the best fitting journal to which to submit, you want to maximize your chance of success during the submission process. First, read the journal submission guidelines (usually presented in the most detail on journal websites) and be meticulous about employing them. You probably read these guidelines when drafting your manuscript, but, before submission, you need to carefully study them to ensure they are correctly implemented. There are many more idiosyncrasies across journals than you might anticipate. For example, *School Psychology Review* requires authors to embed tables in text (versus including them following references as in American Psychological Association [APA] style), and *Psychology in the Schools* discourages authors from using italics in the References section (as journal and book titles are routinely italicized in APA style). Several journals now require a section in the Discussion that addresses implications for practitioners in the field, which is not routinely required.

Second, you will need to explore the web-based manuscript submission portal, as they often differ in their requirements across journals. For example, some portals require you to enter in keywords, whereas other have you select them from a list. Some request that you include a blinded title page, whereas others require you to exclude the title page altogether. Sometimes, there are even worse problems—such as when there are discrepancies between guidelines for authors (often written by the editor) and the requirements of the submission portal (often standard across journals associated with a publisher). Anyway, you should plan to invest a good deal of time reviewing and responding to submission requirements.

Third, craft a strong letter to the editor, which is often called the *submission letter* or *cover letter* (a throwback to days of recent past when manuscripts were submitted by mail in hard copy form (and this letter laid atop the copies)). Across almost 1,000 manuscripts I processed at *Journal of School Psychology*, I found that many authors submitted inadequately developed submission letters. I still recall one that essentially said, "Hi, Randy. I hope that you like our paper. Thank you." I returned this manuscript to the author requesting more details and a resubmission prior to peer review, but there were also poorly developed submission letters that accompanied weak manuscript submissions that I rejected without peer review. With this in mind, you should review chapter 8 (especially p. 232, Figure 8.1) of the *Publication Manual of the American Psychological Association* (APA, 2010) for guidelines for developing these submission letters. I have included one as a model in Table 3.1, which my students and I routinely use. It can be reproduced in its entirety and freely, without fear of being accused of plagiarism. Notice that it addresses page length and word counts, the request for a masked review, blinding of the manuscript, authorship order and the corresponding author, copyright transfer, institutional review board approval, submission to only one journal, prior dissemination of findings, a financial conflict of interest, content to be included in an author note, and contact information. Some of these items are addressed more thoroughly in the next chapter (Chapter 4, Floyd), and opportunities to alert the editor about potential problems (e.g., duplicate publications and conflicts of interest) should not be overlooked. With many submission portals, you could also enter (or otherwise convey) this same information by pasting in text and selecting boxes, but developing a standard submission letter remains important.

I am often asked whether authors should suggest reviewers, as modeled in the sample submission letter in the *Publication Manual* (APA, 2010, p. 232, Figure 8.1). At *Journal of School Psychology*, I cannot recall more than a single case in which authors requested reviewers or asked that editorial board members not serve in this role. Some submission portals, however, require authors to do so. In my experience as an author, I have requested that an editorial board member who served as an editor of another journal and previously rejected my manuscript not serve as a reviewer when I submitted that manuscript to another journal. On two occasions, my co-authors and I requested that an editorial board member who might be prejudiced against our research study not serve as a reviewer. In one case, a co-author of mine had an ongoing professional conflict with an editorial board member, and we requested that this person not serve as a reviewer. In the other case, our research study refuted the conclusions of a publication of one of the journal's associate editors, and we requested that this person not serve as handling editor. It is humorous that,

Table 3.1 An Example Journal Submission Letter Addressing Basic Features and Ethical Imperatives

---

Dear Dr. Editor:

Please accept the submission of our manuscript as a *High Impact Factor Journal* general article. The manuscript is titled "My Life's Work," and it is 22 pages and 5,835 words long (including the title page, references, and a table but not the abstract). We are also submitting three supplemental tables (A–C), including 2,890 words, that are nine pages in length.

My co-authors and I wish the manuscript to be given a masked review. I have removed our names, affiliations, and contact information from the manuscript itself. My co-authors (in order) are Author2 and Author3 from Research Productive University and Author4 from Liberal Arts College. I will be serving as corresponding author for this manuscript. I have assumed responsibility for keeping my co-authors informed of the progress through the editorial review process, the content of the reviews, and any revisions made. I understand that, if accepted for publication, a certification of authorship form will be required that all co-authors will sign.

This research was approved by Research Productive University's institutional review board.

OR

This research used publically available data, rather than human subject data, and is thus considered exempt and need not be subjected to institutional review board review.

The manuscript has not been submitted for concurrent consideration by another journal or published in any part elsewhere. Portions of this research were presented at the National Association of Professionals annual convention as well as a regional research colloquium at Research Productive University.

We have cited a book co-written by one co-author of this manuscript, Author2:

Author2. (2015). *An important book*. Small City, Big State: Publish Anything Press.

Thus, one co-author has financial interest in publishing this manuscript.

If this manuscript is accepted for publication, we would like the following author note to be included: This manuscript is based on a dissertation submitted by the first author under supervision of the second author in partial fulfillment of the requirements for a doctoral degree in school psychology. We thank dissertation committee members Dr. Faculty1, Dr. Faculty2, and Dr. Faculty3 for their helpful comments. We appreciate Examiner1, Examiner2, and Examiner3, for their assistance with data collection and Elementary School and its administrators and teachers for supporting this research.

Please address all correspondence to me at 11 Psychology Building; University A; Big City, Small State 24901 (standard mail); at Author1@university.edu (email), or at 314-159-2654 (phone).

Sincerely,

Author1, Highest Degree

---

in the latter case, our manuscript was assigned to the exact associate editor we identified in our request. The good news is that our manuscript was ultimately accepted for publication by this same associate editor after standard processing. In general, I would not bother requesting reviewers (and if required, I would enter "None requested"), but it makes sense to alert the editor, on

48   *Randy G. Floyd*

occasion, to potential personal and professional conflicts that might bias evaluation of your manuscript. As is apparent from our experience, the editor might not agree with (or even read) your request.

In the end, conduct final edits of your manuscript before uploading it. In particular, for most journals, ensure that your manuscript is sufficiently masked. According to the *Publication Manual* (APA, 2010. p. 226),

> In a masked review, the identity of the author of a manuscript is concealed from reviewers during the review process. . . . Authors are responsible for concealing their identities in manuscripts that are to receive masked review; for example, they should take extra care to format their manuscripts so that their identities as document creators are not easily revealed.

It seems to me that authors are given conflicting information about these efforts, which leads to potentially serious errors. For example, the *Publication Manual* (APA, 2010) suggests, in addressing self-plagiarism (see Chapter 4, Floyd), that authors use first-person pronouns to alert readers to their prior research findings. Following this suggestion, authors should write something like, "In prior research, we examined the effects of peer-mediated reading interventions with second-grade students," but it is unclear if they should cite their prior publication, essentially revealing their identities. The *Publication Manual* also conveys that "As multiple reports from large-scale or longitudinal studies are created, authors are obligated to cite prior reports on the project to help the reader understand the work accurately" (p. 15). If these reports are from the same author team, citing those works would potentially reveal the identities of at least some of the authors of the manuscript under review.

Authors sometimes go overboard to mask their manuscripts. I have seen authors apparently including in-text self-citations and references in the manuscript but blackening them out before submitting. On a few occasions, authors blackened out or otherwise did not report their names in citations in text and in references, but they included the unaltered title of their articles in the references. It was very easy to identify them following an internet search by article title. Thus, these authors unmasked their manuscript rather than promoting a masked review! Instead, I suggest citing your own prior work as you would cite any other reference—referring to you and your co-authors by name—and not using pronouns to indicate the study was yours. Thus, rather than "In prior research, we examined the effects of peer-mediated reading interventions with second-grade students," you would state something like "Author (2015) examined the effects of peer-mediated reading interventions with second-grade students." Reviewers might be able to read through the lines and identify you as the author of your new submission, but you have significantly reduced the probability of such using this simple strategy. After your manuscript is accepted, you can alter the text to use first-person pronouns, if desired. There is no good method to ensure a masked review when citing your own in-press articles that have not yet been posted online or assigned a digital object identifier (DOI, see Chapter 1, Floyd), but the easiest strategy is to omit these articles from your manuscript (a) until after the manuscript under review has been tentatively accepted or (b) until a DOI has been assigned to the in-press article you want to cite.

Review your manuscript with scrupulous attention to detail before submitting. In addition, after you have uploaded your manuscript, review the uploaded file (which is often converted to a PDF). Check your margins, page breaks, consistency of fonts, spelling and grammar, and formatting of tables, figures, and statistical symbols. Make certain that all tracking and comments have been removed; I have seen numerous submissions that contained such markups as the submitting author failed to submit a clean copy with all markups removed. In the end, sweating the details before submission prevents both embarrassment and a delay in your manuscript being processed.

What Should I Expect as an Outcome of My Submission?

After submission, within about a week or two, you will be contacted by someone associated with the journal. It is frequently the editor who makes the first contact, but it might be a handling editor or an editorial assistant. Usually, this first contact (via email) indicates that your manuscript has been received, screened, and assigned to a handling editor. Often, but not always, this contact includes the target decision date or the typical length of the review period. Based on Chapters 5 through 15 in this volume, written by journal editors, this review period is likely to range from three weeks to three months. The goal of a two-month review period is still probably most common across journals (APA, 2010). Alternately, it is possible (and increasingly so, relative to previous decades) that your manuscript will be returned to you (Floyd et al., 2011). You might be asked to remedy some problems that were identified during its screening before resubmitting. Your manuscript might also be returned with a reject decision and without full review. Although rejection without full review is initially disappointing, the benefit to authors is that there is little time wasted when the outcome of the editor's decision would be exactly the same following two or more months of full review (see Albers et al., 2011). The decision letter accompanying the reject decision might include valuable suggestions regarding ways to improve your manuscript and offer other journals to which you could submit the manuscript. Screening, rejecting, and returning manuscripts to authors without full review requires extra effort on the part of the journal editorial team, but it reduces the number of manuscripts processed by handling editors as well as reviews required by editorial board reviewers. Thus, it effectively speeds up the process of full review and allows for journals to nurture authors of the strongest submissions toward publication.

If the manuscript was distributed for peer review, the handling editor will develop a decision letter based primarily on the comments of peer reviewers. These comments are almost always appended to the decision letters (APA, 2010). Although the handling editor also considers the recommendations of the peer reviewers regarding the editorial decision (tentatively accept, reject, etc.), the final editorial decision is not usually based on reviewer consensus or a majority decision. Handling editors—possessing the ability to weigh the strengths and weaknesses of manuscripts relative to journal-specific standards after conducting an independent review of the manuscript—can typically evaluate each manuscript from a better vantage point than any single peer reviewer. As a result, their decisions might not be congruent with reviewers, and authors should not be alarmed by this fact. Peer reviewers provide advisory information to handling editors in most cases. Hence, the highest-functioning journals employ wise, experienced handling editors.

When I receive notification (often via email) that an editorial decision has been rendered on one of my manuscripts, I feel both excitement ("Did we do it right? What if they accepted our submission with only minor revisions?") as well as dread and mild nausea ("What if they totally misunderstood our goals and methods and everyone hated it? It's surely a total reject!"). Based on my discussions with others (and see Dr. Ethan Van Norman's blog post https:// ssspresearch.org/earlycareerforum/demystifying-peer-review-process-advice-associate-editors), this mix of emotions is common. Because most of us have more manuscripts rejected than accepted, the feelings of anxiety and dread (but perhaps not the nausea) are understandable.

Under ideal circumstances, your initial submission is accepted without revisions, but this outcome is extremely rare and essentially a fantasy. Furthermore, tentative (or conditional) acceptance with minor revisions is also just as chimerical for most authors. The status quo with an initial submission to a journal is some form of a decision to reject the manuscript. Usually, the decision letters include either a strong statement conveying that your manuscript does not meet the standards of the journal (as in a decision of *reject*) or reference to an invitation or encouragement to resubmit (as in a decision of *reject: revise and resubmit*). The probability of a rejection letter is extremely high, but do not despair. It happens to all authors—and even more often for authors who submit a lot of manuscripts for review. Silvia (2015) reported viewing rejection letters like sales tax on publications. As the proportion of rejections to submissions is fairly constant across journals, when you submit a greater number of manuscripts, you are faced with more and more rejections. Your dear hope is that you have been given the opportunity to respond to reviewer feedback and resubmit.

Rejection

Following a rejection decision (without the opportunity to resubmit), you have important decisions to make. You could complain or appeal to the editor, forget about the paper and put it in the proverbial file drawer, or submit to another journal. Complaining to the handling editor (or editor of the journal) is never a good idea, as most decisions are final. Complaints cause the most even-keeled editor and editorial team much distress, so do not fire off a complaint or spend days generating one when feeling slighted or misunderstood by reviewers. (Remember that almost everyone on the editorial board is volunteering service to the field.) If you are feeling this way, it is better to get over your hurt feelings, revise the manuscript, and submit it elsewhere than grumble and demand reconsideration of your manuscript. Do not submit your rejected manuscript to the same journal for reconsideration without encouragement to do so.

In contrast to run-of-the-mill complaints reflecting hurt feelings, formal appeals are typically reserved for abject mishandling of a manuscript or evidence of ethical violations apparent during the peer-review process. Although many journals have an appeals procedure and the Committee on Publication Ethics Code of Conduct (1999) implored all journal editors to employ one and make it available to authors, they are often not published and difficult for an author to locate. Such appeals are low incident events, so editors call on these procedures only rarely. Descriptions of appeals procedures appear to have become more nebulous during the past decade (see www.apa. org/pubs/authors/appeals.aspx), but in most cases, the author is first directed to the handling editor in an attempt to resolve the problem. If there is no resolution, the appeal is usually directed to the editor and, if the editor cannot resolve the problem, the appeal is directed to an outside consultant not on the editorial board. In cases in which an appeal might be warranted, you might, unfortunately, need to contact the journal editor to request a description of its appeals procedure.

You should not bury every rejected manuscript, never to return to them again. In many cases, your manuscript might be reasonably strong and publishable, but it was rejected by peer reviewers for whom it did not resonate. They probably simply did not think it was strong enough to warrant publication. All authors have been there! Sometimes, it is more than lack of confidence in the viability of a manuscript: peer reviewers might identify a "fatal flaw" in your study that they believe severely limits the meaning that can be derived from it. Examples include using an extremely small sample, selection bias, lack of random assignment, lack of a comparison group with group-based research, and, with single-case designs, lack of experimental control and lack of a concurrent multiple baseline.

When reviewers mention or otherwise indicate fatal flaws are present in your study, you should not immediately give up. It is possible that they are wrong in drawing this conclusion. In many cases, it is wise to consult with a mentor, colleague, or more senior scholar to determine whether these reviewers are right or wrong. In cases in which they are right, you should consider improving the quality of your study, such as collecting additional data to increase your sample size, conducting more advanced statistical analyses (e.g., removing existing confounds), or if all else fails, recognizing a limitation in the Discussion section would allow the manuscript to be published. Fatal flaws, however, do not include problems with the content of the Introduction or Discussion sections, failure to follow Journal Article Publishing Standards (APA, 2010) when reporting methods and results, or a weak justification for

52 *Randy G. Floyd*

the study. Weaknesses such as these can be remedied with revision and perseverance in the face of prior rejection. However, if the same comments regarding fatal flaws surface across repeated reviews across journals, it might be time to weigh the costs and benefits of pursuing publication of your manuscript. Your time might be better spent trying to publish more viable scholarship.

The chapters in this book, as well as the strategies discussed in Chapter 2 in this book, should make it easy to identify other generalist school psychology journals or specialist journals to which to submit a previously rejected manuscript. Rather than submit the same version of the manuscript again, you should make as many of the suggested changes offered by peer reviewers as possible because it is likely that one of the prior reviewers will review your submission to the next journal. The last thing you want is for a reviewer to react with indignation upon seeing your manuscript and deem you lazy and unresponsive to the feedback from the prior submission. Such reactions usually lead to your manuscript being rejected yet again.

Revise and Resubmit

Although it does not necessarily sound like a good thing, the decision of reject, revise and resubmit is a lot more positive than it might seem. Silvia (2015) suggested that you should view it as the equivalent to conditional acceptance. In receipt of such a decision, you should first closely read the decision letter and determine if the handling editor and reviewers identified significant problems that will decrease the likelihood of your manuscript being accepted following revision and resubmission. Flaws might be apparent—as there are limitations to all research studies and the manuscripts that describe them—but when given the opportunity to resubmit, I suggest you investigate every option for doing so. One benefit of resubmission is that you will likely face the same reviewers who initially reviewed your manuscript. On the surface level, that sounds terrible, but it is not; you now have insights into these reviewers and know exactly what they want to see in a revision. New reviewers are likely to see other problems and want something else from you, so you are effectively starting over when submitting elsewhere. Furthermore, remember that publishers task editors and handling editors with publishing articles in the journal's pages, so your polished, resubmitted manuscript assists them in meeting their goals better than any initial submission possibly could. Your resubmitted manuscript has a much higher probability of being accepted than your original submission. In school psychology, I would estimate that this probability increases from less than 15% for an original submission to better than 75% for a resubmission (see Henson, 2007). Definitely go for the revision!

Acceptance

If you are fortunate enough to have your manuscript accepted for publication (even after numerous resubmissions), congratulations! The editor, editorial assistant, or sometimes a journal manager or copyeditor (with whom you have not previously interacted during the peer-review process and who is not usually listed as being associated with the journal) will ensure you have completed the necessary forms (e.g., a copyright agreement). Within a couple of months of acceptance, you will receive an email providing access to your *page proofs*, which are usually electronic copies of your manuscript formatted as an article—with wide margins and directives (often called *queries*) from a copyeditor. Usually, there are detailed instructions provided by the publisher during this phase, and there is often a request for a very rapid turnaround (e.g., three days) of the page proofs. Consider reviewing chapter 9 in Silvia (2015) and chapter 22 in Day and Gastel (2015) for recommendations for reviewing them. In general, I encourage authors to do more than respond to queries when reviewing proofs. From my experience as editor and author, I know there are frequently errors introduced during formatting or only noticed when content is reviewed in page proofs. As editor, I found numerous problems with column and row alignment in tables, headings formatted incorrectly, and statistical formulas and symbols that were not accurately reproduced. Most commonly, author notes were not transferred from the web portal or submission letter; I always check for the inclusion of author notes in my own page proofs.

How Do I Respond to Reviewer Feedback?

When I receive a decision letter, I tend to scan it as soon as possible (if not immediately). My heart races and my brow furrows, as the reviews sometimes go on and on. Astonishment, frustration, and anger might consume me, and I feel overwhelmed as I consider how to respond to all the comments. There are strategies for coping with all these feelings. First, you must remind yourself of the (a) purpose of peer review—to critically and skeptically evaluate the content in the paper that was submitted—as well as (b) limits in communication via writing. Reviewers are expected to be critical of submissions, and it is also easy for you to overlook limitations in your own studies and fail to convey your intended meaning, despite your best intentions and effort. I have often said that every writer needs a good editor, and I feel strongly that critical reviews and scrupulous review of text improve the quality of what is published. We should reframe our conception of reviewers as consultants rather than critics (Johnson & Mullen, 2007) and reviews as "free writing advice from scholars in your field" (Silvia, 2007, p. 185).

Second, breathe deeply and do not take reviewer comments personally. It is possible that reviewers can determine that you contributed to the paper, but it is doubtful that they had you in mind when reviewing it. It is also likely they were not completely sensitive to your feelings in their wording of their comments, but they almost certainly were not attacking you or your research team. Third, take your time in processing the comments in the review. Read and reflect upon them as early and as deeply as you can, set them aside, and return to them within a week or two. Silvia (2015) recommended responding

54 *Randy G. Floyd*

with a revision within two days of receipt, but I believe that strong revisions take time. Repeated exposure to the reviews and steady progress in addressing them tend to reduce your apprehension (and outrage); reviews never look as bad as when you first read them. If the handling editor has requested a quick turnaround (e.g., 30 days), I suggest kindly requesting an extension after a week or two has passed. Editors usually suggest swift revisions in order to keep authors engaged in the process, to move strong manuscripts toward acceptance, and to ultimately fill journal issues with numerous articles. It is highly unlikely that, in most cases, the editor needs your article so rapidly as to fill the next issue. Trust that the editor will grant your extension, and identify an alternate target date for your resubmission. Finally, sit down to address reviewer comments with the goal of (a) responding to the easiest items and (b) initiating problem-solving to overcome the most challenging items. This step might take courage and a "can-do" mindset (Johnson & Mullen, 2007).

Structure of Response Letters

It is typically the responsibility of the corresponding author (often the first author of the manuscript) to coordinate the revision process and develop the response letter. Even if tasks are delegated to co-authors, it is important to coordinate a cohesive plan for revision. Martinez et al. (2011, p. 702) quoted one researcher who expressed the magnitude of carefully crafting the response letter:

> One highly productive scholar suggested that, "the most important product one produces is the letter to the editor that goes along with a revised/ resubmitted piece." Indeed, doing so "mak[es] it really easy for the editor to see that the revision is desirable." Further, "laying out the rationale for what you did (not) change and why is essential for getting the piece into print."

Although it is sometimes suggested that authors respond only to the comments of the handling editor and to select comments from reviewers they deem relevant, I believe that authors are most successful when they respond, in an appropriate manner, to every editor and reviewer comment. The *Publication Manual* (APA, 2010) indicates the same. However, not every comment should lead to changes to the manuscript text. As noted by Johnson and Mullen (2007), some comments "will be idiosyncratic or superfluous— perhaps reflecting the reviewer's pet peeves, theoretical biases, or down-right misunderstandings" (p. 131). I address how to respond to these comments in the section that follows.

The response letter should be meticulously constructed, and I have seen at least three methods to structure them. The *point-counterpoint method* reproduces the decision letter, and authors insert their responses to each editor and reviewer comment directly following them in the response letter. An example is included in Table 3.2. The initial step with this method is copying the text

Peer-Review & Responding to Feedback 55

Table 3.2 The Initial Sections of an Example Letter Introducing Responses to Reviewers' Comments

---

Dear Dr. Editor:

Thank you very much for your thorough review and encouraging us to resubmit our manuscript ID-2017-0200, entitled "A Truly Great Article about Gifted Assessment."

We have responded to all reviewers' comments in the bolded text that follows. Again, thank you for this opportunity to revise and resubmit our manuscript. We hope our revisions meet your high standards and fully address the reviewers' recommendations.

Reviewer 1

Introduction

1. At the beginning of the manuscript, authors should provide a broader context for understanding the gifted assessment process. First, more theoretical information about intellectual giftedness is needed: What are some of the theories about what giftedness is? What implications do these theories have for how we identify children?

Authors: We reviewed the recent literature on this topic, and without adding excessive length to the Introduction, we included this content (on p. 2) and added two recent references: . . . To us, this sentence opens up this discussion of different theoretical perspectives and assessment methods. Please let us know if more information is needed.

Method

1. The generalizability of the participants in this sample should be outlined. A better explanation of differing identification processes in the literature review should presage the description of this sample, as participants were obtained from a single state and single district.

Authors: Thank you for this recommendation. As we noted previously, we added a sentence about the recent survey from the National Association for Gifted Children (NAGC, 2015) on page 2. In addition, we have added additional information on our participant sample on p. 12: . . . Finally, we addressed the limitations associated with our sampling plan in the Discussion section (p. 23) by stating . . .

---

of the decision letter (as they are almost always communicated via email these days) and pasting it into a word processing program document. The *table method* typically employs a two-column table, where each editor and reviewer comment occupies a row. Their comments are reproduced in the left column, and author comments are included in the right column. Sometimes, there is a third column that includes manuscript page numbers associated with the author responses. Finally, the *summary paragraph method* includes original text from the authors that articulates the edits that they made. This method often does not reference specific comments from the review or cite manuscript page numbers. Instead, it provides a narrative account of the revisions.

As an editor, reviewer, and author, I believe the point-counterpoint method is the best and most efficient of all these methods. (Plus, some submission portal systems do not accommodate tables, as they cannot be pasted into windows in the system.) As an editor and reviewer, when authors use the point-counterpoint method, I can review exactly what I stated previously in my comments.

56 *Randy G. Floyd*

It prevents me from having to find the document containing my prior comments before reviewing the authors' revised manuscript. It also links every editor and reviewer comment to the authors' responses and demonstrates to me that the authors have been thorough and responsive. Thus, this method makes reviewing the revisions relatively easy from the peer-review side. From an author's perspective, the point-counterpoint method is relatively easy to format. The biggest challenge—using the formatting modeled in Table 3.3—is inserting and bolding responses. Of course, this method does not allow much room to avoid reviewer requests; in fact, it forces authors to address them through either revisions or carefully crafted responses (covered in the next section).

The table method is basically the same as the point-counterpoint method, but it is far more difficult to format. Designing a table and copying and pasting every reviewer comment (or otherwise paraphrasing them) in table cells is infinitely more tedious than responding to each point in sequence in standard text. Finally, the summary paragraph method seems to lack the structure and level of detail that are strengths of the other two methods. It was probably the preferred method in the past when it was not possible to copy and paste the whole decision letter into a draft of the response letter (as hard copies were the primary medium of communication); summarizing was far easier than re-typing the decision letter. The summary paragraph method is also limited in that it can lead authors to unintentionally fail to address an important comment, evoking the ire of a reviewer and the editor and hastening a decision of reject. In general, I think that editors and reviewers like seeing their prior comments in their original form, and they often become frustrated when it is not easy for them to do so.

Wording Responses

When writing a response letter, address comments primarily to the handling editor who will render the decision on your manuscript. Thus, most authors will use second-person pronouns ("you") in responses. As an author, your goal is to demonstrate (to both the handling editor and reviewers) what Joireman and Van Lange (2015) referred to as the 3Rs: reflection, rationality, and respect. In addition to these 3Rs, I suggest a fourth R—responsiveness—that highlights evidence of your actions during the revision process. A 4R approach seems highly beneficial.

Following a brief opening statement addressing the handling editor (see Table 3.2), authors can include three classes of adaptive responses that are consistent with the 4R approach. They indicate the following: (1) "We appreciate it," (2) "We were responsive," and (3) the most challenging one, "We considered your point and ways to address it." Table 3.3 provides examples of each class of response. In terms of expressing appreciation, I agree with Joireman and Van Lange (2015, p. 73) who conveyed that

> It may seem hard, or unnecessary, but thanking reviewers can go a long way toward establishing a positive response to the revision. The approach

Peer-Review & Responding to Feedback   57

can be overdone, of course, and different authors will feel more or less comfortable with this approach (with some perhaps feeling it is too deferential). Our advice is to do what is comfortable and (if you can live with it) to err on the side of being overly polite.

Responses expressing appreciation can be brief, as illustrated in Table 3.3. In terms of demonstrating responsiveness, it is important to describe your actions that were directly related to the comments from reviews as well as actions that extended them. Joireman and Van Lange (2015) referred to these extensions as overdelivering, and I can confirm that it is impressive to handling editors when

Table 3.3 Examples of Appropriate Responses to Reviewer Comments and Recommendations

We appreciate it.
- Thank you for these positive comments.
- We appreciate this recommendation and have made this edit as recommended.
- We are grateful that this reviewer identified this error.
- Thank you for pointing out that we should more thoroughly review our results in this manner.

We were responsive.
- This statement has been removed.
- We have done so.
- We worked diligently to identify these errors and altered the text as suggested.
- We understand that our description of coding methods was confusing. We have made an attempt to clarify these terms at the top of page 9. Our new text reads as follows: . . .
- In the first paragraph on page 10, we hope we have revised the text to be clearer (referring a key and a criterion level of coding). The new text reads this way: . . .
- After reviewing this text, we have attempted to clarify this issue. In addition, we added a footnote defining our key terms. Our revised text reads as follows: . . .
- We apologize for causing this confusion. We worked for more than an hour to address this point, and we hope that we did so in a satisfactory manner. First, we altered the first sentence of the paragraph in question to include the percentage of states that employed a blanket statement addressing both reliability and validity standards. Here it is: . . . Second, although we did not convey this point in text, it is important to point out a nuance in coding this variable for specific measures. Mainly, the blanket statement did not necessarily generalize to all measures—especially if a type of measure was not mentioned in any way in the regulations or guidelines. For example, if a measure type was not mentioned in the regulations or guidelines, but a blanket statement referencing reliability and validity standards was included, we did not count this criterion as being met for the given measurement type not mentioned. If the handling editor would like us to make this point more explicit in text, please let us know. At present, statements such as this one (on p. 15) imply such a rule was probably followed: . . .
- We hope that we addressed this point in our earlier comment in response to Reviewer 1. Here it is again: . . .

(continued)

58   Randy G. Floyd

Table 3.3 Examples of Appropriate Responses to Reviewer Comments and Recommendations *(continued)*

We considered your point and ways to address it.

- We have considered this recommendation and hope that the text we included at the beginning of the discussion is sufficient to address it. We agree that adding tables or figures would make it easier to make comparisons but feel that adding them may be redundant with what is in the text and unnecessarily lengthen the manuscript. If this reviewer or the associate editor feels strongly about this matter, we can include a table.
- Thank you for your suggestion. We have given it much consideration but are unsure how to implement it; we welcome more specific directives addressing this point.
- Although we agree with this point, we struggled to implement it without substantially altering the structure of our Method section and significantly lengthening the manuscript. It was our hope that descriptions of the results would inform readers about how content was coded, but we may have failed to sufficiently inform readers. We welcome further suggestions from this reviewer or the associate editor.
- Fearing that we may have made an error as this reviewer suggested, we turned toward the literature on the topic of regression toward the mean. Based on our understanding of the phenomenon, our conception appears to be correct. This reviewer's two examples are appropriate but limited, as the phenomenon also affects measurement outside of experimental and genetic studies. In the school psychology (and related) literature, it has been discussed at some length as applied to assessment of learning disabilities and the IQ-achievement discrepancy analysis. When we turned to the classic text on experimental design by Campbell and Stanley (1963), we found that it addressed these very questions—both in terms of cross-form measurement and intellectual giftedness.

  Campbell, D. T., & Stanley, J. C. (1963). *Experimental and quasi-experimental designs for research.* Boston: Houghton Mifflin. . . .

  In order to address this concern, we altered the text devoted to it on p. 7 and added two references. It now reads as follows: . . . Please let us know if we can improve upon these edits.

---

authors do so. Overdelivering might include expanding the literature review after realizing you have omitted some key findings, completing additional data analyses to control for confounds or to demonstrate that alternate analysis produce equivalent results, and adding limitations to your Discussion after realizing other potential challenges to interpreting your findings. Supporting your responses with references and including quotations from your revised text, as modeled in Table 3.3, strengthen your responses. In general, do not be concerned if your response letter is lengthy, as richer, more thorough responses are consistent with the 4R approach.

The last class of adaptive responses, where authors respond to comments that they were unable to address or that were based on incorrect information, is the most challenging to generate. Reviewers, like everyone else, can be (and often are) wrong in their conclusions. Handling editors know this fact, too. As modeled in Table 3.3, authors should not hesitate to respectfully challenge erroneous statements or gently ask the handling editor or a reviewer to provide more guidance regarding how to address a comment. When I have genuinely asked for additional guidance in a response letter, I do not recall anyone providing it or insisting that I respond to the original comment. If you are really stuck—hit with a major recommendation you cannot overcome—contact the handling editor to schedule a meeting by phone or videoconference. I have used this strategy three or four times as an author in order to clarify expectations for revision, and as editor and handling editor, I fostered use of it to support authors of numerous manuscripts that were ultimately published.

The following weak or otherwise inappropriate responses do not embody the 4Rs of reflection, rationality, respect, and responsiveness very well. My guess is that they increase the probability of your resubmitted manuscript being rejected.

- *We did not make those edits because they are beyond the scope of this study.* This comment does not indicate reflection or responsiveness and is evasive. Some reviewer recommendations are excessive and not easily integrated, but consider the point, note that you considered it, and find a way to address it somehow in the manuscript (e.g., an area of future research in the Discussion).
- *We did not address that point because it will increase the length of the manuscript beyond the allotted pages.* Again, this comment does not indicate reflection or responsiveness. Often, handling editors will allow authors to increase manuscript page length following revision. Moreover, there are almost always ways to cut text to add new text. Try to include some semblance of the content requested—even if it is brief.
- *We employed archival data and do not know the procedures used to collect the data.* This is a lackadaisical and inappropriate response, as there are almost always ways to secure additional information about the data collection process leading to archival data sets.
- *We cannot address this recommendation because we conducted this research in an applied setting and could not control these confounding variables. We noted the limitation in the Discussion.* This response is relatively common, and the authors should provide sound reasons to support the meaningfulness of the results after considering confounds. Some limitations are so severe that they completely undermine the study's results.
- *We do not know how to complete the requested analysis, so we opted for the more basic analysis and noted the limitation in the Discussion.* Again, noting a limitation in isolation is insufficient to many handling editors. Seeking support from other researchers (including adding a co-author) and consulting with the editor regarding support for completion of a more advanced analysis are more appropriate strategies than brushing aside requests for additional analyses.

60 *Randy G. Floyd*

- *We based our decision to use this method on another study's methods.* Without explanation, the handling editor and reviewers do not know the superiority or inferiority of the alternate methods. Relying on precedent versus well-reasoned scientific thinking is a risky strategy as not all peer-reviewed journal articles have been held to the highest standards prior to publishing, and methods and strategies improve over time.
- *Adding this method would require us to reanalyze our data, and we are unwilling to do so.* This comment clearly does not demonstrate responsiveness.
- *We think that the structure of the Introduction is adequate and have not made the requested change.* This one is defiant and opposing the 4R approach.
- *This reviewer is clearly biased—and a veritable idiot. Everyone knows that hypothesis has been falsified.* There is no place for such disrespectful and ad hominem comments during the peer-review process.

Final Editing

Make sure you have edited your revised manuscript with as much rigor as you edited your initial submission. I have often seen revisions introduce errors—including establishing internal contradictions in text (as original and revised text are mixed together). Joireman and Van Lange (2015) conveyed that "after all of the modifications have been made, the paper still must make sense as a whole" (p. 73). The strongest authors make extra efforts to present their revision in the best possible light.

Conclusion

Regardless of whether your goal is publishing in school psychology journals or in other journal outlets, the process toward publication requires access to key resources, self-reflection, attention to detail, civility, and perseverance. Applying a few additional "tricks of the trade" offered by insiders in the field—like those who have authored most chapters in this book—will significantly improve the probability of your achieving this goal.

References

Albers, C. A., Floyd, R. G., Fuhrmann, M. J., & Martinez, R. S. (2011). Publication criteria and recommended areas of improvement within school psychology journals as reported by editors, journal board members, and manuscript authors. *Journal of School Psychology, 49*, 669–689.

American Psychological Association. (2010). *Publication manual of the American Psychological Association* (6th ed.). Washington, DC: American Psychological Association.

Committee on Publication Ethics. (1999). *Guidelines on good publication practice.* Retrieved from https://publicationethics.org/files/u7141/1999pdf13.pdf

Day, R. A., & Gastel, B. (2015). *How to write and publish a scientific paper* (7th ed.). Santa Barbara, CA: Greenwood.

Floyd, R. G., Cooley, K. M., Arnett, J. E., Fagan, T. K., Mercer, S. H., & Hingle, C. (2011). An overview and analysis of journal operations, journal publication patterns, and journal impact in school psychology and related fields. *Journal of School Psychology, 49,* 617–647.

Henson, K. T. (2007). Writing for publication: Steps to excellence. *Phi Delta Kappa,* 88(10), 781–786.

Johnson, W. B., & Mullen, C. A. (2007). *Write to the top! How to become a prolific academic.* New York, NY: Macmillan.

Joireman, J., & Van Lange, P. A. M. (2015). *How to publish high-quality research: Discovering, building, and sharing the contribution.* Washington, DC: American Psychological Association.

Martinez, R. S., Floyd, R. G., & Erichsen, L. (2011). Strategies and attributes of highly productive scholars and contributors to the school psychology literature: Recommendations for increasing scholarly productivity. *Journal of School Psychology, 49,* 691–720.

Silvia, P. (2015). *Write it up: Practical strategies for writing and publishing journal articles.* Washington, DC: American Psychological Association.

4 Ethics in Manuscript Preparation, Publishing, and Dissemination

Randy G. Floyd

As in the practice of psychology and education, school psychologists, students in training, and other professionals must uphold the standards of their field when engaging in research and the publication process (Panter & Sterba, 2011). Consistent with this charge, this chapter addresses ethics and laws in conducting research, writing about its results, submitting manuscripts for publication, and sharing those publications. It will address the American Psychological Association (APA) and National Association of School Psychologists (NASP) codes of ethics, engaging in ethical research and publishing, and communicating with journal editors through submission letters. It will highlight issues related to authorship, techniques for preventing plagiarism, and posting documents on websites and commercial online repositories, such as ResearchGate.

Professional Ethics

One cannot review the ethics codes that guide the field of psychology without concluding that there are high standards for professional behavior in the area of research and publication. Most notably, APA's Ethical Principles of Psychologists and Code of Conduct (2002, including the 2010 Amendments; www.apa.org/ethics/code/index.aspx) address ethics in research and publication under its Standard 8. In addition, NASP's Principles for Professional Ethics (2010; go to www.nasponline.org/standards/2010standards.aspx) address them under its Principle IV.5. Contributing to the School Psychology Knowledge Base. In this section, I highlight five areas of convergence across these ethics codes: institutional approval, duplicate and piecemeal publications, plagiarism, authorship credit, and data sharing. When reviewing each, I will provide recommendations to guide the submission of manuscripts for publication. In addition, I present three areas uniquely addressed in the NASP Principles for Professional Ethics, including presenting results with integrity, correcting errors in publications, and redacting identifying information from case studies.

Institutional Approval

Both APA (2002, 2010a) and NASP (2010) ethics codes require that researchers attest to the fact that they sought and received approval to conduct their research prior to initiating it. APA conveys that "when institutional approval is required, psychologists provide accurate information about their research proposals and obtain approval prior to conducting the research. They conduct the research in accordance with the approved research protocol," and NASP asserts that "school psychologists obtain appropriate review and approval of proposed research prior to beginning their data collection." NASP provides additional details, stating:

> Prior to initiating research, school psychologists and graduate students affiliated with a university, hospital, or other agency subject to the U.S. Department of Health and Human Services (DHHS) regulation of research first obtain approval for their research from their Institutional Review Board for Research Involving Human Subjects (IRB) as well as the school or other agency in which the research will be conducted. Research proposals that have not been subject to IRB approval should be reviewed by individuals knowledgeable about research methodology and ethics and approved by the school administration or other appropriate authority.

Based on these ethics codes, researchers must not only obtain these approvals but also report this approval in their letter to the editor when they submit the manuscript for publication (APA, 2010b). Table 3.1 in this book includes an example of such a letter; it can be duplicated or adapted freely. The following text in that letter certifies that the standards of IRB approval were followed: "This research was approved by Research Productive University's institutional review board." Alternately, if the study did not include human subjects (as when conducting an analysis of archival data or a meta-analysis), the text might read this way: "This research used publically available data, rather than human subject data, and is thus considered exempt and need not be subjected to institutional review board review."

Following prominent recommendations (e.g., APA, 2010b), some authors routinely include a statement about IRB approval in their manuscripts (e.g., in the Method: Participants section or at the beginning of the Method: Procedures section). Although I always address this point in my submission letters, I do not usually include this information in manuscripts I submit. I (as an author and as an editor) have, however, observed reviewers requesting such content be added to manuscripts. Of course, it is easy to add.

64   Randy G. Floyd

Duplicate and Piecemeal Publications

Duplicate Publications

Manuscripts submitted for publication should present original, unique information. APA (2002, 2010a) ethics state that "psychologists do not publish, as original data, data that have been previously published. This does not preclude republishing data when they are accompanied by proper acknowledgment." NASP (2010) echoes this standard in stating:

> [S]chool psychologists only publish data or other information that make original contributions to the professional literature. They do not report the same study in a second publication without acknowledging previous publication of the same data. They do not duplicate significant portions of their own or others' previous publications without permission of copyright holders.

Both of these standards most directly refer to *duplicate publications*, which refers to the products of publishing the same results or ideas in more than one outlet. It is clear that duplicate publications represent copyright violations—covered later in this chapter—and should be avoided. The *Publication Manual of the APA* (2010b) alludes to a variety of publication types that might lend themselves to duplicate publications. *Brief reports* (as published in several journals featured in this book) should not draw upon content from a full-length manuscript or present a more in-depth analysis of a published article. Although it makes sense for *conference abstracts* to be expanded into full-length manuscripts or brief reports, published *conference proceedings* should not be reproduced in journal articles. In the same vein, book chapters should not be reproduced in part or in their entirety in newsletter or journal articles. Although I have made it a common practice to identify, in my submission letters and in acknowledgments in published articles, instances in which the research summarized in a manuscript was presented in local, state, national, or international conferences (without publication of a conference proceeding), this practice might be unnecessary as the conference presentation is not a publication and will not in any way lead to a copyright violation.

When in doubt about whether a prior publication (or one being evaluated concurrent with a manuscript submission) is a duplicate publication, inquire with the journal editor or publisher. When no risk of duplicate publication exists, you can report the following in your submission letter: "The manuscript has not been submitted for concurrent consideration by another journal or published in any part elsewhere." Should you want to report your prior presentation of such results (as I have), you can also add the following: "Portions of this research were presented at the National Association of Professionals annual convention as well as a regional research colloquium at Research Productive University." If you have published some of the results included in a manuscript in part previously, you should report something like this:

Preliminary results from this study were presented at the National Association of Professionals annual convention and published in its conference proceedings. The submitted manuscript represents a significant expansion of the preliminary analysis, including tests of the assumptions of the primary analysis, analysis of moderation across gender and racial groups, and expanded sections across the manuscript. We have included, for your review, copy of this conference proceeding with this submission. We hope that you will agree that the manuscript offers substantial extension of this preliminary study and contributes substantially to the professional literature.

Piecemeal Publications

Another frowned-upon practice that is much more commonplace is *piecemeal publishing*. Levin (2011) has referred to this practice as "carving up a multiple-experiment study into several pieces—what someone has called LPUs, or 'least publishable units'" (p. 486). Authors of multi-study dissertations and researchers with access to large-scale data sets might be prone to engage in this practice. An egregious example of piecemeal publications might include publishing (1) a pilot study examining the relations between predictors and an outcome in a small sample using multiple regression, (2) a study using the same analysis with a much larger sample, (3) a study employing more sophisticated analytic methods (including proper missing data handling and structural equation modeling) with the larger sample, (4) a study adding mediators to the analysis, (5) a study examining moderation by gender, and (6) a study including only the very youngest participants in the sample. Such studies sometimes unfold across time and across independent researchers, but piecemeal publishing is most abhorrent when it occurs across a single research team.

There is no doubt that it is important that research advances through a sequence of studies designed to investigate targeted questions, so there is no harm in engaging in such a program of research. In the same vein, large-scale data sets (especially those that are nationally representative or longitudinal) are probably the best sources of data to answer many important questions; thus, researchers should draw data from them as often as possible to advance understanding. The problem with piecemeal publishing is at least twofold: (a) it saturates the literature with highly similar research studies (often across journals), which makes the results harder to synthesize, and (b) it unduly inflates the status of the authors of piecemeal publications and confounds comparisons across scholars at similar developmental levels.

Authors who are "swimming in data" and eager to share their findings—yet at risk for piecemeal publications—should strive to go overboard to extend prior work and explicitly justify the need for additional study of phenomena under study. When they do submit manuscripts describing follow-up studies for consideration, they should also alert the editor to the existence of similar studies in their submission letters. Here are two examples:

> Please note we have previously published results from this data set in Author1 (2015) and Author1 and Author2 (2016), as have others OtherAuthor (2016). We attest to the fact that this study offers an original contribution to the literature and unique content. We have included, for your review, copies of our two prior publications using the data set along with this submission.

and

> Please note that we have another manuscript under review by a peer-reviewed journal, cited in this one submitted to you, that describes the results of our preliminary analysis of these data. The manuscript submitted to you offers a substantially more rigorous analysis of these data and extends the prior study by conducting moderation analysis by age, gender, and racial group. We have submitted, for your review, a copy of this other manuscript under review.

In addition, authors should cite in their manuscripts their prior studies and those of others who have employed the same data set or used the same study methods. I have concluded that some authors do not include these citations because they believe that citations to their prior studies (a.k.a. *self-citations*) might prevent their manuscripts from being sufficiently blinded to reviewers. This perspective is somewhat egocentric, and I encourage authors to cite their prior studies objectively and in a straightforward manner—as they would cite any other study included in the literature (see Chapter 3, Floyd). These citations do not need to refer to "we" or "our research team" in preceding the citation (although doing so is acceptable; APA, 2010b). They can simply cite their prior work in third person (e.g., "a study by Author and Author (2015) demonstrated that . . ."). Paying attention to potential duplicate and piecemeal publishing, alerting the editor about this potential, and carefully crafting text to address the advancement of science will reduce the effects of these problematic practices.

Plagiarism

Plagiarism is defined as the "appropriation of another person's ideas, processes, results, or words without giving appropriate credit" (Gross, 2016, p. 694). Although APA's ethics code (2002, 2010a) does not refer to plagiarism by name, it states that "Psychologists do not present portions of another's work or data as their own, even if the other work or data source is cited occasionally." NASP (2010) explicitly states that "when publishing or presenting research or other work, school psychologists do not plagiarize the works or ideas of others. They appropriately cite and reference all sources, print or digital, and assign credit to those whose ideas are reflected." Plagiarism is clearly an odious practice, and students, emerging professionals, and long-time researchers should routinely review these guidelines and review recommendations for insuring the originality of their writing. Strong resources addressing plagiarism and its prevention include the *Publication Manual of the APA* (2010b); Levin (2011); Lamoreaux, Darnell, Sheehan, and Tusher (2014); Bramesfeld's Plagiarism Prevention Tutorial (2014); and these online resources:

- The Council of Writing Programs Administrations: http://wpacouncil.org/positions/WPAplagiarism.pdf
- The Purdue Online Writing Center: https://owl.english.purdue.edu/owl/resource/589/01/

Self-plagiarism is a variant of this same infraction, but it is not mentioned explicitly (or actually implied) in the APA (2002, 2010a) or NASP (2010) ethics codes. It is defined as "a type of plagiarism in which the writer republishes a work in its entirety or reuses portions of a previously written text while authoring a new work" (iParadigms, 2011, p. 1). Self-plagiarism is addressed in the *Publication Manual of the APA* (2010b), and the difference between traditional plagiarism and self-plagiarism is made clear: "Whereas plagiarism refers to the practice of claiming credit for the words, ideas, and concepts of others, self-plagiarism refers to the practice of presenting one's own previously published work as though it were new" (p. 170). At its most extreme, self-plagiarism manifests itself as a duplicate publication (as previously discussed).

Self-plagiarism, in the form of text recycling, is a much more pervasive yet often overlooked form of the cardinal sin of plagiarism. I and some of my writing partners sometimes struggle to control urges to employ text we have toiled over, ostensibly perfected (in our minds, at least), and published when we must share similar ideas or study descriptions in our manuscripts. It is very easy to do (via "copy and paste") in the manuscript drafting stage. We are, however, aided in preventing our own self-plagiarism by plagiarism detection programs (discussed in a section that follows), and we strive to uphold recommendations like this one from the *APA Publication Manual* (2010b, p. 16):

> There are . . . limited circumstances (e.g., describing the details of an instrument or an analytic approach) under which authors may wish to duplicate without attribution (citation) their previously used words, feeling that extensive self-referencing is undesirable or awkward. When the duplicated words are limited in scope, this approach is permissible. When the duplication of one's own words is more extensive, citation of the duplicated words should be the norm. What constitutes the maximum acceptable length of duplicated material is difficult to define but must conform with legal notions of fair use. . . . When feasible, all of the author's own words that are cited should be located in a single paragraph or a few paragraphs, with a citation at the end of each.

68   *Randy G. Floyd*

To avoid plagiarism, writers are encouraged to rephrase or paraphrase text while citing sources. Levin (2011) offered a four-step method to preventing plagiarism (and self-plagiarism) that is generally consistent with other recommendations I have encountered over the years: "Read the passage . . . digest what you have read . . . close the source book or article and . . . summarize the passage in your own words" (p. 479). These directives are full of wisdom.

Do not let the pressure to publish lead to foolish decisions to reuse your own (or others') text. To support the screening of the originality of writing, we offer Table 4.1, which contains listings of ten commercial and freeware programs

Table 4.1 Prominent Plagiarism Detection Programs and Their Costs and Features

Program and website	Cost and submission size	Features
Turnitin http://turnitin.com/	$5 per student plus a $1,500 integration fee	Designed for educators in kindergarten to grade 12 and higher education. Upload files to be evaluated. Searches more than 62 billion web pages, 600 million student papers, and 160 million scholarly articles for matches. Provides plagiarism content matching as well as evaluation and grading capabilities. Yields "Similarity Index" as quantification of text overlap.
iThenticate www.ithenticate.com	$100/submission, up to 25,000 words, 5 resubmissions $300 for multiple submissions or one up to 75,000 words	Professional version of Turnitin, designed for editors, publishers, and professional writers. Upload files to be evaluated. Searches more than 62 billion web pages and 160 million scholarly articles and published works for matches. Provides plagiarism content matching. Yields "Similarity Index" as quantification of text overlap.
Writecheck http:// en.writecheck.com/	$7.95/submission, up to 5,000 words, 3 resubmissions $19.95/3 submissions $29.95 5 submissions	Student version of Turnitin. Upload files to be evaluated. Searches more than 62 billion web pages, 600 million student papers, and 160 million scholarly articles for matches. Provides plagiarism content matching. Yields "Similarity Index" as quantification of text overlap. Provides feedback about grammar, spelling, and word usage for additional charge. Customized, professional tutoring available within 24 hrs of submission.

Program and website	Cost and submission size	Features
Grammarly www.grammarly.com/	$29.96/month: monthly plan $19.98/month: quarterly plan $11.66/month: annual plan	Plagiarism and grammar check for students, faculty, writers, and other professionals. Upload file to be evaluated for plagiarism. Searches content over 8 billion web pages. Used for files and online (while writing emails). Identifies 250 types of writing errors. Generates writing score based on number of errors and provides explanation of mistakes. Provides synonym suggestions. Generates citations in MLA, APA, and Chicago styles.
Plagiarismcheck.org https://plagiarismcheck.org/	$5.99/submission, up to 20 pages at 275 words/page: Light $9.99/submission, up to 50 pages: Standard $25.49/submission, up to 150 pages: Premium	Copy-paste text in window. Searches content across all accessible internet pages. Highlights matching content and provides plagiarism score.
Plagiarism Detect http://plagiarismdetect.org/	$0.05/page, up to 275 words/page: Standard $0.25/page, up to 275 words/page: Premium	Upload file or copy-paste text in window. Searches content across accessible web pages. Standard package provides basic detection to common sources used online. Premium package provides advanced detection using all sources. Provides similarity percentage and links to sources.
Plagium www.plagium.com/en/plagiarismchecker	Free, up to 5,000 words: Quick Search, occasional user $0.04/1,000 characters: Quick Search, frequent user $0.08/1,000 characters: Deep Search	Using Quick Search, copy-paste text in window, but no plagiarism report is generated. Using Deep Search, upload files or copy-paste text in window to generate plagiarism report.
PlagScan www.plagscan.com/	**Individual acct:** $5.99/6,500 words, $12.99/25,000 words, $24.99/62,500 words, and $49.99/150,000 words **Institutional acct:** $19.99/month	Upload file or copy-paste text in window. Searches content across billions of documents. Provides "Plaglevel" as quantification of text overlap and links to sources.

(continued)

70 Randy G. Floyd

Table 4.1 Prominent Plagiarism Detection Programs and Their Costs and Features (*continued*)

PlagTracker www.plagtracker.com/	Free, up to 5,000 words $7.49/month, with no word limit: Premium	Using Free package, copy-paste text in window. Using Premium package, upload document. Searches content across 14 billion web pages and databases and 5 million academic papers. Provides plagiarism report with links to sources.
Small SEO Tools Plagiarism Checker http://smallseotools.com/	Free, up to 1,000 words	Upload file or copy-paste text in window. Indicates matching content and provides sources.

Note. Costs were obtained during the period from March to June, 2017.

designed primarily to detect plagiarism in documents. Of these options, I have used only iThenticate (in my role as editor) and Turnitin (in my role as instructor), and they are superb tools. In fact, I use them to screen any manuscript I submit for review and routinely submit for analysis drafts of student milestone projects completed under my supervision. With both programs, I have not paid for each analysis, but using them can be expensive and cost-prohibitive for many students and professionals publishing outside of a university context. Often, users writing lengthy manuscripts (longer than 5,000 words) must pay for multiple submissions for a complete analysis. I recommend those involved in higher education inquire with department and library administrators about access to these programs, as they might be covered by a university-based site license. Otherwise, Grammarly seems like it is the most affordable and versatile of these programs.

Publication Credit

Students are surprised to learn that a description of who deserves to be listed as an author on a journal article or chapter is included in professional ethics codes, as this issue seems far removed from the ideals of beneficence, non-malfeasance, and self-determination represented in professional ethics. Contrary to expectations, publication credit is addressed in three standards in the APA (2002, 2010a) ethics code and once in the NASP (2010) ethics code. Problems related to authorship are clearly challenging enough to warrant such attention. During my five years as editor of *Journal of School Psychology*, the only major conflict I faced involved an author dispute over publication credit.

Authorship

The *Publication Manual of the APA* (APA, 2010b, p. 18) states that

> authorship encompasses . . . not only those who do the actual writing but also those who have made substantial scientific contributions to the study. Substantial professional contributions may include formulating the problems or hypotheses, structuring the experimental design, organizing and conducting the statistical analysis, interpreting the results, or writing a major portion of the paper.

APA (2002, 2010a) encourages researchers to "take responsibility and credit, including authorship credit, only for work they have actually performed or to which they have substantially contributed." Here, a major contribution to the work is key to authorship. The next standard addresses the order in which author names are listed. It states that "principal authorship and other publication credits accurately reflect the relative scientific or professional contributions of the individuals involved, regardless of their relative status." The sole NASP (2010) standard addressing authorship is a general one, saying that

> school psychologists accurately reflect the contributions of authors and other individuals who contributed to presentations and publications. Authorship credit is given only to individuals who have made a substantial professional contribution to the research, publication, or presentation. Authors discuss and resolve issues related to publication credit as early as feasible in the research and publication process.

In the next of APA's (2002, 2010a) standards, it addresses authorship for students completing their major milestones during graduate study and how to address authorship credit, saying:

> Except under exceptional circumstances, a student is listed as principal author on any multiple-authored article that is substantially based on the student's doctoral dissertation. Faculty advisors discuss publication credit with students as early as feasible and throughout the research and publication process as appropriate.

Fine and Kurdek (1993) and Albert and Wager (2003) have thoroughly addressed this challenge of awarding student publication credit. A fellow training director also recently shared a 2015 article by Gaffey (www.apa.org/science/about/psa/2015/06/determining-authorship.aspx) that included an authorship agreement form, an authorship scorecard (Winston, 1985), and a publication contract that are worth considering for adoption. Although these forms are well developed, they—especially the authorship scorecard—should be modified by research teams to better match the types of research projects they are conducting.

72 Randy G. Floyd

In general, it is a wise practice to discuss authorship before beginning a project to make sure that everyone is in agreement. Of course, authorship order (and authorship itself) can change due to the circumstances that arise across what is often a lengthy research and publication process. For example, students might graduate and sever their ties with research labs, and faculty and students might be unable to (or otherwise fail to) contribute in the manner they discussed years before. Early discussion of authors provides all involved with a basic understanding of expectations and helps to prevent problems down the road. Frequent revisiting of the authorship question will undoubtedly amplify this early discussion.

Acknowledgments

APA (2002, 2010a) also addresses what activities do not warrant authorship and how to recognize these persons by stating that "Minor contributions to the research or to the writing for publications are acknowledged appropriately, such as in footnotes or in an introductory statement." These minor contributions might include many of the activities in which undergraduate and graduate students participate, such as recruiting participants; collecting data via interviews, testing, or direct observation; and entering and checking data in a database. Furthermore, university faculty supporting the completion of research projects, such as advising students on data analysis or providing feedback on program milestones (e.g., dissertations), also offer minor contributions that do not typically warrant authorship.

It is my experience that minor contributions to a manuscript are acknowledged in an author note that appears at the bottom of the title page of a manuscript or that is reported in a submission letter (see Table 2.2). The appropriate section of such a submission letter might read as follows:

> If this manuscript is accepted for publication, we would like the following author note to be included: This manuscript is based on a dissertation submitted by the first author under supervision of the second author in partial fulfillment of the requirements for a doctoral degree in school psychology. We thank dissertation committee members Dr. Faculty1, Dr. Faculty2, and Dr. Faculty3 for their helpful comments. We appreciate Examiner1, Examiner2, and Examiner3, for their assistance with data collection and Elementary School and its administrators and teachers for supporting this research.

I have found that there are few costs in being generous in offering authorship credit to those who have contributed sufficiently to a project. Few will decline to be credited, and grudges will be held when there is no discussion of authorship. In the same vein, you should be generous in recognizing minor contributors in an author note. It requires an extra level of conscientiousness, effort, and vigilance, but it is worth it. Based on my experience, many authors appear to be unaware of this requirement to recognize minor contributors or are unwilling to exert the effort to draft an acknowledgment. As discussed in Chapter 3, this information may inadvertently be omitted (e.g., from author notes) during the article formatting process if you are not vigilant; be sure to review your page proofs carefully.

Availability of Data for Verification

During the period in which this book was being developed, psychology as a whole was experiencing what some have called a reproducibility crisis (Pashler & Wagenmakers, 2012). One remedy, according to some, is to make the foundational data supporting published studies available for further review. Gross (2016, p. 708) asserted:

> The widespread adoption of reproducible research tools would be valuable for many purposes. For the individual investigator, it would provide a permanent, accessible history of his or her own data for further analysis, communication, and publication. For collaborators, it would provide a common core of information. For members of the laboratory, it would provide the opportunity to find out what their colleagues have been doing as well as a platform for internal laboratory discussion and critique before the presentation and publication stages. For journals, it would provide tools that would enable all authors to submit all data, all experimental parameters, and all programs used to analyze the data for examination by the journal referees and, if the paper is accepted, by the entire scientific community.

Consistent with Gross's (2016) vision, both APA (2002, 2010a) and NASP (2010) ethics codes address making data available for verification. According to the APA,

> after research results are published, psychologists do not withhold the data on which their conclusions are based from other competent professionals who seek to verify the substantive claims through reanalysis and who intend to use such data only for that purpose, provided that the confidentiality of the participants can be protected and unless legal rights concerning proprietary data preclude their release.

NASP echoes this standard:

> School psychologists make available their data or other information that provided the basis for findings and conclusions reported in publications and presentations, if such data are needed to address a legitimate concern or need and under the condition that the confidentiality and other rights of research participants are protected.

I support the broad initiative to evaluate reproducibility through sharing of data. It does not appear to me, however, that many journals (at least in school psychology and related fields) have developed the infrastructure to support authors in submitting data sets for peer review or sharing. In addition, I believe that the requests described in these ethics codes are relatively uncommon across researchers in school psychology. It has occurred only twice in my 18-year career in university settings, and, in both cases, the request stemmed from articles published in journals outside of the field of school psychology. Authors should be prepared for such requests and to consult with their IRBs regarding provision of de-identified data to other researchers and public data repositories.

Other Ethical Imperatives

NASP (2010) addresses three other issues worth noting. First, they require that school psychologists not present errant or "fake data" in their research and that they correct errors as soon as they are identified. Relevant standards state that school psychologists should "not publish or present fabricated or falsified data or results in their publications and presentations" and stipulate that "if errors are discovered after the publication or presentation of research or other information, school psychologists make efforts to correct errors by publishing errata, retractions, or corrections." NASP (2010) also requires permission and extreme levels of caution in presenting case study data in order to maintain the privacy and confidentiality of those involved in those cases. Accordingly, NASP asserted that "school psychologists who use their assessment, intervention, or consultation cases in lectures, presentations, or publications obtain written prior client consent or they remove and disguise identifying client information." Such case studies are common in book chapters in school psychology. In some instances, whole books have been published that include sample reports based on case studies (Mather & Jaffe, 2016). When case studies are employed, we recommend altering all of the identifying information (including gender; age and grade levels; and the names of persons involved and institutions, such as schools) to avoid revealing details about individuals. We also suggest introducing additional information that would mask identity even further. When in doubt, you should ask someone else to read the case study and ask questions about whether the information is accurate or fabricated in a way to promote masking. If the case study data were collected as part of a research project, it would be wise to consult with IRB representatives to ensure that there are no violations.

Copyright and Sharing of Articles

It has become common practice (and a bit of a competition among scholars) to post publications to commercial online repositories, such as ResearchGate (www.researchgate.net/) and academia.edu, and share resources and insights with other researchers. In particular, these online repositories have been helpful in aiding authors in distributing their research articles to scholars around the world who cannot access their publications through standard library access. In late 2016, ResearchGate and academia.edu reported 10 million and 43 million members, respectively (Rathemacher, Lovett, & Izenstark, 2016). Despite the large discrepancy in their numbers of members, based on recent surveys (e.g., Matthews, 2016) and my experience, ResearchGate is the more well-known site among researchers.

ResearchGate contains three major types of pages: a Home page, a Questions page, and a Job page. The Home page includes a personalized list of suggested readings that have been posted to the site, notifications of recently posted publications from your co-authors and others you follow, as well as alerts about your recent citations and frequently read publications. The Questions page includes a list of questions posed by ResearchGate members as well as responses from others (and opportunities for you to respond). Finally, the Jobs page includes employment listings matched to your ResearchGate profile information; an option to obtain job alerts via email is also available through ResearchGate. This focus on job advertisements should be a reminder that ResearchGate is a commercial venture focused on targeted advertising (Rathemacher et al., 2016). For users, ResearchGate also includes a variety of information as part of the member profile, including scholarly contributions, a timeline of publications and posts, and personal statistics and impact scores.

When considering what to post on ResearchGate and other publically accessible online repositories, you must understand the constraints placed on you as an author when you publish your articles, chapters, and the like. When publishing, authors must sign copyright agreements developed by publishing companies that stipulate (a) the transfer of rights associated with the manuscript from the author to the publisher as well as (b) *fair use* rules (sometimes referred to as "retained rights"). For example, fair use rules typically allow authors to share their published journal articles (a.k.a. *reprints*) in hard copy and electronic form with colleagues and other peers who request them. Some publishers offer authors a webpage link providing free access to their journal article for a limited period (e.g., two months) that can be shared with others and posted to listservs and blogs as well as on social networking sites. In addition, many publishers allow articles to be shared freely to support teaching and training (including course packets) and grant and patent applications under some circumstances. However, far more restrictions exist than fair use provisions.

Pre-Prints, Post-Prints, and Publisher Versions

It is important to understand how copyright law and fair use provisions apply to three forms of publications. Consulting SHERPA/RoMEO (www.sherpa. ac.uk/romeo/index.php), a service hosted by the Center for Research Communications at the University of Nottingham that catalogs copyright and self-archiving information about journal articles across publishers and specific

76 Randy G. Floyd

journal titles, can assist in this understanding. SHERPA/RoMEO distinguishes between *pre-prints*, *post-prints*, and *publisher versions* of manuscripts and journal articles. I have found substantial variation in use of these terms and their definitions across publishers, but I will share the most common themes consistent with the SHERPA/RoMEO distinctions.

Pre-prints refer to manuscripts that have not been peer reviewed via submission to professional conferences or journals. In Psychology, they are typically formatted in APA style—with one-inch margins all around and double spacing. In the eyes of publishers, they are essentially drafts or working papers. Some publishers (such as Taylor & Francis) refer to them as "authors' original manuscripts," which I find more transparent than pre-prints. These pre-prints form the grey literature and are often featured on websites such as arXiv (search.arxiv.org), which highlights research in the fields of Physics, Mathematics, Computer Science, Quantitative Biology, Quantitative Finance, and Statistics. Although arXiv includes documents that cite school psychology journals, my searching revealed none focusing on central elements of school psychology.

Post-prints refer to the final manuscript following peer review (presumably after it has been accepted). Taylor & Francis refer to post-prints as "accepted manuscripts;" this version is submitted for printing. Thus, its content should be identical to the final product, but it exists in a less-polished form. It is the publisher version (a.k.a. *the version of record*) that reflects the article in its formatted form. I assume—but could be wrong—that this category includes *uncorrected page proofs*, which are professionally formatted, pre-press versions of the journal article that are reviewed by authors prior to publication. Although I found some journals (albeit ones with small-scale publishers) that referenced uncorrected page proofs as pre-prints and conveyed that page proofs will be posted online before the final corrected version of the article is posted, page proofs and "articles ahead of print" posted online by publishers would not be considered pre-prints or post-prints by SHERPA/RoMEO or most publishers. Instead, they would be considered the publisher version. As previously noted, most publishers convey that these versions can be shared on an individual basis (without systematic distribution). If someone contacts you via email to request a copy of your recent article, you can share it without reservation.

Sharing

For the most part, pre-prints or post-prints may be shared on personal websites, during professional and educational interactions, and via institutional and non-commercial repositories. However, there are exceptions, and as the manuscript moves increasingly closer to acceptance by a publisher (and your signing over rights to it), the constraints increase. For example, some publishers place an embargo on post-prints, the accepted manuscripts, for a period—often a year or two. Despite these occasional embargoes, most publishers allow you to share post-prints, so upon receipt of an acceptance letter (after celebration), you can add more details about its acceptance and then share the post-print broadly in most cases. For example, guidelines for sharing from Elsevier (www.elsevier.com/about/our-business/policies/sharing) state that, following acceptance of a manuscript and some further processing by the publisher, authors can label the post-print manuscript with a digital object identifier (abbreviated DOI). However, they are asked not to alter the manuscript so that its content mirrors the final publication.

Most publishers will also ask that you include details about the acceptance of the manuscript to the post-print version. Elsevier requires that it bears a "non-commercial Creative Commons user license (CC-BY-NC-ND)." Elsevier's website (www.elsevier.com/about/our-business/policies/sharing) states the following: "On your accepted manuscript add the following to the title page, copyright information page, or header /footer: © YEAR. Licensed under the Creative Commons [insert license details and URL]." Creative Commons licenses can be obtained here: https://creativecommons.org/share-your-work/. Taylor & Francis (http://authorservices.taylorandfrancis.com/sharing-your-work/) recommends adding this text: "This is an Accepted Manuscript of an article published by Taylor & Francis in [JOURNAL TITLE] on [date of publication], available online: http://www.tandfonline.com/[Article DOI]." In a similar manner, Wiley (https://authorservices.wiley.com/author-resources/Journal-Authors/licensing-open-access/open-access/self-archiving.html) recommends the following: "This is the peer reviewed version of the following article: [FULL CITE], which has been published in final form at [Link to final article using the DOI]." It is easy to add such information to the title page of the manuscript following assignment of the DOI and generation of a URL by the publisher.

Based on the SHERPA/RoMEO database, Table 4.2 contains a list of the copyright policies and self-archiving guidelines for the 11 school psychology journals featured in this book. Notice that three of the school psychology journals are not evaluated or included in the database and that the publishers for all but one journal allow for archiving of pre-prints and post-prints. *Psychology in the Schools*, published by Wiley, is the only journal in which there is an embargo on the post-print of 12 months, during which it cannot be shared broadly.

Despite what appears to be a proliferation of publisher versions of journal articles posted to sites such as ResearchGate, I see no justification for posting anything beyond pre-prints to these sites. As (a) rights associated with the manuscript are signed over from the authors to the publisher and (b) copyright agreements do not expire (as embargoes do), fair use is highly constrained. The terms and conditions for such commercial sites make these general principles clear. When posting to ResearchGate, authors must agree to "upload conditions," which read as follows: "By uploading this file . . . you are confirming that you have reviewed this file and that it contains no material protected by intellectual property laws or personal rights unless you own or control such rights or have received all necessary consents." In its Terms and Conditions

Table 4.2 Online Posting Policies of School Psychology Journals Obtained from the SHERPA/RoMEO Database

Journal	Publisher	RoMEO classification	Approved online posting medium		
			Author pre-print (Author's original manuscript)	Author post-print (accepted manuscript)	Publisher version (version of record)
Canadian Journal of School Psychology	SAGE Publishing	Green	Y	Y	N
Contemporary School Psychology	Springer Verlag	Green	Y	Y	N
International Journal of School & Educational Psychology	Taylor & Francis	Green	Y	Y	N
Journal of Applied School Psychology	Taylor & Francis	Green	Y	Y	N
Journal of School Psychology	Elsevier	Green	Y	Y	N
Psychology in the Schools	Wiley	Yellow	Y	E (12 mo)	N
School Psychology Forum	NASP		Not listed		
School Psychology International	SAGE Publishing	Green	Y	Y	N
School Psychology Quarterly	APA	Green	Y	Y	N
School Psychology Review	NASP			Ungraded	
Trainers' Forum	TSP			Not listed	

Note. NASP = National Association of School Psychologists, APA = American Psychological Association, TSP = Trainers of School Psychologists. Green = RoMEO designation indicating approved archiving of author pre-print and author post-print or publisher version, Yellow = RoMEO designation indicating approved archiving of only author pre-print. E = the document is embargoed and cannot be posted for a specified period (as noted). All information was obtained from www.sherpa.ac.uk/romeo/index.php on April 14, 2017.

(www.researchgate.net/application.TermsAndConditions.html), under Article 3: Storage of Information, it states, "Users may only request storage of such information that they may legally store and publish. Users must not request to store any information that infringes any third party's copyright, trademarks, other intellectual property rights or any other rights." Furthermore, in these Terms and Conditions, ResearchGate users agree to indemnify ResearchGate of any liability and accept legal fees as they may surface (Rathemacher et al., 2016). It seems clear to me that most ResearchGate users are violating copyright law.[1]

Conclusion

It is important that students, professional trainers, researchers, and practitioners be aware of and uphold the ethical and legal standards of their field when engaging in research and publication. Often, these standards are either not well understood or otherwise ignored. Both APA and NASP provide detailed guidance in many areas, but tradition and expediency may also upstage these standards, as mentors in research and publication and administrators might operate on outdated and limited experiences. This chapter, and the resource it presents, should assist emerging and emergent scholars in holding themselves to these highest standards and modeling best practices for future generations.

Note

1 During the final days of completing this chapter, the APA began targeting websites such as ResearchGate that allow users to post articles without permission (www. apa.org/news/press/releases/2017/06/curtailing-journal-articles.aspx).

References

Albert, T., & Wager, E. (2003). How to handle authorship disputes: A guide for new researchers. *The COPE Report 2003*, 32–34.

American Psychological Association. (2002). Ethical principles of psychologists and code of conduct. *American Psychologist, 57*, 1060–1073.

American Psychological Association. (2010a). Amendments to the 2002 ethical principles of psychologists and code of conduct. *American Psychologist, 65*, 493.

American Psychological Association. (2010b). *Publication manual of the American Psychological Association* (6th ed.). Washington, DC: American Psychological Association.

Bramesfeld, K. D. (2014). *Plagiarism prevention tutorial: How to avoid common forms of plagiarism* [OTRP Peer Reviewed Teaching Resource]. Available from www.google. com/url?q=http://teachpsych.org/resources/documents/otrp/resources/bramesfeld/ Bramesfeld_Plagiarism%2520Prevention%2520Tutorial2.pptx&sa=U&ved=0ahU KEwjwlIiqlObTAhUmyoMKHeKeCsYQFggEMAA&client=internal-uds-cse&usg= AFQjCNGWfll3AU_yzPO3gksdEYAqOvL5Sw

Fine, M. A., & Kurdek, L. A. (1993). Reflections on determining authorship credit and authorship order on faculty-student collaborations. *American Psychologist, 48,* 1141–1147.

Gaffey, A. (2015, June). Determining and negotiating authorship: Frequent communication and a dynamic approach can help minimize disagreements. Retrieved from www.apa.org/science/about/psa/2015/06/determining-authorship.aspx

Gross, C. (2016). Scientific misconduct. *Annual Review of Psychology, 67,* 693–711. doi: 10.1146/annurev-psych-122414-033437

iParadigms. (2011). *White paper: The ethics of self-plagiarism.* Retrieved from www.ithenticate.com/hs-fs/hub/92785/file-5414624-pdf/media/ith-selfplagiarism-white paper.pdf

Lamoreaux, M., Darnell, K., Sheehan, E., & Tusher, C. (2014). Educating students about plagiarism. Office of Teaching Resources in Psychology for Society for the Teaching of Psychology. Retrieved from http://teachpsych.org/Resources/Documents/otrp/resources/plagiarism/Educating%20Students%20about%20Plagiarism.pdf

Levin, J. R. (2011). Ethical issues in professional research, writing, and publishing. In A. T. Panter & S. K. Sterba (Eds.), *Handbook of ethics in quantitative methodology* (pp. 463–492). New York, NY: Routledge.

Mather, N., & Jaffe, L. E. (2016). *Woodcock-Johnson IV: Reports, recommendations, and strategies* (3rd ed.). New York: Wiley.

Matthews, D. (2016). Do academic social networks share academics' interests? *Times Higher Education.* www.timeshighereducation.com/features/do-academic-social-networks-share-academics-interests

National Association of School Psychologists. (2010). *Principles for professional ethics.* Bethesda, MD: National Association of School Psychologists. Available from www.nasponline.org/standards/2010standards.aspx

Panter, A. T., & Sterba, S. K. (Eds.). (2011). *Handbook of ethics in quantitative methodology.* New York, NY: Routledge.

Pashler, H., & Wagenmakers, E-.J. (2012). Editors' introduction to the special section on replicability in psychological science: A crisis of confidence? *Perspectives on Psychological Science, 7,* 528–530.

Rathemacher, A., Lovett, J., & Izenstark, A. (2016). ResearchGate, copyright, and you. *Technical Services Faculty Presentations. Paper 46.* http://digitalcommons.uri.edu/lib_ts_presentations/46

Winston, Jr., R. B. (1985). A suggested procedure for determining order of authorship in research publications. *Journal of Counseling and Development, 63,* 515–518.

Part 2

Publishing in the School Psychology Generalist Journals

5 Publishing in the *Journal of School Psychology*

Michelle K. Demaray

Overview of the Journal

The *Journal of School Psychology* publishes scientific research relevant to the field of school psychology. The primary goal of the *Journal of School Psychology* is to promote the science of school psychology via upholding rigorous standards for research (Demaray, 2015). The *Journal of School Psychology* is the official journal of the Society for the Study of School Psychology (SSSP). The SSSP is a group of scholars in the field of school psychology who were elected into membership in SSSP based on several criteria surrounding strong scholarship. The mission of the SSSP is focused on recognizing and promoting research and scholarship in the field of school psychology. As the official journal of the SSSP, the *Journal of School Psychology* is closely linked to the goals and mission of SSSP. Both the SSSP and the *Journal of School Psychology* are aligned with their overarching goal to promote science in the field of school psychology. The *Journal of School Psychology* specifically aids the SSSP in promoting science by publishing scientific knowledge to move the field forward. To find about more information about the SSSP, see the following website: www.ssspresearch.org.

The *Journal of School Psychology* has been published for over 50 years, with the first issue published in January of 1963. Currently, the journal is published by Elsevier Publishing Company. For a detailed history of the journal see an article titled, "A History of the Founding and Early Development of the *Journal of School Psychology*" by Fagan and Jack (2012). Additional information about the journal is available on the *Journal of School Psychology* website: www.journals.elsevier.com/journal-of-school-psychology.

Aim and Scope

The aim of the *Journal of School Psychology* is to promote science and advance knowledge in research and practice relevant to the field of school psychology. The *Journal of School Psychology* publishes empirical research articles with implications for the social, emotional, and academic functioning of youth in schools. Thus, research is typically focused on school-aged youth (i.e., 18 years old and younger). Research that is focused on educators (e.g., teachers) and mental-health professionals in schools (e.g., school psychologists) is also within the scope of the journal, but typically these studies also include data on youth or the results are highly impactful for youth in schools.

As noted in recent editorials (Demaray, 2015, 2016), the latest publications have focused on empirically validating academic interventions, including reading, vocabulary, spelling, writing, and math; empirically validating behavior interventions; consultation; advancing the science of curriculum-based measurement; investigating the importance of teacher–student relationships; understanding and reducing bullying and victimization; understanding how school and class climate and instructional practices impact students; advancing the science of assessment; validating the role of parents and peers in social and academic competence; and data-based decision making on grade retention, school absenteeism, and school dropout. This list is not exhaustive but provides some examples of the broad content published in the *Journal of School Psychology*.

Currently, the journal has an editor-in-chief, a consulting editor, ten associate editors (AEs), and one senior statistical and methodological advisor in addition to the editorial board. The current editorial board consists of 14 statistical and methodological advisors, ten senior scientists, and 92 editorial board members. The editor-in-chief reviews all manuscripts submitted prior to assigning each manuscript to an AE to facilitate blinded peer review. An advantage of the large number of AEs involved with the *Journal of School Psychology* is that manuscripts are often assigned to AEs that have expertise in the content area of the manuscript. In addition, the *Journal of School Psychology* has a large number of AEs in order to allow them to only review two initial manuscripts a month (along with revisions). The workload for the *Journal of School Psychology* AEs is strategically kept to two manuscripts a month so they are able to provide detailed and integrated feedback for each manuscript they review. It is a goal of the journal to provide constructive, helpful feedback to every author to promote the science of school psychology.

Manuscripts that are not deemed appropriate to the scope of the journal or not of high methodological quality are returned to the author without review. The process of rejecting manuscripts without review is also a two-part process. The editor-in-chief reviews all manuscripts submitted, and ones deemed for rejection without review are assigned to an AE dedicated to handling manuscripts being considered for rejection without review. In addition to considering the editor-in-chief's comments, this AE also reviews the manuscript. Given this AE handles only manuscripts considered for rejection without review, the AE can provide detailed information on the reasons for the rejection and additional feedback to aid the authors that can shape their future submissions. In recent years, an average of about 35% of submissions were rejected without review (see the section that follows for more details).

One of the strengths of the *Journal of School Psychology* is that each AE works collaboratively with a statistical and methodological advisor to ensure that study methodology and statistical analyses are of the highest quality.

Typically, manuscripts go to a statistical and methodological advisor upon resubmission of a revision, although occasionally first submissions may be sent to a statistical and methodological advisor, especially for methodologically complex papers. The statistical and methodological advisor focuses reviews on the methodological and statistical aspects of the manuscript. Using statistical and methodological advisors helps ensure that AEs have appropriate and knowledgeable reviews on these aspects. The articles published in the *Journal of School Psychology* are primarily focused on quantitative and qualitative empirical research. The *Journal of School Psychology* publishes very few narrative or review papers, and when these papers are published, they are typically commissioned work.

Authorship and Readership

The *Journal of School Psychology* has a large international authorship and readership. In addition, the authorship and readership of the *Journal of School Psychology* crosses a variety of disciplines (education, counseling psychology, developmental psychology, etc.). In 2015, the top ten countries from which manuscripts were submitted included the United States, Australia, the Netherlands, Spain, Canada, Germany, Italy, Turkey, Iran, and China. The top five countries in which authors of accepted manuscripts resided were the United States, the Netherlands, Australia, Belgium, Canada, and Israel. In 2015, the number of downloaded articles was 330,510. In the last five years, most articles were downloaded from these ten locations: the United States (657,393 downloads), the United Kingdom (133, 937), Australia (114,557), Canada (63,379), the Netherlands (57,606), China (40,499), Iran (20,742), Germany (20,523), Malaysia (17,489), and Turkey (16,242).

Impact Factor

The *Journal of School Psychology* has had a 2-year Impact Factor of above 2.0 for the past seven years. The highest impact factors the *Journal of School Psychology* has received were the 2015 2-year Impact Factor (3.36) and the 2015 5-year Impact Factor (4.26). Prior 2-year Impact Factors were 2.26 (2014), 2.28 (2013), 2.88 (2012), 2.24 (2011), 2.68 (2010), 2.31 (2009), and 2.1 (2008).

2015 Journal Statistics and Operations

Manuscript Submissions and Processing

The total number of unsolicited submissions during 2015 (not including resubmissions of previously rejected manuscripts) was 312. Including the resubmissions of previously rejected manuscripts, the total was 357. This number is the highest on record for the journal. Manuscript totals for the prior five years were as follows: 333 (2014), 285 (2013), 269 (2012), 275 (2011),

86 Michelle K. Demaray

Table 5.1 Journal Operations for the *Journal of School Psychology* in 2015

Decision	Number	Percentage
Accept and Accept contingent on revision	41	11.5
Reject (all categories)	316	88.5
Reject, encouraging revision	66	20.9
Reject	128	40.5
Reject without full review	122	38.6

and 229 (2010). The average time to make an editorial decision for manuscripts submitted in 2015 and distributed for full review (not including reject without full review) was 69.8 days (SD = 28.0 days). Time to decision values for the past five years were as follows: 60.0 days (2014), 59.9 days (2013), 57.3 days (2012), 62.6 days (2011), and 65.2 days (2010).

The percentage of manuscripts accepted for publication in 2015 was 11.5% (see Table 5.1). Acceptance rates from previous years were as follows: 10.8% (2014), 6.0% (2013), 12.3% (2012), 9.5% (2011), and 16.6% (2010). Of those manuscripts rejected for publication, 20.9% were accompanied by encouragement to resubmit, whereas 40.5% were rejected following full review. The percentage of manuscripts rejected without full review in 2015 was 38.6%. The prior rates of rejecting without review were as follows: 35.1% (2014), 35.8% (2013), 32.0% (2012), 32.7% (2011), and 15.7% (2010).

Publication Patterns

The *Journal of School Psychology* publishes six issues a year. In the last three years, a range of 30 to 45 articles were published each year. The large majority of articles are empirical. The *Journal of School Psychology* works with Elsevier to utilize Article-Based Publishing (ABP), meaning that once articles are accepted and proofs are finalized, a copy of the manuscript is placed online. The online copy is fully citable, contains a DOI number, and aids in speeding up the citation and publication process.

Elsevier has also recently provided authors with "Share Links," which allows authors to use the provided link to share their article with others via email or social media for free download for 50 days. The *Journal of School Psychology* website is also now providing altmetrics, which provides data on articles that are shared or cited online, including activity on social media, Twitter, Facebook, science blogs, mainstream news, and other online sources. These data can be viewed here: www.journals.elsevier.com/journal-of-school-psychology/altmetric-articles. The *Journal of School Psychology* also has a Facebook account (www.facebook.com/JournalofSchoolPsychology) and Twitter account (https://twitter.com/JofSchoolPsych) that are used to share research and news relevant to the journal via social media.

Historically, the *Journal of School Psychology* has not published many special issues. In 2014, there was a special issue published on *Analysis and Meta-Analysis of Single-Case Designs* (Shadish, 2014) and, in 2012, there was a special issue on *The Process and Products of Publishing in School Psychology Journals* (Eckert & Hintze, 2011). The only other special issue since 2007 was a special issue published in 2010 titled a *Special Series on Statistical Analyses* (Betts, 2010). One goal of my editorship is to strategically increase the number of special issues. Thus, in the first issue of 2016, there was a special section titled, *Lesbian, Gay, Bisexual and Transgender (LGBT) Youth in Schools: Current Issues and Future Directions*. This special issue was driven by some data I saw in a presentation at a convention that demonstrated the lack of research published on LGBT youth in school personnel journals (Graybill & Proctor, 2016). LGBT youth are at risk for many negative outcomes and we need research in school psychology focused on improving the lives of youth who are LGBT (Espelage, 2016). Currently in the planning phase are several special issues focused on (a) current topics in methodology (1st issue 2017); (b) parental involvement in school-based interventions (mid-2017); and (c) advancing the science of personalized interventions to enhance child outcomes (2018). Although there is no formal procedure for submitting ideas for special issues, please feel free to contact the editor-in-chief via email to propose or discuss an idea.

Excellent research published during 2015 that represents the type and quality of articles published in the *Journal of School Psychology* includes the 2015 Article of the Year winner and nominees for the award. The Article of the Year was a meta-analysis titled, "Maximizing the Potential of Early Childhood Education to Prevent Externalizing Behavior Problems: A Meta-analysis" (Schindler et al., 2015). Other high-quality, representative articles nominated for the award were "Increasing Teacher Treatment Integrity of Behavior Support Plans through Consultation and Implementation Planning" (Sanetti, Collier-Meek, Long, Byron, & Kratochwill, 2015); "Classroom Risks and Resources: Teacher Burnout, Classroom Quality and Children's Adjustment in High Needs Elementary Schools" (Hoglund, Klingle, & Hosan, 2015); "Size and Consistency of Problem-Solving Consultation Outcomes: An Empirical Analysis" (Hurwitz, Kratochwill, & Serlin, 2015); and "Profiles of Classroom Behavior in High Schools: Associations with Teacher Behavior Management Strategies and Classroom Composition" (Pas, Cash, O'Brennan, Debnam, & Bradshaw, 2015).

Recommendations for Prospective Authors

Authors can be successful in publishing in the *Journal of School Psychology* by making sure that their research is relevant, methodologically rigorous, clearly described, and impactful. Although all submissions are reviewed by the editor-in-chief prior to review, it is ideal for authors to make sure their work is relevant to the aims and scope of the journal prior to submission. Authors are also welcome to email the editor-in-chief prior to submission to determine relevance. The articles published in the *Journal of School Psychology* are focused more on the science of school psychology than the practice of school psychology.

Given the relatively high rejection rate (88.5% in 2015), authors should submit their best and most methodologically rigorous work to the *Journal of School Psychology*. The journal has high standards for methodological and statistical rigor, and manuscripts that are deemed to include substandard methodology or analyses will be returned without review. It is important to note that all submissions are reviewed by statistical and methodological advisors prior to publication. Thus, authors should submit work that includes assessment tools supported by reliability and validity evidence and utilizes statistical techniques that are current and appropriate to answer the research questions posed. The *Journal of School Psychology* pays close attention to the appropriate handling of missing data (Baraldi & Enders, 2010) and multi-level data (Peugh, 2010). In addition, the most cutting-edge methods to test mediation and moderation (Fairchild & McQuillin, 2010) are recommended. The *Journal of School Psychology* does publish rigorous single-case design (SCD) research; authors planning to submit SCD research should refer to the special issue on this topic published in the *Journal of School Psychology* (Shadish, 2014). Recently, the *Journal of School Psychology* also published the Single-Case Reporting Guidelines in BEhavioural (SCRIBE) interventions 2016 statement that details necessary information for authors to report in SCD research (Tate et al., 2016).

The *Journal of School Psychology* utilizes the journal article reporting standards set out by the American Psychological Association (APA) Publications and Communications Board Working Group on Journal Article Reporting Standards (JARS; APA, 2008). The JARS document is a helpful tool when preparing your manuscripts for submission. An advantage for the *Journal of School Psychology* and authors is that there are currently no page limits for submissions, so manuscripts can be detailed and thorough. Each manuscript should include: (1) a detailed review of relevant theory and literature; (2) clearly posed research questions and hypotheses; (3) detailed methodology, statistical analyses, and results; and (4) an integrated discussion of the findings. Last, the research should be impactful to current research, practices, or both in the field of school psychology.

Common reasons for a manuscript submitted to the *Journal of School Psychology* to be rejected without review include surface-level features: (a) manuscripts that are written poorly; (b) manuscripts that are not in APA style; and (c) lack of detail and clarity in the manuscript. Manuscripts might also be rejected without review due to the focus and type of submissions, including (a) research not deemed broadly relevant to the field of school psychology; (b) narrative or review papers that do not make a significant contribution to the respective research area or field; (c) narrowly focused measurement papers; and (d) manuscripts presenting initial pilot work that is preliminary.

There are also design and method features that could result in a paper being rejected without review, these include (a) research conducted on youth over the age of 18 (e.g., research conducted on college-age youth); (b) lack of methodological rigor; and (c) not utilizing sophisticated and current statistical methods to answer the research questions.

To avoid these common reasons for rejection without review, make sure that your manuscripts are well written and in the current APA style. If your first language is not English, have someone whose language is English carefully read and edit your paper. If you are not sure about the relevance of your paper to the field of school psychology, feel free to contact the editor-in-chief to make sure it is an appropriate match. It might also help to cite some of the relevant literature in the field of school psychology in your manuscript and provide implications for school psychologists. I would also be sure to contact the editor-in-chief if you are thinking of submitting a narrative review or paper focused on a narrow topic (e.g., development of a measure). If necessary, it might help to get feedback from methodological experts to make sure your analyses and method are rigorous.

References

APA Publications and Communications Board Working Group on Journal Article Reporting Standards. (2008). Reporting standards for research in psychology: Why do we need them? What might they be? *The American Psychologist, 63,* 839–851.

Baraldi, A. N., & Enders, C. K. (2010). An introduction to modern missing data analyses. *Journal of School Psychology, 48,* 5–37. doi: 10.1016/j.jsp.2009.10.001

Betts, J. (2010). Expanding school psychology's horizons for understanding and conducting research: Commentary on the special series on statistical analysis. *Journal of School Psychology, 48,* 1–4. doi: 10.1016/j.jsp.2009.11.001

Demaray, M. K. (2015). The state of the *Journal of School Psychology*: Promoting science. *Journal of School Psychology, 53,* 1–6. doi: 10.1016/j.jsp.2014.12.001

Demaray, M. K. (2016). Promoting the science of school psychology. *Journal of School Psychology, 54,* 1–3. doi: 10.1016/j.jsp.2015.12.001

Eckert, T. L., & Hintze, J. M. (2011). School psychology publishing contributions to the advancement of knowledge, science, and its application: An introduction to the themed issue. *Journal of School Psychology, 49,* 613–616. doi: 10.1016/j.jsp.2011.11.002

Espelage, D. L. (2016). Sexual orientation and gender identity in schools: A call for more research in school psychology—No more excuses. *Journal of School Psychology, 54,* 5–8. doi: 10.1016/j.jsp.2015.11.002

Fagan, T. K., & Jack, S. L. (2012). A history of the founding and early development of the *Journal of School Psychology*. *Journal of School Psychology, 50,* 701–735. doi: 10.1016/j.jsp.2012.11.002

Fairchild, A. J., & McQuillin, S. D. (2010). Evaluating mediation and moderation effects in school psychology: A presentation of methods and review of current practice. *Journal of School Psychology, 48,* 53–84. doi: 10.1016/j.jsp.2009.09.001

Graybill, E. C., & Proctor, S. L. (2016). Lesbian, gay, bisexual, and transgender youth: Limited representation in school support personnel journals. *Journal of School Psychology, 54,* 9–16. doi: 10.1016/j.jsp.2015.11.001

Hoglund, W. L. G., Klingle, K. E., & Hosan, N. E. (2015). Classroom risks and resources: Teacher burnout, classroom quality and children's adjustment in high needs elementary schools. *Journal of School Psychology, 53*, 337–357. doi: 10.1016/j.jsp.2015.06.002

Hurwitz, J. T., Kratochwill, T. R., & Serlin, R. C. (2015). Size and consistency of problem-solving consultation outcomes: An empirical analysis. *Journal of School Psychology, 53*, 161–178. doi: 10.1016/j.jsp.2015.01.001

Pas, E. T., Cash, A. H., O'Brennan, L., Debnam, K. J., & Bradshaw, C. P. (2015). Profiles of classroom behavior in high schools: Associations with teacher behavior management strategies and classroom composition. *Journal of School Psychology, 53*, 137–148. doi: 10.1016/j.jsp.2014.12.005

Peugh, J. L. (2010). A practical guide to multilevel modeling. *Journal of School Psychology, 48*, 85–112. doi: 10.1016/j.jsp.2009.09.002

Sanetti, L. M., Collier-Meek, M. A., Long, A. C. J., Byron, J., & Kratochwill, T. R. (2015). Increasing teacher treatment integrity of behavior support plans through consultation and implementation planning. *Journal of School Psychology, 53*, 209–229. doi: 10.1016/j.jsp.2015.03.002

Schindler, H. S., Kholoptseva, J., Oh, S. S., Yoshikawa, H., Duncan, G. J., Magnuson, K. A., & Shonkoff, J. P. (2015). Maximizing the potential of early childhood education to prevent externalizing behavior problems: A meta-analysis. *Journal of School Psychology, 53*, 243–263. doi: 10.1016/j.jsp.2015.04.001

Shadish, W. R. (2014). Analysis and meta-analysis of single-case designs: An introduction. *Journal of School Psychology, 52*, 109–122. doi: 10.1016/j.jsp.2013.11.009

Tate, R. L., Perdices, M., Rosenkoetter, U., Shadish, W., Vohra, S., Barlow, D. H., . . . Wilson B. (2016). The Single-Case Reporting guideline in BEhavioural interventions (SCRIBE) 2015 statement. *Journal of School Psychology, 56*, 133–142. doi: 10.1016/j.jsp.2016.04.001

6 Publishing in *Psychology in the Schools*

David E. McIntosh

Overview of the Journal

Psychology in the Schools is dedicated to publishing research and theoretical manuscripts that have direct implications for school psychologists, counselors, teachers, administrators, and other personnel workers in schools. There also is an emphasis on publishing manuscripts that address issues confronting psychologists and educators within higher education. The journal's 2015 Institute for Scientific Information Journal Citation Reports Ranking was 34 out of 57 (Psychology Educational).

The first issue of *Psychology in the Schools* was published in January 1964, and the journal is considered the longest continuously published journal in school psychology. The journal first published four issues per year and now publishes ten issues a year by Wiley, which includes approximately 1,120 printed pages. In a typical year, two to four special issues and six to eight general issues are published. The journal has had only five editors over the past 50 years (see Table 6.1), which is unusual for most journals. Gerald B. Fuller served as editor for the longest period, approximately 30 years.

Table 6.1 Editors of *Psychology in the Schools*

Editors	Institutional affiliation	Years	Issues per year*
William A. Hunt	Northwestern University	1964–1969	4
Bryon Claude Mathis	Northwestern University	1970	4
Gerald B. Fuller	Central Michigan University	1970–1999	4
LeAdelle Phelps	University at Buffalo-SUNY	1999–2006	6 (1999) & 8 (2004)
David E. McIntosh	Ball State University	2006–present	10 (2008)

Note. * Dates in parentheses are the first year the number of issues per year increased.

92 David E. McIntosh

Psychology in the Schools primarily publishes data-based research manuscripts. Correlational studies are discouraged. Manuscripts between 28 and 32 pages in total length are encouraged. Manuscripts over 35 pages in total length are typically not accepted for publication for general issues, and authors are asked to revise and resubmit. Theoretical manuscripts are not typically published in general issues but are often accepted and published in special issues. Book reviews are no longer published. Authors can submit manuscripts online at http://onlinelibrary.wiley.com/journal/10.1002/(ISSN)1520-6807. Manuscripts are submitted and processed using the ScholarOne Manuscripts platform. In addition to publishing manuscripts, authors have the option to make their articles immediately available using the open access facility called OnlineOpen. Authors are required to pay an article publication charge to cover the cost of publishing with OnlineOpen.

For special issues, authors are encouraged to submit a short proposal outlining the topic and need for a special issue. The proposal also should include a potential list of contributing authors, preliminary topics, and timeline. Special issues typically include between six and eight manuscripts and can be no longer than 224 manuscript pages. Guest editors of a special issue assume full control of the editorial process from soliciting manuscripts, sending manuscripts out for review, and making editorial decisions. However, the editor reviews all manuscripts and the Introduction to the special issue and makes all final decisions regarding the selection of the special issue and the manuscripts accepted for inclusion.

The editorial structure includes an editor, four associate editors, and 72 editorial advisory board members. There are also one to two editorial assistants assigned to the journal. The editor and editorial staff conduct a preliminary review of each submitted manuscript to ensure the topic is a good fit for the journal, that the manuscript adheres to the stylistic guidelines of the sixth edition of the *Publication Manual of the American Psychological Association*, and that a submission letter has been submitted indicating the email address, mailing address, telephone number, and fax number of the author to whom all future correspondence will be addressed. Manuscripts that do not meet the aforementioned criteria are rejected without review. After the preliminary review, manuscripts are submitted to at least two reviewers following a double-blind review process. Depending on the recommendations of the two reviewers, the editor makes an editorial decision. At times, the manuscript is sent to a third reviewer. The journal website provides author submission guidelines (http://onlinelibrary.wiley.com/journal/10.1002/(ISSN)1520-6807/homepage/ForAuthors.html); it also provides resources (e.g., overview of peer-review process, a guide on how to review a manuscript, and advice on becoming a reviewer) to support reviewers and authors.

2015 Journal Statistics and Operations

A total of 309 manuscripts were submitted to *Psychology in the Schools* for consideration from January 1, 2015 to December 31, 2015. In addition to new submissions, 88 manuscripts (previously rejected with resubmission encouraged) were resubmitted for consideration, resulting in a total of 397 manuscripts that were processed by the journal during 2015. The time to editorial decision (not including decisions of Reject Without Full Review) was 92 days on average. It is important to note that the journal aspires to make editorial decisions within six to eight weeks; however, due to a large number of submissions during certain times of the year, editorial advisory board members might not be available to review a manuscript. Specifically, all editorial advisory board members have been assigned at least one or two manuscripts to review, and a manuscript has to wait to be assigned to reviewers until they have completed their current reviews. The review process can also take longer if no reviewer is available matching the topic of the manuscript at the time of submission. Although the journal has an extensive database of ad hoc reviewers, and they are typically used one to three times per year, after August and September most ad hoc reviewers have completed several reviews for the journal and are no longer available. The journal receives the largest number of submissions between mid-August and mid-October. For example, from August to September 2015, the journal received over 50 submissions within a four- to six-week period. The journal also receives a fairly high number of submissions from January to February and from May to June each year. It also is important to note that the majority of manuscripts that are rejected and resubmitted are also sent out to two reviewers (typically the same reviewers who conducted the initial reviews).

As is evident in Table 6.2, only a small percentage (12.4%) of the 306 original manuscripts were accepted during 2015. However, as shown in Table 6.3, the percentage of accepted manuscripts increased to 29.1% when the 88 manuscripts that were rejected and resubmitted were included. The majority of manuscripts that were rejected and resubmitted during 2015 were eventually accepted for publication. A small percentage of the manuscripts that were rejected and resubmitted received a final decision of rejection or major revision.

Table 6.2 Journal Operations for Original Submissions to *Psychology in the Schools* in 2015

Manuscript decisions for original submissions	Number	Percentage
Accept	12	3.9%
Accept pending minor revisions	26	8.5%
Major revision	45	14.7%
Reject	187	61.1%
Reject and resubmit	34	11.1%
Reject without full review	2	0.7%
Total	306	100%

94   David E. McIntosh

Table 6.3 Journal Operations for All Submissions to *Psychology in the Schools* in 2015

Manuscript decisions for all submissions	Number	Percentage
Accept	70	17.9%
Accept pending minor revisions	44	11.2%
Major revision	53	13.5%
Reject	189	48.3%
Reject and resubmit	34	8.7%
Reject without full review	2	0.5%
Total	392	100%

During 2015, seven general issues and three special (themed) issues were published. A total of 76 (51 in general and 25 in special issues) manuscripts were published. The majority (96.1%; $n = 73$) were research articles, while 3.9% ($n = 3$) were Introductions to the special issues. A total of 1,051 pages were published.

Recommendations for Prospective Authors

Psychology in the Schools is primarily focused on publishing high-quality research that has implications for the practice of psychology within schools. Historically, the journal works with authors to improve manuscripts that have the potential to make significant contributions to the literature. In recent years, there also has been an increased focus on increasing the number of international submissions and submissions from non-native English speakers. The following recommendations are intended to assist prospective authors when submitting manuscripts for consideration:

- The majority of manuscripts that are rejected have significant methodological issues. Although it is rare for research conducted within educational settings to employ true experimental designs, researchers often fail to address common confounds when employing quasi-experimental designs. For example, authors should strive to utilize randomization during participant selection to control possible confounds and to demonstrate the effectiveness of psychological treatments or educational interventions.
- Although the journal does publish research that uses single-subject designs, many authors fail to describe the treatment to allow for duplication. Because replication is essential across studies using single-subject designs, the treatment must be described in detail. Essentially, for single-subject designs to demonstrate the effectiveness of a specific treatment and to demonstrate generalizability, replication across studies is required.
- The Introduction to an article should provide a strong theoretical rationale for why the study was conducted and needed. Introductions should include seminal research; however, an exhaustive historical review of the literature

is not required. Authors should assume readers have a general understanding of the topic and published research unless the topic is inimitable.

- Prospective authors should consider the number of participants included in their studies and the generalizability of the results. Studies that use small local samples that have limited generalizability should not be submitted.
- The use of a large number of participants often results in substantial power. Specifically, statistics computed using very large samples are often statistically significant but lack practical significance. For example, very small correlations (e.g., .06, .14, .31) will often be statistically significant but will lack practical significance. Authors should report and discuss the *coefficient of determination* when conducting correlation research. Authors also should report effect sizes (i.e., eta and eta squared) when possible to allow readers to gain a clear understanding of the proportion of variance related to the main effects, interactions, or error depending on the statistics that are computed.
- Using the wrong statistics to answer the research questions or using the wrong statistics given the sample size are common issues. Authors should strive to ensure the statistical results and discussion are aligned to address the research questions outlined within the Introduction. It is not uncommon for authors to lose focus when conducting the data analysis and when discussing the results of a study. Ensuring the appropriate sample size is utilized when conducting parametric analyses (even for non-normal data) is essential. If sample size cannot meet the required guidelines for parametric analyses, authors should consider using nonparametric statistical tests.
- International and non-English-speaking authors should spend additional time editing manuscripts before submission. There are numerous websites where authors can download manuscripts and check grammar. Several of these websites also detect plagiarism. Also, ensure manuscripts follow the stylistic guidelines of the sixth edition of the *Publication Manual of the American Psychological Association*.
- Correlational studies (correlating two measures administered at the same time, correlating test scores and a specific educational intervention, etc.), while interesting, often make minimal contributions to the practice of school psychologists. Therefore, the journal is more likely to publish research that has clear implications for practice within schools.
- Theoretical articles should focus on contributing new knowledge and helping the profession rethink current perspectives. Literature reviews that essentially summarize literature found in published texts, book chapters, or journals should be avoided. It is more likely for the journal to publish theoretical articles in special issues than general issues.
- As mentioned previously, the journal, historically, has worked with beginning faculty and other emerging researchers. Therefore, it is not uncommon for manuscripts to need several revisions (three or four) before final acceptance. Authors are encouraged to resubmit manuscripts that have been rejected but invited to resubmit. However, the revisions and

resubmission should occur within the timeline designated by the editor. Authors also need to follow all editor requests (e.g., decrease the length of the manuscript, update citations, and provide a more detailed description of participants) during the revision of the manuscript. If an author is not able to meet the timeline, the author should request an extension from the editor.

Summary

Psychology in the Schools continues to receive a large number of submissions each year from researchers not only representing the field of school psychology but also the fields of education, counseling, and higher education. The journal also consistently publishes special issues that are guest edited by leading school psychology researchers. Compared to other school psychology journals, *Psychology in the Schools* publishes the highest number of articles per year.

7 Publishing in *School Psychology International*

Amity L. Noltemeyer and
Caven S. McLoughlin

Overview of the Journal

School Psychology International (SPI) is a peer-reviewed journal published six times annually by SAGE Publishing. Publishing its 37th annual volume in 2016, *SPI* has evolved over time from a magazine format into a formal journal with international reach. The aim of *SPI* is to promote effective practice in school and educational psychology globally. This aim is accomplished through the distribution of high-quality academic research, examples of evidence-based practice, and key developments in school psychology around the world. Each year, *SPI* publishes approximately 42 full-length original research and review articles of international interest in a variety of practical and academic areas of K-12 school and educational psychology. The primary readership of *SPI* includes school psychology practitioners, researchers, trainers, and policy makers representing 30+ countries. Therefore, work published in the journal is poised for broad dissemination and exposure across diverse settings.

The *SPI* editorial board is currently comprised of two editors, six senior associate editors, 38 associate editors, 3 methodological advisors, and an editorial assistant. Representation from 14 countries on six continents is included in the current editorial board. There is a two-step peer-review process. Initially each manuscript is reviewed by a senior member of the editorial team (i.e., an editor, action editor, or senior associate editor) to determine the degree of match between the submission and the scope and mission of the journal. This initial review serves as a precursor and filter in advance of full peer review. Double-blind peer review involving appraisals by at least one content reviewer and a methodologist (where applicable) is the standard for *SPI*. We strive for at least one of these reviewers to be from a nation, region, or setting different from any of the manuscript authors. At the conclusion of the peer-review process, the editor provides the author with a final decision and a summary of reviewers' comments. Reviewers' comments are considered to be critically important in reaching a publication decision; nevertheless, the decision about acceptance for publication is made by the editor (or associate editor serving as the action editor). The journal is a member of the Committee on Publication Ethics (COPE) and subscribes to their ethical standards and due process procedures for resolving author and publisher conflicts.

In addition to regular manuscript submissions, *SPI* also considers proposals for guest-edited themed issues developed around a topic aligned with the scope and mission of the journal. These themed issues consist of a set of complementary manuscripts on a shared topic, and aim to advance knowledge and practice related to the topic. Authors interested in guest editing a themed issue are encouraged to email the editor for more information on developing a proposal. Article submissions for approved themed issue proposals undergo the same set of rigorous review procedures as regular submissions; however, the process is overseen by the guest editor under the supervision of the editor. Wherever possible and appropriate, the theme issue content strives to portray perspectives from multiple geographic locations to illustrate different applications and implications.

SPI articles are available in both print and electronic format, via institutional or individual subscriptions or short-term access purchases. Accepted manuscripts are published online before they appear in print, which allows work to be disseminated more quickly. In recent years, the journal has sought to supplement the journal content with additional freely available online resources. For example, *SPI* publishes free-to-access Virtual Special Issue Collections (http://spi.sagepub.com/site/special_issues/directory.xhtml), which include literature reviews featuring a collection of *SPI* articles on a given topic. *SPI* also publishes free podcasts (http://spi.sagepub.com/site/Podcast/podcast_dir.xhtml) and vodcasts (http://spi.sagepub.com/site/Vodcasts/vodcasts_dir.xhtml) to accompany these special issue collections and individual articles, which can extend readers' knowledge of topics covered in the journal. *SPI* also offers authors of accepted manuscripts the opportunity to submit a brief video abstract, which is placed online at the *SPI* website alongside their article. In 2016, *SPI* launched its Twitter (https://twitter.com/SPIjournal) and Facebook (www.facebook.com/groups/117853035274187/) channels that are used to share information about *SPI* and international school psychology.

2015 Journal Statistics and Operations

Manuscript Submissions and Processing

The average time to first decision for all manuscripts in 2015 was 31.66 days, and the average time to final decision was 48.91 days. The total number of original submissions in 2015 was 114, an increase from 2014. Thus far in 2016, between January 1 and June 11, there were 64 original submissions; if this pace of submissions continues it suggests that the number of submissions will once again increase in 2016.

A summary of the frequency and percentage of different types of decisions for manuscripts submitted in 2015 (regardless of when the decision was made) is presented in Table 7.1.

School Psychology International 99

Table 7.1 Journal Operations for *School Psychology International* in 2015

Decisions on 2015 submissions	Number	Percentage
Accepted	44	27.8%
Minor revisions	26	16.4%
Rejected	36	22.6%
Rejected without full review (inappropriate)	10	6.3%
Reject but encourage resubmission	29	18.2%
Reject but recommend to SAGE Open (additional review needed)*	14	8.8%

Note. Data provided reflect both original and revised manuscripts submitted in 2015. *This option allows the *SPI* editor to reject the manuscript from the journal but gives the author the option to have it forwarded for consideration in the journal SAGE Open. If the author consents, it would be considered by the SAGE Open editor and sent out for review if deemed an appropriate submission to that journal.

Publication Patterns

For the 2015 volume year, there were 40 articles published in six issues. Of these, three issues (17 articles; 50% of 2015 issues) were topically themed (*Healthy Students, Better Learners*; *Innovative Preparation Models in School Psychology*; and *Context of Instruction for Student Success*), although two of the topically themed issues also included original articles. Generally, volumes only include one to two themed issues rather than three as occurred in 2015.

In order to illustrate the types of articles published in *SPI*, we classified each of the 2015 published articles as being a research article, expository article, product-focused review, or other type of publication. Table 7.2 displays the

Table 7.2 Number and Percentage of Articles by Type for *School Psychology International* in 2015

Article type	Number	Percentage	Notes
Research	36	76.6%	Primarily quantitative research. There were also 3 qualitative studies, 2 mixed method studies, and a content analysis.
Expository	4	8.5%	Primarily literature reviews. One article was a proposal of a new framework.
Product-focused review	0	0%	
Other	7	14.9%	Included 2 calls for papers, 3 editorial announcements, an erratum, and a memorial statement.

100 *Amity L. Noltemeyer & Caven S. McLoughlin*

Table 7.3 Three Articles from 2015 that Represent *School Psychology International's* Goals

Authors	Title	Volume and issue	Nation(s) of affiliation(s) of author(s)
Vincent Busch, Lydia Laninga-Wijnen, Tom Albert van Yperen, Augustinus Jacobus Petrus Schrijvers, and Johannes Rob Josephus De Leeuw	*Bidirectional Longitudinal Associations of Perpetration and Victimization of Peer Bullying with Psychosocial Problems in Adolescents: A Cross-Lagged Panel Study*	36 (5)	The Netherlands
Sukkyung You, Euikyung Kim, and Unkyung No	*Impact of Violent Video Games on the Social Behaviors of Adolescents: The Mediating Role of Emotional Competence*	36 (1)	Republic of Korea and United States
Amanda B. Clinton, Leihua Edstrom, Heather A. Mildon, and Lesliann Davila	*Social Emotional Learning in a Guatemalan Preschool Sample: Does Socioeconomic Status Moderate the Effects of a School-Based Prevention Program?*	36 (1)	Commonwealth of Puerto Rico and United States

number and proportion of 2015 published articles that were classified as each of these four article types. As evidenced by these results, the vast majority of *SPI* publications are research articles, although expository submissions are also published. *SPI* does not publish product-focused reviews, and articles we classified as "Other" are typically prepared by the *SPI* editorial team and are not encouraged as submissions.

In order to provide exemplars for prospective authors, we identified three articles from 2015 as representative of the journal's goals. These articles are identified in Table 7.3. The highlighted articles generally have strong methodology and global relevance and are of high topical interest to school and educational psychologists. Furthermore, two of the articles are written by author teams from multiple geographical contexts.

Recommendations for Prospective Authors

There are journal-specific requirements for manuscripts submitted to *SPI* (which apply to both regular submissions and themed-issue submissions), and these requirements are fully described in the journal's submission guidelines (https://us.sagepub.com/en-us/nam/journal/school-psychology-international# submission-guidelines). For example, manuscripts must be of international relevance to school and educational psychology. As one of only two journals featured in this text that is explicitly focused on disseminating information intended for international audiences, it might be helpful to highlight the differences between an international journal and a national journal. To be eligible for international dissemination, it is not enough that the author team is located in a different nation or even continent from the publisher's or editors' locations. An international journal requires that the results and implications from a study can, with appropriate cultural modifications, be transferable to settings entirely different from where the data were collected. This element is a vital discriminator between national and international journals. Unless an author team specifically addresses the transferability and universality of their findings to distant settings (albeit generally those with similar characteristics), it is possible that readers will not be able to recognize the applicability of the implications to their daily work or research interests. Prospective authors are strongly encouraged to carefully review the match for both format and content between their manuscript and the journal's submission guidelines; manuscripts that do not accord to the journal style are overrepresented among those declined for publication.

Authors submitting their manuscripts to *SPI* should carefully attend to the length and formatting requirements specified in the submission guidelines. When the potential submission exceeds the maximum word count (6,000 words), authors can consider whether some content of peripheral significance to the main text (e.g., tables of marginally relevant data, appendices, descriptions of complex methodology or sampling required for any replication, and pilot investigations) can be submitted as online supplementary material. This information is featured alongside the electronic article and is readily available to subscribers and researchers. It is not included in the printed article but is available in a permanent online repository. This information does not count towards the submission word limit.

It is particularly important for prospective authors to note that several types of submissions will not be considered for publication by *SPI* and will result in rejection without peer review: book reviews, test or product reviews, obituaries, announcements, and manuscripts describing studies where undergraduate students serve as participants. Furthermore, the journal discourages and rarely accepts the following types of research: (1) survey-research using a poorly justified sample, a psychometrically questionable instrument, or both; (2) manuscripts that primarily serve as analyses of tests or survey instruments (e.g., validation of instrumentation used in cross-cultural research); and (3) studies primarily focused on children's parents or teachers, rather than children themselves (unless multi-setting analyses disclose cultural differences and similarities in psychological or educational services for children).

In addition to the basic journal submission requirements, research described within submissions is evaluated on a variety of other dimensions including rigor, sophistication, clarity, potential to contribute to the literature in a novel or meaningful way, and global appeal. It is important to note that manuscripts submitted to *SPI* vary substantially and that some that appear to meet the

102 *Amity L. Noltemeyer & Caven S. McLoughlin*

basic requirements or constitute solid research might nonetheless be rejected due to editorial priorities. Although incorporating the features below will not ensure publication in *SPI*, manuscripts that attend to these considerations tend to be reviewed more favorably:

- *Include a literature review that is rigorous and internationally comprehensive.* A systematic process should be used to identify, synthesize, and report the extant research on the topic; criteria for inclusion and exclusion of cited research should be stated explicitly. Considering the broad international audience, it is important to assume a global perspective when conducting the literature review rather than narrowly focusing on the literature from a single country or region of the world.
- *Use rigorous research design.* The research design should be appropriate to the research questions and powerful enough to uncover meaningful conclusions and implications. Designs that minimize systematic error or bias and maximize generalizable conclusions are preferred. Furthermore, research designs appropriate for uncovering causal relations are preferred to those resulting in descriptive information.
- *Employ optimal sampling.* The sample size should be adequate for the analyses conducted. Representative sampling is preferred, and convenience sampling is rarely accepted.
- *Use strong instrumentation.* Measures should be chosen wisely and have psychometric data to support their use with the given population. Procedures for the translation of tests used in settings for which they were not designed must be fully described and justified and be reflective of best practice.
- *Employ direct and observable measures.* Self-report measures, including paper-and-pencil surveys, have a place in research; however, they also have limitations. Direct and observable measures or substantiating evidence is preferred.
- *Describe pilot testing.* When appropriate, pilot testing of instruments and procedures strengthens the manuscript. Authors might choose to describe the piloting procedures within the Online Supplemental Materials repository, described earlier.
- *Describe appropriate training of research assistants, interventionists, or data collectors.* Explain how these individuals were trained to ensure consistency in intervention procedures, assessment, and data entry. Control for bias and the incorporation of procedures that validate rigor and objectivity are routinely anticipated by reviewers.
- *Present fidelity data.* Provide information on the degree to which interventions or treatments were implemented with fidelity and consistency, using direct observation procedures when possible.
- *Employ appropriate statistical analyses.* Select robust, strong, statistical analyses that are appropriate for the research questions and data characteristics. Ensure that the measurement and statistical assumptions

for the analyses are met, and describe any assumption violations and how they were handled. Describe information on missing data and how they were accommodated.

- *Engage in accurate statistical reporting and interpretation.* Follow conventions and standards for presenting statistics, figures, and tables. Ensure that results are interpreted accurately and not misrepresented. Avoid selectively reporting statistics for the purpose of supporting hypotheses.
- *Ensure that the study makes a unique contribution.* Studies are preferred that have the potential to significantly advance knowledge and make a novel contribution to the discipline.
- *Include a thorough Discussion section.* Insightfully consider how the findings are consistent with, or different from, previous work. Carefully consider methodological and measurement limitations when discussing the meaning and implications of findings. Research-into-practice implications for psychological service providers in schools should be discussed; research with identifiable value for shaping the practice of school and educational psychology in the service of children is actively sought.
- *Address how results are meaningful across geographical locales.* If the research focuses on a sample of children from a single national setting, it should include a discussion of the relevance of the implications across national boundaries (i.e., generalizable "lessons learned"). Studies without a discussion of the practical implications of the results for psychoeducational services to children in multiple locales are rarely accepted.
- *Offer a compelling story.* Manuscripts submitted for publication in *SPI* should not be boring, dull, unimpressive, or tedious. Rather, an author should aim to submit an article that tells a research "story" that is compelling, novel, timely, and accurate—and likely to derive practical implications for psychologists serving children worldwide.
- *Evidence high-quality writing.* The writing should be well-organized, precise, concise, and reflect APA conventions. The English language is the medium of communication even though it is not necessarily the first language of the author or the reader. Therefore, writing should reflect clarity and be jargon free, easily accessible, and unambiguous. The writer should avoid tortuous multi-clause constructions, limit the use of acronyms specific to a particular setting, and not make assumptions that require knowledge of a culture or an educational system. One example of such an assumption involves the use of the term *grade* in the United States of America, which can refer to an age grouping and also reference a child's level of success in the subject area; such nomenclature is almost wholly confined to the United States. We recommend that contributions from authors for whom English is not their native language should be proofread and edited by an English-language professional skilled in technical writing.
- *Follow research reporting standards.* Prospective authors are referred to the American Psychological Association's Journal Article Reporting Standards (see www.apa.org/pubs/authors/jars.pdf) for more guidance on research reporting standards.

These dimensions reflect a sampling of the standards against which manuscripts are evaluated by the *SPI* editorial team. Whether or not a manuscript is accepted for publication, the editorial team strives to provide constructive and respectful feedback to authors in order to strengthen their current and future work. Because editorial priorities change over time, we urge potential authors to review the *SPI* website for any changes in requirements or priorities before submitting their work.

Conclusion

Successful submissions to *SPI* are prepared by authors who think globally and consider the interests of their international audience; who select elegant, sophisticated, and complex research designs to test their hypotheses; who analyze reliable data accessed from relevant, recent, researched measures using sophisticated statistical procedures; and who parallel the mission, scope, style, and format of the journal.

8 Publishing in *School Psychology Quarterly*

Shane R. Jimerson and Richard C. Gilman

Overview of the Journal

School Psychology Quarterly is published by the American Psychological Association (APA) and is the official journal of the APA Division 16 (School Psychology). As background, Division 16 is dedicated to facilitating the professional practice of school psychology and actively advocates in a variety of domains (e.g., education and health care reform) that have significant implications for the practice of psychology with children, families, and the institutions that serve them. *School Psychology Quarterly* features articles that advance science, practice, and policy relevant to the profession of school psychology.

School Psychology Quarterly publishes premier science related to schooling, child development, pedagogical practices, disability, and related fields (Jimerson, 2013, 2014, 2015, 2016). Scholarship across numerous diverse fields, including educational, cognitive, social, behavioral, preventive, psychological, cross-cultural, and developmental science, continues to inform the field of school psychology. To this end, *School Psychology Quarterly* typically publishes empirical studies and literature reviews of the psychology of education and services for children in school settings, encompassing a full range of methodologies and orientations, including educational, cognitive, social, cognitive-behavioral, preventive, cross-cultural, and developmental perspectives.

As alluded to in Chapter 2, *School Psychology Quarterly* is part of Clarivate Analytics' Journal Citation Reports, and as of 2015 the journal has a 2-year Impact Factor of 2.75, ranking 8th out of 57 journals in the "Psychology—Education" category. Published articles are listed in over 30 of the most comprehensive and widely used databases, including PsycINFO, PsycARTICLES, MEDLINE, and EBSCO. Additional information about *School Psychology Quarterly* can be accessed from a variety of online resources (e.g., www.apa. org/pubs/journals/spq/index.aspx; www.apa.org/monitor/2012/01/journal-spq. aspx; www.apa.org/pubs/journals/features/spq-28-1-1.pdf). Online access to full articles is found at http://psycnet.apa.org/index.cfm?fa=browsePA.volumes &jcode=spq.

Types of Articles Published

School Psychology Quarterly currently reviews manuscripts specific to one or more of the following formats: (a) advances in quantitative, qualitative, and mixed designs, (b) brief reports, (c) empirical research articles, (d) international perspectives, (e) reviews and meta-analyses, (f) letters to the editor and perspective articles, and (g) special topic sections. Each of these categories is briefly described in the sections that follow. Submitted manuscripts should be written for the general readership. Consequently, they might include material that could be considered too basic for those well-versed in the field being covered. The recommended length for manuscripts is approximately 6,000 words, unless otherwise noted (e.g., brief reports are limited to 2,500 words).

Advances in Quantitative, Qualitative, and Mixed Designs

Statistical and methodological designs have advanced and flourished over the past decade. *School Psychology Quarterly* is interested in publishing papers on promising approaches, step-by-step illustrations on the applications of new statistical software packages, and innovative ways to transform traditional methods to examine complex issues facing children, families, and schools. Examples of articles that would be appropriate for this category can be found in recent issues of *School Psychology Quarterly* (e.g., Stormont, Herman, Reinke, David, & Goel, 2013) and elsewhere (e.g., Foster, 2014). Overviews of statistics and methods are also welcomed (e.g., Detry & Ma, 2016).

Brief Reports

A special section is devoted to publishing papers that might be based on a case study, a small sample (e.g., single-case designs), or a limited number of variables. Brief reports are limited to 2,500 words (from the Introduction through the Discussion), a maximum of three tables and figures (total), and up to 25 references. Brief reports begin with a summary of no more than 100 words.

School Psychology Quarterly is particularly interested in case studies, which illustrate step-by-step processes in innovative decision making. Whether specific to an assessment, consultation, or treatment technique, information about the case is presented in stages to simulate the way such information emerges in school psychology practice. The author discusses each problem-solving stage, sharing his or her reasoning with the reader. Example formats for case studies are illustrated in Peterman, Hoff, Gosch, and Kendall (2015) and Schmidt, Iachini, George, Koller, and Weist (2015).

Empirical Research Articles

Empirical research articles are the backbone of the journal and constitute the majority of pages in each published issue. These papers are based on original empirical data that convey the discovery of new knowledge across a variety of domains.

International Perspectives

Cross-cultural and transnational scholarship continues to enhance knowledge and understanding of important topics relevant to school psychology internationally.

Recognizing that learning, psychological, behavioral, and social challenges faced by youth are often universal, *School Psychology Quarterly* regularly features manuscripts from scholars throughout the world, including research from multi-site international projects and work that can be adapted and applied to diverse populations, cultures, and communities. Papers linking innovative empirical research with practice and public policy in the USA and elsewhere will also be considered.

Reviews and Meta-Analyses

School Psychology Quarterly publishes review articles, particularly those that represent a new synthesis of information. All review articles undergo the same peer-review and editorial process as other submissions. Meta-analyses are always welcome (see Burns et al. (2016) as an example). In addition, the journal is interested in publishing reviews that formulate innovative frameworks with which to study learning, psychological, or social development. Examples of such articles are Cicchetti (2016) and Sonuga-Barke, Cortese, Fairchild, and Stringaris (2016).

Letters to the Editor and Perspective Articles

Letters to the editor are specific to articles or editorial comments published in *School Psychology Quarterly* or concern important issues of general interest to school psychology. Authors will be given the opportunity to reply to accepted letters critical of their work. Conversely, perspective articles are not specific to articles published in *School Psychology Quarterly*. Rather, these are brief pieces covering a wide variety of timely topics of relevance to school psychology. Both types of submissions are limited to 1,200 words and may contain one figure or table and a maximum of five references.

Special Topic Sections

Special topic sections aim to bring awareness of, and education on, the nature and correlates associated with a variety of topics of interest to researchers and practitioners. The special topic sections featured in *School Psychology Quarterly* are developed specifically to enrich, invigorate, enhance, and advance science, practice, or policy particularly relevant to the contemporary context of school

108 *Shane R. Jimerson & Richard C. Gilman*

Table 8.1 Recent Special Topic Sections Featured in *School Psychology Quarterly*

Assessment of General Education Teachers' Tier 1 Classroom Practices: Current Science and Practice (Volume 28, issue 4, 2013)

School Climate, Aggression, Peer Victimization, and Bully Perpetration (Volume 29, issue 3, 2014)

Assessing, Understanding, and Supporting Students with ADHD at School (Volume 29, issue 4, 2014)

Mental Health Service Delivery within a Multi-Tiered Problem-Solving Framework (Volume 30, issue 2, 2015)

The Importance of Teachers in Facilitating Student Success (Volume 30, issue 4, 2015)

Immigrants, Schooling, and School Psychology Practice (Volume 31, issue 2, 2016)

Diversification of School Psychology: Developing an Evidence-Base from Current Research and Practice (Volume 31, issue 3, 2016)

Assessing, Understanding, and Supporting Students with Autism at School (Volume 31, issue 4, 2016)

Note. Full contents are available online at http://psycnet.apa.org/index.cfm?fa=browsePA. volumes& jcode=spq.

psychology. Each emphasizes contemporary methods, analytical strategies, and conceptual foundations aimed at providing substantive advancements in knowledge relevant to school psychology (see Table 8.1 for examples of special topic sections).

All scholars are encouraged to submit a proposal for a special topic section to be featured in *School Psychology Quarterly*, including a brief explanation of the theme, purpose, and significance to the field. Each special topic section proposal is then reviewed by editors, as well as editorial board members, to select those that would be optimal. Following the identification of a particular special topic, the call for submissions is distributed to encourage other scholars engaged in relevant research to submit their research for consideration. All submitted manuscripts are processed through the same rigorous peer-review process that all other manuscripts submitted to *School Psychology Quarterly* undergo. Table 8.2 describes the key components of special topic sections in *School Psychology Quarterly*.

Recent Journal Statistics and Operations

The total number of submissions to *School Psychology Quarterly* (including new submissions and resubmissions of revised manuscripts) continues to grow. The most recent statistics, published in 2015, revealed that over 200 new manuscripts were submitted, which is an all-time high (see Table 8.3). Moreover, editors and editorial board members are committed to high-quality and timely decisions, as reflected in the average lag time from submission to

School Psychology Quarterly   109

Table 8.2 Key Components of Special Topic Sections in *School Psychology Quarterly*

Contemporary topics to advance science, practice, and policy. The editor, associate editors, and editorial board members review each proposal for a special topic section with focused analysis on the promise and potential of the topic to advance science, practice, and policy relevant to the field of school psychology.

Emphasis on contemporary methods and procedures. Reviewers consider the use of methods and procedures likely to advance knowledge pertaining to science, practice, and policy relevant to the field of school psychology.

Expertise of guest editors. Guest editors with relevant expertise aim to encourage high-quality submissions and also provide leadership in distributing manuscripts for review and providing recommendations regarding suitability for publication.

An open call for manuscripts is required. Whereas guest editors of proposed special topic sections typically identify potential groups of authors who they will encourage to submit manuscripts for consideration, it is also important to recognize that an open call for manuscripts affords an opportunity for any authors to submit their scholarship for review.

Every manuscript is peer reviewed. As with all submissions, whether they are specifically solicited or not, each manuscript goes through the normal blinded peer-review process, which includes review among editorial board members. Only those receiving favorable recommendations are ultimately published.

Each manuscript is subject to the same policies and guidelines. Authors of manuscripts considered for special topic sections must attend to all relevant *School Psychology Quarterly* policies and guidelines. Further details regarding the preparation of manuscripts are available online at www.apa.org/pubs/journals/spq

There is no set number of manuscripts required. Featuring manuscripts in a "special topic section" permits flexibility regarding the number of articles ultimately featured. One can anticipate the inclusion of at least four articles and possibly many more as determined through peer review of manuscripts submitted.

Table 8.3 Submission Status for 2015 Submissions to *School Psychology Quarterly*

Submission status for 2015 submissions	Number	Percentage
Decisions rendered	204	100%
Accepted	35	17%
Reject (all categories)	169	83%
Reject with reviews	73	36%
Reject without review	96	47%

decision. For example, between 2012 and 2015, the lag time ranged between 20 and 22 days.

Given the prestige of the journal, acceptance rates are competitive and on a par with that of other APA journals. Acceptance rates typically hover around 17% (see Table 8.3 for results from 2015). Further, all submissions are first read by the editor, who screens papers that would not be in keeping with

110   *Shane R. Jimerson & Richard C. Gilman*

quality of methods, writing, subject area, or the aims of the journal; approximately one-third of submitted papers are rejected without external review.

Publication Contents 2015

The 40 articles (totaling 577 pages) published in *School Psychology Quarterly* during 2015 (up from 32 articles and 577 pages in 2014, 27 articles and 404 pages in 2013, and 21 articles and 246 pages in 2012) address important and diverse topics and methods essential for further enriching, invigorating, enhancing, and advancing science, practice, and policy relevant to school psychology. In addition to addressing many facets of facilitating academic achievement and social emotional development of children at school, the following highlights the many important topics featured in *School Psychology Quarterly* during 2015:

- The importance of teachers (e.g., relationships, support, measurement, informants, positive psychological functioning, and contributions to student success).
- Measurement and assessment (e.g., observational, direct behavior ratings, curriculum-based, cognitive, computer adaptive, progress monitoring, writing, math, reading, social, emotional, and teacher).
- Bullying and victimization (e.g., psychosocial adjustment, contextual influences, and process of prevention) and mental health supports (e.g., intervention, assessment, positive behavioral supports, multi-tiered systems of support, and psychopharmacological interventions).
- Developmental psychopathology (e.g., autism, internalizing disorders, and social and emotional disorders) and screening (e.g., social, emotional, and behavioral risk and kindergarten readiness).
- Other important topics such as peer relationships, social emotional skills and self-regulation, self-efficacy, school climate, family factors, patterns of strength and weaknesses, positive psychological functioning, international perspectives, learning disability eligibility, gifted students, homework, and school dropout.

Recent articles also incorporate an assortment of analytical methods (e.g., single-case designs, latent class analysis, factor analysis, randomized controlled designs, structural equation modeling, and regression analyses). Among the 40 articles published in 2015, 36 were research articles producing new findings, two were systematic reviews, and two were editorials.

Recommendations for Prospective Authors

Manuscripts submitted to *School Psychology Quarterly* should typically be limited to 6,000 words (a bit longer than *Psychological Science*, the flagship journal of the Association for Psychological Science, which limits research articles to 4,000 words). Especially in the case of multi-site collaborative projects involving sophisticated modeling analyses, it is understood that there might be a need to exceed 6,000 words. Thus, manuscripts that exceed the 6,000 limit *will* be considered for full review, but they must be accompanied with a submission letter that states the rationale for the need to exceed the word limit. The immediate prescreening by the editors of each article upon submission considers whether the content and associated implications are potentially suitable for publication in *School Psychology Quarterly*. It is important to understand that the length is one dimension that is considered during this prescreening review.

There are several strategies that authors can use to reduce the length of the manuscript prior to submission, for instance, reducing the number of references might significantly reduce the number of words (e.g., instead of five citations, include only the most seminal). Carefully review and revise sections where paragraphs could be eliminated or stated more succinctly to reduce the overall length of the manuscript. Removing sections or paragraphs that might not be necessary is another strategy to reduce the length, and of course, if the reviewers recommend that you need to include additional information, you might choose to include that information in your revised manuscript. Also please consider whether any tables could be suitably placed online as supplementary information; this way, the information is available to readers immediately when reading the manuscript online. Examples of supplementary materials that can be posted online include oversized tables, lengthy appendices, detailed intervention protocols, supplementary data sets. See "Supplementing Your Article With Online Material" for further information (www.apa.org/pubs/authors/supp-material.aspx). Through the review process, the quality of the manuscript will be the highest premium.

Authors are encouraged to clearly articulate the unique contributions of their manuscript, with particular emphasis on how the manuscript advances science, practice, or policy relevant to school psychology. Additional details regarding the preparation of manuscripts for submission to *School Psychology Quarterly* are available online at www.apa.org/pubs/journals/spq/index.aspx?tab=4

Conclusion

Featuring articles that advance science, practice, and policy relevant to the profession of school psychology, *School Psychology Quarterly* publishes premier science related to schooling, child development, pedagogical practices, disability, and related fields. *School Psychology Quarterly* continues to emphasize science and scholarship across numerous diverse fields that inform the field of school psychology. The contents of *School Psychology Quarterly* are featured in the leading indexes and databases, providing distribution dissemination and access to practitioners and scholars throughout the world.

References

Burns, M. K., Petersen-Brown, S., Haegele, K., Rodriquez, M., Schmitt, B., Cooper, M. et al. (2016). Meta-analysis of academic interventions derived from neuropsychological data. *School Psychology Quarterly, 31*, 28–42. http://dx.doi.org/10.1037/spq0000117

Cicchetti, D. (2016). Socioemotional, personality, and biological development: Illustrations from a multilevel developmental psychopathology perspective on child maltreatment. *Annual Review of Psychology, 67*, 187–211. doi: 10.1146/annurev-psych-122414-033259

Detry, M. A., & Ma, Y. (2016). Analyzing repeated measurements using mixed models. *The Journal of the American Medical Association, 315*, 407–408.

Foster, E. M. (2014). Mediation, identification, and plausibility: An illustration using children's mental health services. *Journal of Consulting and Clinical Psychology, 82*, 803–812. doi: org/10.1037/a0031980

Jimerson, S. R. (2013). Advancing science, practice, and policy relevant to school psychology. *School Psychology Quarterly, 28*, 1–6. doi: 10.1037/spq0000021

Jimerson, S. R. (2014). Enhancing science, practice, and policy relevant to school psychology around the world. *School Psychology Quarterly, 29*, 1–6. doi: 10.1037/spq0000066

Jimerson, S. R. (2015). Invigorating science, practice, and policy relevant to school psychology throughout the world. *School Psychology Quarterly, 30*, 1–7. http://dx.doi.org/10.1037/spq0000119

Jimerson, S. R. (2016). Enriching science, practice, and policy relevant to school psychology around the globe. *School Psychology Quarterly, 31*, 1–7. doi: 10.1037/spq0000153

Peterman, J. S., Hoff, A. L., Gosch, E., & Kendall, P. C. (2015). Cognitive-behavioral therapy for anxious youth with a physical disability: A case study. *Clinical Case Studies, 14*, 210–226. doi.org/10.1177/1534650114552556

Schmidt, R. C., Iachini, A. L., George, M., Koller, J., & Weist, M. (2015). Integrating a suicide prevention program into a school mental health system: A case example from a rural school district. *Children & Schools, 37*, 18–26. doi.org/10.1093/cs/cdu026

Sonuga-Barke, E. J. S., Cortese, S., Fairchild, G., & Stringaris, A. (2016). Annual research review: Transdiagnostic neuroscience of child and adolescent mental disorders—Differentiating decision making in attention-deficit/hyperactivity disorder, conduct disorder, depression, and anxiety. *Journal of Child Psychology and Psychiatry, 57*, 321–349. doi.org/10.1111/jcpp.12496

Stormont, M., Herman, K. C., Reinke, W. M., David, K. B., & Goel, N. (2013). Latent profile analysis of teacher perceptions of parent contact and comfort. *School Psychology Quarterly, 28*, 195–209. http://dx.doi.org/10.1037/spq0000004

9 Publishing in *School Psychology Review*

Amy L. Reschly

Overview of the Journal

School Psychology Review is a refereed scholarly journal published by the National Association of School Psychologists (NASP). Founded in 1969, NASP provided a national identity and stable leadership for the burgeoning field of school psychology (Fagan & Wise, 1994). NASP is now the world's largest professional organization of school psychologists, representing approximately 25,000 school psychologists, as well as graduate students and other related service professionals in the United States and 25 other countries. NASP's mission is to advance effective practices in order to improve students' learning, behavior, and mental health (www.nasponline.org/utility/about-nasp).

It appears that there has always been a desire to link research to practice within the profession of school psychology. An editorial by an early NASP leader noted, "He [school psychologists] must also translate theoretical and empirical findings of basic social science disciplines into specific services for school children" (Guidubaldi, 1972, p. 1). Furthermore, a survey of members of the newly founded NASP indicated a strong desire to have greater access to a broad range of scholarly research. Thus, the *School Psychology Digest* was launched in 1972 (Guidubaldi, 1972).

Perusal of over 40 years of the journal reflects the ever-increasing importance and sophistication of research in education and psychology in general and within the field of school psychology in particular. At its founding, the *Digest* included some original work but was primarily populated with summaries of research articles that had been published in other outlets and reviews of professional books. Within the first few years, however, the *Digest* became longer, including more content as well as more original research. The themed and special series issues that remain a staple of the journal can also be traced back to the first ten years of its existence. To reflect the increasing sophistication and growing scholarship within the field of school psychology, the *Digest* was renamed *School Psychology Review* in 1980 with the first issue of volume 9.

The desire to access research to inform school psychology practice in order to improve lives and outcomes of youth was evident in the founding of *School Psychology Review*; it is a desire that remains an integral part of NASP's vision.

114 Amy L. Reschly

In the last 47 years, NASP has developed a variety of publications (e.g., books, a regular newsletter [*Communiqué*, see Chapter 22], an applied online journal [*School Psychology Forum*, see Chapter 14], and curricula) and resources (e.g., podcasts and an online learning center) for school psychologists and related service professionals. Of these resources, *School Psychology Review* anchors the research-to-practice mission of the organization. As such, articles that appear in the journal have undergone a rigorous peer-review process. As was true when the journal was founded, *School Psychology Review* seeks to draw from a broad range of disciplines (e.g., developmental psychology, special education, educational psychology, and clinical child psychology). Preference is given to original, data-based manuscripts, with a particular interest in prevention and intervention strategies. Additional editorial goals this term include (a) the creation of formal guidelines for editorial board members to mentor advanced graduate students or new professionals in the peer-review process, (b) pairing young scholars with experienced former editors and associate editors to serve as guest associate editors on one or more manuscripts, and (c) utilizing NASP's other outlets (e.g., podcasts and *Communiqué*) to promote and publicize research in *School Psychology Review* and highlight implications for practice.

School Psychology Review is published quarterly. The journal converted to a digital-only format in 2015. Members of NASP have access to the journal through the NASP website (www.nasponline.org) and NASP Publications App for iPad or Android tablets. Membership circulation is approximately 25,000, not including library subscriptions. Currently, editorial leadership for *School Psychology Review* is provided by an editor, a consulting associate editor, associate editors (six to eight), a scientific advisory panel, and an editorial board. An editorial assistant provides assistance to authors with submission requirements, difficulties with the online journal portal, collection of copyright release forms, etc. All manuscripts are screened by the editor for appropriateness to the journal, including relevance of topic, quality of methods and writing, and fit with journal publication priorities. Manuscripts that are determined to be a poor fit for the journal in topic, relevance (e.g., studies of music theory with undergraduate students) or methodology (e.g., most case studies, survey studies, and literature reviews) are returned without being submitted to the peer-review process. The screening by the editor is a time-saving measure for *School Psychology Review* associate editors and editorial board members as well as authors, in that it allows them to quickly identify a more appropriate outlet for their work. After the editor screens a submitted manuscript and determines that it should be submitted to peer review, the manuscript is assigned to one of the associate editors, who selects three to five reviewers for the manuscript. *School Psychology Review* uses a masked peer-review process. Associate editors typically render a publication recommendation (e.g., reject, rejection–revision encouraged, accept with minor revisions) and accompanying decision letter within 60 days. Final editorial decisions are made by the editor.

There are three types of issues in *School Psychology Review*: general, special topic, and special series. General issue articles have been accepted following the peer-review process. Articles in a general issue were independent submissions and likely represent a range of topics (e.g., academic interventions, screening for emotional and behavioral difficulties, results of a parent–child intervention for homework completion, and teacher consultation for classroom management). A special topic issue is also composed of articles that were independent submissions and subjected to peer review; however, the editor grouped these articles together at the time of publication because of a similar theme or topic across the articles, such as reading assessment and intervention or advances in Curriculum-Based Measurement.

A special series is a guest-edited issue of the journal that includes several articles and invited commentaries on a particular theme relevant to school psychology. The purpose of a special series is to provide comprehensive coverage of a timely and important topic. There are specific guidelines for the preparation of a special series proposal. Upon submission, the special series proposal is reviewed by the editor, selected associate editors, and members of the journal's scientific advisory panel, who rate the proposal in terms of interest, organization and coverage of the topic, match with the NASP Model for Comprehensive and Integrated School Psychological Services (NASP, 2010), scientific merit, qualifications of guest editors and proposed contributors, and so forth. If a special issue proposal is accepted, manuscripts slated for the issue are still subjected to peer review. Up to two issues a year might be special series; however, typically one special series is published annually.

Across its different types of issues, *School Psychology Review* publishes several types of articles. Most manuscripts are submitted as general articles. *School Psychology Review* also accepts research briefs, which are concise presentations (approximately 15 manuscript pages), of research studies, such as pilot or replication studies. Manuscripts may be submitted for consideration in the Research into Practice or Children, Research, and Public Policy sections. The focus of a Research into Practice manuscript is on application or evaluation within an applied setting. The Children, Research, and Public Policy section is for manuscripts that address public health issues and policy development relevant to education (www.nasponline.org/resources-and-publications/publications/spr-author-guidelines). Finally, the editor of the journal also periodically invites a distinguished scholar to submit a manuscript as a Featured Research Commentary (e.g., Masten, Fiat, Labella, & Strack, 2015).

2015 Journal Statistics and Operations

Manuscript Submissions and Processing

Excluding those manuscripts included in special series, editorials, and invited commentaries, 129 new manuscripts were submitted to the journal in 2015 (see Table 9.1). The time to editorial decision for these manuscripts (not including those rejected without review) was 61.37 days (SD = 15.76). The percentage of manuscripts accepted for publication was 7.9%. Of those

116   Amy L. Reschly

Table 9.1 Journal Operations for *School Psychology Review* in 2015

Submission status for 2015 submissions	Number	Percentage
No decision yet	1	0.8%
Decisions rendered		99.2%
Accept and accept contingent on revision	10	7.9%*
Reject (all categories)	117	92.1%*
Reject encouraging revision	30	23.6%*
Reject	64	50.4%*
Reject without full review	23	18.1%*

Note. One manuscript was withdrawn prior to a decision being rendered (*n* = 128). * = percentage of decisions rendered.

manuscripts rejected for publication, 23.6% were accompanied by encouragement to resubmit, whereas 50.4% were rejected following full review. The percentage of manuscripts rejected without full review was 18.1%.

Publication Patterns

In 2015, *School Psychology Review* published one special series, *Bullying Research from a Social-Ecological Perspective*; two special topic issues; and one general issue. A total of 30 articles were published in 2015: 21 were research articles (70%) and nine were expository articles (30%). Of those classified as expository in nature, one was included in the special issue (i.e., measurement issues related to bullying), one was a general article, four were invited commentaries, and three were editorials by the editor or guest editors of the special series. *School Psychology Review* does not publish book or test reviews.

Several features are noteworthy about articles published in 2015. First, there were two meta-analyses that appeared in the journal, one on the relationships between school suspension and student outcomes (Noltemeyer, Ward, & Mcloughlin, 2015) and the other on the association between empathy and defending in the bullying literature (Nickerson, Aloe, & Werth, 2015). Research articles were largely quantitative in nature, including both group and single-subject designs. Furthermore, articles drew broadly from scholars across disciplines and addressed a variety of topics relevant to advancing effective practices to improve outcomes for youth, such as screening for academic or behavioral problems as well as academic, behavior, and mental health interventions across ages (i.e., early childhood through high school) and at both systems (e.g., class-wide) and individual levels (e.g., interventions for youth with emotional and behavior disorders).

Recommendations for Prospective Authors

Most manuscripts submitted to *School Psychology Review* are as general article submissions. With the exception of research briefs, all manuscript submissions to the General, Research into Practice section or Children, Research, and Public Policy sections should be approximately 35 pages in length. Longer manuscripts might be considered for review following consultation with the editor. It is expected that authors address (a) relevant theory in the Literature Review and Discussion sections and (b) implications for practice or public policy. In terms of style, authors should follow the *Publication Manual of the American Psychological Association, Sixth Edition* (American Psychological Association, 2010).

There is a similar mission across NASP publications: advancing effective practices to improve outcomes for students. However, *School Psychology Review* can be differentiated from other NASP publications in several ways. As outlined in the original mission of *School Psychology Review*, the journal draws broadly from scholars in related disciplines, in addition to school psychology. Furthermore, articles published in *School Psychology Review* are methodologically rigorous and trend toward original data-based articles that include discussions of both theory and practice implications. Conversely other outlets, such as *School Psychology Forum* or the *Communiqué*, are more applied and practice-focused.

Approximately 18% of manuscripts are rejected out-of-hand by the editor (see Table 9.1). The primary reason a manuscript is rejected without being subjected to the peer-review process is that the manuscript is determined by the editor to be inconsistent with the journal focus either in terms of topic, relevance, or methodology. As noted in our publication guidelines, *School Psychology Review* rarely publishes narrative reviews or survey research (www.nasponline.org/resources-and-publications/publications/spr-author-guidelines). In most cases, *School Psychology Review* does not publish manuscripts that are primarily descriptions of psychometric studies of a single, specific assessment tool. It is this latter decision that has generated the most controversy from prospective authors. Manuscripts that provide psychometric information about an assessment instrument but also include information that is relevant for informing effective practices (e.g., linking assessment to intervention, decision rules in progress monitoring, and meta-analyses) are considered appropriate for *School Psychology Review*. Once manuscripts are subjected to the peer-review process, methodological rigor (i.e., "inappropriate/weak research design") is the most common reason a manuscript is rejected. *School Psychology Review* reviewers expect well-articulated hypotheses and congruence between research questions and analyses, explicitly described methods, high internal validity, and when applicable, measures of treatment integrity. In addition, authors should be cautious not to overstate the importance or implications of their results.

Conclusion

School Psychology Review is the flagship journal of the world's largest professional organization of school psychologists. It was founded to facilitate access to and translation of research into practice with the purpose of improving services and outcomes for youth. *School Psychology Review* publishes primarily original, data-based articles that have undergone masked peer-review and met the rigorous standards of its associate editors and editorial advisory board. With a NASP membership of over 25,000, in addition to library subscriptions, *School Psychology Review* has a large distribution that aids in accomplishing this goal of drawing broadly from research in multiple disciplines to improve outcomes for youth.

References

American Psychological Association. (2010). *Publication manual of the American Psychological Association* (6th ed.). Washington, DC: American Psychological Association.

Fagan, T., & Wise, P. (1994). *School psychology: Past, present, and future*. White Plains, NY: Longman.

Guidubaldi, J. (1972). School psychology: A development diagnosis. *School Psychology Digest, 1*, 1–3.

Masten, A. S., Fiat, A. E., Labella, M. H., & Strack, R. A. (2015). Educating homeless and highly mobile students: Implications of research on risk and resilience. *School Psychology Review, 44*, 315–330.

National Association of School Psychologists (2010). *Model for comprehensive and integrated school psychological services*. Bethesda, MD: National Association of School Psychologists.

Nickerson, A. B., Aloe, A. M., & Werth, J. M. (2015). The relation of empathy and defending in bullying: A meta-analytic investigation. *School Psychology Review, 44*, 372–390.

Noltemeyer, A. L., Ward, R. M., & Mcloughlin, C. (2015). Relationship between school suspension and student outcomes: A meta-analysis. *School Psychology Review, 44*, 224–240.

10 Publishing in the *Canadian Journal of School Psychology*

Donald H. Saklofske

Overview of the Journal

The *Canadian Journal of School Psychology* (*CJSP*) was first published in the early 1980s at the University of British Columbia (UBC). In 1985, Dr. G. Gerald Koe at UBC consolidated the journal as editor and continued in this role for the next seven years. The journal was published somewhat sporadically but did provide an opportunity for school psychologists to both publish and access articles reflecting topics of relevance to the Canadian context and beyond. At the start of the 1990s, editorship and ownership of *CJSP* was transferred to the Canadian Association of School Psychologists (CASP), a national organization created in 1984 and somewhat mirroring the National Association of School Psychologists in the USA. *CJSP* was continuing to attract attention from researchers and practitioners in Canada but also the USA, and many of its articles reflected a more North American view of school psychology. During this time, Dr. Hank Janzen (University of Alberta) and I, Dr. Donald Saklofske (University of Western Ontario), were appointed co-editors and held this position until the appointment of the next two editors, Dr. Marvin Simner (University of Western Ontario) and Dr. Jeff Derevensky (McGill University). In 2006, I was again asked to take on the editorship of *CJSP* at which time Dr. Joseph Snyder (Concordia University) joined me as co-editor. Another significant change occurred at this time, and with the support of Dr. Cecil Reynolds (Texas A&M University), I transacted for the CASP the arrangement for SAGE to publish *CJSP*. Although there was a backlog of papers and issues at the point of this transfer, publication of *CJSP* by SAGE began in 2007 and carries through to the present.

In 2016, another series of major changes were made to *CJSP*. The journal continues to be the official journal of the CASP and to be published by SAGE, but it has now transitioned to a fully online submission system. Following the publication pattern established by Saklofske and Snyder, *CJSP* is committed to publishing four issues per year with an annual page count of 320 journal pages. A system of associate editors as well as a much more diverse editorial board was put in place to manage not only the increased number of submissions but also the diversity of papers reflecting the growth of school psychology around the world. The current editorial composition of *CJSP*, effective 2016,

120 Donald H. Saklofske

includes Donald Saklofske (University of Western Ontario) as editor and Adam McCrimmon (University of Calgary), Janine Montgomery (University of Manitoba), Steven Shaw (McGill University), Joseph Snyder (Concordia University), and Shannon Stewart (University of Western Ontario) as associate editors.

At present, there are 53 members serving on the editorial board of *CJSP*. All current board members are from Canada (42) and the USA (11) and hold either university appointments or are established school psychology practitioners.

Current information, descriptions, and the online version of the *CJSP* can be found at http://cjsp.sagepub.com/. The journal publishes both print copies as well as the online version focusing on the theory, research, and practice of school psychology and its application to all areas of education. Thus, *CJSP* provides an important forum for practitioners, researchers, trainers, and graduate students in school and educational psychology and other branches of psychology that contribute to the academic, cognitive, social, and emotional well-being of children and youth within educational contexts. Each quarterly issue of *CJSP* includes broad-based, multidisciplinary original research studies, applied and practice articles, and both test and book reviews. *CJSP* is a major reference for school and applied psychologists and has extended its content coverage to be more reflective of school psychology in the international context. A recent increase in articles submitted from Europe, Asia, the Middle East, Australia, and other areas will likely require a concurrent change in the composition of the editorial board over time, much like the trends observed in *Journal of Psychoeducational Assessment*, which I also edit.

Submitting Manuscripts to CJSP

Preparation of manuscripts should follow the most recent edition of the *Publication Manual of the American Psychological Association*. Manuscripts must be submitted electronically at http://mc.manuscriptcentral.com/jopa where authors will be required to set up an online account in the SAGETRACK system powered by ScholarOne. Manuscripts that do not comply with submission guidelines will be returned to the author for editing prior to beginning the review process. Authors' names and affiliations, including complete contact information, should appear on a separate cover page, and the manuscript should be formatted for anonymous review; there should not be any identifying information in the manuscript, including headers and footers. A cover page should include statements attesting that the information in the manuscript has not been published elsewhere, that it is not currently being considered for publication elsewhere, and that all ethical guidelines were followed as required for conducting human research. Authors may provide names and email addresses of potential reviewers for their paper.

Article Types

Following the restructuring of *CJSP* in 2016, manuscript submissions fall into four categories: regular articles, special issue articles, brief articles, and test and book reviews.

Regular articles. *CJSP* is particularly focused on publishing original articles reflecting the theory, research, and practice of psychology in education and the specialization of school psychology. Regular manuscripts should not exceed 5,500 words, including text, tables, figures, and references, and include an abstract of between 100 and 150 words as well as four or five keywords identifying the major themes of the article. An advantage of the online format, besides the fact that articles are now accessible to readers well in advance of the published hard copy of the journal (via "publish ahead of print"), is that some information such as tables and figures that would normally exceed the word count can now be included as supplemental material in the online version. Also, in some instances (such as major review or expository papers, meta-analyses, or papers that present two or more studies), the word count allowance may be increased but this should be discussed first with the editor, Dr. Don Saklofske (dsaklofs@uwo.ca).

Special issues articles. Special issues are comprised of a collection of papers (usually five to seven) focused on a particular area of current interest and relevance to school psychologists. Guest editors most often propose the special issue theme and a listing of authors and article titles to the editor, although the editor might invite a well-known expert to develop a special issue. Once the issue has been approved, the guest editor will assume responsibility for the issue in consultation with the editor. Special issues of *CJSP* have been previously published on topics such as mental health, positive behavioral interventions, bullying, learning disabilities, ADHD, report writing, and resiliency. Currently, three special issues of *CJSP* are planned for 2016–2017: "Clinical Reasoning in School Psychology: From Assessment to Intervention," "School and Educational Psychology in Canada: A 2016 Perspective," and "Contemporary School-Based Issues Related to Identification and Intervention for Students with Autism Spectrum Disorder."

Brief articles. This format is for papers that have a narrower or more limited focus or where preliminary results from larger or in-progress studies would be of interest to readers and fit well with the aims and scope of *CJSP*. Replication studies and analyses of contemporary tests that inform assessment practices would be appropriate for this format. Brief articles should not exceed 2,200 words inclusive of text, references, tables, and figures and also include an abstract and four to five keywords. The number of tables, figures, and references should be limited, and the text should combine headings (e.g., Results and Discussion) where appropriate.

Book and test reviews. Reviews should follow the standard format for such reviews as found in other SAGE publications such as the *Journal of Psychoeducational Assessment*. The typical length is 1,600 to 2,000 words. Reviews contain identifying information about the test or book, including

122   Donald H. Saklofske

author, title, and publisher, and describe issues of particular relevance to practitioners. Contributors of test reviews must be familiar with and address the test construction guidelines described in *The Standards for Educational and Psychological Tests* (American Educational Research Association, American Psychological Association, & National Council on Measurement in Education, 2014). In order to ensure that the reviews are contemporary, the test or book under review should have been published within the past two years. For more specific guidelines and inquiries on test and book reviews, please contact associate editor, Dr. Janine Montgomery at Janine.Montgomery@umanitoba.ca or the editor at dsaklofs@uwo.ca.

Manuscript Submissions and Processing

All articles submitted to *CJSP* are first received at the SAGE office and are reviewed for key points, such as American Psychological Association format and word count, by an editorial assistant before being sent to the editor. It is the editor who then determines if the paper is a good fit with the aims and scope of the journal and decides if it should be rejected, returned to the author for prescribed modifications (e.g., resubmit as a brief article), or forwarded to an associate editor who will obtain at least two peer reviews. If the manuscript is forwarded for review, the associate editor will then recommend acceptance, revision and resubmission (with or without further review), or rejection, although the final decision in all cases rests with the editor. With the transition and changes made to *CJSP* in 2016, the method of record keeping and tracking papers also changed. The description in Table 10.1 is an estimate of completed journal operations in 2015. The total number of paper submissions in 2015 was 53, including 45 regular article submissions, five test review submissions, and three book review submissions. It is estimated that about ten of the articles were revisions of papers submitted the year before with an initial decision to revise and resubmit. None were special issue article submissions. Table 10.1, focusing on regular article submission, shows that the acceptance rate in 2015 was close to 50% and that about a quarter of these submissions were rejected without full review. Although not reported in Table 10.1, four test reviews (80% of submissions) and two book reviews (66% of submissions) were accepted for publication.

Table 10.1 Journal Operations for *Canadian Journal of School Psychology* in 2015

Submission status for 2015 regular article submissions	Number	Percentage
Accept	22	49%
Accept pending revision	–	–
Reject with review	12	27%
Reject without review	11	24%

Publication Patterns

A change in the number of submissions has already been observed for 2016, in part due to three special issues described previously—with one published late in 2016 and two more in 2017. All special issue manuscripts undergo a full review, but invariably, most all are published, given the close oversight by the guest editor and editor as well as the fact that invited authors are experts in their respective areas. For other submissions in 2016 that have been considered for review, the acceptance rate to date is approximately 40%.

In 2016, about 35% of all initial submissions were rejected by the editor or associate editor without review. The basis for such rejections is usually due to several key factors: the submission is not a good fit with the aims and scope of *CJSP* (e.g., a study of personality characteristics of military recruits), it makes a minimal contribution to either the science or practice of school psychology (e.g., a factor analysis of an obscure and dated questionnaire using a small and restricted sample), it is poorly written and fails to follow submission guidelines such as word count and American Psychological Association format, and the study is methodologically flawed (employing incorrect data analyses, an unknown sample, or a poorly implemented research design).

Together with the special issue papers and regular submissions to *CJSP* since the start of 2016 (to July), 23 submissions had been accepted, and there were four regular articles under review. At least six more submissions earmarked for a 2017 special issue were expected by the end of 2016. (This special issue, titled *Contemporary Issues in School-Based Practices for Students with Autism Spectrum Disorder* was published in the fourth issue of the journal in 2017.) The majority of papers submitted to *CJSP* that are not slated for special issues tend to report research studies, most often of an applied nature and that have applications for building and informing evidence-based practices. These studies can be quantitative, qualitative, or mixed method in design and data analysis, but the key factors to publishing a paper are again based on the contribution, presentation, and methodological rigor of the study. Most papers in the special issues, by the nature of the topic, tend to be more of the expository kind. For example, an earlier special issue on school-based mental health (2103) or the currently in-press special issues papers describing school psychology across Canada might report a number of findings and relevant "statistics" but are essentially position papers or description of current issues, best practices, etc.

Recommendations to Authors

All reputable journals have clear guidelines for writing and submitting manuscripts, and fortunately there is considerable overlap making obvious the task of authors. Many of my suggestions are clearly made in other chapters in this book, so I shall limit them to just a few.

Although the title of the journal (*Canadian Journal of School Psychology*) has been retained since the journal was first published more than 30 years ago, the journal is open to receiving and publishing articles contributed by and of

124 *Donald H. Saklofske*

relevance to school psychologists from outside of Canada and indeed North America. This change is due to two facts. Much of both the science and practice of school psychology is without borders, whether describing best practices in assessment, evidence-based interventions, or issues surrounding consultation, collaboration, program efficacy and efficiency, etc. Second, Canada is a multicultural country with new families and their children arriving daily from every region of the world. In cities such as Toronto, it is often said that one can hear dozens of different languages spoken in the same school. In Vancouver, the Sikh population is the second largest outside of India, and languages including Cantonese, Mandarin, Farsi, and Korean are commonplace. Canada is a bilingual country with two official languages (French and English), and First Nations are recognized as the founding people of Canada. We have recently welcomed more than 25,000 Syrian refugees to Canada. Thus, *CJSP* invites papers that will inform Canadian school psychologists in their everyday professional work with all children and, in turn, allow for the sharing of our knowledge and expertise with school psychologists from around the world.

Manuscript submission processing is a multi-step process with *CJSP*. The editorial assistant who first receives online submissions will review each submission essentially for its presentation, as mentioned earlier, and either forward it to the editor or return it to the author (if it does not comply with the journal requirements) with a request to make the required format changes. Once a paper meets submission guidelines, it is sent to the editor who has the responsibility to decide if it has the potential to be published in *CJSP*. This judgment of potential includes evaluation of the potential relevance and impact of the paper for readers of the journal and an initial review of methodology, research design, and related criteria. If a paper is deemed ready for peer review, the editor will most often assign the paper to an associate editor (although I do also handle the review of some papers). It is the associate editor's task to initiate and complete the review process by requesting a minimum of two reviews from editorial board members (or ad hoc reviewers) who are the most informed and able to review the content and methodology of the paper. When there is disagreement between reviewers resulting in different recommendations, the associate editor will make an informed decision after insuring the reviews are fair, comprehensive, and most importantly prescriptive, and then render the decision. If there is some uncertainty around the best decision, the editor and associate editor will discuss the editorial decision to arrive at a consensus, although the editor assumes the final responsibility for all decisions related to the journal.

The majority of papers rejected for publication at *CJSP* lack clarity, do not have a meaningful impact on the field, or most seriously are methodologically weak or flawed. Poorly written papers are frustrating and confusing to read for reviewers, and while I commend those authors whose first language is not English for the considerable effort they must put into writing their papers, the language of *CJSP* is English. I caution authors who use some of the online services that provide translation and editing; some are just not very good.

With the advice of SAGE, *CJSP* includes the following statement about English language editing services:

> As more submissions are being received from countries where English may not be the main language or first language of the author, we wish to provide as much support as we can to assist these authors who are wanting to submit their papers for review or have had papers accepted for publication following peer review. Authors who want to refine the use of English in their manuscripts may consider using the services of SPi, a non-affiliated company that offers Professional Editing Services to authors of journal articles in the areas of science, technology, medicine or the social sciences. SPi specializes in editing and correcting English-language manuscripts written by authors with a primary language other than English. Visit http://www.prof-editing.com for more information about SPi's Professional Editing Services, pricing, and turn-around times, or to obtain a free quote or submit a manuscript for language polishing. Please be aware that SAGE or *CJSP* has no affiliation with SPi and makes no endorsement of the company. An author's use of SPi's services in no way guarantees that his or her submission will ultimately be accepted.

Should an author be invited to revise and resubmit a paper, they are asked to consider very carefully the recommendations and requests of the reviewers and handling editor and reply with a fully detailed covering letter regarding how they elect to address the suggestions in the revised paper. Although an author might disagree with a reviewer on a particular point, they should be respectful in replying and make a good case to support their actions during revision. Authors should take time to carefully proofread their paper so that errors, such as incorrect statistical results, poorly presented figures, tables out of alignment, and missing references, do not detract peer reviewers and handling editors from evaluating the content of their submissions. Remember, these papers are intended to inform others who will use the findings and information presented; there is an ethical and professional responsibility to report accurately, completely, and without bias. And finally, ask yourself if your paper makes a contribution and who will want to read, cite, implement your recommendations, or at least be informed by your article. The vast majority of rejected articles are ones that fall short of telling us much that is important or new.

Conclusion

The *Canadian Journal of School Psychology* has been publishing for more than 30 years and joins the other journals described in this book in contributing to the science and practices of psychology in schools and educational contexts. The journal continues to have a strong applied focus so that articles, special issues, and test and book reviews will have relevance to practicing school psychologists, trainers and graduate students in school psychology

126 *Donald H. Saklofske*

programs, and allied professionals including teachers, special educators, and school administrators. Recent changes, including publication by SAGE, online submissions, and "publish ahead of print," together with a new editorial structure, will ensure a more efficient journal in every respect. Finally, *CJSP* has broadened its mandate and invites articles and reviews from authors outside of Canada that have relevance to a wider and more international audience of school psychologists and interested readers.

Reference

American Educational Research Association, American Psychological Association, & National Council on Measurement in Education. (2014). *Standards for educational and psychological testing*. Washington, DC: American Educational Research Association.

11 Publishing in *Contemporary School Psychology*

Michael R. Hass

Overview of the Journal

Contemporary School Psychology (CSP) began in 1996 as the *California School Psychologist*. The *California School Psychologist* was originally established by the Board of the California Association of School Psychologists (CASP) as a service for its members. The goal was to disseminate timely and relevant scholarship to support the practice of school psychology in California and elsewhere in the nation. From 1996 until 2013, the *California School Psychologist* was published once a year. Many of these issues were devoted to important special topics such as (a) reading success, (b) school engagement, (c) strength-based assessment, (d) response to intervention, (e) autism, (f) students with emotional or behavioral disorders, and (g) university–school collaboration to promote student success.

Faculty members from California's School Psychology graduate programs, especially the University of California, Santa Barbara, provided important editorial leadership during the first decade of the journal's existence. Pauline Mercado, Mike Furlong, Marilyn Wilson, Shane Jimerson, Stephen Brock, and Kristin Powers all served as editors or associate editors from 1996 to 2010. In 2010, editorial leadership passed to me and associate editors Kelly Kennedy and Brian Leung. A year later, Pedro Olvera also joined the editorial team as associate editor.

In June of 2010, CASP Board of Directors agreed to a name change, and the *California School Psychologist* became *Contemporary School Psychology* (CSP). The goal was to give the journal a name that would both reflect its past breadth of scholarship—many authors were from outside of California—and enhance the journal's ability to attract more high-quality scholarship from a wider pool of authors. These efforts continued when the CASP Board agreed to have Springer publish the journal. Beginning with the first issue with Springer in March of 2014, the journal began to accomplish its goals of increasing both the number of high-quality articles published and breadth of scholarship. For example, in 2013, of the 11 articles published, three (27%) were written by authors from outside of California, whereas in 2015, of the 33 articles published, 24 (72%) were written by national (outside California) and international authors.

CSP is currently indexed by PsycINFO, Google Scholar, ERIC System Database, and Online Computer Library Center, Inc. (OCLC), and Summon by ProQuest. Articles are submitted via the editorial manager at www.editorial-manager.com/casp/default.aspx. CSP offers fast track publication by publishing articles online within a few weeks of acceptance. Upon acceptance, authors can also choose to have their manuscripts published with open access. CSP accepts electronic multimedia files (e.g., animations, movies, and audio) and other supplementary files to be published online with an article. This feature, known as Springer's Electronic Supplementary Material, enables authors to add additional features to their articles.

Although CSP continues to serve the membership of CASP, which is the largest state organization in the country serving the interests of school psychologists, it also seeks to inform school psychology practice throughout the United States and the world. Our goal is to reach multiple audiences, including researchers, practitioners, and students. Given this, CSP is devoted to current issues in school psychology with the goal of publishing diverse, high-quality articles that connect theory to practice. The journal seeks to provide a broad multidisciplinary and international perspective on the practice of school psychology. The editorial team is open to different kinds of writing that accomplish this goal and has published critical reviews, program evaluations, case studies, discussions of promising practices, thoughtful commentaries on issues important to the profession, long-form book reviews, as well as original quantitative and qualitative research. We purposefully seek to broaden the discussion and highlight the diversity of viewpoints in the profession and of the students, parents, and communities served by school psychologists.

As part of this effort, we have published several timely special issues since 2014, including *School Psychology and the Common Core State Standards* (Guest Editor, Barbara J. D'Incau); *School Psychologists Working with Bilingual and Bicultural Youth* (Guest Editor, Pedro Olvera); and *School-Based Approaches to Promote Complete Mental Health: School Psychologists Working to Foster Students' Thriving Well-being* (Guest Editor, Michael Furlong). Future special issues include *School-Based Threat Assessment* (Guest Editors, Steve Brock and Melissa Reeves); *School-Based Approaches to Cultivating Mindfulness* (Guest Editors, Tyler Renshaw, David Klingbeil, and Aaron Fischer), and *Culturally Responsive School-Based Mental Health Practices* (Guest Editor, Sara Castro-Olivo). The majority of articles submitted to special issues are unsolicited although some have been solicited by guest editors. All articles, whether solicited or unsolicited are blind reviewed. The topics for special issues have been developed collaboratively by both the editorial team and potential guest editors. Those interested in proposing a special issue topic are welcome to contact the editor-in-chief with their ideas.

In addition to broadening the discussion of issues important to school psychologists, CSP is committed to improving scholarship and innovation in the practice of school psychology by providing timely, positive, and constructive feedback to authors, even if we do not accept their work. As

Contemporary School Psychology   129

editor-in-chief, I view each peer review as having at least three purposes, including contributing to development of knowledge in the field, development of a particular piece of work, and development of a particular writer and researcher.

Manuscript Submissions and Processing

In 2015, the total number of unsolicited submissions (including new submissions and resubmissions of previously rejected manuscripts) was 30 (see Table 11.1). One manuscript submitted in 2015 was still in the review process at the time of developing this manuscript in mid-2016. Decisions have been rendered on 29 manuscripts. Eleven manuscripts (24%) were accepted or accepted contingent on revision. Thirteen manuscripts (45%) were rejected but revision and resubmission was encouraged. Of these manuscripts, 11 were eventually accepted, often after multiple revisions. Three manuscripts were rejected following review, and one was rejected without review. The average time to editorial decision (not including the decision of Reject without full review) was 77 days (SD = 33.4 days) across these submissions.

2015 Publication Patterns

In 2015, CSP published four issues, including two general issues along with two special issues, with a total of 33 articles. Two of the four issues were the special issues mentioned above related to well-being and the common core state standards. Of the 33 articles published, 15 (45%) presented original research, and 18 (54%) were expository articles, including narrative literature reviews, practice protocols based on a review of the literature, and case studies. In addition to articles assigned to an issue, another five articles were published "online first" in 2015. Of these articles, three were original research and two were expository pieces. Although published (with DOI numbers), these articles will be assigned to a print issue in 2016.

Table 11.1 Journal Operations for *Contemporary School Psychology* in 2015

Submission status for 2015 submissions	Number	Percentage of decisions
No decision yet	1	2%
Decisions rendered	29	100%
Accept and accept contingent on revision	11	38%*
Reject (all categories)	18	62%*
Reject encouraging revision	13	45%*
Reject	3	10%*
Reject without full review	2	0.1%*

Note. * = percentage of decisions rendered as of June 29, 2016.

130 *Michael R. Hass*

CSP publishes articles on a variety of topics related to school psychology. Some noteworthy articles published in 2015 include *Methods for Assessing Single-case School-based Intervention Outcomes* (Busse, McGill, & Kennedy, 2015); *Increasing Elementary School Students' Subjective Well-being through a Classwide Positive Psychology Intervention: Results of a Pilot Study* (Suldo et al., 2015); *School Climate, Discrimination, and Depressive Symptoms Among Asian American Adolescents* (Wang & Atwal, 2015); and *Development and Initial Examination of the School Psychology Multicultural Competence Scale* (Malone et al., 2015). These articles are simply a sampling of the many *CSP* articles that made significant contributions to the profession of school psychology in 2015.

Recommendations for Prospective Authors

CSP's description on the journal's website (http://link.springer.com/journal/40688), states that the journal:

> publishes high-quality articles that link theory to practice. The journal offers articles which critically review research on topics of general interest to school psychologists in California and nationwide; which report research relevant to practicing school psychologists; which present promising practices or programs that address the needs of children and youth and which critically reflect on the profession of school psychology and the challenges faced by its practitioners.

Given this mission, we encourage national and international authors to submit high-quality articles that promote better outcomes for children, schools, and communities. What "high-quality" means is of course sometimes difficult to pin down, but I share the following guidelines to assist authors in making that judgment:

- Pay close attention to the clarity of writing. We expect that authors' ideas should be easily understood by both practitioners and academics. The best target is to write to an audience that does not do research for a living and does not have Ph.D.s. Even readers who are experienced researchers will appreciate your lucidity.
- Format manuscripts according to the *Publication Manual of the American Psychological Association, Sixth Edition* (APA, 2010). Follow all of the guidelines for developing manuscripts according to APA style—not just rules for references and citations (including page formatting, margins, headings, etc.).
- Include a submission letter also formatted according to recommendations from the APA (2009). The letter should specifically (a) state that the manuscript will not be submitted elsewhere during the review process, (b) provide notice of any interests or activities that might have influenced the research (e.g., financial interests), and (c) offer verification that

participants were treated in accordance with ethical standards. *CSP* is a member of the Committee on Publication Ethics (COPE), so the journal will follow the COPE guidelines on how to deal with potential acts of misconduct.

- Do not worry too much about page length. Most articles are 20 to 30 pages in length, although authors do not need to be overly concerned about the length of their manuscript. Decisions about page length will be made on a case-by-case basis.
- Clearly link conclusions to practice. Authors can do this directly by making specific recommendations for practitioners for implementing your conclusions or results. If conclusions are tentative or point to gaps in the literature, make clear how future research will build the bridge to practice.
- Use high-quality methodology. If presenting quantitative or qualitative research, authors should clearly explain their choice of methodologies and how their research design meets quality standards for that particular research tradition. Given that qualitative research is less common in school psychology, we urge those considering qualitative research to pay close attention to the guidelines proposed by Nastasi and Schensul (2005). A good source for guidelines on statistical analysis is Wilkinson (1999).
- Contact me. If you have questions about the fit of a manuscript for *CSP*, please send me an abstract and any question you might have to mhass@ chapman.edu.

Conclusion

The editorial board of *CSP* is proud of what we have accomplished over the last several years. As I discussed above, we have increased the number of articles published by the journal threefold. We have also widened our author pool so that the large majority of articles accepted are written by international and national authors outside California. Our editorial board now includes well-known scholars who are actively involved in the *National Association of School Psychologists*, the *American Psychological Association* and the *International School Psychology Association*. Our long-term goals are to expand our editorial board even more, continue to produce timely special issues, and move toward increasing the journal's impact on the scholarly community. We will continue our commitment to support practice through scholarship and to both broaden and deepen the discussion issues important to school psychology.

References

American Psychological Association. (2010). *Publication manual of the American Psychological Association* (6th ed.). Washington, DC: American Psychological Association.

Busse, R. T., McGill, R. J., & Kennedy, K. S. (2015). Methods for assessing single-case school-based intervention outcomes. *Contemporary School Psychology, 19*, 136–144.

Malone, C. M., Briggs, C., Ricks, E., Middleton, K., Fisher, S., & Connell, J. (2015). Development and initial examination of the School Psychology Multicultural Competence Scale. *Contemporary School Psychology, 19*, 1–10.

Nastasi, B. K., & Schensul, S. L. (2005). Contributions of qualitative research to the validity of intervention research. *Journal of School Psychology, 43*, 177–195.

Suldo, S. M., Hearon, B. V., Bander, B., McCullough, M., Garofano, J., Roth, R. A., & Tan, S. Y. (2015). Increasing elementary school students' subjective well-being through a classwide positive psychology intervention: Results of a pilot study. *Contemporary School Psychology, 19*, 300–311.

Wang, C., & Atwal, K. (2015). School climate, discrimination, and depressive symptoms among Asian American adolescents. *Contemporary School Psychology, 19*, 205–217.

Wilkinson, L. (1999). Statistical methods in psychology journals: Guidelines and explanations. *American Psychologist, 54*, 594–604. doi:10.1037/0003-066X.54.8.594

12 Publishing in the *International Journal of School & Educational Psychology*

Rik Carl D'Amato and Yuan Yuan Wang

Overview of the Journal

School and educational psychology has been an important area in psychology, which has attracted increasing research attention from all over the world (D'Amato, 2013). The field of school psychology has viewed change in the schools as leading to needed changes in classrooms, changes in children, and finally changes in the world (D'Amato, Zafiris, McConnell, & Dean, 2011). The *International Journal of School & Educational Psychology* was launched in 2013, and it is the official journal of the International School Psychology Association (ISPA). The ISPA has promoted the work of school psychologists around the globe since the early 1970s and provides resources, membership, annual meetings, a newsletter, and a community to help develop a specialty within a worldwide network of psychologists. This is the most prominent group of international school and educational psychologists in the world. Similar to ISPA, the *International Journal of School & Educational Psychology* seeks to bridge the gap between Eastern and Western psychology, special education, counseling, learning, and other school-related practices (D'Amato, 2013). The *International Journal of School & Educational Psychology* accepts research that has global implications; findings suggesting how best to serve children, youth, and families; as well as studies that could help developing countries, demonstrating the importance of global issues such as test and intervention development, with a focus on evidence-based cross-cultural initiatives. Researchers and practitioners are invited to submit papers that focus on applied educational psychology, educational research, new models of instruction, and other educational psychology-related areas. The *International Journal of School & Educational Psychology* accepts original studies, literature reviews, single-subject design intervention studies, as well as seminal methodological or theoretical statements.

In 2012, the Taylor & Francis Publishing Group was selected as the official journal outlet, and Dr. Rik Carl D'Amato was appointed editor-in-chief. Previously, D'Amato served as editor of *School Psychology Quarterly*. The editor-in-chief is responsible for overseeing complete production of the journal and appoints associate editors and the editorial board. Current journal associate editors consist of Drs. Melissa Bray, Mary (Rina) Chittooran, Beth Doll, John

134 *Rik Carl D'Amato & Yuan Yuan Wang*

Kranzler, Barry Mallin, and Gertina van Schalkwyk. The editorial board is cross-culturally diverse and unique in that it consists of prominent scientists, senior practitioners, and a group of outstanding student reviewers from all over the world. Diversity in *roles* and *places* is evident. These individuals review manuscripts and make recommendations about the publication of all articles or special issues.

The journal sets as a goal offering one special issue approximately each year, focused on a topic of international interest. A total of four special issues have been offered in the last four years. Upcoming and previous special issues have included the following: (1) *International Perspectives on the Academic and Professional Preparation of School & Educational Psychologists*; (2) *Holistic School Psychology: Understanding the Mind-Body Connection to Address Student Concerns—Part I*; (3) *Holistic School Psychology: Understanding the Mind-Body Connection to Address Student Concerns—Part II*; and (4) *Current Practices and Future Directions for the Assessment of Child and Adolescent Intelligence*. Special issues should be discussed with the editor-in-chief before submission of proposals. In general, topics should be international in focus and should cover areas of interest to contemporary or historical school or educational psychology.

In 2016, we began a special section, called Point-Counterpoint, which featured a seminar article by a well-known author, a critique and response by another expert featuring a divergent view of the topic, and finally a follow-up by the initial author. It is only by such discussion, critique, and analysis that we are able to continue our quest for life-long learning. This section is also a highlight in the journal because of our audience. Many scholars in emerging countries will use this section to help themselves grow. So too, it will be a vehicle that may be regularly used when training school psychologists from around the world.

2015 Journal Statistics and Operations

Manuscript Submissions and Processing

As listed in Table 12.1, in 2015, there were 108 manuscripts submitted to the *International Journal of School & Educational Psychology* that were not associated with a special issue. A total of eight manuscripts did not fit the focus of the journal or were not ready to be reviewed. It is critical to note that the *International Journal of School & Educational Psychology* views the development of young scholars from around the world as a priority. Thus, papers that would be initially rejected in other journals are reviewed to help our community of scholars. We believe that providing constructive feedback to beginning scholars is a critical part of what we offer. Based on these editorial decisions, 100 of the submitted manuscripts were distributed for a full review, and a total of 42 manuscripts were accepted, giving an acceptance rate of almost 40%. In 2015, the average time to editorial decision (not including initial rejection by the editor), from submission to final decision, was 41 days. This average

Table 12.1 Journal Operations for the *International Journal of School & Educational Psychology* in 2015

Submission status for 2015 submissions	Number	Percentage
Accepted (all categories)	42	38%
Accept	20	18%
Accept with editorial revisions	12	11%
Accept with minor revisions	10	9%
Rejected (all categories)	66	60%
Reject encouraging major revision	24	22%

Note. Numbers have been rounded off, so the total is equal to 98%. Three papers related to a special issue have been removed from the analysis.

time to decision also did not include any manuscripts submitted as part of special issues.

Publication Patterns

From January 2013 until the present, the *International Journal of School & Educational Psychology* has published four issues each year, with each issue containing about seven articles and each article consisting of about 8 to 13 pages. A total of 25 articles were published in 2015. Of these, there were 21 (84%) research articles, four (16%) expository or review articles, and no product-focused reviews. Given that we are a relatively new journal we have yet to select any best articles of the year. Table 12.2 lists the titles of articles published in the first issue of 2015.

Recommendations for Prospective Authors

The *International Journal of School & Educational Psychology* accepts all kinds of outstanding articles, qualitative or quantitative research, and original studies or literature reviews, with no page limit requirements. We provide international scholars a great deal of freedom to publish their seminal work and assist them in influencing and changing the world. Our aim is to make the *International Journal of School & Educational Psychology* the leading and most influential journal in the area of international school and educational psychology.

Considering that we encourage all styles and lengths of research papers, with few theme restrictions, both seasoned and emerging scholars have the chance to publish their work with few constraints. Moreover, the editor, associate editors, and editorial board all have experience living in both Eastern and Western cultures and are from different countries and cultural backgrounds, which is an advantage for accepting cross-cultural research from a worldwide academic community. The *International Journal of School & Educational Psychology* is looking for articles that show the uniqueness of various countries and related psychological services. Potential authors should

136   *Rik Carl D'Amato & Yuan Yuan Wang*

Table 12.2 Articles Published in the *International Journal of School & Educational Psychology* in the First Issue of 2015

Article title	Article type
"DSM-5 Diagnostic Criteria for Autism Spectrum Disorder with Implications for School Psychologists" (Esler & Ruble, 2015)	E
"Effects of a Multimedia Social Skills Program in Increasing Social Responses and Initiations of Children with Autism Spectrum Disorder" (Block, Radley, Jenson, Clark, & O'Neill, 2015)	R
"Measuring Heedful Interrelating in Collaborative Educational Settings" (Daniel & Jordan, 2015)	R
"Cultural and Gender Differences in Experiences and Expression of Test Anxiety Among Chinese, Finnish, and Swedish Grade 3 Pupils" (Nyroos et al., 2015)	R
"The Shortened Visuospatial Questionnaire for Children: A Useful Tool to Identify Students with Low Visuospatial Abilities" (Fastame, Cherchi, & Penna, 2015)	R
"Perceived Stressors of Suicide and Potential Prevention Strategies for Suicide Among Youths in Malaysia" (Kok, van Schalkwyk, & Chan, 2015)	E
"Psychometric Properties of the Revised Teachers' Attitude Toward Inclusion Scale" (Monsen, Ewing, & Boyle, 2015)	R

Note. R = Research articles and E = Expository or Review articles.

consider showcasing work that reveals the richness of international education from the great variety of their countries around the world. Distinctive projects come from unique programs in diverse countries.

The year the journal began, the editor-in-chief summarized his view of the new journal and his hope for the future:

> I no longer want to focus my energy on people who live in a single country. I have developed a much broader vision for education; and I believe, if we work together, we can make changes that will influence the world. Please send us your best research projects. And, read the *International Journal of School & Educational Psychology* so you can see what is happening in education from around the world. Obviously, we need your help if we are to succeed. Will you help us change our world? Just wait, you will see, we will do it!
>
> (D'Amato, 2013, p. 2)

Conclusion

When we consider that the *International Journal of School & Educational Psychology* is the newest school psychology journal, and the fact that it has an extremely broad base of journal readers and article publishers, it seems to be well on its way to achieving some of its initial goals. Many journal initiatives, such as special issues and special sections, have become popular. Submission of quality articles also grows each year. But still, as a new journal, we need your continued support if we are to change schools, change children, change countries, and change the world.

References

Block, H. M., Radley, K. C., Jenson, W. R., Clark, E., & O'Neill, R. E. (2015). Effects of a multimedia social skills program in increasing social responses and initiations of children with Autism Spectrum Disorder. *International Journal of School & Educational Psychology, 3*, 16–24. doi: 10.1080/21683603.2014.923355

D'Amato, R. C. (2013). Will you help us change our world? *International Journal of School & Educational Psychology, 1*, 1–2. doi: 10.1080/21683603.2013.799026

D'Amato, R. C., Zafiris, C., McConnell, E., & Dean, R. S. (2011). The history of school psychology: Understanding the past to not repeat it. In M. Bray & T. Kehle (Eds.), *Oxford handbook of school psychology* (pp. 9–60). New York, NY: Oxford University Press.

Daniel, S. R., & Jordan, M. E. (2015). Measuring heedful interrelating in collaborative educational settings. *International Journal of School & Educational Psychology, 3*, 25–36. doi: 10.1080/21683603.2014.909342

Esler, A. N., & Ruble, L. A. (2015). DSM-5 diagnostic criteria for autism spectrum disorder with implications for school psychologists. *International Journal of School & Educational Psychology, 3*, 1–15. doi: 10.1080/21683603.2014.890148

Fastame, M. C., Cherchi, R., & Penna, M. P. (2015). The Shortened Visuospatial Questionnaire for Children: A useful tool to identify students with low visuospatial abilities. *International Journal of School & Educational Psychology, 3*, 49–54. doi: 10.1080/21683603.2014.917061

Kok, J. K., van Schalkwyk, G. J., & Chan, A. H. W. (2015). Perceived stressors of suicide and potential prevention strategies for suicide among youths in Malaysia. *International Journal of School & Educational Psychology, 3*, 55–63. doi: 10.1080/21683603.2014.920285

Monsen, J. J., Ewing, D. L., & Boyle, J. (2015). Psychometric properties of the Revised Teachers' Attitude Toward Inclusion Scale. *International Journal of School & Educational Psychology, 3*, 64–71. doi: 10.1080/21683603.2014.938383

Nyroos, M., Korhonen, J., Peng, A., Linnanmäki, K., Svens-Liavåg, C., Bagger, A., & Sjöberg, G. (2015). Cultural and gender differences in experiences and expression of test anxiety among Chinese, Finnish, and Swedish Grade 3 Pupils. *International Journal of School & Educational Psychology, 3*, 37–48. doi: 10.1080/21683603.2014.915773

13 Publishing in the *Journal of Applied School Psychology*

Frank J. Sansosti

Overview of the Journal

The *Journal of Applied School Psychology* (JASP) is the official journal of the American Academy of School Psychology (AASP). The academy is organized for the purpose of contributing to the development and maintenance of school psychology practice at its highest level. Specifically, the AASP is committed to furthering the American Board of Professional Psychology's (ABPP) recognition of excellence in the practice of school psychology (see www.abpp.org). Consequently, manuscripts published in *JASP* are intended to provide school psychologists, mental health professionals, applied school psychology researchers, and all others interested in the application of school psychology in school-based contexts with hands-on tips, techniques, methods, and ideas for improving assessment, instruction, and management of all students.

Formerly known as *Special Services in the Schools* (1982–2002), the journal began as a quarterly publication that emphasized the wide range of special services (i.e., pre-referral evaluation, instructional programming, and counseling) delivered to children and youth in school-based contexts. The intended focus was to provide professionals employed in schools and related educational settings with information about current and future trends for the broad delivery of special services. In 2002, the name of the journal was changed to *JASP*. The new name for the journal reflected a shift from content that dealt with the broad range of special services within schools to a more direct focus on the practice of school psychology at the individual, group, and organizational levels. Such reconfiguration was viewed as necessary to recognize school psychology as a field that had expanded its description from primarily assessment and special education gate-keeping functions to broader areas of practice such as consultation, systemic change, social-emotional learning, and program evaluation, among other foci. Within this contemporary context, *JASP* was, and still is, focused on the communication of practical application of school psychology by practitioners in their work.

As the official journal of the AASP, *JASP* aims to promote and publish high-quality articles focused on the direct application of practice in school psychology. This broad goal emanates from the belief that for school psychology to reach its fullest potential, a commitment to cultivating, completing, and disseminating applied research must be made. This is not to say that the field of school psychology has not achieved many substantial objectives in terms of applying research to practice. Rather, a chasm exists between the innovative research conducted in school psychology and the application of such innovations in contemporary school-based settings. Such a research-to-practice gap is not new, as this problem has been raised by other prominent individuals in the field (e.g., Riley-Tillman, Chafouleas, Eckert, & Kelleher, 2005; Sansosti, 2014; Wodrich, 2009). In an era of educational reform and accountability, schools increasingly are called upon to use highly rigorous data to identify areas of student need (at individual and systemic levels); develop, implement, and monitor plans targeting instructional practice within a multi-tiered system of supports; and establish a culture that continually evaluates organizational data to alter instructional practice and improve student performance (Sansosti, 2014). Consequently, each submission should rest on solid theoretical or empirical support and convey information of use in applied school settings, related educational systems, or community locations where school psychologists might work. Thus, manuscripts appropriate for publication in *JASP* reflect psychological applications concerning individual students, groups of students, teachers, parents, or administrators with relevance to practicing school psychologists.

Types of Articles Published

The goal of *JASP* is to promote and publish high-quality articles focused on the direct application of practice in school psychology. Specifically, articles ultimately published within *JASP* possess the authority to impact the field of school psychology through delineation of essential practices ("the what") and real-world applications ("the how") aligned within contemporary education reform. As such, the journal offers four categories of submissions.

Original Research

Such articles will consist of detailed reports of investigative efforts concerning all forms of school psychological practice that utilize group comparisons, rigorous single-case experimental design, or meta-analyses of extant literature. With Original Research articles, an emphasis must be made by authors to state explicitly the implications for practice. As such, all Original Research articles must demonstrate methodological soundness *and* relevance to the practice of school psychology.

Case Studies

Such articles will consist of detailed reports of innovative evaluation and/or intervention techniques implemented with an individual student or a small group of students for which there is a concern. Articles of this type should focus on the use of rigorous single-case experimental strategies that demonstrate a functional relationship clearly, as well as provide scientific measures of effectiveness (such as, but not limited to improvement rate difference and Tau-U). Manuscripts that employ an evaluation of impact using percent of non-overlapping data, or other such methods, will not be accepted, as they are not considered to be sensitive enough to detect the important characteristics of trends and variability within time-series data (Parker, Vannest, & Davis, 2011). Authors interested in applying rigorous, single-case design procedures that will be valued within *JASP* should follow the various methodological and statistical methods discussed in Kratochwill and Levin (2014).

Service Delivery Briefs

Articles of this sort will consist of brief reports of innovative district-wide programs (e.g., in-service trainings; evaluation team processes; and response to intervention, RTI; and positive behavioral intervention and supports, PBIS) that have a demonstrable impact on a variety of stakeholders associated with schools (e.g., parents, teachers, administrators, and students). Articles of this type should provide evidence of high-quality investigation but will not require the need for careful reviews of the extant literature nor well-controlled trials.

Science to Practice

Such articles will consist of comprehensive compilations of the extant literature as well as interpretations and advanced discussions of empirically validated school-based practices. Articles of this type must focus on the application of empirically promoted strategies, with discussion that emphasizes the practicality (or lack thereof) of application of a particular practice within schools.

Prime Content of JASP

Both Original Research and Case Studies submissions will be considered as the prime foci of *JASP*, making up approximately 80% of published articles. It is desired for both types of submissions to possess methodological and scientific soundness as well as relevance to practical application. That is, Original Research and Case Studies submissions should provide evidence of rigorous scholarship and applied value. The remaining published articles will be composed equally of Service Delivery Briefs and Science to Practice articles that provide commentary and create discussion among trainers and practitioners alike.

Journal of Applied School Psychology   141

2015 Journal Statistics and Operations

Manuscript Submissions and Processing

The total number of new manuscript submissions to *JASP* in 2015 was 60. When considering resubmissions of revised manuscripts, a total of 67 manuscripts were submitted. Overall, this number of submissions to *JASP* represents an increase of 12% from the previous year. The average number of days from submission to first decision (not including those manuscripts returned to authors without full review) was 70.4, whereas the average number of days from submission to final decision (manuscripts that were revised and resubmitted) was 57.7. On average, reviewers submitted their manuscript evaluations to the editor within 46.7 days.

During the 2015 publishing year, a total of 14 (23.7%) manuscripts were accepted for publication, with an additional six (10.2%) manuscripts accepted pending minor revisions. Combined, the overall acceptance rate was approximately 33%. A smaller number of manuscripts were recommended for major revision (with resubmission highly encouraged). The majority of manuscripts (54.2%) submitted during 2015 were rejected without encouragement to resubmit. Of this large percentage, a significant majority of rejections were returned to authors without full review because the manuscript did not align with the aims and scope of the journal or they were methodologically unsound. A summary of this information is provided in Table 13.1.

Publication Patterns

During 2015, as is true of each publication year, *JASP* released four issues. There were no special issues released during the 2015 publication year. However, one issue will be devoted annually to a contemporary topic in the field of school psychology (i.e., mental health service delivery). For 2015, a total of 14 manuscripts were published. Of these 14 manuscripts, ten were

Table 13.1 Journal Operations for the *Journal of Applied School Psychology* in 2015

Submission status for 2015 submissions	Number	Percentage of decisions
Accept	14	23.3%
Minor revision	7	11.7%
Major revision	7	11.7%
Reject (all categories)	32	53.3%
Reject and resubmit	2	6.25%*
Reject	12	37.5%*
Reject without full review	17	53.1%*

Note. * = percentage of category.

142   *Frank J. Sansosti*

Original Research; two were Case Studies; and two were Science to Practice. No Service Delivery Briefs were accepted for publication in 2015. Several of these articles not only were strong representations of the aims and scope of the journal but also serve as exemplary articles for the field to bridge the research-to-practice gap. For example, Walick and Sullivan (2015) provided a review of the research on school-based supports for meeting the educational needs of Somali immigrants and refugee students. Such a review is timely and genera-tive as the demographics of students continue to become increasingly diverse across all parts of the country. DeJager and Filter (2015) presented the effective-ness of a student intervention that utilized prevent-teach-reinforce for three kindergarten students exhibiting behavior problems. Through careful data collection and analysis, including calculation of Tau-U effect sizes, the authors demonstrated the utility of such an intervention within school-based contexts.

Recommendations for Prospective Authors

Submission of a manuscript to *JASP* will imply that it represents an original contribution to the field. Specifically, the manuscript will address a contempo-rary issue in the day-to-day practice of school psychology and link data to real-world issues within the practice of school psychology. As such, the priority for manuscripts will be the investigation of effectiveness across a variety of settings including, but not limited to, schools, communities, and non-traditional educational centers by offering specific practice recommendations that can be gleaned from the results. Highly valued manuscripts are those that focus on topics such as (a) systemic educational practice, including school-wide applications of RTI, PBIS, and a multi-tiered system of supports; (b) applied examples of effective problem-solving within a collaborative consultation model; (c) selection, implementation, and evaluation of evidence-based instructional and/or mental health services within school-based contexts; (d) creation and/or implementation of methods for demonstrating treatment fidelity within applied settings; (e) preventive services including, but not limited to, bullying prevention, social skills programs, and various social-emotional instructional programs; (f) evaluation of the impact of school psy-chological services; and (g) empirical demonstrations of various technological approaches (i.e., computer-assisted instruction and mobile technology) for delivering and/or enhancing instruction strategies or collecting data.

For each of the aforementioned, manuscripts of the highest value are those that use data (quantitative or qualitative) for determining educational decisions and/or demonstrating impact of services to children and families within school-based settings. Scholarly, robust articles must be methodologi-cally sound and be conducted and interpreted so that they can shape and guide practice. Authors should focus on research designs and data collection procedures that not only are experimentally sound, but also are applicable and replicable within school-based settings. Moreover, scholarly robust articles must describe research methods, findings, and conclusions in a manner that can be understood and utilized by practitioners. It also is anticipated that articles will provide information on the assessment and interpretation on feasibility, treatment integrity, and social validity.

Each manuscript submission must provide a detailed discussion of the practical implications gleaned from the data reported within your manuscript. Because *JASP* is focused on the direct application of data-based practices that are responsive to and address the contemporary issues of real concern among practitioners working within school-based contexts, information that provides explicit and direct application to the practice of school psychology is required. That is, articles published will focus on the implementation of data-driven professional practices that serve to promote the professional competence of school psychologists working in the field. Manuscripts that fail to provide such information likely will be returned without full review. Typically, manuscripts will include an Implications for Practice subsection that appears at the conclusion of the Discussion section.

Due to the highly applied nature of *JASP*, it is likely that manuscripts ultimately published are not free from limitations. Although it is expected that authors will use empirical data to substantiate the phenomena under study, manuscripts also should provide consideration for and inclusion of alternate explanations for findings and limitations of the current research (see Lilienfeld, Ammirati, & David, 2012 for guidelines).

All manuscript submissions should be formatted according to the *Publication Manual of the American Psychology Association, Sixth Edition* (American Psychological Association, 2010). Due to the diversity of potential applied topics combined with the four different categories of submissions within the journal itself, no journal-specific formatting exists. As such, both national and international authors should format the entire manuscript (not only the citations and references) in accordance with the requirements of the *Publication Manual of the American Psychological Association* (see www.apastyle.org for assistance). Although there is no word count or page length requirement, it is anticipated that manuscript submissions will be about 25 to 30 pages in length, inclusive of tables, figures, and references. (Longer manuscripts, however, are permitted.) Manuscripts from international authors for whom English is not their primary language are encouraged to consider using the services of a professional English-language editing company prior to submitting for review. Please be aware that authors' use of such services is their responsibility and in no way guarantees that their manuscript will be accepted.

Conclusion

The goal of *JASP* is to provide school-based personnel with hands-on tips, techniques, methods, and ideas for refining the practice of school psychology within applied settings. A great deal of respect is due to the editorial team members and the executive board of the AASP for their continued focus on bridging the research-to-practice gap in school psychology. Moreover, a great

144 *Frank J. Sansosti*

deal of reverence is due to prospective authors who engage in applied school psychological research. Authors intending to submit a manuscript are encouraged to contact the editor via email (fsansost@kent.edu) to discuss the potential fit of their manuscript with the aims and scope of the journal.

References

American Psychological Association. (2010). *Publication manual of the American Psychological Association* (6th ed.). Washington, DC: American Psychological Association.

DeJager, B. W., & Filter, K. J. (2015). Effects of Prevent-Teach-Reinforce on academic engagement and disruptive behavior. *Journal of Applied School Psychology, 31,* 369–391.

Kratochwill, T. R., & Levin, J. R. (2014). *Single-cased intervention research: Methodological and statistical advances.* Washington, DC: American Psychological Association.

Lilienfeld, S. O., Ammirati, R., & David, M. (2012). Distinguishing science from pseudoscience in school psychology: Science and scientific thinking as safeguard against human error. *Journal of School Psychology, 50,* 7–36.

Parker, R. I., Vannest, K. J., & Davis, J. L. (2011). Effect size in single-case research: A review of nine nonoverlap techniques. *Behavior Modification, 35,* 303–322.

Riley-Tillman, T. C., Chafouleas, S. M., Eckert, T. L., & Kelleher, C. (2005). Bridging the gap between research and practice: A framework for building research agendas in school psychology. *Psychology in the Schools, 42,* 459–473.

Sansosti, F. J. (2014). Furthering highly rigorous applied research in school psychology in an era of education reform and accountability. *Journal of Applied School Psychology, 30,* 1–6.

Walick, C. M., & Sullivan, A. L. (2015). Educating Somali immigrant and refugee students: A review of cultural-historical issues and related psychoeducational supports. *Journal of Applied School Psychology, 31,* 347–368.

Wodrich, D. L. (2009). Addressing school psychology's need for rigorous scholarship with applied value. *Journal of Applied School Psychology, 25,* 1–4.

14 Publishing in *School Psychology Forum: Research in Practice*

Oliver W. Edwards and Steven R. Shaw

Overview of the Journal

School Psychology Forum: Research in Practice (SPF) is a quarterly refereed journal published electronically by the National Association of School Psychologists (NASP; www.nasponline.org/resources-and-publications/publications/about-SPF). The primary readers of *SPF* are NASP members, specifically, psychologists working in schools, hospitals, mental health centers, and independent practice. *SPF* is as follows:

- a translational research journal that links research to application of best practices;
- a scholarly outlet that translates and speeds the application of new knowledge to practice;
- a periodical and forum for hosting the scholarly treatment and scientific evaluation of current clinical, legal, school, policy, practice, and professional issues;
- an interactive environment for scholars, practicing school psychologists, policy makers, and all *SPF* readers to contribute by making suggestions, discussing posted articles, and engaging in active leadership that promotes and advances the discipline;
- an innovative scholarly publication that permits authors to include supplemental materials in their submissions (see Table 14.1).

Aims and Purpose

The purpose of *SPF* is to provide readers a forum to access, discuss, and expand on current critical issues related to children's learning and mental health with the explicit goal of supporting school-based practitioners' ability to improve outcomes for students, families, and schools. *SPF* has themed issues consisting of invited articles surrounding specific themes as well as general issues consisting of unsolicited manuscripts. *SPF* publishes original research, program evaluations, literature reviews, and reviews of evidence-based practices.

146 Oliver W. Edwards & Steven R. Shaw

Table 14.1 Supplemental Materials: Opportunities for Innovative Formats and Presentation of Materials with *School Psychology Forum*

Format	Description
Interview	Usually conducted over the phone and posted on the *SPF* website, interviews present authors with the opportunity to elaborate on the specific article and other aspects of their research.
Other materials	Photographs, video, raw data, PowerPoint presentations, computer software, and other information can be posted to illustrate articles for consumers.
Related links	Links to NASP materials related to the article may be posted for the benefit of readers.
NASP Communities	All articles have an area for commentary on the NASP Communities. Commentaries are invited and may be published for each article. Unsolicited commentary and questions concerning articles are welcome and are considered for publication. Authors of the primary articles provide responses to questions or comments raised by readers, practitioners, and scholars.
Continuing Professional Development	Some articles in *SPF* are selected for a webinar made available to NASP members through the Online Learning Center (https://nasp.inreachce.com/).

Core Mission

The core mission of *SPF* is to address important professional issues relative to the roles and practice of school psychologists, respond to the revolutionary changes in service delivery, and provide an outlet for school psychologists and educators that most academic journals do not offer (Sanetti & Kratochwill, 2009). Certainly, the scale and scope of school psychology practice has advanced well beyond the more than 50-year-old scientist–practitioner model established at the Boulder Conference (Frank, 1984). Substantial diversity and complexity currently define the school psychologist's role and practice. These roles include prevention implementation, multi-tiered systems of supports or response-to-intervention, special education eligibility and test administration, neuropsychological assessment, counseling, consultation, training, and action research (Edwards, 2006; Edwards, Mumford, & Serra-Roldan, 2007; Gracyzk, Domitrovich, Small, & Zins, 2006). The daily practice of school psychologists requires a comprehensive knowledge base and specific skillset necessary to fill these roles with a degree of competence that any one professional might find challenging to demonstrate consistently (Puyana & Edwards, 2016). The knowledge base and specific skillset include the following: applying data-based decision-making, managing accountability data, assessing and addressing treatment integrity, managing paperwork, participating in meetings, providing and receiving supervision, applying technology, interacting with attorneys, understanding the politics and culture of schools and the school district, and serving as a liaison between the community, parents, and the school.

SPF was introduced in 2006 under the editorship of Ray Christner to assist practitioners who have difficulty finding resources regarding this comprehensive knowledge base as applied to specific professional skills. Subsequently, Steven Shaw assumed editorship through 2016 and Oliver Edwards was appointed as editor to begin serving a term in January of 2017. With each new editor, *SPF* continued to progress to keep pace with the evolving roles of school psychologists and the expanding practice of school psychology. The current framework of *SPF* addresses the dynamic roles and practice of school psychologists, concomitantly bridging the burgeoning gap between research and its translation to real-world settings.

Translational Research: Connecting Research and Practice

SPF uses a translational research framework to help advance the discipline and practice of school psychology. Translational research applies findings from basic science to enhance mental health, physical health, academic achievement, and overall well-being. To improve functioning, research findings must be translated into best practice methods (Puyana & Edwards, 2016; Woolf, 2008). As a translational research journal, *SPF* works to swiftly advance the implementation of best practices into school, community, and other applied settings. In *SPF*, the traditional sections of the scholarly article are altered slightly. Each article must contain an explicit section describing how the concepts or findings in the article can be applied to practice. In this manner, the connection between research and practice is addressed.

External validity of findings is emphasized when deciding whether to accept a manuscript for publication. Published scholarly work often straddles the line between internal and external validity. Laboratory research studies that control variables carefully, have narrowly defined hypotheses, and use well-defined participant populations, are common in high-quality research. Thus, most published research studies have high internal validity but may minimize external validity (i.e., context and applicability to real-world situations). Usually, this research is of high scientific quality but has limited generalizability and thus holds nominal clinical relevance.

Field studies, policy implementation, pilot studies, program evaluation, qualitative designs, and the like are extremely complex types of research. Controlling all of the variables in a real-world setting is difficult and often impossible. These studies sometimes sacrifice internal validity for external validity. Nonetheless, this type of research, whether qualitative or quantitative, should involve sound logic and quality design. Exemplary research of this type can assist school staff and students modify their behaviors to advance favorable school-related outcomes. *SPF* welcomes manuscripts that apply these complex types of studies via the translational research framework that

148 *Oliver W. Edwards & Steven R. Shaw*

links research to best practice methods. Further, SPF editorial staff invite and welcome comments, critiques, and ideas regarding the application of articles in SPF. Devices such as podcasts, PowerPoint presentations, and online video presentations can be introduced by authors. Dynamic and analytical discussion is encouraged. We believe that nothing is more relevant to advancing school psychology practice than employing this translational approach of interactive and manifold engagement of ideas and concept-sharing among professionals and pre-professionals.

2015 Journal Statistics and Operations

Manuscript Submissions and Processing

All articles in SPF explicitly advance the practice of school psychology with concrete and actionable recommendations. The journal has an editor and typically three associate editors in addition to the editorial advisory board. The editorial board usually consists of 32 editorial advisory board members. All manuscripts are submitted electronically via the journal's manuscript submission site (mc04.manuscriptcentral.com/nasp_spf). The editor reviews all manuscripts submitted prior to assigning each manuscript to an associate editor to facilitate blinded peer review. Manuscripts not aligned with the purpose of the journal or manuscripts of inadequate quality are returned to the author without further review. Associate editors solicit reviews from at least two peer reviewers prior to rendering a decision. The reviewers are typically members of the SPF editorial advisory board. This board includes university-based scholars, practicing school psychologists, graduate students, and post-doctoral scholars.

In 2015, a total of 57 solicited and unsolicited manuscripts were submitted to SPF (see Table 14.2). The median time to editorial decision was 67 days across these submissions. Of the 30 unsolicited manuscripts submitted to the journal, 11 (36.6%) were accepted for publication. The majority of the unsolicited manuscripts submitted to the journal (40.0%) were rejected with encouragement to resubmit.

Table 14.2 Journal Operations for *School Psychology Forum* in 2015

Submission status for 2015 submissions	Number	Percentage
Total submissions	57	
Solicited	27	47.4%
Unsolicited	30	52.6%
Accepted (unsolicited)	11	36.6%
Rejected (unsolicited)	19	63.3%
Rejected encouraging revision	12	40.0%
Rejected	6	20.0%
Rejected without full review	1	3.3%

Publication Patterns

SPF published three issues in 2015. Of the 34 articles published across these issues, 12 (35%) were studies involving original research with reporting original data, and 22 (65%) were comprehensive literature reviews related to applied school psychology, conceptual analyses, and scholarly commentaries.

Recommendations for Prospective Authors

General Article Guidelines

SPF requires two manuscript features that differ from most scholarly journals. First, there must be a heading and section that explicitly describes how the current manuscript can be applied to the practice of school psychology. This section can include practice guidelines, cautions for school-based practice, recommendations for policy development, improvement on current best practices, or other approaches that advance school psychology practice. Second, information must be included regarding where readers can find additional resources on the topic. Where applicable and feasible, authors provide resources for readers that would enhance practice. These resources could include tips for parents or teachers, guidelines for administrators, worksheets, links to websites, or lists of books.

Many articles in *SPF* are part of themed issues that are solicited by a guest editor. To become a guest editor, the scholar proposes a special topic with suggested contributors to that topic. This process is usually conducted via email with the editor. Topic proposals are reviewed by the editor, associate editors, and members of the editorial advisory board for approval or suggestions for improvement. In addition, solicited manuscripts are reviewed by at least two members of the editorial advisory board or ad hoc reviewers.

Selection of Manuscripts

The primary criterion used to determine whether manuscripts are accepted for publication in *SPF* is as follows: Does this article advance the daily practice of school psychology with quality scholarship? Manuscripts that are accepted for publication have the following characteristics: they clearly advance the knowledge base and practice of school psychology; they communicate effectively and professionally; the design and methodology apply acceptable scientific standards; and the results of the paper have fundamental implications for the day-to-day practice of school psychology. Manuscripts commonly rejected for publication do not evince findings that contribute to the knowledge base and day-to-day practice of school psychology. In addition, we frequently receive manuscripts about local practices and ideas implemented in a specific region that do not generalize to most school psychologists in North America. Unless those local practices are truly innovative or represent an important underserved community, their usefulness for our readership is very limited.

150   *Oliver W. Edwards & Steven R. Shaw*

Manuscripts offering a broad review of techniques or procedures that describe rather than provide a model for innovative school psychology practice are unlikely to contribute substantially to our profession and are not published in *SPF*. Simple survey studies are generally not published in *SPF*. This is because a survey is frequently an individual's or group's perception of a phenomenon. We often receive surveys regarding teachers' opinions about whether a specific technique was successful. Teachers' perceptions and opinions are not nearly as important as data indicating that the technique was actually successful.

Relationship among NASP Publications

NASP has four major outlets for scholarly publications. These include the following: *School Psychology Review*, the *Communiqué*, *School Psychology Forum*, and books published by NASP. *School Psychology Review* is a well-established and well-regarded scholarly journal (see Chapter 9). This journal typically publishes large-scale empirical articles and comprehensive literature reviews related to professional school psychology. The *Communiqué* normally publishes news, responses to new legislation and regulation, and some research that is considered newsworthy to NASP members (see Chapter 22). Books are large-scale projects that guide practice. *SPF* fills an important niche by publishing scholarly articles that are empirical or literature reviews that focus on translating research to practice. Whereas *School Psychology Review* seems to emphasize a scientific foundation for our profession and the *Communiqué* provides recent and relevant news and scholarly information, *SPF* links the two publications by providing a scholarly basis that translates and speeds the application of new knowledge to practice.

Illustration Issue

Although there have been multiple outstanding special issues of *SPF*, perhaps the most emblematic of high-quality translational research is the spring 2016 issue (Volume 10, Number 1) on school climate and violence prevention and intervention that was guest edited by Joel Myers and Kris Varjas (Parris, LaSalle, Varjas, & Meyers, 2016). This issue offers eight themed articles representing both complex and detailed research as well as innovative pilot research in the area of violence prevention in schools. This special issue illustrates precisely what *SPF* attempts to accomplish in providing outstanding research to best practice demonstrating evidence-based and effective innovation that can be implemented by school psychologists and educators in their actual environments.

Conclusion

SPF is a quarterly online journal published by NASP. This journal fills a niche in the field of school psychology by publishing articles that emphasize research knowledge that enhances the day-to-day practice of school psychology. Consequently, the focus is on translational research that has high potential for direct application to improve outcomes for students, parents, staff, and schools served by school psychologists. *SPF* provides a unique opportunity for researchers and practitioners to disseminate innovative ideas and high-quality translational research that informs, and serves to transform, the practice of school psychology.

References

Edwards, O. W. (2006). Special education disproportionality and the influence of intelligence test selection. *Journal of Intellectual & Developmental Disability, 31*, 246–248. doi: 10.1080/13668250600999178

Edwards, O. W., Mumford, V. E., & Serra-Roldan, R. (2007). A positive youth development model for students considered at-risk. *School Psychology International, 28*, 29–45. doi: 10.1177/0143034307075673

Frank, G. (1984). The Boulder Model: History, rationale, and critique. *Professional Psychology: Research and Practice, 15*, 417–435. doi: 10.1037/0735-7028.15.3.417

Graczyk, P. A., Domitrovich, C. E., Small, M., & Zins, J. E. (2006). Serving all children: An implementation model framework. *School Psychology Review, 35*, 266–274.

Parris, L., LaSalle, T. P., Varjas, K., & Meyers, J. (2016). Introduction to the special issue: Improving student outcomes: Research on school climate and violence prevention and intervention. *School Psychology Forum, 10*, 1–3.

Puyana, O. E., & Edwards, O. W. (2016). Identifying school psychologists' intercultural sensitivity. *School Psychology Forum: Research in Practice, 10*, 410–421.

Sanetti, L., & Kratochwill, T. (2009). Toward developing a science of treatment integrity: Introduction to the Special Series. *School Psychology Review, 38*, 445–459.

Woolf, S. H. (2008). The meaning of translational research and why it matters. *Journal of the American Medical Association, 299*, 211–213.

15 Publishing in *Trainers' Forum*

Kelly Kennedy[1]

Overview of the Journal

Trainers' Forum began as the newsletter for the Trainers of School Psychologists (TSP) organization. To best understand the *Forum*, it helps to understand TSP. This organization's mission is as follows:

> TSP is committed to innovation and excellence in graduate training programs for specialist and doctoral school psychologists. Our purpose is to foster high quality training in school psychology programs. We work toward this goal by examining current trends in graduate education programs, providing professional growth opportunities to school psychology faculty, facilitating communication with field based supervisors, and supporting legislative efforts that promote excellence in training.
>
> (https://tsp.wildapricot.org)

The *Trainers' Forum* newsletter was published four times per year as a service for its members. In 2006, *Trainers' Forum* established a peer-review process, and in 2009, it was re-established as a journal. In 2012, *Trainers' Forum* moved to a semi-annual publication schedule. As the *Forum* continues to function as a service for TSP members, articles remain the property of TSP for two years after publication, after which time issues are posted on the TSP webpage. The *Forum* is available for library subscriptions and is indexed by ProQuest.

Editors of the *Forum* serve as ex-officio members of the TSP executive board. Past editors include Gilbert Gredler, David Mealor, Anthony Paolitto, David McIntosh, Mardis Dunham, Enedina García Vázquez, and Fred Krieg. I have been the editor since 2012, with Michael Hass and Paul Jantz as associate editors. A special mention should be made to Enedina García Vázquez, whose leadership brought the *Forum* from a newsletter to the peer-reviewed journal that it is today.

The review process of the *Forum* is a fairly simple one. All manuscripts come to the editor, and the editor and editorial assistant assign reviewers. The editorial assistant tracks the progress of each manuscript under review and sends correspondence to authors and reviewers as the process unfolds.

Over the course of my editorship, I have made nearly all publication decisions, with the exception of 2015 when the associate editors made a number of decisions for me as I took a maternity leave.

During the course of our peer-review process, reviewers are asked to recommend that a manuscript be rejected outright, resubmitted with revisions, accepted with revisions, or accepted as is. As editor, I take these recommendations into account as I make editorial decisions. When the two reviewers make different decisions, I use my own review of the manuscript in concert with the narrative feedback and suggested revisions provided by both reviewers to make the final acceptance decision. As a journal focused on trainers, the *Forum* editorial staff is deeply committed to supporting authors. As the editor, I make every effort to ensure that every author gets useful feedback and guidance in manuscript development. The vast majority of our published articles go through multiple revisions and often multiple rounds of review. I always examine each reviewer's response with each manuscript and typically provide my own suggestions about which areas of feedback to focus on, how to interpret various comments or suggestions made by the reviewers, etc. From my perspective, all writers are in one stage of development or another, and it is our job to support all of our colleagues' efforts to share their research with our community.

As described on the TSP website (https://tsp.wildapricot.org), *Trainers' Forum* "features articles relevant to the preparation of school psychologists" and is "designed for a readership of academics who shape the field of school psychology." Additionally, the website invites authors to submit data-driven and conceptual pieces that are "consistent with best practices in the training of school psychologists." The primary audience of the *Forum* is the membership of the TSP organization, and these guidelines solidify its purpose in providing that audience with articles that are directly relevant to their role as trainers. A potential author may ask a simple question that would help determine if a certain manuscript is appropriate for the *Forum*: "Would reading this article be beneficial to a trainer of future school psychologists?"

As described previously, the *Forum*'s scope includes articles that are relevant to trainers in the field of school psychology. Over the years, many articles have focused on training practices (e.g., how or how much are certain topics taught across training programs) or examples of specific approaches to training (e.g., a case study describing the effectiveness of one program's methods). Other articles focus on topics in the field that are of interest to trainers, which can be much broader in scope (e.g., online learning and changes in education law). Many articles in the *Forum* examine current practices in the field of school psychology (e.g., trends in counseling services provided by school psychologists) and present results in a manner that makes direct recommendations for training (e.g., training programs need to spend more time teaching counseling strategies). Although this represents a fairly wide breadth of potential manuscripts, the most important factor for future authors submitting

154 *Kelly Kennedy*

to the *Forum* to keep in mind is the relevance of their piece to training. As demonstrated in my examples, not every piece needs to include data regarding training programs or current students, but all discussions need to be focused on how the information presented in the piece can be applied to training programs.

2015 Manuscript Submissions and Processing

In 2015, the total number of submissions (including new submissions and resubmissions of previously rejected manuscripts) to the *Forum* was 26. Ten manuscripts (38%) were accepted or accepted with contingent revisions. For 14 manuscripts (54%), authors received notification of rejection but were encouraged to resubmit with revisions. Seven of these manuscripts were resubmitted and eventually accepted, and three others were resubmitted the following year. Two manuscripts were rejected outright. Acceptances and rejections are outlined in Table 15.1.

The decision time from manuscript submission to editorial decision is outlined in Table 15.2. As shown, the average length of time from a manuscript's submission to the decision date was 67 days. The average time elapsed between a submission and the return of the blind peer reviews was about 52 days, with a large range (15 to 126 days). For four manuscripts submitted in 2015, additional reviewers were assigned after original reviewers were unable to complete reviews in a reasonable time. The average length of time for an editor's decision was 15 days, with a wide range (1 to 54 days), which captures the editor's unavailability during a maternity leave.

Table 15.1 Journal Operations for *Trainers' Forum* in 2015

Submission status for 2015 submissions	Number	Percentage
Decisions rendered	26	
Accept and accept contingent on revision	10	38%
Reject (all categories)	16	62%
Reject encouraging revision	14	54%
Reject	2	8%

Table 15.2 Decision Time in Days for Submissions to *Trainers' Forum* in 2015

	Reviews returned (days)	Editor decision (days)	Total review time (days)
Mean	51.82	15.05	67.06
Standard deviation	21.15	14.07	34.62
Range	15–126	1–54	23–141

2015 Publication Patterns

Trainers' Forum published two issues in 2015, each with five articles. Of the ten articles published, six (60%) presented original research, and four (40%) were expository articles. Of the research articles, three (50%) used descriptive survey designs, and three (50%) used case study designs featuring training programs. Of the expository articles, two (50%) were literature reviews, and two were position pieces.

The articles published in 2015 followed the historical trends of the *Forum* in terms of content (i.e., training practices and topics of interest to trainers), including "Counseling Training Practices in School Psychology Programs" (Fernald & Hanchon, 2015), "Integrating the Scientist-Practitioner Model into Specialist Level School Psychology Training" (Castro-Villareal et al., 2015), "Bringing the Triangle to Life: Teaching RTI Practices to School Psychologists" (Dixon, 2015), "Multicultural Transformation of a School Psychology Course: Process and Outcomes" (Lasser, Dark, Beam, Morris, & Shatila, 2015), and "The Nature and Extent of Research on Autism Spectrum Disorder in School Psychology Journals" (Henze, Jaspers, Wilson, & Fasko, 2015).

Recommendations for Prospective Authors

As described earlier, the *Forum*'s scope includes data-based and discussion-based manuscripts that directly relate to the training of school psychologists. Potential authors should understand that this scope does not preclude submissions that do not involve a training program or current school psychology students; many submissions utilize data provided by current school psychologists rather than trainees. Literature reviews and meta-analyses are also relevant to the *Forum* to the degree that the results can inform training practices. Position papers are also welcome to the degree that they are applicable to the training of future school psychologists.

The most relevant and best-received articles in the *Forum* tend to be those that provide trainers with explicit information that can be applied to their own practices. For example, an article might describe how a specific course was developed for a training program to meet standards, describe the impact of the implementation of that course on student learning outcomes, and also provide a thorough description of the content of that course, such that a faculty member teaching a similar course could implement similar content. Similarly, an article might describe the gaps in knowledge of practicing school psychologists when working with a specific population (e.g., students with specific learning disabilities) and then provide a list of recommended training materials or resources. In many ways, the *Forum* is a practical journal that is contributed to and consumed by a large network of colleagues who aim to share resources, ideas, and data-based strategies to serve a collective goal of preparing stronger, more well-rounded, and more competent school psychologists. Manuscripts that share this goal are nearly always eventually accepted (pending revisions) for publication.

156 *Kelly Kennedy*

The review form used by the *Forum* asks reviewers to provide ratings on several aspects of each article: (a) clarity and organization, (b) significance of the topic/importance to the *Forum* readership, (c) quality of background literature, (d) relevance to training, (e) format appropriateness, and (f) quality of research methodology. One of the most common reasons for rejections or requests for revisions includes a failure of authors to adequately address the article's relevance to training. Authors considering submitting a manuscript to the *Forum* should ensure that their article clearly confers training implications, applications, or recommendations for trainers or training programs based on their findings.

For any reader of this book who might be considering publishing in the *Forum*, I encourage you to do so. Nearly everything a scholar in the field of school psychology studies or writes about has relevance to the training of school psychologists, and it is a great way to contribute to the future of our profession. If potential authors have any questions about their manuscript's suitability for *Trainers' Forum* or would like any additional information about publishing in this journal, please contact the current editorial team. The editors' contact information will always be available on the *Trainers' Forum* page of the TSP website (https://tsp.wildapricot.org/forum).

Note

1 Kelly Kennedy served as the editor of *Trainers' Forum* from 2012–2017. Paul Jantz (Texas State University) succeeded her as editor. Thus, correspondence and manuscripts for submission should be sent to pj16@txstate.edu

References

Castro-Villareal, F., Rodriguez, B., Sullivan, J., Guerra, N., Garza, S., & Harris, E. (2015). Integrating the scientist-practitioner model into specialist level school psychology training. *Trainers' Forum, 33*(2), 7–25.

Dixon, R. (2015). Bringing the triangle to life: Teaching RTI practices to school psychologists. *Trainers' Forum, 33*(2), 72–87.

Fernald, L., & Hanchon, T. (2015). Counseling training practices in school psychology programs. *Trainers' Forum, 33*(3), 57–81.

Henze, E., Jaspers, K., Wilson, K., & Fasko, S. (2015). The nature and extent of research on Autism Spectrum Disorder in school psychology journals. *Trainers' Forum, 33*(3), 36–56.

Lasser, J., Dark, L., Beam, K., Morris, M., & Shatila, A. (2015). Multicultural transformation of a school psychology course: Process and outcomes. *Trainers' Forum, 33*(3), 27–35.

Part 3

Publishing in Specialty Journals in School Psychology and Related Fields

16 Publishing in Behavioral Research Journals

Scott P. Ardoin and Kevin M. Ayres

A primary reason that teachers leave the field of education is due to the challenges they face in managing the behavior of students within their classrooms (Hong, 2012). It is therefore important that school psychologists and educational researchers continue to investigate (a) effective classroom behavioral management procedures, (b) assessment procedures for quickly and easily determining the function of student problem behavior within school settings, (c) means by which to increase teachers' fidelity of intervention implementation, and (d) interventions for teaching students how to behave in the school setting. The research methodology employed to examine these questions often differs from that of the majority of quantitative research conducted within the field of school psychology that relies on large-N research designs.

Much of the research examining behavioral assessment and behavioral intervention practices analyzes behavior at the level of the individual student. The goal of such research is to determine (a) what consequences in the environment are maintaining a student's levels of inappropriate and appropriate behavior, (b) how to teach appropriate behavior, and (c) how the environment might be altered to decrease rates of inappropriate behavior and increase rates of appropriate behavior (Martens, Daly, & Ardoin, 2015). Because the behaviors being measured are of primary interest (as opposed to constructs) and because behavior itself is the central focus of intervention, analysis must be conducted at the level of the individual. Single-case design (SCD) methodology provides a means by which to experimentally evaluate whether the changes being observed in the behavior of an individual are a function of the intervention being conducted. For these reasons, another important segment of quantitative research is SCD research (Odom & Strain, 2002).

SCD methodology is especially conducive for the conducting of research within school settings (Horner, Swaminathan, Sugai, & Smolkowski, 2012). By definition, the SCDs allow for evaluation and demonstration of a functional relationship between a selected intervention and changes in behavior of an individual participant. Data are not collapsed across participants (except in cases where groups of students are treated at a single unit), but rather time series are data collected, and data collected during the intervention phase(s) are compared to data collected during the nonintervention (baseline) phase(s).

These characteristics are conducive to the conducting of research within school settings for multiple reasons. First, researchers do not have to ask for access to large samples of students or to be able to randomly assign participants who might benefit from intervention to a control condition. Rather, the researcher can ask for access to participants who might benefit from the intervention of interests, and promise that at a minimum all participants will be exposed to the intervention under investigation. Furthermore, the researcher can offer the school information regarding whether the selected intervention improved student behavior, and promise that if data suggest the intervention is ineffective, the intervention will be discontinued to allow for another potentially more effective intervention to be implemented. Second, administrators can generally recognize the potential benefit of allowing SCD studies to be conducted in their school, as the studies are typically designed to improve the behavior of participants who need the selected intervention. A third reason SCD is conducive to school-based research is that a study can potentially be conducted with as few as one participant at a time. In fact, some journals will occasionally publish brief reports with only one participant. The ability to empirically demonstrate a causal relationship between the intervention and behavior with only a few participants allows for empirical research to be conducted (a) with populations for which it would be difficult to obtain a large sample size and (b) when one might lack the necessary resources to implement an intervention with large samples of students, across multiple classrooms, or both.

Publishing SCD Research

Employing SCD methodology to evaluate intervention with the hope of publishing resulting data requires that researchers understand the benefits and drawbacks of the various SCDs (see Gast & Ledford, 2014). Selecting the wrong design can potentially result in the inability of the research to demonstrate a causal relationship between the intervention and change in behavior. Likewise, researchers must carefully select dependent variables and ensure the variable is a directly observable behavior that is operationally defined with clear procedures for measuring. Making poor choices in these areas can result in data being collected that do not accurately represent changes in participant behavior. Fortunately, there are resources from which individuals can learn these critical elements for conducting quality and publishable SCD research (Gast & Ledford, 2014; Horner et al., 2005).

What Works Clearinghouse (WWC) has published a set of standards that has emerged as one of the more prominent sets of guidelines for SCD. Kratochwill et al. (2010) structured these standards to help with the review of SCD studies for establishing evidence-based practice, but they can also be used to assist the novice researcher with meeting some minimal level of quality and rigor in their design. Researchers should note, however, that these standards do not have universal acceptance (e.g., Wolery, 2013), and there are aspects of designing an SCD study that are critical but not included in the WWC design standards (e.g., procedural fidelity). The panel who wrote the standards established a two-stage system to evaluate a study. The first stage evaluates the quality of the design itself and includes multiple components. If a study meets design standards or meets with reservations, then the reviewer considers the quality of the evidence yielded by the study. For a researcher intending to develop a study, attending to the design component of the WWC standards is important, but the WWC standards should not be viewed as the final word on design as the nuance of some very rigorous studies might not meet the standards for reasons that would not impinge on internal validity. As with any field there are, however, some unwritten rules that can make publishing SCD research challenging for those with little experience. Although a good study is likely to be published, failure to adhere to unwritten rules decreases reviewers' confidence in an author's works and thus potentially increases their likelihood of recommending rejection of a manuscript that they might otherwise recommend be resubmitted with revisions.

One of the unwritten rules—and a rule that is critical when publishing an SCD study—involves the collection and reporting of (a) the fidelity with which the components of a condition are implemented and (b) inter-rater reliability data. Both sources of data speak largely to the quality of the data (and study as a whole), and if they are not up to standard, the associated manuscript is generally not publishable. If the conditions that make up a study (including baseline) are not implemented as designed (i.e., with high fidelity), then the descriptions of the conditions within the manuscript are essentially meaningless, and one cannot be certain of the mechanisms that account for changes in behavior across conditions. Likewise, if inter-rater reliability is poor, one cannot be certain if the data presented within the manuscript accurately represent what occurred during observation and thus whether intervention truly changed behavior. Researchers need to report these two indicators of study quality; in addition, they need to list the procedures used to ensure each met acceptable levels (e.g., statements regarding training of observers). For instance, Klubnik and Ardoin (2010) reported that in order to ensure high procedural fidelity, those implementing the intervention were first trained to 100% procedural integrity, and when providing intervention, they employed scripts to ensure maintenance of fidelity. Fidelity was then assessed by having an independent observer mark the number of steps completed by the interventionist and dividing by the total number of steps possible. Likewise, researchers need to report the formula for calculating these values as the method used to calculate them can result in differences in reported integrity and reliability. Finally, it is essential that data be reported per condition by participant as adherence to condition procedures as well as inter-rater reliability may vary across time and participant.

Another unwritten rule with which those new to SCD research might be unfamiliar is the proper display of data in graphical form. Although there are resources for developing SCD graphs (Dixon et al., 2009; Pritchard, 2008), researchers might be unaware of some of the details and that certain graphing conventions are not considered optional by researchers. Frequently made mistakes include (a) presenting the first observation on the y-axis, (b) failing to ensure that phase change lines end perfectly on the x-axis, (c) improperly labeling axes and conditions, and (d) placing lines where they do not belong (e.g., including a border line around the entire graph, horizontal axis lines at y-axis data values, and a horizontal line at the top of the y-axis). Although an editor can easily recommend that an author correct these mistakes, such errors might reduce the confidence peer reviewers have in the author's work and thus should be avoided.

Failure to properly interpret SCD data is another challenge new researchers face when attempting to publish SCD studies. It is important to remember when presenting findings from SCD studies that data must first, and primarily, be interpreted at the individual participant level. Although one might report in their Discussion section that results indicate intervention was effective for all participants, it is never appropriate to collapse data across participants so as to compare mean performance of participants during a baseline condition to an intervention condition. Likewise, it is generally not appropriate to calculate a mean percentage increase across participants or for a single participant across settings or behaviors within a multiple baseline design. Given that the data used in SCDs represent behavior across time, averaging within a condition does not usually provide a meaningful summary about what occurred— especially when data have trends within a phase. Moreover, because the analysis should focus on level, trend, and variability, reporting mean values alone ignores the latter two. That said, in SCD, researchers rarely if ever report standard deviation or slope for the data.

Researchers should also be mindful that performance under one phase should only be compared to the adjacent phases; thus, if an ABAB design is employed, it would not be appropriate to compare a student's behavior during the second intervention condition to the first baseline condition. The primary comparison of a participant's level of behavior during the second intervention condition should be compared to the second baseline condition. It is also important, when analyzing the impact of intervention on student or teacher behavior, that the primary focus is on changes in level, trend, and variability. Although within the last several years there has been an increased emphasis on employing statistical analyses of SCD data (Parker & Vannest, 2012; Solomon, 2014; Swaminathan, Rogers, & Horner, 2014), it is important that, if such analyses are employed, they are used as a supplemental and secondary means by which to evaluate the effects of intervention. The primary means of analyzing SCD data should be visual analyses, as summarizing intervention effects by other means is not only unconventional but also can be difficult and potentially misleading for others to interpret.

Selecting Journals that Publish Behavioral Research

Researchers can increase the probability of publishing their SCD research by submitting their manuscripts to the most appropriate journal in regards to topic area, setting of research, participants involved, and the extent to which the study extends the literature. Although the major school psychology journals publish behavioral intervention studies (see Collins et al., 2016; DuPaul, Eckert, & Vilardo, 2012; Pfiffner, Villodas, Kaiser, Rooney, & McBurnett, 2013), researchers might have greater luck publishing their behavioral research in other outlets that focus on the intervention work conducted.

Table 16.1 provides the 2015 2-year and 5-year Impact Factor values, and types of manuscripts accepted by six journals that publish research conducted by school psychology researchers and that frequently cite work published within school psychology journals. Information provided within Table 16.1 was obtained through the respective journals' websites. In an effort to gain a better understanding of the type of research published within these journals, we reviewed and coded all articles published in each journal during 2015. Variables coded included the keywords listed by the authors, the setting in which the study was conducted, the population studied, and the type of study

Table 16.1 Behavioral Research Journals that Publish Research Conducted by School Psychology Researchers and that Frequently Cite Work Published within School Psychology Journals

Journal	2015 IF 2-year/5-year	Type of manuscripts accepted
Behavioral Interventions	0.5/.74	Book reviews, Brief reports, Discussion articles, Literature reviews, Research articles
Behavior Modification	1.22/2.04	Clinical articles, Program descriptions, Research articles, Review articles, Treatment manuals
Behavior Therapy	3.28/4.33	Clinical replication series, Empirical research, Literature reviews, Methodological papers, Single case design studies, Theoretical papers
Journal of Applied Behavior Analysis	1.39/1.59	Research articles, Reports, Discussion Articles, Brief Reviews, Technical Articles, Book Reviews
Journal of Behavioral Education	None	Critical reviews, Discussion articles, Research articles
Journal of Positive Behavior Interventions	1.56/2.43	Conceptual papers, Empirical research, Discussions, Literature reviews, Media reviews

Note. IF = impact factors. Impact factors were obtained from each of the respective journals' websites on 07/10/2016.

(i.e., SCD, case study, measurement study, and large-N design). Although the information gathered from each journal might be skewed as a function of special issues published during 2015, the topics of special issues are generally consistent with the type of articles and topics that are of interest to the readers of the journal.

Behavioral Interventions, published quarterly, publishes research and practice articles that employ behavioral techniques as a form of treatment, education, and assessments directed toward students, clients, and staff (http://online library.wiley.com/journal/10.1002/(ISSN)1099-078X). Topics frequently covered by articles published in 2015 included differential reinforcement, staff training, and video modeling.[1] Other topics covered included auditory integration training, discrimination training, intraverbal training, and imitation training. Of the 22 articles published in 2015, the overwhelming majority involved intervention research, assessment research (i.e., functional assessment), or reviews of the literature involving individuals with classifications such as autism, developmental delay, and intellectual disability. The remaining articles focused on staff training, review of gender bias in gerontology research, review of SCD research, and precision teaching of reading fluency within a regular education setting. With the exception of four review articles and one measurement article examining a behavioral rating scale, the remaining articles were SCD studies.

Behavior Modification publishes six issues annually with the intention of providing valuable information to both researchers and practitioners interested in the application of behavioral modification techniques in psychiatric, clinical, educational, and rehabilitative settings. Based upon the description on the journal website (https://us.sagepub.com/en-us/nam/behavior-modification/journal200900#description), it publishes research that extends beyond the topics covered by similar journals (including those discussed within this chapter). Examples of such topics of interest include anxiety, child abuse, divorce and children, sleep disorders, learning disabilities, and weight-loss maintenance. Although the keywords identified by authors in the manuscripts published within 2015 were generally consistent with what one might expect (e.g., autism, contingency, functional analysis, SCD, and video modeling and feedback), there were also a substantial number of topics that might be surprising to see within other behavioral journals (e.g., anxiety, acceptance and commitment therapy, cohabiting stepfamilies, decoupling, depression, emotion dysregulation, mindfulness, and psychological flexibility). Similarly, there was great variation in the population, setting in which the research was conducted, and methodology employed. Participants included children, adolescents, and adults with autism and other developmental disabilities; teachers of regular and special education students; elementary students without disabilities; adults with depressions; and college students with social anxiety. Although more than a third of the 39 articles published in 2015 were SCD studies, there were also several reviews of the literature, meta-analyses, a pilot study, a case study, a randomized control trial, and multiple measurement studies. Of those journals reviewed in this chapter, *Behavior Modification* is, without question,

Behavioral Research Journals   165

the most diverse of the journals in regards to topics and types of manuscripts it will publish.

Behavior Therapy publishes six issues annually and has the highest impact factor of those articles discussed within this chapter (see Table 16.1). The journal's website (http://onlinelibrary.wiley.com/journal/10.1002/(ISSN) 1099-078X) suggests it publishes research focusing on the application of behavioral and cognitive sciences in the conceptualization, assessment, and treatment of psychopathology and related clinical problems. A synthesis of the keywords that frequently appeared within its 2015 articles suggests a considerable focus on anxiety, with 14 of the 67 studies (21%) including anxiety as a keyword. Other keywords that appeared multiple times across the 2015 studies include autism, cognitive behavior therapy, depression, emotion, fear activation/conditioning/generalization, obsessive-compulsive disorder, and phobia. The most prominent setting was a clinical setting, followed by studies conducted with college-aged students within a university setting. Only four (6%) of the 67 studies were conducted in a school setting. Unlike any of the other behavioral journals discussed within this chapter, none of the studies published in 2015 with *Behavior Therapy* were SCD studies. Most of the manuscripts involved evaluation of a measurement or examination of an intervention through a randomized control trial. There were also seven literature reviews and four longitudinal studies published.

In comparison to the journals described above, *Journal of Applied Behavior Analysis* tends to be more focused. The journal's website (http://onlinelibrary. wiley.com/journal/10.1002/(ISSN)1938-3703) indicates that it publishes research across four quarterly issues that focus on the application of experimental analysis to problems of social importance. As suggested by the title of the journal, the emphasis of the journal is on the application of behavioral analysis to real-world problems. Keywords frequently included terms associated with the field of applied behavioral analysis including reinforcement (e.g., automatic reinforcement, differential reinforcement, establishing operations, and functional analysis), functional communication training, self-injury, and stimulus equivalence. Although the participants in nearly a third of the full research articles were diagnosed as having autism or a related disability and studies were conducted in what would best be described as clinical settings, several involved preschool- and school-aged children without disabilities in general education environments. The journal also occasionally publishes articles that examine the application of behavioral analysis with populations that those outside of the field might not typically associate with applied behavior analysis (e.g., blackjack players and professional footballers). Of the 42 full articles coded, 30 employed SCD methodology (71%), four were descriptive studies (10%), and the remaining were classified as measurement, meta-analyses, randomized control trials, and reviews of the literature. In addition to full-length research articles, each issue of the *Journal of Applied Behavior Analysis* includes multiple brief reports. According to the journal's guidelines for authors, brief reports are typically innovative pilot work, replication of previous studies, or controlled case studies. Publishing such work is believed to be essential to the advancement of the field. Although the brief reports published in 2015 were not coded as were the full research articles, the topics, participants, and settings of brief reports generally seemed to mimic those of the full research articles.

Journal of Behavioral Education, which is published quarterly, publishes research that examines the application of behavioral principles and technology to education as well as the employment of SCD methodology to investigate issues, practices, and problems associated with education (http://link.springer.com/journal/10864). It is the only journal of the six discussed in this chapter that does not have an impact factor (see Table 16.1). Given the title and stated focus of the journal, it is not surprising that the keywords most frequently employed by authors include terms associated with educational environments (e.g., classroom management) and intervention implemented within both regular and special education classrooms (e.g., discrete trial training, incremental rehearsal, reading intervention, and treatment intensity). Although more than a quarter of its 22 articles included as participants either children with autism or their teachers, the majority focused on assessment or intervention research conducted with regular education students or students with mild educational disabilities. All studies involved either school-aged children or individuals within schools who were providing either behavioral or academic intervention services to children. In contrast to many other behaviorally focused journals in which the primary focus of intervention is on the behavior or basic skill development of individuals with severe disabilities, the *Journal of Behavioral Education* publishes many studies that employ principles of behavioral analysis in the design and evaluation of academic interventions targeting the skills of students with and without disabilities. The majority of its articles were SCD studies ($n = 14$; 64%) and reviews of the literature ($n = 5$; 23%) with the remaining studies being large-N-design studies developed to examine the effects of behaviorally based academic and behavioral interventions.

Journal of Positive Behavior Interventions publishes articles quarterly that focus on positive behavioral support and interventions implemented within home, school, and community settings (http://pbi.sagepub.com/). Given its purpose, many of its articles are associated with the implementation of the evidence-based practice of Positive Behavioral Intervention and Supports in schools (Horner et al., 2009). Keywords that were frequently employed included challenging behavior, functional analysis, interventions, positive behavior interventions and supports, self-monitoring, teachers, and other behavioral terms frequently heard within school settings. All but one of the studies published in this journal during 2015 were conducted within school settings, and all studies included school-aged children or their teachers as participants. The one study conducted outside of the school setting was conducted within the home of three children, and it examined the impact of coaching on the implementation of a function-based intervention on parents' fidelity of implementation and student behavior (Fettig, Schultz, & Sreckovic, 2015). Of the 20 manuscripts published, nine were SCD studies (45%), and four

(20%) were literature reviews, with the remaining manuscripts being surveys, examination of measurements, two large-N-design studies, and one case study.

Final Recommendations

Although the six journals highlighted in this chapter are clearly behaviorally oriented, a review of their targeted topic areas, the types of articles they publish, keywords employed by their authors, participant characteristics, settings of studies, and research designs illuminates their differences. In order to both expedite the publication of their work as well as to inform the proper audiences of their work, authors should give considerable thought to which journal they will submit their work to. In addition to the information provided within this chapter, authors should examine their own reference lists and see what journals they cite most frequently. Recognizing numerous references to a particular journal provides an excellent clue as to what journal's research you are most extending. After determining to which journal a manuscript should be submitted, it is then wise to (a) identify some of the best articles within that journal as well as articles that employed similar methodology within the journal and (b) use those articles as models for structuring the manuscript. Finally, after reviewing the manuscript multiple times in an effort to ensure that all formatting rules are followed and that there are minimal to no typographical and other editing errors, researchers should give strong consideration to selecting keywords. The keywords selected by authors are often used by editors in the selection of the reviewers who will evaluate the details of the manuscript. Having reviewers who understand and appreciate the area of research one is attempting to extend is likely to increase the desire of a reviewer to see a manuscript published.

Note

1   *Behavioral Interventions* does not provide a listing of keywords for the articles published within the journal. Thus, keywords could not be used in the synthesis of topics covered by *Behavioral Interventions* in 2015.

References

Collins, T. A., Cook, C. R., Dart, E. H., Socie, D. G., Renshaw, T. L., & Long, A. C. (2016). Improving classroom engagement among high school students with disruptive behavior: Evaluation of the class pass intervention. *Psychology in the Schools, 53*, 204–219.

Dixon, M. R., Jackson, J. W., Small, S. L., Horner-King, M. J., Lik, N. M. K., Garcia, Y., & Rosales, R. (2009). Creating single-subject design graphs in Microsoft Excel™ 2007. *Journal of Applied Behavior Analysis, 42*, 277–293. doi: 10.1901/jaba.2009.42-277

DuPaul, G. J., Eckert, T. L., & Vilardo, B. (2012). The effects of school-based interventions for attention deficit hyperactivity disorder: a meta-analysis 1996–2010. *School Psychology Review, 41*, 387.

Fettig, A., Schultz, T. R., & Sreckovic, M. A. (2015). Effects of coaching on the implementation of functional assessment-based parent intervention in reducing challenging behaviors. *Journal of Positive Behavior Interventions, 17*, 170–180.

Gast, D. L., & Ledford, J. R. (2014). *Single case research methodology: Applications in special education and behavioral sciences.* New York, NY: Routledge.

Hong, J. Y. (2012). Why do some beginning teachers leave the school, and others stay? Understanding teacher resilience through psychological lenses. *Teachers and Teaching, 18*(4), 417–440. doi: 10.1080/13540602.2012.696044

Horner, R. H., Carr, E. G., Halle, J., McGee, G., Odom, S., & Wolery, M. (2005). The use of single-subject research to identify evidence-based practice in special education. *Exceptional Children, 71*, 165–179.

Horner, R. H., Sugai, G., Smolkowski, K., Eber, L., Nakasato, J., Todd, A. W., & Esperanza, J. (2009). A randomized, wait-list controlled effectiveness trial assessing school-wide positive behavior support in elementary schools. *Journal of Positive Behavior Interventions, 11*(3), 133–144.

Horner, R. H., Swaminathan, H., Sugai, G., & Smolkowski, K. (2012). Considerations for the systematic analysis and use of single-case research. *Education and Treatment of Children, 35*(2), 269–290.

Klubnik, C., & Ardoin, S. P. (2010). Examining immediate and maintenance effects of a reading intervention package on generalization materials: Individual versus group implementation. *Journal of Behavioral Education, 19*, 7–29.

Kratochwill, T. R., Hitchcock, J., Horner, R. H., Levin, J. R., Odom, S. L., Rindskopf, D. M., & Shadish, W. R. (2010). Single-case designs technical documentation. Retrieved from What Works Clearinghouse website: http://ies.ed.gov/ncee/wwc/Docs/ReferenceResources/wwc_scd.pdf

Martens, B. K., Daly, E. J., III, & Ardoin, S. P. (2015). Applications of applied behavior analysis to school-based instructional intervention. In H. S. Roane, J. E. Ringdahl, & T. S. Falcomata (Eds.), *Clinical and organizational applications of applied behavior analysis* (pp. 125–150). San Diego, CA, US: Elsevier Academic Press.

Odom, S. L., & Strain, P. S. (2002). Evidence-based practice in early intervention/early childhood special education: Single-subject design research. *Journal of Early Intervention, 25*, 151–160. doi: 10.1177/105381510202500212

Parker, R. I., & Vannest, K. J. (2012). Bottom-up analysis of single-case research designs. *Journal of Behavioral Education, 21*, 254–265. doi: 10.1007/s10864-012-9153-1

Pfiffner, L. J., Villodas, M., Kaiser, N., Rooney, M., & McBurnett, K. (2013). Educational outcomes of a collaborative school–home behavioral intervention for ADHD. *School Psychology Quarterly, 28*, 25.

Pritchard, J. K. (2008). A decade later: Creating single-subject design graphs with Microsoft Excel 2007™. *The Behavior Analyst Today, 9*(3–4), 153–161. doi: 10.1037/h0100655

Solomon, B. G. (2014). Violations of assumptions in school-based single-case data: Implications for the selection and interpretation of effect sizes. *Behavior Modification, 38*, 477–496. doi: 10.1177/0145445513510931

Swaminathan, H., Rogers, H. J., & Horner, R. H. (2014). An effect size measure and Bayesian analysis of single-case designs. *Journal of School Psychology, 52*, 213–230. doi: 10.1016/j.jsp.2013.12

Wolery, M. (2013). A commentary: Single-case design technical document of the What Works Clearinghouse. *Remedial and Special Education, 34*, 39–43.

17 Publishing in Assessment and Measurement Journals

Matthew R. Reynolds, Christopher R. Niileksela, and Emily M. Meyer

High-quality psychological assessment requires the use of high-quality measurement instruments. The development of high-quality measurement instruments is contingent upon the application of sound psychological and measurement theory. School psychologists rely directly on measurement instruments in their assessment practice, making assessment and measurement fundamental to the practice of school psychology. Further, school psychology researchers should utilize measurement (and hopefully psychological) theory when conducting assessment research.

The extent of measurement and assessment influences, nonetheless, spreads beyond school psychology; these influences permeate all aspects of practice and research in psychology. *They affect training.* Measures used by school psychologists, such as intelligence tests and rating scales, are likely part of any graduate program curriculum geared toward educating future licensed psychologists. Likewise, courses in measurement theory and statistics are standard in any psychology graduate program. *They affect practice*—and not only assessment practice. For example, accurate evaluation of intervention effects, whether in practice or in reading the literature, requires knowledge of sound measurement and assessment practices. Last, *they affect psychological research.* The validity of research findings depends on the use of sound measurement and assessment practices. Thus, school psychology researchers who conduct research in assessment and measurement might wish to report research findings to a more general audience of psychologists by publishing in journals outside of traditional school psychology journals. Further, school psychology researchers and practitioners who want a well-rounded education in the scientific basis of assessment and measurement would do well by reading outside of school psychology journals.

The purpose of this chapter is to describe several important assessment and measurement journals in psychology and education. Although a couple of the journals described in this chapter publish studies conducted primarily by school psychology researchers, none of the journals described is considered a "major" school psychology journal (Kranzler, Grapin, & Daley, 2011) as highlighted earlier in this book.

Journal Selection Process

We used several steps to identify journals to include in this chapter. First, we reviewed a list of journals provided by this book's editor. This list from Clarivate Analytics' Journal Citation Reports included journal statistics from eight categories relevant to school psychology: educational psychology, developmental psychology, clinical psychology, education and educational research, special education, multidisciplinary psychology, applied psychology, and family studies. We searched and highlighted journals with *assessment* or *measurement* in the titles. Second, we searched a PsycINFO output file that included data from over 2,000 journals. Again, we searched for the terms *assessment* and *measurement*, along with *psychometrics*. Last, we conducted the same search with over 30,000 journals in Scopus Sources. Highlighted journals that were related to education or psychology were initially considered. A total of 16 assessment journals and ten measurement journals were initially identified. After reviewing various journal websites, we decided to highlight six assessment journals and six measurement journals. The final selection process was mostly subjective. Please do not interpret our selection of these journals as indicating that they are the best ones available. They were the journals that we found most relevant for this book.

Assessment Journals

Assessment issues comprise a major research theme emanating from school psychology faculty research (Kranzler et al., 2011). Although assessment issues are often published in core school psychology journals, other journals exist that are focused primarily on assessment in psychology and education. Of the 16 assessment journals that we originally identified, we pre-identified four for inclusion. We included the three assessment journals with which we were most familiar (i.e., *Assessment*, *Journal of Psychoeducational Assessment*, and *Psychological Assessment*). We also included *Assessment for Effective Intervention* because research by school psychologists is frequently published in that journal (Kranzler et al., 2011). Ten journals were eliminated because the scope was outside of school psychology (e.g., career assessment), most of the research was in a setting not prominently occupied by school psychologists (e.g., higher education), or most of the research was geared toward adults.

The six assessment journals we included are listed in Table 17.1. Two are school psychology-focused (*Assessment for Effective Intervention* and *Journal of Psychoeducational Assessment*); two are clinical psychology-focused but are of high quality, have strong impact factors, and have included research from school psychology researchers (*Assessment* and *Psychological Assessment*); and two are potential outlets for school psychology researchers—one geared toward clinical psychology (*Journal of Psychopathology and Behavioral Assessment*) and the other toward educational assessment (*Educational Assessment*).

Assessment & Measurement Journals   171

Table 17.1 Specialty Journals Publishing Articles on Assessment

Journal and website	Journal description and types of articles published	2015 2-yr IF/5-yr IF
Journal of Psychoeducational Assessment (JPA) http://jpa.sagepub. com/	Publishes studies related to psychological and educational assessment, with a focus on empirically based research. Addresses innovative assessment strategies, multimethod assessment strategies, relations among assessment strategies, analysis of assessment methods, cross-cultural assessment methods, links between assessment and outcomes, and reliability and validity. **Types of articles:** Standard articles, brief articles, test/book reviews, and special issues (4 since 2010).	1.0/1.6
Assessment for Effective Intervention (AEI) http://aei.sagepub. com/	Publishes studies of applied assessment practices that inform instruction and diagnosis with implications for practitioners. Addresses relations among assessment instruments, links between assessment and intervention/instruction, and the utility of assessment techniques and instruments. Practical implications of research are emphasized. **Types of articles:** Research studies, brief/ psychometric reports, and special series with editor-chosen topics (~10 since 2010).	None
Assessment http://asm.sagepub. com/	Publishes research on the clinical assessment of personality, cognitive/neuropsychological functions, and psychopathology. Addresses the development, validation, and interpretation of assessment measures; the practical application of assessment; and how assessment research informs understanding of psychopathology. **Types of articles:** Standard research articles and those selected for special issues/sections about topics chosen by editor (3 since 2010).	2.9/3.5
Psychological Assessment http://www.apa.org/ pubs/journals/pas/	Publishes empirical research related to all areas of clinical assessment in psychology. Addresses clinical judgment and decision-making, translating basic psychological research into clinical assessments, and the development and validation of assessments. **Types of articles:** Standard research articles, brief reports, and special issues (2 since 2010).	2.9/3.8

(continued)

172 *Reynolds, Niileksela, & Meyer*

Table 17.1 Specialty Journals Publishing Articles on Assessment (*continued*)

Journal and website	Journal description and types of articles published	2015 2-yr IF/5-yr IF
Journal of Psychopathology and Behavioral Assessment http://www.springer.com/psychology/journal/10862	Publishes research that promotes understanding of psychopathology and mental disorders as they manifest across the lifespan. Addresses assessment, diagnosis, psychobiological factors, and theories of psychopathology and behavior change. **Types of articles:** Original papers, review articles, editorials, and special sections (3 since 2010).	2.0/2.5
Educational Assessment http://www.tandfonline.com/toc/heda20/current	Publishes research on assessment design, analysis, and use for individuals, groups, and programs within educational settings. Includes theoretical content and qualitative or quantitative empirical studies with implications for educational policy and practice. **Types of articles:** Standard manuscripts and special issues (2 since 2010).	None

Note. IF = impact factor. Descriptions of each journal were obtained from the journal's website, following headings such as "aim and scope" and "author guidelines." These descriptions were edited for content. The 2015 journal impact factor values were obtained from Clarivate Analytics' Journal Citation Reports database.

School Psychology Focus

The *Journal of Psychoeducational Assessment* and *Assessment for Effective Intervention* were included in a recent analysis of school psychology program publishing trends because of the frequency with which school psychology researchers publish in them (Kranzler et al., 2011). These journals are likely familiar to school psychology researchers.

The *Journal of Psychoeducational Assessment* (JPA) is intended for a broad assessment audience. The name itself implies that it is relevant to school psychology. A list of authors from studies published in the inaugural 1983 issue reads like a "who's who" list of legends in school psychology, signifying school psychology's heavy influence at its inception. It has continued to be a popular outlet for school psychology research (Carper & Williams, 2004; Kranzler et al., 2011). The JPA publishes an array of studies related to both psychology and education, including studies related to measurement instruments and different assessment models (see Table 17.1). It also includes reviews of important measurement instruments. Historically, the JPA was issued four times a year. In 2009, it began publishing six issues a year, eventually increasing that number to eight issues a year in 2014. In the first few years, the page counts were about 400 pages annually. More recent page count estimates are approximately 720 pages annually. The journal is currently ranked 36th out of 57 in educational psychology journals according to its impact factor.

The second journal listed in Table 17.1, published in association with the Council for Educational Diagnostic Services Division of the Council for Exceptional Children, has a rather presumptuous title: *Assessment for Effective Intervention (AEI)*. Despite the title, a review of studies published in the journal from 2008–2011 revealed very few research studies (<4%) that included assessment data to evaluate interventions (Burns, Scholin, & Zaslofsky, 2011). Although this pattern might have changed since then, researchers should nevertheless not eschew the journal because their research does not demonstrate how assessment data may be used for intervention. It appears to publish many types of studies (e.g., development and psychometric properties of instruments and the predictive validity of scores). *AEI*, which was called *Diagnostique* until 2000, was first published in 1979. Until 2003, the number of issues per year ranged from one to four. Since 2004, however, there have been about four issues a year. The annual page count is about 250 pages. *AEI* does not produce an impact factor, something that might be considered when deciding whether to publish in it.

Clinical Psychology Focus

The next two journals listed in Table 17.1, *Assessment* and *Psychological Assessment*, have a clinical psychology focus. *Assessment* is sponsored by Division 12 (Society of Clinical Psychology: Section IX Assessment Psychology) of the American Psychological Association (APA). It publishes many studies relevant to school psychology. The first year it was published, it included studies with the Wechsler tests, Kaufman tests, and the Stanford-Binet. Even in the most recent issue (June 2016) there are two studies that involved the Wechsler tests. Although these studies might be most relevant to us, the relevance of the research published in the journal is broad. For example, there are a number of studies utilizing instruments commonly used by school psychologists (e.g., behavior rating scales). Of course, such instruments are often used in contexts outside of the schools, and the research in *Assessment* often reflects that. The current editor (Pincus, 2014) has called for an increased emphasis on studies focused on assessment science, which is research designed "to advance the field by examining new assessment methodologies and techniques for both researchers and practitioners" (p. 259). The first issue of *Assessment* was published in 1994. It was initially published quarterly, but in 2013 it began publishing bimonthly (~775 pages annually since 2013). Its impact factor is ranked 22nd out of 121 clinical psychology journals. School psychology researchers who are interested in increasing the visibility of their research might wish to submit studies to *Assessment*.

Psychological Assessment is sponsored by Division 5 (Quantitative and Qualitative Methods) of the APA. It too has a focus on clinical psychology but publishes research that is relevant to school psychology. The inaugural issue in 1989 included several studies germane to school psychology, including a study that compared children's self-reports on a behavior rating scale to parent and teacher reports. The most recent issue as of writing this chapter (June, 2016) included several studies with measures used with children and adolescents. According to the current editor, *Psychological Assessment* wants to publish cutting edge research relevant to clinical and consulting psychology within the subareas of "cognitive/neuropsychological, forensic, health, multicultural, personality, psychopathology, and screening of candidates for high-risk public safety positions" (Ben-Porath, 2016, p. 1).[1] *Psychological Assessment* had been published quarterly since its inception in 1989, but it began publishing monthly in 2016. The number of pages printed annually has seen a large increase. Since 2013, it has published about 1,400 to 1,500 pages a year compared with the ~1,000 pages published from 2010–2012 and ~500 per year prior to that. The journal boasts healthy 2- and 5-year Impact Factors and is ranked 21st out of 121 clinical psychology journals.

Potential Outlets

The *Journal of Psychopathology and Behavioral Assessment* was not as familiar to us, but it seems like a viable outlet (see Table 17.1). The research focus is across the lifespan, but a large proportion of studies are with preschool- and school-aged children and adolescents. The tables of contents reveal a broad scope of studies, a number of which are relevant to school psychology (e.g., school readiness for preschoolers with behavior problems, executive functioning in preschoolers, and peer victimization in high school) and some of which have been conducted in a school setting. The journal has a strong focus on testing well-constructed theories of psychopathology with empirical data. As stated in a recent editorial, "An article that is accepted into the *Journal of Psychopathology and Behavioral Assessment* generally reflects mastery of the assessment, psychopathology, and intervention area that the author is studying" (Salekin, 2014, p. 1). The editor listed types of submissions that would strengthen the journal. One type, the "economics of assessment and intervention," might be especially appealing to school psychology researchers as they have access to parents, teachers, and a large number of children and adolescents. The first issues of the *Journal of Psychopathology and Behavioral Assessment* were published in 1979, when it was called the *Journal of Behavior Assessment*. It changed to its current title in 1985. Since its inception it has been published four times a year (~500 pages a year). Its impact factor is ranked 48th out of 121 in clinical psychology journals.

The last journal in Table 17.1 is *Educational Assessment*. This journal, unlike other journals described thus far, is focused much more on the educational side of assessment. Topics of specific interest to school psychology researchers include teacher and classroom assessment, test accessibility for special populations, and studies with curriculum-based measures. The first issue was published in 1993. Although there have been exceptions, the journal is typically published about four times a year, with roughly 350 pages printed per year. The journal does not have an impact factor. School psychology research that is broadly related to education, rather than clinical concerns, fits better with this journal.

Measurement Journals

School psychology researchers are less likely to publish in measurement journals than they are in assessment journals described in this chapter. Further, unlike the topics in assessment journals, topics found in measurement journals are often not found in major school psychology journals. Several of the measurement journals described here only publish studies that reflect technical and narrow expertise. Nonetheless, school psychology researchers who have strong backgrounds in measurement and statistics, or who collaborate with those who do, could potentially use these journals as outlets for studies of measurement and statistical issues in school psychology that do not fit well in assessment or standard school psychology journals. Further, research findings published in these journals should be used by school psychology researchers to improve technical aspects of their own measurement and assessment research.

Of the ten measurement journals originally identified, we chose six to highlight for this chapter. The six measurement journals are described in no particular order in Table 17.2. The first journal in Table 17.2 is the *Journal of Educational Measurement*. The journal is associated with the National Council on Measurement in Education. Large-scale educational assessment is a common topic of research, with attention on equating, linking, and item analysis. The first volume was published in 1964. The first two volumes included two issues, but since then it has been published four times a year with approximately 475 pages a year. Its impact factor is ranked 7th out of 13 in mathematical psychology, 23rd out of 57 in educational psychology, and 34th out of 79 in applied psychology.

Educational and Psychological Measurement (see Table 17.2) includes topics that are more diverse than *Journal of Educational Measurement*, consistent with both the educational and psychological focus. It is impressive to review the tables of contents and see the different types of measurements used in psychology and education. The topics are relevant to school psychology, though the type of research (e.g., measurement issues and statistical technique-focused) seem outside the scope of most research conducted by school psychology researchers. *Educational and Psychological Measurement* was first published in 1941. In 1945, it began publishing four issues a year, and since 1995, six issues a year. It publishes slightly over 1,000 pages a year. According to its impact factor, *Educational and Psychological Measurement* ranks 8th out of 13 in mathematical psychology, 25th out of 57 in educational psychology, and 39th out of 101 in interdisciplinary applications in mathematics.

The third journal listed in Table 17.2, *Psychometrika*, is associated with the Psychometric Society. The journal publishes highly technical articles, but

Table 17.2 Specialty Journals Publishing Articles on Measurement

Journal and website	Journal description and types of articles published	2015 2-yr IF/5-yr IF
Journal of Educational Measurement (JEM) http://onlinelibrary.wiley.com/journal/10.1111/%28ISSN%291745-3984	Publishes measurement research with broad applicability to theoretical and applied measurement professionals. Addresses techniques, processes, and instruments for educational measurement, innovative uses of measurement, psychometric evaluation of new instruments, procedures for reporting results, and the philosophy and practice of educational measurement. **Types of articles:** Standard research articles, special issues on topics chosen by editors (1 since 2010—traditionally 1 per editor term), special report (1 per year maximum) and book and software reviews.	1.5/1.3
Educational and Psychological Measurement (EPM) http://epm.sagepub.com/	Publishes measurement research from any academic area for which educational measurement is relevant. Includes theoretical articles that broaden the scope and understanding of measurement and the innovative application of measurement techniques. **Types of articles:** Standard research articles.	1.5/1.9
Psychometrika http://link.springer.com/journal/11336	Publishes articles on statistical methods, mathematics, and theory for data analysis in the social and behavioral sciences. Addresses methods and techniques used for analyzing data rather than development and validation of tests or measures. **Types of articles:** Theory and methods (quantitative models and methodology, application of techniques), application reviews and case studies (application of data analysis and modeling), and book reviews. There has been one special issue since 2010.	1.8/2.6
Applied Psychological Measurement (APM) http://journals.sagepub.com/home/apm	Publishes on measurement topics in psychology and related social sciences. Addresses the development of measurement procedures, methods that solve measurement problems, comparisons and applications of measurement techniques, research on reliability and validity, and critical reviews of measurement procedures. **Types of articles:** Standard research articles, brief reports (small exploratory or replication studies), computer program exchange (programs and subroutines for measurement, must include software), software notes (experiences and observations with commercial software), computer software reviews, and book reviews.	1.0/1.3

Journal and website	Journal description and types of articles published	2015 2-yr IF/5-yr IF
Educational Measurement: Issues and Practice (EM:IP) http://onlinelibrary.wiley.com/journal/10.1111/(ISSN)1745-3992	Publishes articles to improve understanding of educational measurement and research designed to be applicable to those interested in measurement in academic and applied settings. Addresses practical issues in evaluation and assessment that might influence policy and practice in educational measurement and promote discussion and debate. **Types of articles:** Standard research papers, *Instructional Topics in Educational Measurement Series* (ITEMS). Commentary articles without original research are considered, though should be brief.	0.8/NA
Measurement and Evaluation in Counseling Development (MECD) http://www.tandfonline.com/toc/uecd20/current	Publishes articles focused on measurement and evaluation issues in applied settings, especially those in counseling and related fields. Addresses the development and use of measures in counseling psychology, assessment practices and concepts, and methods related to counseling assessment. **Types of articles:** Assessment, development and validation, applications of assessment, and methods plainly speaking.	0.9/1.5

Note. IF = impact factor. Descriptions of each journal were obtained from the journal's website, following headings such as "aim and scope" and "author guidelines." These descriptions were edited for content. The 2015 journal impact factor values were obtained from Clarivate Analytics' Journal Citation Reports database.

the methods are applicable to education, psychology, and the social sciences. Although it publishes excellent research, it seems unlikely that school psychology researchers would publish in this journal unless they collaborated with an expert in measurement or statistics. Some of the great debates on intelligence were published years ago in *Psychometrika*, with attempts at clear linkages between substance and method. Those linkages are not always apparent now, perhaps reflecting how technically advanced the measurement and statistical fields have become (especially relative to substantive psychology). Although this is an outstanding journal, more direct linkages with substantive areas of psychology might result in greater adoption of psychometric advances in psychological research (see Borsboom, 2006). *Psychometrika* was first published in 1936. Since that time, it has published an impressive 3,350 articles. It is published four times a year. The annual pages published since 2010 have ranged from 716 to 1,159. The impact factor is the highest out of the measurement journals discussed in this chapter and it is ranked 26th out of 101 in interdisciplinary applications of mathematics.

Next, *Applied Psychological Measurement* is also a journal that focuses on the many technical aspects of measurement and statistics, with a focus on publishing research on new applications of measurement. It also encourages international communication (Chang, 2012). A distinctive aspect of this journal is that it includes articles related to computer software (see Table 17.2). Such articles might be useful for researchers interested in using more complex statistical techniques or for researchers to share programs that they have developed. The first issue was published in 1977. In that year it published four issues and about 600 pages. Now it is published eight times a year with roughly 650 to 700 pages published annually. According to its impact factor, *Applied Psychological Measurement* ranked 11th out of 13 in mathematical psychology and 28th out of 49 in mathematical methods in the social sciences.

The fifth journal listed in Table 17.2, *Educational Measurement: Issues and Practice (EM:IP)*, published in association with National Council for Measurement in Education, includes studies broadly related to educational measurement. The studies in this journal focus more on application of measurement in practice and are less technical than those in the *Journal of Educational Measurement*, which is its companion journal. The articles should promote "understanding of and reasoned debate on assessment, evaluation, testing and related issues of practical importance to educators and the public" (Objectives of *EM:IP*, cited in Everson, 2016, p. 4). It also publishes the *Instructional Topics in Educational Measurement Series* (ITEMS), which are brief articles written as instructional guides for measurement topics. *EM:IP* was first published in 1982. It is published four times a year and, since 2010, has published 169 to 195 pages a year. The impact factor is ranked 44th out of 57 journals in educational psychology and 140th out of 230 journals in education and educational research.

The last journal discussed in this chapter is *Measurement and Evaluation in Counseling and Development*. The journal is associated with the Association for Research and Assessment in Counseling. Although due to its name it is listed under the measurement journals, the content is similar to assessment journals. The focus is more on the development and validation of scales for research and practice than it is on the refinement of measurement and statistical techniques. *Measurement and Evaluation in Counseling and Development* was first published in 1968. It is typically published four times a year (~300 pages annually). The journal seems like a viable outlet for studies related to scale development. Its impact factor is ranked 41st out of 57 in educational psychology and 56th out of 79 in applied psychology.

Recommendations

Assessment and measurement are vital to research and practice in all of psychology. School psychology researchers might want to branch out and publish their assessment- and measurement-focused studies outside of "major" school psychology journals. Based on our summary, we have concluded that for publishing original research, assessment journals are likely a better fit than are measurement journals (perhaps other than the *Measurement and Evaluation in Counseling and Development*). Nonetheless, all of the journals are worth reading to keep up with assessment and methodology advances. All of the journals include research that is citable.

Is it even worth trying, as a school psychology researcher, to publish in an assessment or measurement journal? If a researcher is focused on creating, developing, and using assessments, then why not try to publish in journals that focus on advancing assessment and measurement? For example, despite a clinical focus in the assessment journals, there is large overlap of instruments used in school and clinical psychology—even though they might be used in different settings. Knowledge of how to use instruments across settings would benefit those in both school and clinical psychology. For example, school psychology researchers might have easier access to large samples of children in schools, samples that include students with and without clinical diagnoses. These populations might not be readily available to clinical researchers, but they are of interest to them. Alternatively, clinical psychologists likely have easier access to larger samples of children with clinical diagnoses. These populations might not be readily available to school psychology researchers, but they are of interest to them (i.e., the few students who take up a disproportionate amount of school psychologists' time in schools!). Thus, research published across settings would be mutually beneficial for clinical and school psychologists. Authors should consider making that case clearly in the submission letter and in the manuscript when submitting to those journals.

Regardless, researchers should examine the journal in which they wish to submit their research. Read through the table of contents. Tables of contents from multiple issues provide insight into what has been published in the past. Read editorials written by journal editors.[2] Editorials provide a glimpse of what the journal would like to publish in the near future—if your research lines up

180 Reynolds, Niileksela, & Meyer

with what the editor would like, make that clear in the submission letter. Review the editorial board. Do you find that you have cited these people in your own work? Further, read through published studies. Evaluate the scientific rigor of those studies. Take note of how much theory is emphasized. It is important to find a good match—and the journal title is not enough to determine that. Do not make the mistake of submitting a manuscript that has no chance of getting published because it does not fit with the scope or quality of the journal. But if a journal seems inappropriate for your research at the time, think about how your research or theory can be improved or modified in the future so that it is appropriate for journals outside of school psychology.[3] If it is good for school psychology, it should be good for all of psychology.

In general, unless the study is a bad fit and submitting would waste everyone's time,[4] researchers should welcome the challenge of publishing outside of school psychology to increase the visibility of their work. They should welcome feedback obtained from expert reviewers who might not be as familiar with their current or past work (although do not submit just to get feedback). Although most journal review processes are blinded, the field of school psychology is fairly small, restricted, and circumscribed. By publishing in journals intended for a broad psychology audience, researchers could avoid the incestuous trap of having their research reviewed only by a few others in their field who do exactly the same research. Although doing so might (or might not) help with productivity, it could also stunt new developments. It is easy to be drawn into an unfulfilling research pattern (even if it is productive with publication counts) without incorporating other ideas, theories, or methods. Another possible advantage of publishing outside major school psychology journals is to avoid the problem of having research that is continually evaluated by others who are either outside or inside similar schools of thought in school psychology—that is, those who hold similar rigid beliefs about how school psychology should be practiced—so the reviewers either fundamentally love or fundamentally hate the research. In this case, despite great efforts, reviewers might lack objectivity and subsequently reject or accept the study based on their school psychology worldview rather than strictly on the scientific merit. Neither situation is likely healthy for a scientist—or a field.

Last, researchers should be excited to share what they have learned from their own research with others. Initially, researchers in school psychology might want to share that information with other school psychologists. Great! They should! But, there is also something to be said for thinking more broadly. Share what has been learned with all psychologists!

Notes

1 The previous editor of *Psychological Assessment*, Cecil Reynolds (editor from 2009 to 2015), is a prominent figure in school psychology.

2 We have cited several editorials in this chapter and there are several examples in our reference list.

3   The *Journal Article Reporting Standards* (JARS; APA Publication and Communications Board Working Group on Journal Article Reporting Standards, 2008), especially those adapted to methods used in measurement and assessment research (e.g., Hoyle & Isherwood, 2013), and *The Reviewer's Guide to Quantitative Methods in the Social Sciences* (Hancock & Mueller, 2010) are excellent resources for incorporating standard reporting practices.
4   If that is the case, hopefully the editor will send the manuscript back to you before sending to reviewers.

References

APA Publication and Communications Board Working Group on Journal Article Reporting Standards. (2008). Reporting standards for research in psychology: Why do we need them? What might they be? *American Psychologist, 63*, 839–851.

Ben-Porath, Y. S. (2016). Inaugural editorial for *Psychological Assessment*. *Psychological Assessment, 28*, 1–2.

Borsboom, D. (2006). The attack of the psychometricians. *Psychometrika, 71*, 425–440.

Burns, M. K., Scholin, S. E., & Zaslofsky, A. F. (2011). Advances in assessment through research: What have we learned in the past 3 years? *Assessment for Effective Intervention, 36*, 107–112.

Carper, R. M., & Williams, R. L. (2004). Article publications, journal outlets, and article themes for current faculty in APA-accredited school psychology programs: 1995–1999. *School Psychology Quarterly, 19*, 141–165.

Chang, H.-H. (2012). New editor's statement. *Applied Psychological Measurement, 36*, 631.

Everson, H. T. (2016). Editorial. *Educational Measurement: Issues and Practice, 35*, 3–4.

Hancock, G. R., & Mueller, R. O. (2010). *The reviewer's guide to quantitative methods in the social sciences*. New York, NY: Routledge.

Hoyle, R. H., & Isherwood, J. C. (2013). Reporting results from structural equation modeling analyses in *Archives of Scientific Psychology*. *Archives of Scientific Psychology, 1*, 14–22.

Kranzler, J. H., Grapin, S. L., & Daley, M. L. (2011). Research productivity and scholarly impact of APA-accredited school psychology programs: 2005–2009. *Journal of School Psychology, 49*, 721–738.

Pincus, A. L. (2014). Incoming editorial. *Assessment, 21*, 259.

Salekin, R. T. (2014). Some new directions for publication in the *Journal of Psychopathology and Behavioral Assessment*: New constructs, physiological assessment, worldwide contribution, and economics. *Journal of Psychopathology and Behavioral Assessment, 36*, 1–3.

18 Publishing in Educational Psychology and Education Journals

Daniel H. Robinson

In this chapter, I provide a list of journals that focus on the enhancement of learning in educational settings. I follow with some insights for authors trained in school psychology who are interested in publishing in these journals. I consider myself an educational psychologist. I served as a faculty member for over 20 years, teaching mainly learning and statistics. I was editor of *Educational Psychology Review* from 2006 to 2015 and now serve as an associate editor of the *Journal of Educational Psychology*. My purpose in this chapter is to give you an idea of what is going on in educational and educational psychology research.

This is not the first time I have written for a school psychology audience (Robinson, 2011). Educational psychology is different from school psychology in a few ways. Subject-wise, one could say that educational psychology is sort of a subset of school psychology. School psychology is a broad field that applies principles of several fields, including educational psychology, to promote child and adolescent behavioral health and learning. Educational psychology is simply concerned with the social, emotional, and cognitive processes involved in human learning. Academically, however, school psychology is usually a subset of educational psychology. Typically, Educational Psychology departments exist within Colleges or Schools of Education. Conversely, there are very few Departments of School Psychology, and rather, school psychology programs typically reside within Educational Psychology departments. Educational Psychology departments may contain programs in Counseling Psychology, Measurement and Statistics, Development and Personality, and Learning, Cognition, and Motivation, in addition to School Psychology.

It is no secret that I have been very critical of the type of research that has been published in education and educational psychology journals over the past 30 years (see, for example, www.youtube.com/watch?v=DSHyFmtE69Y). The *Educational Researcher*, flagship journal of the American Educational Opinion (sorry, I mean Research) Association (AERA), has published articles on the use of poetry (Cahnmann, 2003) and autoethnography (Hughes, Pennington, & Makris, 2012) in educational research. Beyond this, and to give you a better sense of my frustration with AERA as an organization and education as a scientific field of study, the 1994 AERA conference even featured a session in which one researcher read a poem about another researcher engaged in a professional activity, while the other researcher displayed a painting of the first researcher similarly engaged (Levin & O'Donnell, 1999). Look through any recent AERA conference program, and I challenge you to find evidence that the study of education in higher education is worthy of taxpayer dollars. Suffice it to say that this chapter will not pull any punches.

According to Clarivate Analytics' Journal Citation Reports, the following are the top ten education journals in the two categories of "Education & Educational Research" and "Psychology, Educational" followed by their 2015 2-year Impact Factor values:

1	*Educational Psychologist*	5.69
2	*Review of Educational Research*	5.24
3	*Educational Research Review*	3.86
4	*Child Development*	3.79
5	*Learning & Instruction*	3.69
6	*Journal of School Psychology*	3.36
7	*Journal of Educational Psychology*	3.26
8	*Journal of Counseling Psychology*	3.15
9	*Journal of the Learning Sciences*	3.14
10	*Journal of Research on Science Teaching*	3.05

Note that the list contains a few journals that are obviously educational psychology journals such as the *Educational Psychologist* and the *Journal of Educational Psychology*. However, the list also includes several journals that would not be considered educational psychology journals, such as *Child Development*, the *Journal of School Psychology* (see Chapter 5), and the *Journal of Counseling Psychology*. For a very subjective list of "purely" educational psychology journals, I offer the journals listed in Table 18.1. This list of journals has as its main focus publishing articles pertaining to learning in educational settings. The best way to get a sense of what types of articles a journal publishes is to simply take a look at a few recent issues. Those of you school psychology folks who feel that the topic of your study might fit best in an educational psychology journal should email the editor (see Table 18.1) and include the abstract. As an editor, I welcome such inquiries and usually can give the author a thumbs-up or -down, in terms of appropriateness, by just reading the abstract.

Finally, I was directed to also provide a list of additional educational psychology journals that do not register an impact factor. These journals are helpful when authors cannot seem to get their work published in the "better" journals. I have extensive experience in this journal "dumpster diving" as there has been more than one occasion when I had to hold my nose and resort to publishing my work in places that had extremely high acceptance rates and very little turnaround time to publication. In the old days, such journals were called "vanity press" as you would get an acceptance decision almost milliseconds after you submitted. Of course, this came with a price. For you to publish your work, you had to fork out "page costs," which could be as much

Table 18.1 Impact Factor Values, Aims and Scope (Taken from Journal Websites), and Editor Email Addresses for the Top Ten Educational Psychology Journals (According to Me)

Journal and 2-yr impact factor (2015)	Aims and scope	Email the editor (2015)
Educational Psychologist (5.69)	Publishes scholarly essays, reviews, critiques, and articles of a theoretical/conceptual nature that contribute to our understanding of the issues, problems, and research associated with the field of educational psychology. Does not publish articles whose primary purpose is to report the method and results of an empirical study.	Kathryn Wentzel, edpsy@umd.edu
Learning and Instruction (3.69)	An international, multi-disciplinary, peer-refereed journal that publishes the most advanced scientific research in the areas of learning, development, instruction and teaching. Publishes original empirical investigations, referring to any age level, from infants to adults and to a diversity of learning and instructional settings, from classroom to informal learning.	Jan Vermunt, jli@elsevier.com
Journal of Educational Psychology (3.26)	Publishes original, primary psychological research pertaining to education across all ages and educational levels. Occasionally publishes exceptionally important theoretical and review articles that are pertinent to educational psychology. Does not typically publish reliability and validity studies of specific tests or assessment instruments.	Steve Graham, steve.graham@asu.edu
Journal of the Learning Sciences (3.14)	A multidisciplinary forum for research on education and learning as theoretical and design sciences. Publishes research that elucidates processes of learning and the ways in which technologies, instructional practices, and learning environments can be designed to support learning in different contexts.	Iris Tabak and Josh Radinsky, journalofthelearningsciences@gmail.com
Educational Psychology Review (2.59)	An international forum for the publication of peer-reviewed integrative review articles, special thematic issues, reflections or comments on previous research or new research directions, interviews, replications, and intervention articles—all pertaining to the field of educational psychology. Provides breadth of coverage appropriate to a wide readership in educational psychology and sufficient depth to inform specialists in that area.	Fred Paas, paas@fsw.eur.nl

Journal and 2-yr impact factor (2015)	Aims and scope	Email the editor (2015)
Contemporary Educational Psychology (2.49)	Publishes articles that involve the application of psychological theory and science to the educational process. Places great value on the quality of research methodology. Publishes quantitative, qualitative, and single-subject design studies that involve the application of psychological science to an important educational process, issue, or problem. Does not limit its scope to any age range and does not focus on a particular educational setting.	Patricia Alexander, palexand@umd.edu
Metacognition and Learning (2.40)	Addresses various components of metacognition, such as metacognitive awareness, experiences, knowledge, and executive skills, employed in learning situations. Submitted papers judged on theoretical relevance, methodological thoroughness, and appeal to an international audience.	Roger Azevedo, roger.azevedo@ mcgill.ca
Cognition and Instruction (2.17)	Addresses foundational issues concerning the mental, socio-cultural, and mediational processes and conditions of learning and intellectual competence. Preferentially attends to the "how" of learning and intellectual practices. Research at multiple levels and involving multiple methods welcomed.	Rogers Hall, rogers. hall@vanderbilt.edu
British Journal of Educational Psychology (2.00)	Publishes psychological research that makes a significant contribution to the understanding and practice of education as well as advances the field in terms of theory related to educational psychology. Accepts empirical and methodological papers, experimental studies, observations of classroom behaviors, interviews, and surveys. Quality of argument and execution, clarity in presentation, and educational significance are valued.	Alice Jones Bartoli, a.jones@gold.ac.uk
Journal of Experimental Education (1.64)	Publishes basic and applied research studies in the laboratory as well as in authentic environments that use the range of quantitative and qualitative methodologies found in the behavioral, cognitive, and social sciences. Accepts investigations that address all levels of schooling and a broad variety of educational contexts in the United States and abroad.	Avi Kaplan, akaplan@temple. edu

as $500 per page. Nowadays, we have renamed such journals "open access," although they still charge authors to publish.

Just so you know, I have published a few recent papers in open access journals and have been pleased with the results. Hopefully, you know that virtually no one outside academia reads our articles in the high-impact journals because they would have to pay to read them. However, if you publish in an open access journal, anyone can read it. Thus, a few years ago, I decided to hand over some grant money to publish a few articles. Rather than measuring the results of this venture via requests for reprints, numbers of citations, etc., instead I began to receive several email inquiries from the business sector requesting my assistance as a paid consultant or evaluator. So, for those of you who could use some extra cash in addition to your lucrative nine-month faculty salary, you might consider similar "dumpster diving." Do so at your own peril. Here are the "dumpster" journals (with no impact factor) in no order or preference where I have published:

- *Springer Plus* (open access)
- *Sage Open* (open access)
- *Journal of Advanced Academics*
- *Journal of Technology, Learning, and Assessment*
- *Research in the Schools*
- *New Directions for Teaching and Learning*
- *International Journal of Higher Education*
- *Newsletter for Educational Psychologists*
- *The Journal of Research in Education*
- *Reading Research and Instruction*

My goal in this chapter is to provide you with some lesser-known insights concerning trends in research published in those educational psychology journals that register an impact factor. My colleagues and I have conducted a few descriptive studies to identify these trends (Hsieh et al., 2005; Reinhart, Haring, Levin, Patall, & Robinson, 2013; Robinson, Levin, Thomas, Pituch, & Vaughn, 2007; Shaw, Walls, Dacy, Levin, & Robinson, 2010). Based on these studies, I offer the following six conclusions.

1   *Educational intervention and experimental research is disappearing*
Intervention research is defined as measuring the effects of a researcher-manipulated independent variable on a learner dependent variable. This kind of research has decreased from 44% of all empirical articles appearing in a group of four educational psychology journals (*Contemporary Educational Psychology, Cognition and Instruction,* the *Journal of Educational Psychology,* and the *Journal of Experimental Education*) and the *American Educational Research Journal* to 26% in 2010. Intervention research that used random assignment (a.k.a. experimental research) decreased from 47% in 1983 to 22% in 2010. For those of you who conduct intervention

and experimental research, these findings do not mean that your studies would not be welcomed in educational psychology journals. On the contrary, when I was editor of *Educational Psychology Review*, we began welcoming intervention studies in an attempt to counter this decline.

2   *Intervention research is being replaced by descriptive research, accompanied by recommendations for practice*
In contrast to intervention research, ex post facto or causal comparative research (called *descriptive research* here) does not involve a researcher-manipulated independent variable. For example, comparing student achievement in 2008 to 2011, or comparing boys to girls, is not an intervention. Descriptive research does not provide strong evidence of causality, which is typically required before a recommendation for practice is warranted. In 1994, only 30% of descriptive articles included such recommendations. However, by 2010, this percentage had increased to 46%. Thus, if you consider this group of journals as representative of the field, almost half of the educational psychology contributions to practice were based on research methods that have weak evidence for causal claims.
A few years ago, I received an email from a junior author who recently published in the *Journal of Educational Psychology*. This person had read some of our work on these trends and shared an experience:

> My original submission didn't include any recommendations for practice, but the reviewers/editor pushed me to include such recommendations in the discussion section. Perhaps you can talk about the role of reviewers/editors in pushing such recommendations. Or perhaps comment on the distinct motivations of reviewers/editor versus publishing scholars to include recommendations for practice.

I have several anecdotal examples of such "pushing" from editors to go beyond my findings. I often lament that when I was a junior faculty member, journal reviewers would frequently chide me for going beyond my data in the results section of my papers. Today, I am chided for *not* going beyond my data. So, a word of caution: you might be encouraged to go beyond your data. But stick to your guns. Don't.

3   *Statistical modeling of descriptive data is on the rise and these articles are more likely to contain recommendations than are articles based on descriptive data that do not use modeling*
This increase in the tendency of authors to make recommendations based on descriptive research coincided with the explosion in the use of statistical modeling techniques (e.g., structural equation modeling, multilevel modeling, etc.) with descriptive data. In 2000, only nine articles out of 135 employed statistical modeling analyses with descriptive data. Six of those articles included recommendations for practice. By 2010, 50 articles

out of 141 used modeling with descriptive data. Twenty-nine of those articles included recommendations for practice. These findings reflect a depressing trend in the field of educational psychology. Authors of empirical articles in educational psychology journals are becoming more likely to base their recommendations for practice on descriptive data accompanied by statistical modeling analyses. Can we blame the modeling analyses? No. Just like other tools, such as null hypothesis significance testing and meta-analysis, modeling is not the problem. It is the people who believe that modeling can somehow magically take descriptive data and crank out causal conclusions. They might be encouraged to do so by editors and reviewers. Perhaps their training in graduate school leads to these false beliefs. In any case, it is shameful.

Have I played a role in these trends? I have served as an associate editor of an empirical journal, the *Journal of Educational Psychology*, since 2014. We looked closely at two years' worth of data, ten years apart to get a sense of the increase in use of statistical modeling. In 1999–2000, only six out of 120 empirical articles used modeling with descriptive data, and only three of those articles included recommendations for practice. By 2009–2010, 56 out of 136 articles used modeling with descriptive data, and 32 included recommendations for practice. This is a trend we need to reverse—fast. I can tell you that none of the articles for which I served as action editor in the past two plus years have been published with recommendations for practice based on descriptive research.

4 *Recommendations based on descriptive data can be repeated in later articles*
Nineteen descriptive articles published in 1994 included a recommendation for practice. Within the next ten years, these 19 articles were cited in 255 later articles. The original recommendation for practice was repeated in 30 of those articles, a rate of 12%. So, the actual "damage" of original recommendations for practice based on weak causal evidence does not simply end with the original publication. Other researchers might repeat the weak claim. Talk about a new definition of "impact" or should we say "swindled" factor! As an author, be careful when citing previous studies to support your hypotheses. Make sure those studies were conducted using methods that permit strong causal evidence.

5 *There is an increasingly global representation in terms of the most productive authors publishing in educational psychology journals*
We should end with something positive for the last two conclusions. In a very recent study (Greenbaum et al., 2016), we found that, in a list of the most productive authors in educational psychology, a clear majority resided outside the United States. Specifically, 16 of the top 19 researchers' institutions were outside the United States, compared to only ten of the top 32 during 2003–2008 and three of the top 20 during 1991–1996. Thus, one could argue that the field of educational psychology has moved

Educational Psych & Education Journals 189

from being largely dominated by prolific United States researchers to becoming ever more international. The field of educational psychology is becoming more international. Keep that audience in mind when writing your papers.

6 *Participation of women in the field of educational psychology in terms of authorships, editorial board memberships, and editorships continues to move closer to matching participation in terms of society membership*
Fong, Yoo, Jones, Torres, and Decker (2009) found that women's membership in the two major organizations that most educational psychologists belong to increased from 28% in 1976 to 63% in 2008. During the same period, women's participation in authorships, editorial board memberships, and editorships increased from 24%, 13%, and 22% to 54%, 47%, and 67%, respectively. Thus, women continue to make gains in the field of educational psychology. This is an encouraging sign and signals that the field welcomes contributions from both genders.

Final Recommendations to Authors

If you are interested in publishing an article that involves research on human learning, broadly defined, there are several decent educational psychology journals that have respectable impact factor ratings. In this chapter, I have listed those journals and also discussed publication trends in educational psychology, some that are encouraging and some that are discouraging. Perhaps school psychology as a field has similar trends. Nonetheless, my advice is to first contact the journal editor to see if your paper is appropriate for the journal. Send your title and abstract. Most editors welcome this as an effective screen. Also, browse a few recent issues of a journal to get a feel for what is published. Do not be angrily surprised if the reviewers do not resonate with research that is behaviorally based. My experience is that most educational psychologists unfairly equate behaviorism with punishment and think it is obsolete. And if you think that most educational psychologists favor cognitive psychology, think again. My cognitive psychology friends have numerous accounts of submitting their work to educational psychology journals and receiving reviews of their papers that reveal ignorance. From my vantage point, motivation is very popular in educational psychology journals. The buzz terms are "mindfulness," "self-regulation," and "goal theory." Many reviewers are socio-constructivists. Qualitative research is increasingly popular in the *American Educational Research Journal*. Yet, those of us who feel educational psychology can be a strong scientific field march on undaunted. As someone who serves as but one gatekeeper for the field of educational psychology, I can only tell you that there are those of us who are striving to make it better.

If I were to look back at all the papers I have rejected as an editor, several common author mistakes come to mind. Lack of a theoretical framework is a common criticism. This can mean that you simply failed to review pertinent

190 *Daniel H. Robinson*

literature. But it more likely means that you did not set up your study in a way so that it tests meaningful hypotheses. Another common criticism is the "who cares?" question. You may have a well-executed study, but your study and its findings do not contribute to the field. Does your study produce new knowledge that advances our thinking? Finally, and related to something discussed earlier, is the criticism that your recommendations are not supported by your data. Lots of authors like to pull out the soapbox for the final paragraphs and preach about how we can improve the world. But please limit these pontifications to what your present data support. If you have weak causal evidence, refrain from making recommendations.

I encourage you to check out the educational psychology journals I have listed in this chapter. Perhaps your research can inform our field and encourage interdisciplinary exchange. As an editor, I would welcome your inquiries. But please, no poetry.

References

Cahnmann, M. (2003). The craft, practice, and possibility of poetry in educational research. *Educational Researcher, 32*(3), 29–36.

Fong, C. J., Yoo, J. H., Jones, S. J., Torres, L. G., & Decker, M. L. (2009). Trends in female authorships, editorial board memberships, and editorships in educational psychology journals from 2003–2008. *Educational Psychology Review, 21*, 267–277.

Greenbaum, H., Meyer, L., Smith, M. C., Barber, A., Henderson, H., Riel, D., & Robinson, D. H. (2016). Individual and institutional productivity in educational psychology journals from 2009–2014. *Educational Psychology Review, 28*, 215–223. doi: 10.1007/s10648-016-9360-8

Hsieh, P.-H., Hsieh, Y.-P., Chung, W.-H., Acee, T., Thomas, G. D., Kim, H.-J., et al. (2005). Is educational intervention research on the decline? *Journal of Educational Psychology, 97*, 523–529.

Hughes, S., Pennington, J. L., & Makris, S. (2012). Translating autoethnography across the AERA standards: Toward understanding autoethnographic scholarship as empirical research. *Educational Researcher, 41*(6), 209–219.

Levin, J. R., & O'Donnell, A. M. (1999). What to do about educational research's credibility gaps? *Issues in Education: Contributions from Educational Psychology, 5*, 177–229.

Reinhart, A. L., Haring, S. H., Levin, J. R., Patall, E. A., & Robinson, D. H. (2013). Models of not-so-good behavior: Yet another way to squeeze causality and recommendations for practice out of correlational data. *Journal of Educational Psychology, 105*, 241–247.

Robinson, D. H. (2011). Thoughts and recommendations concerning impact and productivity in school psychology journals. *Journal of School Psychology, 49*, 745–749.

Robinson, D. H., Levin, J. R., Thomas, G. D., Pituch, K. A., & Vaughn, S. R. (2007). The incidence of "causal" statements in teaching and learning research journals. *American Educational Research Journal, 44*, 400–413.

Shaw, S. M., Walls, S. M., Dacy, B. S., Levin, J. R., & Robinson, D. H. (2010). A follow-up note on prescriptive statements in nonintervention research studies. *Journal of Educational Psychology, 102*, 982–988.

19 Publishing in Special Education and Literacy Journals

Elizabeth B. Meisinger and
Melissa F. Robinson

The field of school psychology is interdisciplinary in nature, and this diversity is reflected in the scholarly works we produce. The majority of journal articles (70%) from 2005–2009 generated by faculty from school psychology programs accredited by the American Psychological Association were published across a wide range of social and behavioral sciences journals rather than in major school psychology outlets (Kranzler, Grapin, & Daley, 2011). School psychologists routinely work with students who are either currently receiving, or who could be eligible for, special education services, along with their parents, teachers, and school administrators, to promote a positive learning environment. In particular, concerns regarding reading difficulties represent the most common reason for a student to be referred to their school psychologist (Bramlett, Murphy, Johnson, Wallingsford, & Hall, 2002) with as many as 79% of students referred to their school psychologist experiencing difficulties in reading (Nelson & Machek, 2007). Therefore, it is likely that school psychologists might have a particularly keen interest in publishing in special education and literacy journals. This chapter will review special education and literacy journals, with the goal of providing information to guide scholars in the field of school psychology in the selection of publication outlets in these areas.

Special Education Journals

Special education journals were identified for inclusion in this chapter by conducting a search using the Journal Citation Reports, PsycINFO, and Scopus databases. Journals that focused on a narrow topic area within special education (i.e., *American Annals of the Deaf*) were excluded for the sake of parsimony. Although the majority of the journals were identified by all three database searches, each search resulted in a handful of non-redundant titles. This procedure identified a total of 19 special education journals. A description of each journal's aim and scope, the 2015 Thomson Reuters 2- and 5-year Impact Factors from the Journal Citation Reports database, the type of submissions accepted, and the recommended manuscript length are provided in Table 19.1. Given the variation in special education laws, policies, and

Table 19.1 Journals Addressing Special Education

Journal	Description and website page	2015 2-yr/5-yr impact factor	Submission types	Recommended manuscript length
British Journal of Special Education*	Covers the range of learning difficulties of children in mainstream and special schools. Targets members of the National Association for Special Educational Needs, administrators, advisers, teacher educators, and researchers in the United Kingdom. http://onlinelibrary.wiley.com/journal/10.1111/(ISSN)1467-8578	None	A, B	4,000–6,000 words
Education & Treatment of Children	Addresses the development of services for children and youth. Strives to offer content of direct value to educators, parents, child care providers, or mental health professionals. www.educationandtreatmentofchildren.net/	0.49/None	A, B, C, E, J	20–30 pages
European Journal of Special Needs Education*	Provides a forum for reporting and reviewing scholarly research and significant developments in the field of special education. Written for teachers and researchers. www.tandfonline.com/toc/rejs20/current	0.61/None	B, C, E	7,000 words
Exceptional Children	Publishes papers on the education and development of children and youth with exceptionalities. www.cec.sped.org/Publications/CEC-Journals/Exceptional-Children	2.80/3.23	A, B	NR
Exceptionality	Provides a forum for presentation of current research and professional scholarship in special education. Welcomes basic, experimental, applied, naturalistic, ethnographic, and historical investigations and papers describing assessment, diagnosis, placement, teacher education, and service delivery. www.tandfonline.com/loi/hexc20	0.32/0.95	A, B, C, D, F, G, I	NR
Exceptionality Education International*	Publishes original, peer-reviewed articles and reviews addressing pedagogy, school and system organization and management, curricula, policy, inclusion, marginalization, international and national trends, classroom practice, adult education, educational innovations and initiatives, and teacher education. http://ir.lib.uwo.ca/eei/	None	A, B	30 pages

Journal	Description and website page	2015 2-yr/5-yr impact factor	Submission types	Recommended manuscript length
Infants & Young Children*	Focuses on children with or at risk for disabilities from age birth to five years. Emphasizes innovative interventions, summaries of research developments, updates for high priority topic areas, balanced presentations of controversial issues, and articles that address issues involving policy, professional training, and new conceptual models. http://journals.lww.com/iycjournal/pages/default.aspx	0.59/1.05	A, B, C	25 pages
International Journal of Disability Development & Education*	Addresses the education and development of persons with disabilities. Publishes research and review articles concerned with education, human development, special education, and rehabilitation. www.tandfonline.com/toc/cijd20/current	0.74/0.88	A, B	5,000–7,000 words
International Journal of Special Education*	Publishes original experimental and theoretical articles concerning special education, with an international focus. www.internationaljournalofspecialeducation.com/	None	A, B, C, F, G, I	NR
Intervention in School & Clinic	Equips teachers and clinicians with hands-on tips, techniques, methods, and ideas for improving assessment, instruction, and management for individuals with learning disabilities or behavior disorders. Articles focus on curricular, instructional, social, behavioral, assessment, and vocational strategies and techniques that have a direct application to the classroom settings. http://isc.sagepub.com/	0.20/0.40	A, B, C, I	9–18 pages
Journal of Early Intervention	Offers articles related to research and practice in early intervention for infants and young children with special needs. Addresses procedures that facilitate the development of infants and young children who have special needs or who are at risk for developmental disabilities. http://jei.sagepub.com/	0.66/1.78	A, B	35 pages

(continued)

Table 19.1 Journals Addressing Special Education (*continued*)

Journal	Description and website page	2015 2-yr/5-yr impact factor	Submission types	Recommended manuscript length
Journal of Research in Special Educational Needs	Publishes papers on meeting special educational needs. Offers a forum for researchers to reflect on, and share ideas regarding, issues of particular importance. http://onlinelibrary.wiley.com/journal/10.1111/(ISSN)1471-3802	None	A, B	6,000–8,000 words
Journal of Special Education	Provides research articles and scholarly reviews on special education for individuals with mild to severe disabilities. Publishes traditional, ethnographic, and single-subject research; intervention studies; integrative reviews; critical commentaries; and special thematic issues. http://sed.sagepub.com/	1.42/2.09	A, B, C, F, G, H, I	30 pages
Remedial & Special Education	Emphasizes the interpretation of research literature and recommendations for the practice of remedial and special education. Addresses definitions, identification, assessment, characteristics, management, and instruction of underachieving and exceptional children, youth, and adults; related services; family involvement; service delivery systems; legislation; litigation; and professional standards and training. http://rse.sagepub.com/	2.02/1.81	A, B	20–30 pages
Research and Practice for Persons with Severe Disabilities	Publishes articles on topics such as inclusion, augmentative and alternative communication, supported living and employment, early childhood issues, self-advocacy, positive behavioral supports, and disability rights. http://rps.sagepub.com/	0.74/1.16	A, B, C, E, I	25–35 pages

Journal	Description and website page	2015 2-yr/5-yr impact factor	Submission types	Recommended manuscript length
*Research in Developmental Disabilities**	Focuses on original, interdisciplinary research that has a direct bearing on the understanding or remediation of problems associated with developmental disabilities. Publishes primarily empirical studies addressing aspects of developmental difficulties using rigorous research methods. http://www.journals.elsevier.com/research-in-developmental-disabilities/	1.88/2.18	A, B	8,000 words
Support for Learning	Examines the practical and theoretical issues surrounding the education of pupils with special educational needs in mainstream schools. Addresses curriculum delivery, classroom management, and the use of support services. Strategies to eliminate underachievement and promote best practice are featured. http://onlinelibrary.wiley.com/journal/10.1111/(ISSN)1467-9604	None	A, B	3,000–5,000 words
Topics in Early Childhood Special Education	Focuses on information that will improve the lives of young children with special needs. Features original research, literature reviews, conceptual statements, position papers, and program descriptions. http://tec.sagepub.com/	1.14/1.66	A, B, C, D, F	35 pages

Note. Descriptions of each journal were obtained from the journals' websites, following headings such as "aim and scope" and "author guidelines," and edited for content. The 2015 journal impact factor values were obtained from Clarivate Analytics' Journal Citation Reports database. * = international journals; NR = not reported. Based on Floyd et al. (2011), A = full-length research articles (i.e., descriptive, correlational, meta-analysis, causal-comparative, and causal-experimental), B = full-length narrative articles (e.g., narrative review articles, theoretical articles, professional developmental articles), C = brief research articles, D = test reviews, E = book reviews, F = historical articles, G = narrative case studies (not employing research designs), H = obituaries and commemorative reports, I = comments, commentary, reaction articles, or letters to the editor, J = award addresses, and K = other.

196 *Meisinger & Robinson*

practices across countries, it seemed important to further denote the eight journals with an international focus. An examination of the 2- and 5-year Impact Factors for the special education journals reveals a wide range of values (0.20 to 2.80 and 0.40 to 3.23, respectively), and it is notable that six of the 19 journals (32%) do not generate impact factors. Although it is important to keep in mind the impact factors represent only one metric for gauging the quality of a journal, it is notable that *Exceptional Children, Remedial and Special Education*, and *Research in Developmental Disabilities*, produced the strongest values and are widely considered to be top outlets in this field.

When selecting an outlet for your work, it might be helpful to consider the overlap between a particular special education journal with the school psychology literature. One way to address this intersectionality is to examine how often a particular special education journal cites articles published in primary school psychology journals (and vice versa). Five school psychology journals are indexed in Clarivate Analytics' Journal Citation Reports (i.e., *Journal of School Psychology, Psychology in the Schools, School Psychology International, School Psychology Review*, and *School Psychology Quarterly*). The 100 most frequently citing or most frequently cited journals for each of these five school psychology journals (across the past 10+ years) were identified and sorted by the number of citations, selecting the 200 most frequently citing or cited journals. Of those special education journals listed in Table 19.1, a total of 11 journals were identified among the 200 journals that most frequently cite these school psychology journals. Six of the 11 special education journals were found to have 20 or more citations from at least three school psychology journals; these six journals were *Education and Treatment of Children, Intervention in School and Clinic, Exceptional Children, Research in Developmental Disabilities, Journal of Special Education*, and *Remedial and Special Education*. Seven special education journals reviewed in this chapter were also represented among the top 200 journals most frequently cited by school psychology literature (as represented by the five school psychology journals previously listed). Five of the seven were cited 20 times or more across at least three school psychology journals; these five journals are *Exceptional Children, Journal of Special Education, Remedial and Special Education, Education and Treatment of Children*, and *Journal of Behavioral Education*.[1] It is notable that nearly all the special education journals most often cited by school psychology journals (six out of seven) were also listed among the 11 special education journals that most often cite the school psychology literature. (*Journal of Behavioral Education* was the sole exception.) In sum, although variation exists in the frequency with which special education journals cite works from school psychology journals (and vice versa), the overlap across citing and cited journals in special education suggests some clear cross-disciplinary citation patterns.

Literacy Journals

Literacy journals were identified using the same general methods as we previously described, and journals that publish a smattering of articles on literacy (e.g., *Journal of Educational Psychology*) or that focus on the neurobiological basis of cognitive processes (e.g., *Neuropsychologia*) were excluded. A total of 16 literacy journals were identified for inclusion in this chapter. Table 19.2 provides a description of the aim and scope, the 2015 2- and 5-year Impact Factors from the Clarivate Analytics' Journal Citation Reports databases, the types of submissions accepted, and the recommended manuscript length for each journal. Journals with an international focus or which primarily address reading disabilities are further denoted. An examination of the 2- and 5-year Impact Factors for the literacy journals reveals a wide range of values (0.45 to 2.75 and 0.55 to 3.17, respectively). Consistent with their reputation as top literacy outlets, *Reading Research Quarterly* and *Scientific Studies of Reading* had the highest 2- and 5-year Impact Factors.

When selecting a literacy outlet for your work, it might also be useful to consider the cross-disciplinary interplay between that journal and the school psychology literature. Using the same procedure described in the special education section, we found that only three of these literacy journals were identified among the 200 journals that most frequently cite the five primary school psychology journals (*Reading & Writing: An Interdisciplinary Journal, Dyslexia: An International Journal of Research & Practice*, and *Learning Disability Quarterly*). Conversely, only five of these literacy journals were among those journals that are most often cited by the school psychology literature (*Scientific Studies of Reading, Journal of Learning Disabilities, Reading and Writing Quarterly, Learning Disability Quarterly*, and *Reading & Writing: An Interdisciplinary Journal*). Further, only two journals are presented on both lists of journals that cite and are cited by school psychology journals, *Reading and Writing: An Interdisciplinary Journal* and *Learning Disabilities Quarterly*. Together, these data suggest that there is little exchange between the literacy and school psychology literatures, which is rather surprising given the amount of time school psychologists devote to working with students with reading difficulties. It is also notable that if journals focusing on reading disabilities had not been included in this section, no literacy journal would have been identified as frequently citing articles in school psychology journals, and only two journals would have been identified as frequently cited by school psychology outlets. These findings suggest the overlap among these literatures is concentrated in the area of reading disabilities rather than typical reading development and curriculum.

Recommendations for Authors

Based on the information presented in Tables 19.1 and 19.2, several recommendations can be offered to scholars in the field of school psychology who wish to submit their work to special education or literacy journals. First, the summary information provided in these tables can be used to develop a preliminary list of journals that might be well suited to your manuscript. For

Table 19.2 Journals Addressing Literacy

Journal	Description and website page	2015 2-yr IF/5-yr IF	Submission types	Recommended manuscript length
Annals of Dyslexia[b]	Focuses on the scientific study of dyslexia, its comorbid conditions, and theory-based practices on remediation and intervention of dyslexia and related areas of written language disorders. https://dyslexiaida.org/annals-of-dyslexia/	1.00/1.77	A, B	NR
Dyslexia: An International Journal of Research & Practice[a b]	Provides reviews and reports of research, assessment and intervention practice. Addresses interesting developments, both theoretical and practical, reported internationally. http://onlinelibrary.wiley.com/journal/10.1002/(ISSN)1099-0909	1.43/1.56	A, B, C, I	15 pages
Journal of Adolescent & Adult Literacy	Published exclusively for teachers of older learners. http://onlinelibrary.wiley.com/journal/10.1002/(ISSN)1936-2706	0.72/0.80	A, B, C, G, I	4,000–6,000 words
Journal of Early Childhood Literacy	Addresses research related to the nature, function, and use of literacy in early childhood. http://ecl.sagepub.com/	None	A, B, C, F	6,000–8,000 words
Journal of Learning Disabilities[b]	Publishes articles on practice, research, and theory related to learning disabilities. Offers an international, multi-disciplinary perspective. http://ldx.sagepub.com/	1.64/2.38	A	35–40 pages
Journal of Literacy Research	Publishes research related to literacy, language, and literacy and language education from preschool through adulthood. http://jlr.sagepub.com/	0.73 1.25	A, B, I	9,500 words
Journal of Research in Reading[a]	Provides an international forum for researchers that is devoted to reports of original empirical research in reading and related fields such as writing and spelling. http://onlinelibrary.wiley.com/journal/10.1111/(ISSN)1467-9817	0.92/1.35	A, B, C	5,000–8,000 words

Journal	Description and website page	2015 2-yr IF/5-yr IF	Submission types	Recommended manuscript length
Learning Disability Quarterly[b]	Publishes research and scholarship concerning children, youth, and adults with learning disabilities that has the potential to impact and improve educational outcomes, opportunities, and services. http://ldq.sagepub.com/	0.73/1.24	A, B, I	35 pages
Literacy	Offers educators a forum for those interested in the study and development of literacy and for debate through scrutinizing research evidence, reflecting on analyzed accounts of innovative practice, and examining recent policy developments. http://onlinelibrary.wiley.com/journal/10.1111/(ISSN)1741-4369	0.89/0.73	A, B, C, I	3,000–5,000 words
Literacy Research & Instruction	Publishes articles on aspects of literacy related to the four major areas of the organization: teacher education, college reading, clinical, and adult learning. www.tandfonline.com/toc/ulri20/current	None	A, B	25 pages
Reading & Writing Quarterly: Overcoming Learning Difficulties[b]	Provides direction for educating preschool through grade 12 students for literacy. It disseminates critical information to improve instruction for regular and special education students who have, or who are at-risk for having, difficulty learning to read and write. Interdisciplinary in scope, the journal addresses the causes, prevention, evaluation, and remediation of reading and writing difficulties in regular and special education settings. www.tandfonline.com/loi/urwl20	0.45/0.55	A, B, E	30 pages
Reading & Writing: An Interdisciplinary Journal	Publishes high-quality scientific articles pertaining to the processes, acquisition, and the loss of reading and writing skills. http://www.springer.com/linguistics/journal/11145	1.31/1.83	A, B, C, D, E	30 pages

(continued)

Table 19.2 Journals Addressing Literacy (*continued*)

Journal	Description and website page	2015 2-yr IF/5-yr IF	Submission types	Recommended manuscript length
Reading Psychology	Publishes original manuscripts in the fields of literacy, reading, and related psychology disciplines. Articles appear in the form of completed research; practitioner-based "experiential" methods or philosophical statements; teacher and counselor preparation services for guiding all levels of reading skill development, attitudes, and interests; programs or materials; and literary or humorous contributions. www.tandfonline.com/toc/urpy20/current	None	A, B, I	NR
Reading Research Quarterly	Highlights global scholarship on literacy among learners of all ages. http://onlinelibrary.wiley.com/journal/10.1002/(ISSN)1936-2722	2.09/3.17	A, B, C	16,000 words
The Reading Teacher	Addresses professional reading for everyone who works with children up to age 12. http://onlinelibrary.wiley.com/journal/10.1002/%28ISSN%291936-2714	0.70/0.89	A, B, C, I	5,000–6,000 words
Scientific Studies of Reading	Publishes original empirical investigations on all aspects of reading and literacy. www.tandfonline.com/toc/hssr20/current	2.75/2.89	A, C	6,000 words

Note. Descriptions of each journal were obtained from the journals' websites, following headings such as "aim and scope" and "author guidelines," and edited for content. The 2015 journal impact factor values were obtained from Clarivate Analytics' Journal Citation Reports database. a = international journals; b = journals that focus on reading disabilities. NR = not reported. Based on Floyd et al. (2011), A = full-length research articles (i.e., descriptive, correlational, meta-analysis, causal-comparative, and causal-experimental), B = full-length narrative articles (e.g., narrative review articles, theoretical articles, professional developmental articles), C = brief research articles, D = test reviews, E = book reviews, F = historical articles, G = narrative case studies (not employing research designs), H = obituaries and commemorative reports, I = comments, commentary, reaction articles, or letters to the editor, J = award addresses, and K = other.

example, not all journals accept narrative case studies or test reviews, so even a cursory review of these tables might help authors narrow their search for appropriate outlets. If you are preparing a rather lengthy manuscript describing a meta-analysis, a journal with a more conservative page length (e.g., *British Journal of Special Education*) or one that has a primarily practitioner audience (e.g., *The Reading Teacher*) might be a poor fit. Impact factors might be useful in determining the suitability of a journal in light of the quality of a particular manuscript. However, variation exists across literatures regarding what is considered an acceptable value, and sometimes journals with strong reputations within their own field have lower-than-expected values or do not produce impact factors. In general, do not be afraid to submit your work to a journal that does not produce an impact factor value. After all, it is better to publish your work in any peer-reviewed outlet than not to have it published at all!

Carefully consider the match between the purpose of your paper and the aim and scope of the journal. If the manuscript utilized an international sample (from outside of United States) of special education students, then one of the eight special educational journals with an international focus might be a reasonable place to start. Similarly, if the manuscript you are preparing for submission to a literacy journal utilized a clinical or at-risk sample, then a journal focusing on reading disabilities might be an appropriate option.

Once a list of preliminary outlets has been identified, it might be useful to consider the degree of overlap between the journal and the school psychology literature in terms of their citation history. With regard to special education literature, the six journals that are listed as being often citing and cited by the school psychology journals might represent particularly good potential outlets for scholars in the field of school psychology, given their history of cross-disciplinary interplay with the school psychology literature. Given the limited citation overlap between the school psychology and literacy literatures, particular consideration regarding the alignment of the manuscript's topic to the literacy journal might be needed. Based on our own experience publishing across these literatures, the field of school psychology appears to be more assessment focused and behaviorally oriented than the reading literature, and it is now largely embedded in the response to intervention (RTI) framework. We often ask ourselves whether the topic is broad enough to warrant submission to a literacy outlet. Thus, would this paper be of interest to a reading educator or a reading researcher whose approach might not be entirely congruent with the RTI framework? As such, if the paper is heavily assessment oriented and addresses issues primarily related to RTI, we tend to focus on a school psychology outlet.

Once your list has been further narrowed, consider examining a few recent issues of the targeted journals. This sort of up-close examination will give you a feel for the sample sizes, methodology, and content that are typical. It might even be helpful to review the list of editorial board members to determine whether the literature cited in the paper overlaps with that produced by the board members who are likely to review your paper. For example, if you have cited several papers published in that journal and can easily integrate citations from works produced by editorial board members in your paper, then it is likely a good match to your work. If you are unsure as to whether your topic is appropriate, consider contacting the journal editor for guidance. On a related note, do not wait until you are done writing your paper to select the journal outlet. If you know your intended audience and potential reviewers, then you will be better able to tailor your manuscript to that journal. If you are seeking to publish in a journal that is a bit outside your specific area of expertise, inviting a coauthor with expertise in that literature can be another way to ensure that the submission will meet the expectations of that literature.

Once you have selected the potential outlet for your work, familiarize yourself with any peer-review guidelines available from that journal's website. Although there is a fair amount of commonality across journals in terms of the key aspects addressed in reviewer guidelines, considerable variation exists in terms of the specific criteria used to assess the manuscript's features (see Maggin, Chafouleas, Berggren, & Sugai, 2013). Also, be sure to review submission guidelines carefully as failing to following these guidelines could lead to an outright rejection of your work. Last, carefully proofread your paper to ensure adherence to recommendations in the *Publication Manual of the American Psychological Association*, clarity, cohesion, and the absence of grammatical or typographical errors.

In sum, the time and energy devoted to selecting an appropriate outlet for your work and in preparing your manuscript to meet the guidelines and expectations for that journal is well spent. Selecting an appropriate outlet for your paper will increase the likelihood of having it accepted for publication and could prevent the frustration associated with having a paper repeatedly rejected due to poor fit. We hope that the information in this chapter will assist you in selecting appropriate publication outlets in special education and literacy for your work.

Note

1 *Journal of Behavioral Education* is not reviewed in this chapter as a summary is provided in Chapter 16 offered by Ardoin and Ayers.

References

Bramlett, R. K., Murphy, J. J., Johnson, J., Wallingsford, L., & Hall, J. D. (2002). Contemporary practices in school psychology: A national survey of roles and referral problems. *Psychology in the Schools, 39*, 327–335.

Floyd, R. G., Cooley, K. M., Arnett, J. E., Fagan, T. K., Mercer, S. H., & Hingle, C. (2011). An overview and analysis of journal operations, journal publication patterns, and journal impact in school psychology and related fields. *Journal of School Psychology, 49*, 617–647.

Kranzler, J. H., Grapin, S. L., & Daley, M. L. (2011). Research productivity and scholarly impact of APA-accredited school psychology programs: 2005–2009. *Journal of School Psychology, 49*, 721–738.

Maggin, D. M., Chafouleas, S. M., Berggren, M., & Sugai, G. (2013). A systematic appraisal of peer review guidelines for special education journals. *Exceptionality, 21,* 87–102.

Nelson, J. M., & Machek, G. R. (2007). A survey of training, practice, and competence in reading assessment and intervention. *School Psychology Review, 36,* 311–327.

20 Publishing in Clinical and Pediatric Journals

Thomas J. Power and Katy E. Tresco

School psychologists publish in a wide range of journals outside the field of school psychology, including clinical child and pediatric psychology journals as well as journals in medicine and prevention science. Why would a school psychologist want to publish in clinical and pediatric journals? First, school psychologists might be interested in disseminating their work to a network of researchers, educators, and clinicians who are engaged in activities related to a particular theme or child condition, such as attention-deficit/hyperactivity disorder (ADHD), autism spectrum disorder (ASD), anxiety and depression, violence prevention, chronic illness, and health promotion. Journals publishing research, reviews, and case illustrations on these topics often operate outside the field of school psychology and might be geared to professionals across many disciplines. School psychologists might decide that their work can have the greatest impact on science, practice, and policy by publishing in these types of journals.

Second, researchers and professionals from many disciplines are invested in improving children's health and development by helping children learn and succeed in school. Some of this work is conducted in non-school settings (e.g., hospitals, pediatric primary care practices, and mental health agencies), even though the services can have an effect on adjustment in school (e.g., Canter & Roberts, 2012; Logan, Simons, & Kacsynski, 2009; Power et al., 2012). In addition, some important research has focused on the intersection of schools and health practices to promote coordinated care for children (e.g., Bradley-Klug et al., 2013). Sometimes research and clinical activities that are school-linked versus school-based might be a better fit with clinical or pediatric journals as opposed to school psychology publications.

Third, journals vary widely in their impact on science, as indicated by the journal impact factor, which is a function of the number of times that articles in a journal are cited in the literature. Although some school psychology journals have relatively high impact factors compared to other journals in the same discipline, Clarivate Analytics' Journal Citation Reports impact factors of some journals in clinical psychology, pediatrics, and prevention are higher than those in school psychology. As such, publishing in certain journals outside of school psychology could have a greater impact on science, or at least be perceived that way.

Fourth, there are some journals, particularly those in medicine (e.g., *Pediatrics*), that have an excellent track record of disseminating the findings of published studies in high-profile media outlets. Publishing in these journals can enhance the impact of the study on policy and practice. Fifth, publishing in clinical and pediatric journals might be career enhancing for some researchers in school psychology. In research-intensive universities, the impact factor of faculty publications is often given strong consideration in promotion decisions. Indeed, the faculty in many research-oriented school psychology programs often publish in clinical and pediatric journals (Kranzler, Grapin, & Daley, 2011). Further, some school psychologists are on the faculty in schools of medicine within university settings. Publishing in medical journals might be highly valued in these settings and could accelerate the rate of promotion and enhance one's standing in the university.

Clinical and Pediatric Journals

This chapter presents a wide range of journals in the clinical and pediatric areas. Because of the high volume of journals in each category, only a limited sample could be included. The term "clinical" is used in this chapter to refer to the broad range of journals in clinical psychology, psychiatry, and mental health; "pediatric" is used to refer to journals in pediatric psychology, pediatrics, and prevention.

Factors Considered in Selecting Journals

Several factors were considered in selecting journals to be reviewed and included in this chapter. First, we identified clinical and pediatric journals that had the most influence on school psychology research, as indicated by the journals most often cited in school psychology journals according to the Web of Science database. Second, we identified clinical and pediatric journals most influenced by school psychology research, as indicated by the journals that most often cite articles published in school psychology journals according to the Web of Science database. Third, we considered the major publication outlets of school psychology researchers, as identified in the study published by Kranzler and colleagues (2011). Fourth, we identified journals affiliated with professional associations affiliated with school psychology, including Divisions 53 (Clinical Child and Adolescent Psychology) and 54 (Pediatric Psychology) of the American Psychological Association, the American Academy of Child and Adolescent Psychiatry, the American Academy of Pediatrics, the Society for Developmental and Behavioral Pediatrics, the Association of Psychologists in Academic Health Centers, and the International Society of Research in Child and Adolescent Psychopathology. Fifth, we purposefully included a diverse range of journals for school psychologists interested in publishing original research, literature reviews, illustrations of research into practice, and case illustrations. Finally, we included journals with a wide range of impact

206 *Thomas J. Power & Katy E. Tresco*

factors and degree of difficulty with regard to acceptance rates, so that the listing might be useful for researchers, educators, and practitioners with diverse interests in publication.

Brief Description of the Journals

The journals described in this chapter were divided into three sections: clinical, pediatric, and special populations. Examples of journals in each category are described in Tables 20.1 to 20.3.

Clinical

Several moderate- to high-impact clinical journals are available as outlets for original research (see Table 20.1). *Journal of Consulting and Clinical Psychology* is a highly regarded journal that publishes research with both child and adult populations. Many of the publications in this journal use randomized controlled trials supported by federal grants. Two highly rated clinical journals with a specific focus on child and adolescent populations are *Journal of Clinical Child and Adolescent Psychology* and *Journal of Abnormal Child Psychology* (JACP). Both of these journals publish articles with strong relevance to clinical researchers, but JACP also includes articles with high theoretical relevance. Another high-impact journal focusing on children and adolescents is the *Journal of the American Academy of Child and Adolescent Psychiatry*. Although the primary target audience of this journal is child psychiatrists, the readership includes academicians and clinicians in psychology.

Several journals have particular relevance for school psychologists engaged in school mental health research, and school psychologists often publish in these journals. *School Mental Health* is an interdisciplinary journal that places a priority on original intervention and prevention research. The *Journal of Emotional and Behavioral Disorders* places a priority on mental health research across a range of settings, but a relatively high percentage of the articles included in this publication focus on school-based mental health research.

Two additional journals, *Child & Youth Care Forum* and *Children and Youth Services Review*, were included because the articles in these publications quite often cite papers in the major school psychology journals. Although school psychologists might not commonly publish in these journals, they might want to consider doing so; these journals appear to be highly influenced by research being conducted in the field of school psychology.

Pediatric

School psychologists have several options for publishing their work in health psychology journals (see Table 20.2). *Journal of Pediatric Psychology*, which has

Table 20.1 Clinical Journals

Journal and website	Journal description and types of articles published	2015 2-year IF/ 5-year IF
Journal of Consulting and Clinical Psychology www.apa.org/pubs/journals/ccp/	Publishes articles on treatment and prevention in clinical and clinical-health psychology that appeal to a broad clinical-scientist and practitioner audience, including populations that fall anywhere within the lifespan. Focuses on implications for clinical practice and includes the development, validity, and use of techniques of diagnosis and treatment of disordered behavior; populations of interest; cross-cultural, diversity or demographic factors; personality and its assessment and development; and psychosocial aspects of health behaviors. Considers critical analyses and meta-analyses of treatment approaches and methodologically sound single-case designs. **Types of articles:** Original research, brief reports, commentaries, and conceptual papers **Professional affiliation:** American Psychological Association	4.71/6.66
Journal of Clinical Child and Adolescent Psychology www.tandfonline.com/loi/hcap20	Publishes articles focusing on the development and evaluation of assessment and intervention techniques for use with clinical child and adolescent populations, the development and maintenance of clinical child and adolescent problems, cross-cultural and sociodemographic issues that have a clear bearing on clinical child and adolescent psychology, and training and professional practice in clinical child and adolescent psychology and child advocacy. Considers theoretical and/or methodological issues on topics pertinent to clinical child and adolescent psychology. **Types of Articles:** Original research, brief reports, and future directions (by invitation only) **Professional Affiliation:** Society of Clinical Child and Adolescent Psychology (APA Div. 53)	4.03/3.95
Journal of Abnormal Child Psychology http://link.springer.com/journal/10802	Publishes research on psychopathology in childhood and adolescence, with an emphasis on empirical studies of the major childhood disorders. Features studies highlighting risk and protective factors, the ecology and correlates of children's behavior problems, and advances in prevention and treatment. **Types of articles:** Original research **Professional affiliation:** International Society for Research in Child and Adolescent Psychopathology	3.58/4.12

(continued)

Table 20.1 Clinical Journals (*countinued*)

Journal and website	Journal description and types of articles published	2015 2-year IF/ 5-year IF
Journal of the American Academy of Child and Adolescent Psychiatry www.jaacap.com/	Seeks to advance the science of pediatric mental health and promoting the care of youth and their families. Relevant topics focus on the mental health of children, adolescents, and families as well as health policy, legislation, advocacy, culture and society, and service provision. **Types of articles:** Original research, review articles, clinical review articles, and letters to the editor (published at editor's discretion) **Professional affiliation:** American Academy of Child and Adolescent Psychiatry	7.18/8.72
School Mental Health http://link.springer.com/ journal/12310	Publishes research on prevention, education, and treatment practices that target the emotional and behavioral health of children in the education system. Addresses innovative school-based treatment practices; training procedures; educational techniques for children with emotional and behavioral disorders; racial, ethnic, and cultural issues; and the role of families in school mental health. Welcomes perspectives from fields of education, pediatrics, psychiatry, psychology, counseling, social work, and nursing. **Types of articles:** Original research, review articles, and theoretical papers	1.21/Not available
Journal of Emotional and Behavioral Disorders http://ebx.sagepub.com/	Publishes interdisciplinary research, practice, and commentary related to individuals with emotional and behavioral disabilities. Focuses on child and adolescent characteristics, assessment, prevention, intervention, treatment, legal or policy issues, and evaluation. Welcomes perspectives from a wide range of disciplines. **Types of articles:** Original research, review articles, discussion papers, and descriptions of programs or practices **Professional affiliation:** Hammill Institute on Disabilities	1.95/1.95

Journal and website	Journal description and types of articles published	2015 2-year IF/ 5-year IF
Child & Youth Care Forum http://link.springer.com/ journal/10566	Publishes research that has implications for child and adolescent mental health, psychosocial development, assessment, interventions, and services. Addresses influences on children, youth, and families and welcomes contributions from scholars across disciplines as well as government agencies and corporate and nonprofit organizations. **Types of articles:** Original research, theoretical reviews, and invited commentaries	1.00/1.33
Children and Youth Services Review www.journals.elsevier.com/ children-and-youth- services-review/	Aims to provide an interdisciplinary forum for critical scholarship regarding service programs for children and youth. **Types of articles:** Original research, current research and policy notes, and book reviews	0.97/1.52

Note. Descriptions of each journal and type of manuscripts accepted were obtained from the journal's website, following headings such as "aim and scope" and "author guidelines." These descriptions were edited for content. The 2015 journal impact factor values were obtained from Clarivate Analytics' Journal Citation Reports database and rounded to two decimal places.

Table 20.2 Pediatric Journals

Journal and website	Journal description and types of articles published	2015 2-year IF/ 5-year IF
Journal of Pediatric Psychology http://jpepsy. oxfordjournals.org/	Publishes articles related to theory, research, and professional practice in pediatric psychology, which is an interdisciplinary field addressing physical, cognitive, social, and emotional functioning and development as they relate to health and illness issues in children, adolescents, and families. Addresses topics exploring the interrelationship between psychological and physical well-being, including psychosocial and developmental factors contributing to the etiology, course, treatment, and outcome of pediatric conditions; assessment and treatment of behavioral and emotional concomitants of illness and developmental disorders; the promotion of health and health-related behaviors; and the prevention of illness and injury. **Types of articles:** Original research, scholarly reviews, case reports, and commentaries **Professional affiliation:** Society of Pediatric Psychology, Division 54 of the American Psychological Association	2.62/3.30
Journal of Clinical Psychology in Medical Settings http://link.springer. com/journal/10880	Publishes articles focusing on clinical research related to the work of psychologists in medical settings with all patient groups. Addresses innovative training programs and course materials; licensing, credentialing, and privileging in hospital practice; ethics; the role of psychologists in medical settings; professional practice issues; practice management; marketing and the politics of health care in general. **Types of articles:** Original research (including single-case designs), review articles, and descriptions of training models **Professional affiliation:** Association of Psychologists in Academic Health Centers	1.08/1.54
Clinical Practice in Pediatric Psychology www.apa.org/pubs/ journals/cpp/	Publishes articles representing the professional and applied activities of pediatric psychology. Complements scientific development with information on the applied side, provides modeling that addresses the ways practicing psychologists can incorporate findings from the empirical literature into their activities, and provides a forum for those primarily engaged in clinical activities to report on their work and inform future research. **Types of articles:** Original research, review articles, clinical case reports, and commentaries **Professional affiliation:** Society of Pediatric Psychology, Division 54 of the American Psychological Association	Not available

Journal and website	Journal description and types of articles published	2015 2-year IF/ 5-year IF
Pediatrics www. aappublications.org/ content/pediatrics	Publishes articles of broad impact to clinicians and researchers that address the needs of the whole child in his or her physiologic, mental, emotional, and social structure. Welcomes submissions from related disciplines such as nutrition, surgery, dentistry, public health, child health services, human genetics, basic sciences, psychology, psychiatry, education, sociology, and nursing. Targets general and specialist pediatricians, pediatric researchers and educators, and child health policymakers. **Types of articles:** Original research, clinical observations, special feature articles, and case reports **Professional affiliation:** American Academic of Pediatrics	5.20/6.04
Journal of Developmental & Behavioral Pediatrics http://journals.lww. com/jrnldbp/pages/ default.aspx	Publishes articles addressing some of the most challenging issues affecting child development and behavior, including mental health and medical conditions, psychosocial determinants of health, health disparities, stress and adversity, neurodevelopmental disabilities, learning disabilities, parenting and family factors, gene–environment interactions, clinical screening, and assessment. Targets clinicians, teachers, and researchers involved in pediatric health care and child development. **Types of articles:** Original research, review articles, case reports, challenging cases, commentaries, book reviews, and letters to the editor **Professional affiliation:** Society of Developmental and Behavioral Pediatrics	2.32/2.54
Preventive Medicine www.journals. elsevier.com/ preventive-medicine/	Publishes articles on the science and practice of disease prevention, health promotion, and public health policymaking. Welcomes insightful observational studies, thoughtful explorations of health data, unsuspected new angles for existing hypotheses, robust randomized controlled trials, and impartial systematic reviews. Aims to publish research that will have an impact on the work of practitioners of disease prevention and health promotion, as well as of related disciplines. **Types of articles:** Original research, brief reports, review articles, commentaries, book reviews, and letters to the editor	2.89/3.75

Note. Descriptions of each journal and type of manuscripts accepted were obtained from the journal's website, following headings such as "aim and scope" and "author guidelines." These descriptions were edited for content. The 2015 journal impact factor values were obtained from Clarivate Analytics' Journal Citation Reports database and rounded to two decimal places.

212 Thomas J. Power & Katy E. Tresco

a moderately high impact factor, publishes research on children with, or at risk for, illness and injury, including research that is school-based and school-linked. An alternative, *Journal of Clinical Psychology in Medical Settings*, includes papers about child and adult populations with, or at risk for, medical conditions, and is unique in that it publishes articles focused on training models. For example, training initiatives in pediatric school psychology (Power & Bradley-Klug, 2013) might be of interest to this journal. School psychologists seeking to publish on the link between research and practice for children with, or at risk of, medical conditions are encouraged to examine *Clinical Practice in Pediatric Psychology*, a new journal sponsored by the Society of Pediatric Psychology.

Several options are available to school psychologists seeking to publish in medical journals. One option is *Pediatrics*, which is a high-impact journal with a broad readership that publishes articles with relevance to practice and policy for children and adolescents with, or at risk of, health problems. Another option is *Journal of Developmental and Behavioral Pediatrics*, which publishes original research and reviews on topics related to disabilities and behavioral health problems in pediatrics, including studies about ADHD, ASD, developmental delay, factors contributing to developmental disability, and behavioral concerns manifesting in primary care practices (e.g., sleep, feeding, enuresis, and encopresis). In addition, many school psychologists are engaged in prevention and health promotion research in schools related to violence prevention and nutrition education (Hoffman et al., 2011). Many interdisciplinary journals with a focus on prevention, such as *Preventive Medicine*, are potential outlets for school psychologists engaged in this type of work.

Special Populations

Many journals publish articles focused on children and adolescents with specific diagnoses or sets of problems (see Table 20.3). The *Journal of Attention Disorders* is dedicated to publishing a wide range of research (e.g., genetics and neurobiology, epidemiology, assessment and diagnosis, and intervention services) focused on children with ADHD and the broader construct of attention. Similarly, the *Journal of Autism and Developmental Disorders* is an interdisciplinary journal publishing articles on a broad range of topics related to children with ASD and developmental disabilities. In addition, several journals focus on issues related to aggression, bullying, and violence, a common topic of research among school psychologists. For example, *Aggressive Behavior* and *Journal of School Violence* are journals that quite frequently cite publications in major school psychology journals. In addition, *Aggressive Behavior* is frequently cited by school psychology journals, indicating that the research conducted by school psychologists is often influenced by research published in this journal.

Table 20.3 Journals Targeting Specific Populations

Journal and website	Journal description and types of articles published	2015 2-year IF/5-year IF
Journal of Attention Disorders http://jad.sagepub.com/	Publishes basic and applied science and clinical issues related to attention in children, adolescents, and adults. Provides an objective and diverse cross-section of studies by scholars in the field of attention and addresses practice, policy, and theory.	3.38/3.28
	Types of articles: Original research, research into practice, research briefs, literature reviews, letters to the editor (published at the editor's discretion), and opinion essays (by invitation only)	
Journal of Autism and Developmental Disorders (JADD) http://link.springer.com/ journal/10803	Publishes articles advancing the understanding of autism, including potential causes and prevalence; diagnosis advancements; and effective clinical care, education, and treatment. Addresses health policy, legislation, advocacy, culture and society, and service provision.	3.49/4.26
	Types of articles: Original research, brief reports, special issue articles, commentaries, and letters to the editor	
Aggressive Behavior http://onlinelibrary.wiley. com/journal/10.1002/ (ISSN)1098-2337	Publishes articles addressing the mechanisms underlying or influencing behaviors generally regarded as aggressive as well as the consequences of being subject to such behaviors. Encourages interdisciplinary behavioral and neuro-physiological studies concerning the underpinnings of human and animal aggression. Focuses on empirical studies, but broad theoretical reviews are also welcomed.	2.47/3.38
	Types of articles: Original research and literature reviews	
	Professional affiliation: International Society for Research on Aggression	
Journal of School Violence www.tandfonline.com/loi/ wjsv20	Publishes empirical articles related to school violence and victimization from a variety of social science methodologies. Focuses on a range of contemporary issues centering on violence in the school environment including the nature, extent, prevention, and consequences of school violence for students, teachers, and staff.	Not available
	Types of articles: Original research	

Note

Descriptions of each journal and type of manuscripts accepted were obtained from the journal's website, following headings such as "aim and scope" and "author guidelines." These descriptions were edited for content. The 2015 journal impact factor values were obtained from Clarivate Analytics' Journal Citation Reports database and rounded to two decimal places.

Recommendations for Publishing in Clinical and Pediatric Journals

Identifying potential outlets for publishing your work entails careful consideration of the fit between your manuscript and the journal. To examine potential fit, it is critically important to learn as much as possible about journals that might be potential outlets for your work. Several resources are available to authors. First, some key publications provide information and guidelines useful to authors. In particular, Floyd and colleagues (2011) amassed a wealth of information about a wide range of publications that are potential outlets for school psychologists. Their article provides information about types of submissions, length of manuscripts, rejection rates, duration of review period, and lag time from acceptance to publication of numerous journals, including many in the clinical area. Another highly useful resource is Cabells Directories of Publishing Opportunities (www.cabells.com/index/aspx), which provides information about the mission and submission guidelines of journals. An additional source of useful information is colleagues who have published in clinical, pediatric, and prevention journals. For example, numerous scholars in school psychology have published in clinical journals about ADHD, ASD, depression, and aggression. Similarly, there are several school psychology researchers, including those who identify themselves as pediatric school psychologists and prevention experts, who publish research in pediatric psychology, medical, and prevention journals.

Once an author has identified potential publication outlets, there are numerous factors to consider in prioritizing journal options. First, it is important to examine the match between your manuscript and the journals being considered. Your manuscript must coincide with the types of manuscripts published and the topics addressed in the journal. In addition, the methodologies used in your project must fit within the range of articles in the journal. As a rule, it is important to acquaint yourself with articles published in each journal when you are prioritizing journal outlets. This information is readily available if you conduct an online search of the journal.

Second, identify your target audience. Are you primarily interested in influencing researchers conducting investigations related to a particular theme or childhood problem? Are you interested in influencing policymakers and practitioners? Are you targeting researchers and professionals across a broad range of disciplines? Information regarding intended audiences, professional affiliations, and circulation is also readily available through online searches.

Third, consider how a publication in each journal might help you in pursuing your career goals. Could publication in a particular journal help to establish or strengthen your network of relationships with researchers and professionals who are critical for career enhancement? Are certain journals given stronger consideration when applying for grant funding, research conferences, or other career advancement opportunities?

Fourth, consider the impact factor of the journal, which is often used by universities to determine journal quality, although it clearly has limitations

(Floyd et al., 2011). How does your institution view the impact factor of journals? To what extent is the impact factor considered in tenure and promotion decisions? Although institutions vary widely in their emphasis on impact factors, this variable is sometimes considered by external reviewers when evaluating candidates for promotion and it can contribute to one's national reputation.

Fifth, it is important to consider the difficulty level of publishing in each journal. Although there is no ideal metric of this factor, the rejection rate of submitted manuscripts is a useful index to examine. As a general rule, we encourage authors to aim high, that is, to target a journal of high quality with a high rejection rate and high impact factor. However, authors need to be realistic about their chances of publishing in certain journals. Quite frankly, it makes no sense to submit to a journal that is extremely likely to reject your manuscript.

Finally, consider pragmatic issues such as whether a journal provides a rapid screen for the appropriateness of the submission, the lag time between submission and review, and the lag time between manuscript acceptance and publication. Your work is important and publishing in a timely way is a priority. As a rule, it is wise to submit to journals that provide rapid feedback and are able to get your accepted work published in a timely manner. Medical journals usually are more efficient than psychology journals in reviewing manuscripts and publishing articles. Nonetheless, there is substantial variability among journals in each category. Another pragmatic issue to consider is the formatting of manuscripts for journal submission. Psychology journals follow the publication manual of the American Psychological Association, whereas medical journals typically follow the American Medical Association (AMA) manual. Converting a manuscript into AMA format can be somewhat challenging, although electronic reference management programs have made this much easier to accomplish.

Conclusions

This chapter reviews clinical, pediatric, and medical journals that might serve as an outlet for the scholarly activities of school psychologists. Although there are high volumes of journals in these areas, we identified a sample of journals with a wide range of impact factors, levels of difficulty with regard to acceptance, and types of articles published in order to increase the relevance of the chapter for school psychologists with diverse interests in publication. The chapter concludes by outlining a series of factors to consider in identifying potential publication outlets and prioritizing among journal options.

References

Bradley-Klug, K. L., Jeffries-Deloatche, J., Walsh, A. S. J., Bateman, L. P., Nadeau, J., ..., Cunningham, J. (2013). School psychologists' perceptions of primary care partnerships: Implications for building the collaborative bridge. *Advances in School Mental Health Promotion, 6*, 51–67. doi: 10.1080/1754730X.2012.760921

Canter, K. S., & Roberts, M. C. (2012). Systematic and quantitative review of interventions to facilitate school reentry for children with chronic conditions. *Journal of Pediatric Psychology, 37*, 1065–1075.

Floyd, R. G., Cooley, K. M., Arnett, J. E., Fagan, T. K., Mercer, S. H., & Hingle, C. (2011). An overview and analysis of journal operations, journal publication patterns, and journal impact in school psychology and related fields. *Journal of School Psychology, 49*, 617–647.

Hoffman, J. A., Thompson, D. R., Franko, D. L., Power, T. J., Leff, S. S., & Stallings, V. (2011). Decaying effects in a randomized multi-year fruit and vegetable intake intervention. *Preventive Medicine, 52*, 370–375. doi: 10:1016/j.amepre.2016.02.031

Kranzler, J. H., Grapin, S. L., & Daley, M. L. (2011). Research productivity and scholarly impact of APA-accredited school psychology programs: 2005–2009. *Journal of School Psychology, 49*, 721–738. doi: 10.1016/j.jsp.2011.10.004

Logan, D., Simons, L. E., & Kaczynski, K. J. (2009). School functioning in adolescents with chronic pain: The role of depressive symptoms in school impairment. *Journal of Pediatric Psychology, 34*, 882–892.

Power, T. J., & Bradley-Klug, K. (2013). *Pediatric school psychology: Conceptualization, applications, and strategies for leadership development*. New York, NY: Routledge.

Power, T. J., Mautone, J. A., Soffer, S. L., Clarke, A. T., Marshall, S. A., Sharman, J., . . ., Jawad, A. F. (2012). Family-school intervention for children with ADHD: Results of randomized clinical trial. *Journal of Consulting and Clinical Psychology, 80*, 611–623. doi: 10.1037/a0028188

21 Publishing in Developmental Psychology Journals

Ibrahim H. Acar and
Kathleen Moritz Rudasill

The field of school psychology is closely linked to developmental psychology. As argued by Pianta (2009), schooling and development are inseparable. According to the bioecological model of development, children develop within complex systems, including families, neighborhoods, schools, and cultures; as children age, school becomes a primary system within which the child interacts (Bronfenbrenner & Morris, 2006). Similarly, the American Psychological Association's description of the school psychology field highlights the importance of development, illustrating an emphasis on children's development in school and other critical contexts, such as families and peer networks (www.apa.org/ed/graduate/specialize/school.aspx). Indeed, the very purpose of the educational system is to positively guide children's cognitive, behavioral, and social-emotional development. When developmental problems arise, school psychologists are often called in to help (Pianta, 2009). At the same time, researchers who study child development regularly find themselves in schools and classrooms. Thus, school psychologists and child developmentalists often work in the same realm. Indeed, the last two decades have seen a surge in developmentally grounded research programs focused on classroom and school effects (Pianta, 2009). For these reasons, scholars in the two fields frequently publish in journals in both school psychology and developmental areas.

An examination of citations in school psychology publications reveals that authors of articles in these journals cite quite a few journals with a developmental focus. Over the past decade, the developmental psychology journals most frequently cited in school psychology journals were *Developmental Psychology*, *Journal of Applied Developmental Psychology*, *Child Development*, *Journal of Research on Adolescence*, *Journal of Youth and Adolescence*, *Early Childhood Research Quarterly*, and *Early Education and Development*. These journals tend to be frequently referenced by scholars in school psychology because of either their high impact factors, applied focus, or both. Similarly, authors of articles in developmental journals cite school psychology journals. The journals most cited over the past decade were the *Journal of School Psychology*, *Psychology in the Schools*, *School Psychology International*, *School Psychology Quarterly*, and *School Psychology Review*.

Developmental Psychology Journals

Developmental psychology journals fall into several categories. *Developmental Psychology* and the *Journal of Applied Developmental Psychology* are outlets for publications on development across the lifespan, although both journals publish many articles that are focused on child and adolescent development. *Child Development* is well known for publishing articles about development from infancy through adolescence. As their names suggest, the *Journal of Research on Adolescence* and the *Journal of Youth and Adolescence* publish articles centered on adolescent development, whereas *Early Childhood Research Quarterly* and *Early Education and Development* cover childhood. The *Journal of Applied Developmental Psychology* and *Early Education and Development* include an emphasis on application. What follows are more detailed descriptions of the ten top developmental journals for school psychology scholars.

In Table 21.1, we have provided a comprehensive list of developmental journals that might be useful to scholars in school psychology. We have included the oft-cited journals, as well as many more that are cited less often, and some that might slip under the radar but may be useful for certain manuscripts that are more specialized or limited in scope. For every journal, we have provided the 2015 2- and 5-year Impact Factor values, a brief description of the journal and its website, and the types of articles published. This list of journals is not exhaustive (for example, it omits some education- and health-focused journals), but it is an attempt to provide a comprehensive list of options.

1   *Child Development* is a main journal of the Society for Research in Child Development (SRCD), published six times per year. *Child Development* is a leading journal within developmental psychology and has the highest impact factor in this area. This journal does not identify a specific category of topical research, but rather it tends to cover many topics regarding child development. As a result, multiple school-based studies are published in *Child Development*; it is an important publication platform and resource for researchers from school psychology.

2   *Developmental Psychology* is a monthly journal published by the American Psychological Association. This journal publishes studies regarding development across the lifespan, but many are focused on child and adolescent development. Articles published in *Developmental Psychology* are generally focused on seminal empirical work and rarely theoretical and methodological. This is a highly prestigious and competitive journal for researchers from developmental psychology fields. It is appropriate for research from school psychology when a developmental perspective has been embedded in studies.

3   *Early Childhood Research Quarterly* is one of the most prominent and influential journals in the area of early childhood development. This journal covers topics in all aspects of development in early childhood (0 to 8 years old), childcare quality, policy related studies, and professional development for early childhood practitioners. Because this journal is at

Table 21.1 Developmental Psychology Journals

Journal	2015 Impact Factor		Description and website	Article types
	2 yr.	5yr.		
Child Development	4.06	5.80	Publishes about topics in child and adolescent development. http://onlinelibrary.wiley.com/journal/10.1111/(ISSN)1467-8624	Articles; essays; reviews; tutorials
Developmental Psychology	4.14	4.28	Publishes work on development across the lifespan that focuses on the biological, social, and cultural factors that affect development. www.apa.org/pubs/journals/dev/	Scholarly reviews; theoretical or methodological articles
Early Childhood Research Quarterly	1.73	2.91	Publishes work on early childhood education and development, theory, and educational practice targeting children from birth through age 8 years. www.journals.elsevier.com/early-childhood-research-quarterly/	Empirical research (quantitative or qualitative methods); occasionally practitioner and/or policy perspectives, book reviews, and significant reviews of research
Early Education and Development	0.76	1.47	Publishes research emphasizing the implications for practice of solid scientific information across early childhood. www.tandfonline.com/action/journalInformation?show=aimsScope&journalCode=heed20#.V2WD5bsrK00	Empirical qualitative, quantitative methods, mixed-methods studies
Social Development	1.80	2.59	International journal which publishes work dealing with all aspects of children's social development (peer relationships, social interaction, attachment formation, emotional development, and theory of mind). http://onlinelibrary.wiley.com/journal/10.1111/(ISSN)1467-9507	Empirical reports; debates and comments on theoretical and empirical issues; literature reviews and in-depth book reviews
Journal of Research on Adolescence	2.48	3.72	Publishes rigorous quantitative or qualitative work focused on adolescent development. http://onlinelibrary.wiley.com/journal/10.1111/(ISSN)1532-7795	Empirical articles; brief reports; reviews

(continued)

Table 21.1 Developmental Psychology Journals (*countinued*)

Journal	2015 Impact Factor		Description and website	Article types
	2 yr.	5yr.		
Journal of Adolescence	2.10	2.70	International journal on development between puberty and adulthood; emphasizes research and practice. www.journals.elsevier.com/journal-of-adolescence/	Research articles; review articles; brief reports; international notes
The Journal of Early Adolescence	1.30	2.23	Publishes research that increases understanding of individuals from 10 through 14 years of age regarding advances and issues from diverse developmental lenses. http://jea.sagepub.com/	Major theoretical papers; state-of-the-art papers; current research; reviews of important professional books and early adolescent films and literature
Journal of Youth and Adolescence	3.56	3.81	Publishes research on policy needs and implications for the way society formally or informally responds to the period of youth and adolescence. http://link.springer.com/journal/10964	Quantitative analyses, theoretical papers, and comprehensive review articles
The International Journal of Behavioral Development	1.31	2.14	Publishes work on developmental processes at all stages of the lifespan—infancy, childhood, adolescence, adulthood, and old age. http://jbd.sagepub.com/	Empirical articles, methodological, theoretical, and review papers
Applied Developmental Science	1.36	1.70	Publishes synthesis of research and application to promote positive development across the lifespan and across the globe. www.tandfonline.com/action/journalInformation?journalCode=hads20#.V2W9OrsrK70	Empirical articles; theoretical and conceptual articles
British Journal of Developmental Psychology	1.71	2.30	All developmental areas of childhood, adolescence, and adulthood; theoretical approaches to development, including neo-Piagetian, information processing, naive theory, dynamic systems, ecological, and sociocultural approaches. http://onlinelibrary.wiley.com/journal/10.1111/(ISSN)2044-835X	Empirical, conceptual and theoretical papers; review and discussion papers; methodological papers; brief reports

Journal	2015 Impact Factor		Description and website	Article types
	2 yr.	5yr.		
Childhood	0.84	0.97	Publishes research about children in global society that spans divisions between geographical regions, disciplines, and social and cultural contexts. http://chd.sagepub.com/	Theoretical and empirical articles; reviews and scholarly comments on children's social relations and culture
Child Development Perspectives	3.26	3.90	Addresses emerging lines of inquiry in developmental science. http://onlinelibrary.wiley.com/journal/10.1111/(ISSN)1750-8606	Brief, well synthesized reviews of research; essays on policy; statistics and methods
Cognitive Development	1.57	2.10	Publishes work on development of perception, memory, language, concepts, thinking, problem solving, metacognition, and social cognition. www.journals.elsevier.com/cognitive-development	Reports of empirical research; methodological advances; theoretical essays; critical reviews
Developmental Review	4.80	6.38	Publishes about human developmental processes and research relevant to developmental psychology, and research with fundamental implications to pediatrics, psychiatry, and neuroscience, and increases the understanding of socialization processes. www.journals.elsevier.com/developmental-review	Theoretical statements; reviews of literature; summaries of programmatic research; empirical articles; collections of papers on a single theme; analyses of social policy; historical analyses; essays on major books; analyses of method and design
European Journal of Developmental Psychology	0.79	1.58	Publishes work on psychological development and developmental psychopathology during infancy, childhood, and adolescence. Preference for papers relevant to European developmental psychology that consider European history, policy, or cultural diversity. www.tandfonline.com/action/journalInformation?journalCode=pedp20#.V2WOXbsrK70	Innovative original theoretical, empirical, methodological and review papers

(continued)

Table 21.1 Developmental Psychology Journals (*countinued*)

Journal	2015 Impact Factor		Description and website	Article types
	2 yr.	5yr.		
Journal of Cognition and Development	1.77	2.25	Addresses policy issues and practical applications that mainly focus on cognitive development during all stages of life and the understanding of ontogenetic processes in both humans and nonhumans. www.tandfonline.com/loi/hjcd20#.V2XKzbsrK70	Empirical reports; theoretical essays (occasionally accompanied by peer commentaries); essay reviews of new and significant books
Merrill-Palmer Quarterly: Journal of Developmental Psychology	1.28	2.42	Publishes research on child development and family–child relationships. www.wsupress.wayne.edu/journals/detail/merrill-palmer-quarterly	Empirical and theoretical papers; summaries and integrations of research; commentaries by experts; reviews of important new books in development
Monographs of the Society for Research in Child Development	1.88	2.48	Publishes in-depth research studies and significant findings in child development and its related disciplines. http://onlinelibrary.wiley.com/journal/10.1111/(ISSN)1540-5834	Single study or a group of papers on a single theme, accompanied usually by commentary and discussion
New Directions for Child and Adolescent Development	0.96	1.76	Publishes issues and concepts in the field of child and adolescent development. Each volume focuses on a new direction or research topic. http://onlinelibrary.wiley.com/journal/10.1002/(ISSN)1534-8687	Empirical work; theoretical reviews; research reviews; methodological papers on specific issues
Research in Human Development	1.97	1.74	Publishes conceptual, empirical, and methodological integrative and interdisciplinary approaches to the study of human development across the lifespan. www.tandfonline.com/action/journalInformation?journalCode=hrhd20#.V2W8lLsrK70	Empirical articles; theoretical and conceptual articles

the intersection of developmental and educational studies in early childhood, school psychologists might benefit by publishing their work here as it will attract attention from scholars in both developmental and educational fields.

4 *Early Education and Development* aims to serve communities of researchers, school psychologists, and developmental specialists in the field of early childhood. As such, this journal publishes work related to factors influencing early child development and education. Researchers in school psychology frequently cite studies in this journal and publish in this journal. Because *Early Education and Development* places such an emphasis on implications and policy perspectives of research, there is a particular benefit to school psychologists for publishing in this journal.

5 *Social Development* is an international journal focused on social development of children. This journal is published four times per year. Empirical reports, comments, literature reviews, and book reviews can be published with this journal, which is considered to be a primary platform for work conducted by developmental and social psychologists. Main topics covered in this journal are in the areas of social cognition, peer relations, social interaction, attachment, and emotional development. Thus, many of these topics fall within the purview of school psychology, particularly peer relations and emotional development.

6 The *Journal of Applied Developmental Psychology* is a well-regarded journal that publishes research on applications of behavioral science pertaining to development across the lifespan. The main focus of the journal is to show how knowledge derived from research can be applied in policy, education, clinical settings, and social contexts. The applied focus of this journal makes it a good fit for scholars in school psychology.

7 The *Journal of Research on Adolescence* is published by the Society for Research on Adolescence and is a leading journal in the area of adolescent development. With four publications per year, the journal is an outlet for rigorous, empirical articles that add to our understanding of development from ages 10–20. Studies using quantitative or qualitative methods are welcome.

8 *Journal of Adolescence* is an international journal that publishes work focused on the period between puberty and adulthood. The aims of the journal are to foster research and cultivate positive practice in working with adolescents. Because of relatively liberal copyright guidelines, this journal might be particularly appealing to school psychologists who are concerned with spreading their message to a wide audience of practitioners and researchers.

9 The *Journal of Early Adolescence* is published eight times per year. This journal covers studies in early adolescence (from ages 10 to 14 years). It focuses on a variety of developmental changes that occur within different contexts such as with peers, at school, with the family, and within the broader culture. It accepts empirical papers, literature reviews, and practical papers.

224 Ibrahim H. Acar & Kathleen Moritz Rudasill

10 The *Journal of Youth and Adolescence* is a prestigious journal in the field of adolescence that primarily focuses on studies addressing policy implications of research. The journal publishes quantitative empirical studies, theoretical papers, and comprehensive articles. Scholars in school psychology interested in policies affecting individuals during adolescence might find this journal to be a good fit for their research.

11 *The International Journal of Behavioral Development* is an international journal published by the International Society for the Study of Behavioural Development. It publishes studies focusing on all developmental stages from infancy to old age. This journal prioritizes studies conducted cross-nationally with an emphasis on cross-cultural issues regarding behavioral development. In addition to empirical articles, this journal accepts theoretical and review papers as well as methodological papers regarding behavioral development. School psychology researchers who are conducting cross-national and cross-cultural behavioral research might want to consider this journal to disseminate their research and implications.

Recommendations for Publishing in Developmental Journals

Scholars working primarily in the area of school psychology who are interested in publishing in developmental journals might find it helpful to keep several recommendations in mind. Fortunately, concepts, terms, and theoretical perspectives are similar across the developmental and school psychology realms, thus facilitating cross-fertilization between fields. For example, scholars in both fields apply a bioecological framework to the study of children's outcomes because this approach fits well with the conceptualization of development as dynamic and occurring within complex sets of systems, such as families and schools (Pianta, 2009). However, the emphasis on change over time in developmental journals brings with it a high regard for research studies with longitudinal designs and, ideally, multiple observations of the same construct. In developmental journals, it is difficult to publish a cross-sectional study based on measures from a single reporter, and there is a tendency in the most prestigious developmental journals to favor complex designs, sophisticated methodological approaches, and, by necessity, studies with large samples.

There is also a trend in developmental journals to require authors to fully describe the ethnic characteristics of their participants and the extent to which the participants are representative of the population from which they were drawn, as well as delineate the extent to which samples from studies described in the literature review and discussion sections are from the United States or other countries. This is part of an emphasis on cultural sensitivity in the developmental field. Another difference between the developmental and school psychology journals is the emphasis on implications of the research. Whereas most school psychology journals emphasize practical implications for research findings, this is not true for all developmental journals. It is important to check the submission requirements for particular journals, but many in the

Developmental Psychology Journals   225

developmental arena are decisively research focused, so implications would be for future research rather than practice or policy.

Within developmental psychology, there are several high-impact journals. In fact, developmental psychology is filled with really competitive journals, such as *Child Development* and *Developmental Psychology*, which can be intimidating for entry-level or junior scholars. These high-impact journals may be very difficult to get published in, but, as illustrated in Table 21.1, there are other great options in the field that are cited frequently in school psychology and are quite useful to scholars in both developmental and school psychology. As an example, the *Journal of Applied Developmental Psychology* (2-year Impact Factor in 2015 = 1.4) was one of the journals, within the past ten years, that was cited frequently in school psychology journals and in which articles published in school psychology journals were frequently cited.

To delve into the world of developmental psychology publishing outlets, it is good practice to keep in mind the strategies that work in school psychology publishing as well. Take a look at the types of topics and articles that have been recently published in that journal to see if your work seems to fit with the purview of the journal; consider the prestige of the journal and whether your sample and methods will constrain your reach; think about the value of your findings for research, practice, or policy implications—the emphasis on the type of implications might steer you toward a certain type of journal; and finally, consider the recommendations of your colleagues. Often, colleagues have favorite journals or are on editorial review boards of journals and can provide helpful insight.

Conclusion

Considering developmental and school psychologists go hand in hand as they cover overlapping topics of interest in their research, publishing in developmental psychology journals can reward school psychologists in several ways: (1) sharing implication-based results from school psychology in developmental psychology journals may inform developmentalists' research and practice, (2) creating common ground for disentangling issues in both developmental and school psychology regarding child development, (3) taking advantage of similar requirements presented by developmental and school psychology journals, (4) benefiting from the wide range of journal options in developmental psychology, and (5) using journals that publish articles focused on both education and development.

References

Bronfenbrenner, U., & Morris, P. A. (2006). *The bioecological model of human development.* In R. M. Lerner (Ed.), *Theoretical models of human development* (6th ed., Vol. 1, pp. 793–828). New York, NY: Wiley.

Pianta, R. C. (2009). School psychology and developmental psychology: Moving from programs to processes. In T. B. Gutkin & C. R. Reynolds (Eds.), *The handbook of school psychology* (4th ed., pp. 107–123). Hoboken, NJ: Wiley.

Part 4

Publishing in Other Outlets

22 Publishing in Professional Newsletters

Rosemary Flanagan, John Desrochers, and Greg Machek

Professional newsletters are a source of timely information. Newsletters are commonly published by associations, and in some ways, are the face of the association. For some, newsletters are members' only connection to the association. Some association newsletters are made available to individuals outside of the association, possibly as a membership recruitment tool. Two major newsletters in school psychology are *The School Psychologist*, published by Division 16 of the American Psychological Association (APA), and the *Communiqué*, published by the National Association of School Psychologists (NASP). In addition, *World-Go-Round* is published by the International School Psychology Association (ISPA). The circulation of the newsletters varies as does the size of the organizational membership. Based on membership figures *Communiqué* has the highest circulation, exceeding 25,000 copies per issue, followed by *The School Psychologist* at over 2,200 copies. The circulation of *World-Go-Round* is to over 600 members (personal communication, Sue Lijkwan March 29, 2016) of ISPA. This chapter will focus on *Communiqué* and *The School Psychologist*.

The range of information is potentially broad in that professional newsletters are the primary vehicle that the association uses to communicate with members. Newsletters document the field and its changes over time. *Communiqué* is published eight times per year, and *The School Psychologist* is published three times per year. Although newsletter content varies, there is predictable structure and sections. A president's column introduces the newsletter; it is most often about a timely issue or concern. Sections are typically dedicated to different groups in an association such as students or early career psychologists. An array of content is found in newsletters. Content might include articles about contemporary practice and research, education and training, and professional practice issues, such as ethics, supervision, laws and regulations that impact practice. Articles about career issues, and practice innovations are common. Book and test reviews are also appropriate content. Such brief articles are intended to be of interest to most members. On occasion, a newsletter article will lead to the submission and publication of other articles on the same topic. Also possible are articles espousing contrasting views or notions, which is a useful way to share multiple perspectives and increase involvement in the profession outside of the primary work setting. Other information in newsletters includes seminar and workshop announcements, networking and service opportunities at professional meetings (such as the APA and NASP conventions), advertisements for tests and books, employment listings, and current information about association activities, initiatives, and accomplishments. Surveys (Ash, 1965; Hutzell & Graca, 1986) of the editors of APA Division Newsletters and State Psychological Association newsletters suggest that newsletter content has held steady over the years in that content includes reports of association business, convention programming, letters to the editor/editorials, employment notices, and research.

Newsletters are a means to keep members updated on the activities of colleagues, and until the advent of email lists and social media, they were the primary means to accomplish this end. Thus, columns for member updates of accomplishments and changes in employment are common, as are announcements of award winners and election results. Obituaries of individuals who have made substantial contributions to the field over their careers appear in newsletters. The annual conventions are advertised to members through newsletters, and reports about the convention are similarly shared with members. Newsletters are important because not all members attend annual meetings.

Newsletter content is broad because school psychology newsletters such as *The School Psychologist* and *Communiqué* serve a wide audience that ranges from students to early career psychologists to seasoned senior school psychologists, all working in various settings. Within the school psychology community, newsletters serve practitioners in school and non-school settings, as well as those in academia. It is also a way for retirees to read about the field and maintain an ongoing connection. From the vantage point of publication, newsletters tend to be published more rapidly than other hard copy print media, such as journals and books. In that regard, newsletters are more similar to magazines.

Publishing in newsletters is a worthwhile activity and, although not bearing the weight of publishing in a peer-reviewed journal, it can still have a positive impact on one's curriculum vitae. Writing for newsletters is a good way to practice writing for professional audiences, which is particularly useful for advanced doctoral students and early career individuals. It is also a way for practitioners to contribute to the field in a way other than by providing direct client service. Newsletters are also an appropriate venue for contributions by senior practitioners and academics reflecting the professional wisdom obtained via years of experience. Newsletter articles are cited like any other publication and are a convenient way to obtain professional exposure and make connections with others having similar professional interests. One can publish on a wide array of scholarly and professional practice topics, including pilot studies and works in progress. Newsletters are not commonly indexed in searchable databases such as PsycINFO (www.apa.org/pubs/databases/psycinfo/), but their content can nonetheless be substantive. Academic institutions vary in their consideration of this type of scholarly activity (Persinger & Daniels, 2011), as discussed further in a section that follows.

The editorial process for a newsletter is generally less rigorous than that of a refereed journal, but not all newsletter submissions are accepted. Newsletters have editorial boards, and those individuals review submissions. A difference between newsletters and refereed journals is that newsletter editors will often work with those making submissions to refine their work, making the editorial process less formal, but collegial; nevertheless standards remain. This fact is particularly important because those newer to scholarly writing, such as students and early career individuals, can be encouraged to write; this similarly applies to all those whose primary professional work is practice. Consequently, the role of editor is a substantial time commitment for which the workload varies. Newsletter editors serve without pay, although honoraria are common.

Similar to refereed journals, submission information and expectations are included in each issue. Prospective authors are urged to contact the editor when seeking direction about submission content. It is important that the submission make a contribution to the field; thus, student papers that are literature reviews are generally not acceptable unless the review is suggesting a novel interpretation. Thought-provoking and mildly controversial content is often welcome. Particularly appropriate are articles representing opposing viewpoints on a current topic of interest; those articles are often more scholarly. On occasion, articles are invited from individuals who have made either a specific contribution or numerous contributions over a career (such as award recipients); such contributions generally carry important messages but would not be published in peer-reviewed journals.

An Insider's Guide to *The School Psychologist*

Overview and Content

The School Psychologist is a newsletter published by Division 16 (School Psychology) of the APA. Each issue of *The School Psychologist* is currently composed of four recurring sections: People and Places, which highlights personal accomplishments within the field (hires, awards, and recognitions), as well as program accomplishments (accreditation, new program development, etc.); Student Corner, which is written by SASP (Student Affiliates in School Psychology) members and covers issues and tips for graduate students; Early Career Psychologist's Column, which addresses career development and is written by early career psychologists; and the President's Message, which allows for a formal avenue to update readers on a number of issues affecting Division 16 members. In addition, *The School Psychologist* publishes original scholarly content. Scholarly pieces go through a more thorough, blinded peer-review process; thus, *The School Psychologist*'s content is composed of briefer, recurring pieces, as well as original works that undergo submission guidelines in accordance with other peer-reviewed publications, making them acceptable for recognition in tenure and promotion decisions, analogous to the *Communiqué* (Persinger & Daniels, 2011).

For the peer-reviewed, scholarly pieces, submissions of 12 double-spaced manuscript pages are preferred, and the content of submissions should have a strong applied theme. For example, empirical pieces conducted in school settings and which highlight practical treatment effects are valued. Any other empirical pieces should have a strong research-to-practice linkage. Non-empirical pieces will also be reviewed for possible publication, but they are expected to have a strong applied element to them as well. For example, research that measures the effect of a particular academic intervention, applied in the school setting, would be appropriate here. *The School Psychologist* will also consider briefer (up to five pages) applied articles (e.g., non-empirical papers addressing best practice in service delivery), test reviews, and book reviews for publication. All submissions should be double-spaced in Times New Roman 12-point font and emailed to the editor.

Editorial Processes and Outcomes

Although not an indexed journal, *The School Psychologist* endeavors to adhere to a number of suggested practices to ensure quality in its peer-reviewed pieces. Some of these practices are emphasized by Park (2009), who lists primary differences between publishing in traditional psychology journals as compared to journals devoted to neurosciences or "basic" sciences. The former, the author contends, tends to have a more "tedious" (p. 37) review process, whereas the latter has (a) a more efficient review process; (b) short time to publication; and (c) shorter articles. As noted previously, *The School Psychologist* limits empirical and other research-based manuscripts to 12 double-spaced pages. Review is usually accomplished within four weeks, and time to publication is usually within two to three months.

The review process consists of an initial screening by the senior editorial team (editor and associate editor) to make sure the manuscript conforms to the goals and guidelines of the newsletter, is of acceptable quality, and content and methodology are meaningful and timely for the publication's readership. If the manuscript is acceptable according to the initial screening, it is sent out to at least one, and sometimes two, peer reviewers. Peer reviewers are professional school psychologists from the newsletter's advisory editor team. *The School Psychologist* uses a reviewer form, which provides a checklist for the reviewer to relay information on (a) the topical relevancy of the piece; (b) the clarity of title, abstract, literature review, results and discussion; (c) the appropriateness of methods and procedures; and (d) formatting and style, among other areas. It also allows the reviewer to posit a recommendation for acceptance as well as space to provide specific comments to the editor and space to provide specific comments to the author(s). The peer-review process is double blinded, meaning that advisory editors who serve as peer reviewers do not see author names, and authors are not aware of the reviewers' names. Because article length is shorter than in typical school psychology journals, reviewers are asked to give feedback within two to three weeks. The initial review cycle produces one of the following decisions: accept, resubmit with minor revisions, resubmit with major revisions, or reject.

The 2015 operations of *The School Psychologist* included submissions that were published in html format and were limited in length because APA allocated limited web space to Division newsletters. Unfortunately, there were fewer submissions as potential contributors learned of the space limitations. During 2015, *The School Psychologist* resumed publication in PDF format. The return to PDF format led to increased publication of unsolicited manuscripts. Thus, the January and April issues each contained two unsolicited manuscripts. In contrast, the August 2015 issue contained five unsolicited manuscripts. To provide a clearer notion of the numbers of unsolicited manuscripts, data from 2013 are informative, in that 16 unsolicited manuscripts were published. Because there has been a commitment to providing opportunities to publish, contributors were given feedback and encouraged to resubmit. The submissions varied in quality, with suggestions to improve the writing and encouragement to provide more scholarly information and citations to ensure accuracy being the most common types of revisions requested. Time in review was generally two to four weeks.

Distribution

The School Psychologist is primarily targeted to scholars and practitioners within the field of school psychology. Beginning in fall 2015, *The School Psychologist* changed its process of distribution and dissemination, a process that has been aided significantly by the hire of a Director of Communications for Division 16, School Psychology, with significant newsletter editing and social media management capabilities. Specifically, Division 16 offers a multi-tier distribution route for ensuring *The School Psychologist* reaches the broadest audience possible. The newsletter is first sent to all current members of Division 16 via its listserv as soon as the final copy is prepared. This method allows members to have initial access to the content. About one week later, the newsletter is posted to the Division website, where it will remain archived: http://apadivision16.org/the-school-psychologist-tsp/. A link to the latest content is posted and shared through social media outlets such as Facebook (www.facebook.com/apadivision16/), Twitter (https://twitter.com/apadivision16), and LinkedIn (www.linkedin.com/groups/6935561/profile). This social media distribution captures roughly 3,000 followers. Finally, a link to the latest edition will be part of the *Division 16 Digest*, with encouragement for members to share with colleagues or other interested parties.

Future Directions and Recommendations for Prospective Authors

The newsletter has evidenced a number of changes in the last four years. It has gone from a PDF-based platform to an entirely online format and back to a PDF distribution. In the process, overall content capacity has also fluctuated, as has the publication cycle, from four editions a year to three. Currently, the newsletter has three major aims for the next three to five years. The first is to increase the number of quality scholarly submissions. This goal will be accomplished by increasing both readership and solicitation of research-to-practice pieces using distribution methods described previously. Second (and also in service to the first goal), the newsletter seeks to begin annual special editions on timely and salient topics in the field. It will make use of guest editors, and these editions will, in essence, yield a fourth annual issue of the newsletter. Third, *The School Psychologist* has re-introduced advertising opportunities to offset the cost of publishing.

Prospective authors wishing to submit unsolicited manuscripts are encouraged to adhere to some general guidelines. First, staying within the posted length parameters is important. If authors think that their piece would be significantly constrained by doing so, they can contact the editor directly to discuss a possible length accommodation before submitting. Second, the relevancy of the topic is important. Because one important goal of *The School Psychologist* is to disseminate information that is salient to practitioners, pieces should be based on contemporary literature and current best practice. Pieces that put forward fresh perspectives should have a strong theoretical grounding. Third, good writing is a must, particularly because the review period does not offer the opportunity for substantial revision time. Therefore, organization (making good use of headings and subheadings) and writing clarity are important. For empirical pieces, defensible methods and procedures are also important. Further, prospective authors are encouraged to contact the editor to discuss potential contributions. This contact affords the editor the opportunity to share the newsletter's goals, set parameters regarding quality, and vet the appropriateness of content.

An Insider's Guide to *Communiqué*

Overview and Content

Communiqué is one of the major publications of NASP. With a subscription base in excess of 25,000, it is likely the most widely read publication in school psychology. Its primary mission is to report on news and professional trends of interest to school psychologists, keep members apprised of the activities of NASP, and provide professional development in the form of substantive articles relevant to best practices in the field. A typical issue of *Communiqué* will contain articles about best practices in school psychology, professional topics (e.g., legal and ethical issues, advocacy and communication, and standards); informed opinion (Viewpoint and Letters to the editor); book reviews; obituaries; association activities (e.g., Convention News and NASP News); and information appearing in regular columns (e.g., Welcoming and Safe Schools, IDEA in Practice, Just a Click Away, and Student Connections). Brief articles from the NASP president and the editor of *Communiqué* are also found in each issue. *Communiqué* generally does not publish empirical research articles.

Editorial Processes and Outcomes

Communiqué is not a peer-reviewed publication, although its articles are sometimes accepted by university tenure and promotion committees (e.g., see Persinger & Daniels, 2011). Most articles are reviewed by editorial board members; some are sent to ad hoc reviewers. All editorial decisions are made by the editorial board, similar to such publications as *Educational Leadership* and *Phi Delta Kappan.*

Because *Communiqué* publishes a wide variety of different kinds of articles, the editorial process for these articles can be somewhat different depending on the nature of the manuscript. Unsolicited manuscripts of all types are welcomed and frequently published in *Communiqué*, but most news articles, regular columns, and articles reporting on NASP business are submitted by contributing editors or leaders in NASP and are published with only minor revision. Unsolicited manuscripts are initially screened by the editor and, if moved forward, assigned to an editor who coordinates the editorial process, including solicitation of any ad hoc reviews that might be needed and management of the revision process. Final decisions regarding publication are made by the editor in consultation with editorial board members.

The acceptance rate for unsolicited manuscripts varies greatly from year to year because of the relatively small number of such submissions. In 2015, 54 unsolicited manuscripts were submitted, and 36 were accepted for publication (67%). An overall estimate of the average rate of acceptance in recent years would be between 70% and 80%. The time to editorial decision also varies depending on the time of year (spring is slowest) and complexity of the review process needed, but most decisions to accept, reject, or accept with revision are made within two weeks.

Distribution

Communiqué is published in eight 40-page issues per year in both print and electronic formats. Its audience consists of school psychology practitioners, students, and graduate educators, although teachers, administrators, and parents are often given copies of the handouts and other articles by practitioners. Paper copies are routinely mailed to all NASP members, electronic copies are posted on the NASP website, and selected articles are disseminated through NASP's various electronic distribution channels. Total paid subscriptions exceed 25,000.

Future Directions and Recommendations for Prospective Authors

Manuscripts should be submitted to the editor (desroc@optonline.net) as Microsoft Word documents using 12-point Times New Roman font without unusual formatting (e.g., mixed font styles and borders around text). Style is according to the *Publication Manual of the American Psychological Association, Sixth Edition* (APA, 2010).

Guidance on submitting manuscripts can be found in *Communiqué Author Guidelines* on the NASP website (www.nasponline.org/resources-and-publications/publications/cq-author-guidelines). This document also provides a description of the various categories of articles that typically appear in *Communiqué*:

- Columns
- Communication Matters
- Research-Based Practice
- Professional Practice
- Advocacy
- Crisis Management
- Transitions
- Opinion
- Student Connections
- Graduate Education
- Handouts
- Book Reviews

Although there is some flexibility regarding length of manuscripts, the following approximate guidelines pertain to the most common types of unsolicited manuscripts:

- Letters to the editor: 350 to 725 words
- Viewpoint: 725 to 1,450 words
- Student Connections: 1,450 words
- Others: 1,450 to 3,000 words

These word counts are inclusive of references and graphic elements. Special cases may be discussed with the editor (e.g., two-part articles are sometimes published). Articles are subject to final editing for space or layout considerations.

Articles likely to be accepted for publication in *Communiqué* will be written in a clear, concise, and engaging way designed to give school psychologists important information that will help them improve their day-to-day practice. The style should be authoritative but relevant, readable, and interesting to busy practitioners. Consider submitting supplementary material (e.g., a brief handout for teachers) to accompany the main article. Most important is that implications, examples, and recommendations for practice be included as a part of the manuscript. *Communiqué* editors frequently will work with authors to help them bring their manuscripts to publication. The best advice for prospective writers is to read several articles in *Communiqué* that are similar to the kind you want to write and observe how the authors crafted them. This review will provide some idea of the style of writing that might be most appropriate for new manuscripts. Topics may cover the gamut of interests held by school psychologists, but articles that focus on mental and behavioral health, the NASP Practice Model (www.nasponline.org/standards-and-certification/nasp-practice-model), the school psychologist shortage, and leadership development within the field are currently most sought after. Calls for specific kinds of articles are also published from time to time in *Communiqué*. Specific proposals or questions may be addressed to the editor. For more information about publishing in *Communiqué*, see Desrochers (2015), and for specific information on submitting articles for the Student Connections column, see Klotz and Frank (2016).

Conclusions

Publishing in professional newsletters is a satisfying and worthy activity that contributes to the field. The benefits to associations and their members are numerous and varied. Newsletters document the field and its growth and development and serve as archival sources of information. The opportunity to publish serves multiple agendas in that it is a professional development and socialization activity, knowledge is disseminated, and a wide constituency of school psychologists are brought together to share ideas and remain connected to the scholarly aspects of our field.

References

American Psychological Association. (2010). *Publication manual of the American Psychological Association* (6th ed.). Washington, DC: American Psychological Association.

Ash, P. (1965). Newsletters of APA divisions. *American Psychologist, 20*, 840–841.

Desrochers, J. E. (2015). Write for *Communiqué! Communiqué, 44*(3), 12–13.

Hutzell, R. R., & Graca, J. J. (1986). Newsletters of state psychological associations. *Professional Psychology: Research and Practice, 17*, 80–81.

Klotz, M. B., & Frank, M. (2016). Seeking new submissions for the Student Connections column. *Communiqué, 44*(7), 35.

Park, D. C. (2009). Publishing in the psychological sciences: Enhancing journal impact while decreasing author fatigue. *Perspectives on Psychological Science, 4*, 36–37.

Persinger, J., & Daniels, C. (2011). Publish or perish: Is an article in *Communiqué* a "publication?" *Communiqué, 40*(1), 26–27.

23 Publishing Books

Dawn P. Flanagan and Megan C. Sy

When I (DPF) was asked to write a chapter on how to publish books and what steps one needs to take to "break into" book publishing, it did not strike me as a particularly interesting topic. But, if you want to publish a book in the field of psychology, then it is important to understand the best way to proceed. I actually find the process of writing a book and how that process affects the author to be a more interesting topic. Knowing how to secure a book contract and actually writing a book are two completely different experiences. Both will be addressed here because knowledge of the book writing experience itself will assist prospective authors in deciding whether or not publishing a book is something they truly wish to pursue. Specifically, this chapter will focus on (1) the steps that are necessary to secure a book contract in the field of psychology and (2) how the process of writing and publishing books affects authors in both positive and negative ways.

Although I have been an author of books that have been published over a period of 20 years, I cannot say with any degree of certainty whether my experience is similar to that of others who have also written books over most of their careers. Some of the greatest "highs" in my life were associated with "book publishing." And, some of the greatest "lows" in my life were the result of writing a book, and more specifically, meeting a book deadline. But, are these the experiences of all authors who have published a lot of books?

To find out, I teamed up with a highly competent graduate student to assist me with this chapter. When you enter the realm of book publishing (or publishing of any kind), graduate students are not only necessary, they are invaluable. Together, we "interviewed" well-known book authors in the field of psychology by emailing them a set of questions designed to elicit their experiences with writing and publishing books. About 90% of the authors we surveyed (i.e., 10 out of 12) responded to our request and answered our questions. This chapter is organized according to the questions we asked. We first summarize book authors' answers to our questions, then we offer some of our thoughts on the qualities and characteristics of book authors that will likely facilitate the process of writing and publishing books. This chapter commences with some concrete guidelines that may be followed by anyone interested in pursuing book publishing.

What Are the Rewards of Writing a Book?

Dissemination of Knowledge

When asked to identify the rewards gained by authoring or editing a book, all respondents reported that the greatest benefit is the ability to share knowledge and ideas (often new and creative ideas) with others. Writing a book can potentially provide the opportunity to guide and mentor thousands of people, including graduate students in training, academics, and practicing psychologists. In turn, the ideas, methods, and practices disseminated in books are often used by professionals to help school districts, students, clients, and patients. Books have the potential to push the edge of the envelope of a field as whole.

Personal Satisfaction

According to several book authors, it is very fulfilling when other professionals share stories about how a book has been helpful or useful to them or to the students, families, or clients with whom they work. Nearly all authors reported feeling a great sense of satisfaction upon publication of their books. In answer to the question regarding what is rewarding about writing a book, one author stated, "The satisfaction of having a discrete body of work that represents a vision."

Increased Opportunities

Publishing books affords authors increased opportunities to present at state and national conferences, leads to prestige in professional circles, and results in having more flexibility in negotiating future book contracts and royalties with publishing companies. Also, the more well-known your book becomes, the more well-known you become, which often results in invitations to collaborate on a variety of different professional projects. Some authors reported that their books led to opportunities that propelled their careers forward.

What Are the Challenges Associated with Writing a Book?

There are certainly a number of rewards that come with writing a book as well as opportunities that could change the direction of your career in ways you did not dream possible. However, there are also challenges and sacrifices.

Time

It takes a tremendous amount of time to write a book manuscript and meet a book deadline. Most new book authors do not realize how much time they will actually need to complete a book. Many factors go into estimating how long it will take to write a book, including content, length, personal writing style, amount of research necessary, other personal and work-related responsibilities, and so forth. Once those factors have been considered and you believe you have a realistic deadline, *add six to eight months* to it. As a favorite colleague of mine often says, "life happens." When you do not build in time for the unexpected, it can make the book writing process exceedingly stressful and meeting a book deadline unlikely. Publishers typically do not set book deadlines; they leave that judgment up to book authors. It has been my experience that just about every initial book deadline I estimated was an underestimate. Remember, it is better to submit a book manuscript early than late. First impressions are important, so *overestimate* how much time it will take. Chances are you will be thankful you overestimated because you might just meet that deadline.

Self-Discipline

It is often difficult to motivate oneself to complete a task. Writing a book requires a great deal of self-motivation, self-control, and self-discipline. It is not easy to meet the writing goals you have set for yourself, avoid temptations, and remove distractions. Most book authors find that creating a routine is the most effective way to stay on schedule and maintain consistent progress. For example, one author reported that she writes for about two hours every morning before her children get up for school—and that meant getting up at 3:45 a.m. every day. However, other authors reported that they prefer large chunks of time to write, such as four to six hours at a time, which often occurred in the evenings or on weekends. For authors who hold full-time positions, are the primary caretaker of their children, or have both responsibilities, finding the time to write is very challenging.

Co-Authors and Contributing Authors

You often do not know whether a colleague (even a close colleague) shares your passion, drive, and determination with regard to completing a book well and on time until you write with him or her. Co-authors have their own lives which often get in the way of the schedule you, as the primary author, might have set for the book project. Also, as dedicated as co-authors might be, the bulk of the responsibility for getting the book done falls on the shoulders of the primary author. Select co-authors carefully, as they will become an important part of your life for several months or years.

The difficulties that can arise with book co-authors may be compounded with an edited book. The greatest challenge in editing a book is in finding contributing authors who follow through and do what they say they are going to do. Contributing authors can delay a book significantly by not respecting deadlines. When contributing authors do not respect deadlines, the book is held up for several months or even a year or more. Such a situation is frustrating to book editors, unfair to other contributing authors who met the deadline (or came reasonably close), and interferes with the book production schedule.

The authors we surveyed indicated that as their experience as an editor grew, they were able to make better decisions about which authors would deliver a quality chapter on time. Sometimes, editors might have to make the difficult decision to get a book published without certain chapters or waiting for those chapters. On the other hand, outstanding chapters are often the ones being written by leading experts and are usually worth the wait. For the first book I edited, I waited a year for a chapter and it was delivered 70 pages over the limit and written on a completely different topic than the one requested. I sent it back. Incidentally, the author I waited for was Dr. John L. Horn. He revised his chapter and it was published in my book, *Contemporary Intellectual Assessment*. Horn's chapter played a very prominent role in moving the field of intelligence testing forward. I was glad I waited.

What Are the Sacrifices Associated with Writing a Book?

Time Away from Family and Friends

Nearly every author we surveyed said that the greatest sacrifice of book writing was time spent away from their family and friends. Most authors also commented that writing a book detracted significantly from their personal lives and, at times, their personal health and well-being. The sacrifice of time away from loved ones was summarized well by one of the authors we surveyed, "In every preface of every book I thank the many people who have helped to make it a success—and I always say thanks to my family 'for the hours away'— definitely a sacrifice on my part and especially their part."

One of the authors we surveyed relayed a story that resonated well with my own experience as a book author and a parent. This respondent told a story of spending time with his daughter (age 10) on a class assignment that required her to find three words that best described her as a person. After he and his daughter completed the assignment, he indicated that he "made the mistake" of asking her to find three words that described him—he reported, "Without missing a beat, she said: Work, Work, Work!!!" This anecdote epitomizes what most authors mean by "sacrifice."

Pressure to Keep Writing

When a book is successful, the publisher makes money (and *a lot more* money than the authors). As such, there is what amounts to an obligation to write the next edition. And, if or when the second edition is successful, there is pressure to write a third and a fourth edition, and so on. Writing a book is often not a one-time endeavor. The pressure to keep up with subsequent editions of books can be overwhelming at times, especially when there are changes in the field that impact book content significantly. For example, I write books that include

242 *Dawn P. Flanagan & Megan C. Sy*

tests of intelligence and cognitive abilities. Although these tests are revised roughly every 10 to 12 years, they were not all developed at the same time, so their publications are staggered such that a new edition of an important test is published every few years. The greater the impact of the test on the field, the greater the pressure to revise a book to include the test.

Because several new tests were revised in recent years, I worked on three books at the same time, and all were at different stages of production. I also had a fourth book that I was preparing for a second edition. When one is caught up in such a cycle, there is little if any time for other professional activities. Book publishing becomes your primary and at times sole contribution to the field, especially when you are juggling more than one book at a time. There are of course pros and cons to this cycle. One of the pros is knowing that your books are successful and influencing your field of study. According to the authors surveyed, the major cons are feeling like you are "never really done" and that you do not have the time to contribute to your field via other outlets.

Not a Money-Maker

You will not get rich publishing a book in a specialized field of psychology; publishing companies typically give authors 10% to 15% royalties. If you have one or more co-authors, then you of course split royalties in any way you deem appropriate. Sadly, if you add up all the hours spent working on a book, it is likely that you are working for less than minimum wage.

Recently, one of my co-authors moved across the country. Even with the benefits of technology, the distance made it difficult to co-author a book; we needed time together to "sit with the material" and brainstorm ideas. As such, we met at a half-way point a few times. The amount of money we spent on airfare, hotels, meals, and the like was "out of pocket." If our book does well, it will take two years of royalties to break even. For this and other reasons, many authors contemplate self-publishing (discussed in a section that follows). Also, it is important to keep in mind that books in specialized fields of study have a "shelf life" of about five years. One of the most disappointing aspects of publishing in a specialized field is that royalties typically spiral down rapidly after the first couple of years unless they are adopted on graduate courses.

Based on my 20 years of experience in the book publishing arena, along with the responses we received from other book authors with similar longevity, it is clear that there are challenges, sacrifices, and disappointments that go hand-in-hand with book writing and publishing, but there are also triumphs and rewards. One of the stories relayed to us by a prominent book author in the field of school psychology captured beautifully the difficulty and the joy that accompanies book writing:

> It was 1978. I was writing the first chapter of "Intelligent Testing with the WISC-R." It was hard labor, causing much pain and frustration, very much like pulling teeth. After months of writing, I finished it. I read it. I hated

it. Then I looked over my shoulder, and I saw him standing there, watching me intently: David Wechsler. I threw that image out of my mind. I threw out the entire first chapter. I decided that I could not please him and stopped trying to. Then I started over and the entire book wrote itself in a few months. And the "new" first chapter was, to me, the best thing I ever wrote. When I used to do workshops, many new psychologists and graduate students would come up to me after my talk to tell me how that first chapter changed their way of thinking. And it always brought back memories of Dr. Wechsler standing over my shoulder, watching me write every word of the first version of the chapter—and my feeling of triumph when I ripped the pages in half and threw them in the trash. It was the bravest thing I ever did!

(Alan S. Kaufman, October 3, 2016, personal communication)

What Have You Learned from Your Book Publishing Experiences?

All authors we surveyed reported that writing a book is not easy for a variety of reasons. In addition to the time an author needs to devote to the project, much of the process is also dependent on the publisher. In fact, several of the authors we surveyed identified publisher-related factors that either hindered or facilitated a book project. Sometimes it can take years before a project is even picked up by a publishing company. One of the authors surveyed reported that it took her ten years just to convince a publisher that she was writing about an important subject: cross-cultural neuropsychology. At the same time, many of the authors have had positive experiences with helpful, creative, and talented editors.

It is important to talk to book authors about their book publishing experiences. It will assist you greatly in understanding how to break into book publishing. If you know a well-published author, have her recommend you to the editor of the company that publishes her books. If she does not know your work, ask her if she is willing to read something that you have written and discuss your ideas for a book. This will assist her in understanding the importance of your book topic for the field. Publishing companies want to know *why* your book will sell. You could also consider contacting an expert in your field of study who has published a book or two and inquire about his availability and willingness to co-author a book with you. Prior to making such contact, you should have a detailed outline of your vision for the book and be prepared to discuss the contribution that you would like for him to make. If he is not interested or is over-committed, ask him to recommend someone else. Perhaps my first book publishing experience will be helpful or inspiring to you in some way.

244 Dawn P. Flanagan & Megan C. Sy

A Trip down Memory Lane

Twenty years ago, I was new to my field. My mentor liked my ideas and told me I should write a book. I did not have a name in my field; I was only a few years out of school. No publisher would take a chance on me. But, I had a vision for a book that I could not let go. The only way to bring my ideas to the forefront was to edit a book with people who were known in the field and to bring together the absolute best and brightest scholars. I worked tirelessly on a Table of Contents (TOC). Next to each chapter I placed the name of a prominent scholar—people I only dreamed of actually meeting one day. I wondered why anyone would agree to write a chapter for me—a no-name.

Upon completing the TOC, I wondered how I was going to contact the people I listed. That same day I came across a flyer in a pile of mail that had been sitting on my desk. The flyer described a symposium on an intelligence test (the Woodcock-Johnson Psycho-Educational Battery, Revised; WJ-R) that was taking place in VT the next day; I lived in NY. Three people I listed as authors for chapters were part of the symposium! I had to go. I got up at 4 a.m. and drove to VT. I walked into the hotel where the symposium was being held and the first person I saw was Dr. Kevin McGrew—a scholar who had written a lot about the WJ-R and assisted the author of that test, Dr. Richard Woodcock, with creating its norms. I took a deep breath and introduced myself. I then asked him if he would be willing to look over the TOC of the book I was proposing and write a chapter for it. He seemed put off but agreed to meet with me. We sat down. He looked over the TOC and much to my surprise, he began writing all over it. As he wrote, he offered ideas and made suggestions for other chapters and authors. He also said he was too busy to write a chapter. My heart sank. He told me that Dr. Woodcock was at the symposium and encouraged me to talk to him. But, I could not get up the nerve to approach *the* Richard Woodcock.

Instead, I approached another person I had hoped would write a chapter in the book, Dr. Nancy Mather—a well-known scholar who wrote about the use of the WJ-R in identification of learning disabilities. She told me she was too busy to write book chapters. She was not even interested in looking at the TOC. Strike two. As disappointed as I was, I sat through the symposium and wondered how people like Drs. McGrew and Mather could be *that busy*. [My thoughts at the time are a reflection of how naive I was.] After strolling through the exhibit hall at the conference, I decided to go home—defeated. Just then, Dr. McGrew came up to me and said, "Dr. Woodcock is looking forward to meeting you. He is interested in your book." WHAT?! He walked me over to him and introduced me.

There I was, sitting on a couch with the author of a famous test. A test that inspired me to do research. A test that changed my way of thinking about intelligence. With trembling hands, I opened up the folder I was holding that contained several copies of my TOC. I reached for a clean copy and then stopped myself. Instead, I handed Dr. Woodcock the copy that Dr. McGrew wrote all over. I wanted him to see how interested his close colleague was in the project. The only words I was able to remember from my conversation with Dr. Woodcock were, "I'll write that chapter." Elation! Those four words were the single best thing that happened to me in my career.

Once I had Dr. Woodcock on board, I started contacting other test authors. They all said yes, one by one—probably not so much because they had the time for the project and truly desired to be part of it, but because they wanted their test represented in the book. No one wanted to be left out. The more scholars I could list as having agreed to write chapters, the easier it was to convince people to be part of the project. The book soon became a "Who's Who" in intelligence testing. The first edition was published in 1997. Drs. McGrew and Mather ended up contributing chapters to the book as well as two subsequent editions. I am currently working on the fourth edition and they, along with many other original authors, continue to be part of this project. Over the course of my career, I became friends and colleagues with several of the original contributors and wrote books with some of them.

My first book set the stage for my career. Proposing the list of scholars was bold; asking them to write chapters for me was brave; having over 25 "big names" agree to write chapters for me before I even had a publisher was a dream come true. Several weeks ago, I stumbled upon a copy of that book proposal that I hand-delivered to Guilford in New York City in 1995. It brought back memories of how hard I worked on that proposal—I had attached a brief reference list of each proposed author's most important contributions to the field, a very detailed description of their chapter, and documentation of their willingness to write the chapter for the book. I remember meeting the president of the publishing company and hearing the editor say that it was the first time that anyone had ever delivered a proposal to them in person. I remember signing the book contract. Those were career highs for sure. I enjoyed editing that book and, over the years, I enjoyed writing books as well. It is not for everyone though. There are professional and personal prerequisites for book writing. We discuss these next.

Prerequisites for Book Writing

Spiegler (2011) described a number of professional and personal prerequisites for writing a textbook. From a professional standpoint, knowledge and expertise in the subject area is one of the primary and most obvious prerequisites. Authors typically will have experience teaching courses, conducting workshops, or presenting at conferences on a variety of issues related to the topic. It is important to note that textbooks are often written for students or other individuals with less experience in the subject area; thus, specific writing skills are also necessary in order to successfully engage the reader and stimulate learning. Furthermore, because writing a book requires a significant amount of time, authors will benefit from a supportive professional environment (e.g., release time from their institution, ability to go on sabbatical, or a course reduction).

Perhaps equally important are the personal characteristics that enable an author to be successful. Spiegler (2011) identified a number of these, including flexibility, perseverance, stamina, and good work habits. In addition, certain cognitive skills (e.g., attention to detail and logical thinking) and personality traits (e.g., openness to criticism and comfort with solitary work) are also helpful. Notably, all of the authors we surveyed described the importance of time management and commitment in the writing process, which is often slow and tedious. As one of our contributors stated, book writing is "a marathon, not a sprint."

Deciding How to Publish: Commercial vs. Self-Publishing

After making the decision to pursue a book contract and ensuring that the prerequisites are in place, authors generally have two options for publishing their work; these are commercial publishing companies and self-publication. There are advantages and disadvantages to each and there is certainly not one correct path. By and large, the most significant disadvantage to working with a commercial publishing house is that the system benefits the companies much more than the authors. Individuals who publish their work with a commercial company lose ownership of their work and have less control over how the book is produced or marketed. Furthermore, as one of the individuals we surveyed described it, "The book publishing industry is not set up to help the author make money." Royalties are typically a small percentage of the cost of the book and new authors often do not have leverage in terms of negotiating their rates. Certainly, when a book is well-received or when a second edition is requested, authors might be in a better position to bargain and negotiate. However, the collective wisdom from the authors we surveyed was not to expect to get rich from writing books. Despite this disadvantage, working with a commercial publishing house can remain a rewarding experience. Authors will often form close collegial relationships with the editorial team. Aside from being able to collaborate with other creative and talented individuals, these connections might also make it easier to publish subsequent projects.

For authors who might not be inclined to work with a commercial publishing company, self-publication can also be a worthwhile option. The main advantages of self-publishing include retaining the rights to one's work and intellectual property and having more control over profits. On the other hand, self-publishing can require plenty of time, upfront expenses, and coordination of various logistics. Commercial publishing houses assume most of the responsibility for aspects like marketing the book, shipping to relevant retailers, and ensuring stocks and availability. Authors who self-publish do not have access to these resources and support. That being said, the widespread use of social media as a marketing tool can make it easier for authors to promote their work.

Pursuing Commercial Publication

For new authors interested in pursuing commercial book publication, it might be difficult to know where to start. Based on the collective experience of the authors we surveyed, here are a few steps to get you started:

Step 1: Seek advice and learn from more experienced authors and editors.

Step 2: Review the books in your field that are similar to or related to the topic on which you would like to write a book. Make a list of the publishers of those books. Contact one or more authors of those books and ask them about their experience with their publisher and the lead editor with whom they worked. Understand that authors are busy, so you might have difficulty connecting with many of them. Be sure to cast a wide net.

Step 3: Once you have an idea of which publishing companies might be right for you, review their guidelines for submitting a book proposal. These are often found online through the company's website. Tables 23.1 and 23.2 provide some examples of the important components of a book proposal, as required by prominent publishing companies.

Step 4: Write your proposal. Keep in mind that publishing companies want to make money. Therefore, they will pay close attention to the following: (a) market for the book, (b) competing titles and how yours is different or unique, and (c) the need for your book (i.e., Why would people want to buy your book? And what are its major selling points?). Ask authors of books for a copy of a book proposal they have written. Although, keep in mind that well-established authors do not need to write lengthy and convincing book proposals, so try to obtain copies of proposals that were written by people who are more junior in their field.

Step 5: If you do not yet have a well-established program of research or if you are not yet well known for your area of expertise, you will need to convince a publisher that you are worth the investment. It takes a long time to establish a reputation of excellence in your field of study. If you are not there yet, then consider seeking out a co-author who is. Having a co-author who is recognized in the field will increase your chances of securing a book contract.

I was once asked to write a book with one of the "giants" in my field of study. I was excited to say the least. However, the arrangement was that I would write the entire book, he would review and edit it, and we would split the royalties evenly. Suddenly, it did not sound as attractive or appealing, but only because of where I was in my career—I was not at all new to the field. However, if you are new to your field of study, this type of arrangement, although labor-intensive, would almost guarantee a book contract and, upon publication, greatly enhance your visibility in your field of study. Before talking with anyone about co-authorship, be prepared with a detailed description and TOC for your book and be open to suggestions.

Alternatively, consider editing a book in your area of expertise prior to writing your own. Write a chapter for your edited book that will provide a

Table 23.1 Required Elements in a Book Proposal for Wiley and Routledge/Taylor & Francis Group

Wiley	Routledge/Taylor & Francis Group
Product vision • Goals of the project, implications for how students and instructors will benefit • Unmet needs the project will fulfill • Intended audience • Format—how will the content be presented? • Unique characteristics of the project • Environment—how and where will the product be used (e.g., online, classroom)? *Learning design* • Overall experience—what elements (e.g., text, exercises, interactive material) are needed to provide an ideal learning experience? • Learning elements—what elements will be included to assess learning? • Customization—how much can the content be customized by faculty? • Visuals—describe visual illustrations *Product outline* • Outline of the product—table of contents with chapter titles and chapter headings/subheadings • Define any components of print and media associated with the title *Additional information* • Curriculum vitae of author or editor • Identify the text you currently use for this topic and why you chose it • Information about currently available texts on the topic • Summary of any market research for project	*Statement of aims* • Main themes and objectives of the project • Description of how the book is innovative or different from currently available texts • 150- to 200-word abstract *Detailed synopsis and chapter summaries* • Table of contents with chapter titles and subheadings • Chapter headings, with explanation of intended content • Basic structure and features of each chapter • Expected authors, if edited collection *Description of target market* • Intended audience for the book • Primary purpose • List of aligned journals, publications, and relevant organizations • International appeal of the book *Review of main competing titles* • Competing titles and strengths and weaknesses of these books • What distinguishes the book from existing competition? *Format and timeline* • Date for final manuscript submission • Anticipated length of book • Anticipated number of diagrams, illustrations, and tables • Anticipated third-party materials *Additional information* • Curriculum vitae of author or editor • Online resources—would this book benefit from a companion website? • List of academic referees—3 to 5 qualified reviewers

Note. Wiley: www.wiley.com/WileyCDA/Section/id-301850.html; Routledge/Taylor & Francis Group: https://s3-us-west-2.amazonaws.com/tandfbis/rt-files/docs/Proposal+Guidelines_Textbooks+PDF.pdf

Publishing Books 249

Table 23.2 Required Elements in a Book Proposal for Guilford Press and Oxford University Press

Guilford Press	Oxford University Press
Prospectus • Table of contents • Detailed chapter outline • Introduction to the book summarizing principal themes and unique features • Major selling points—how the work is superior to existing books • Details—length, use of visuals, format issues, proposed schedule for completion	*Book description* • Description of the project • Detailed chapter outline • Outstanding features—what are the outstanding, distinctive, or unique features of the work? • Visuals, cases, questions, appendices, and supplementary material • Competition—how the book will be similar to and different from existing works
Author information • Curriculum vitae of author or editor *Sample chapters* • One or two chapters that best represent the work or writing samples on the same subject	*Market considerations* • The major market for the book • For what course and level of student is the book intended? • How may the market best be reached?
	Status of the work • Timetable for completing the book • Estimated length of the book • Plans to class-test the material
	Sample chapters • One or two chapters that are an integral part of the book
	Additional information • Curriculum vitae of author or editor • Experts in the field suited to evaluate the proposal

Note. Guilford Press: www.guilford.com/authors/submit-proposal; Oxford University Press: https://global.oup.com/academic/authors/submissions/?cc=us&lang=en&

springboard for the book you wish to write independently. Note that if you decide to edit a book, it is critically important to include well-known experts. More importantly, you must include documentation showing that at least 50% of the people you invited to write a chapter for your book have agreed to do so. Publishing companies will not give you a "good faith" contract.

Step 6: Submit your proposal to the publishing company that seems like the best match. Before you send your proposal to more than one publishing company, make sure that the publisher allows simultaneous submissions. This information is likely available on the publisher's website. If possible, meet with an editor of your preferred publishing company at a national conference where you are presenting your work. Most major publishing companies have exhibits

250   *Dawn P. Flanagan & Megan C. Sy*

at national conferences and editors are typically in attendance. If you know an author of a book published by the company you are interested in, have him or her introduce you to an editor at a conference.

Step 7: Be patient. There are many book publishing companies. You only need one to say yes.

Concluding Thoughts and Advice for New Authors

Writing and editing books can be an extremely rewarding endeavor that provides opportunities to reach many students, colleagues, and practitioners. However, the process is not without its challenges and disappointments. It is clear that a book project requires hours upon hours of time, tireless effort, and personal sacrifices. We hope that the collective wisdom from all the individuals we surveyed will help any aspiring authors decide whether publishing is right for them and will provide some information on how to get started. On a final note, we asked the authors we surveyed for any advice they wish to impart to new authors. Below are their responses:

- Make sure you have the discipline and commitment to get the manuscript done on schedule. Set aside certain hours each day to write without interruptions and stick with that schedule.
- Make sure you are comfortable working alone for long hours for days at a time.
- Be organized.
- Choose co-authors with a similar work style and work ethic that you can count on to do their part. Find people you enjoy writing with. All authors need to be committed to the project and need to try to stick to the agreed-upon schedule. For edited books, invite people you know will follow through and who are able to write clearly.
- Choose a topic you are really interested in or very experienced in or both! It is much easier to complete a book if you are truly passionate about the subject.
- Be very careful with references and citations and keep track of them as you work. Otherwise, you spend a great deal of time trying to find sources at the end of the project.
- Learn from those who have been there before you.
- Do not let publishing houses tell you what content is important. They are thinking about sales; you are thinking about integrity.
- Do not let publishing houses create your cover without your input or approval. It is essential that the cover represent your vision.
- Consider the sacrifices involved in book writing very carefully so you know what you are getting into. Significant time away from family and friends for months on end is difficult. Be sure to build in time for family and friends as their support is invaluable.
- Find ways to make the process of writing a book as enjoyable as possible. For example, set up a cozy, comfortable corner of your home that you

retreat to only when working on your book. That space, along with the passion you bring to it, will help to ensure that the endeavor is fulfilling.

Reference

Spiegler, M. D. (2011). Writing a psychology textbook: Is it right for you? *Observer*, 24(10). Retrieved from www.psychologicalscience.org/index.php/publications/observer/2011/december-11/writing-a-psychology-textbook.html

24 Publishing Tests and Assessment Instruments

Bruce A. Bracken

Edward Thorndike (1926) is known for many significant contributions to psychology and education, but within the measurement realm he is known for espousing possibly the most famous axiom ever: "If anything exists, it exists in some amount. If it exists in some amount, it can be measured" (p. 38). Thorndike's oft-repeated claim seems to have become a rationale and catalyst for educators' and psychologists' efforts to measure seemingly every conceivable form of behavior, concept, construct, or content known to man. The subsequent proliferation of tests throughout the 20th and 21st centuries has been truly remarkable—to the point that one has to wonder if we have gone too far in what we measure as opposed to what we treat. I worked briefly with a director of special education in Georgia who said it best, "You can weigh a pig ten times a day, but if you don't feed him he won't gain any weight." Despite seeking balance in the services provided by school psychologists to offset assessment with more diverse roles and activities, there remains profound interest in educational and psychological assessment and test development. This chapter will focus on the process of test publishing for individuals who are passionate about measuring the multitude of psychological and educational entities that presumably exist—and if they exist, exist in some quantity, and therefore can be measured.

Pursuing Test Publication

There seem to be three types of people who develop tests: clinicians and educators who know a good bit about human characteristics and the target content but know little about measurement methods; measurement specialists well-steeped in measurement theory but not very knowledgeable about human characteristics (e.g., cognitive, behavioral, developmental) or the target content; and test developers who understand the intricate interplay between measurement, the target content, human characteristics, clinical theory, and practice. It is this last group of test developers who are most successful at publishing tests of high psychometric quality and practical value.

Where does one go to acquire that requisite balance between clinical and technical knowledge? The fundamental answer is higher education—graduate

Publishing Tests & Assessment Instruments   253

programs in education and psychology. However, beyond higher education, there are supplemental sources, such as professional organizations that offer guidelines, recommendations, and words of wisdom. Examples of these professional organizations include the American Educational Research Association (AERA), the American Psychological Association (APA), the American Test Publishers (ATP), the International Test Commission (ITC), and the National Council on Measurement in Education (NCME). Individually and collectively, these organizations influence test construction by publishing related textbooks, journals, in-house publications (e.g., *The ITC Guidelines on Adapting Tests*; ITC, 2005), and cross-organizational joint publications (e.g., *Standards for Educational and Psychological Testing*; AERA, APA, & NCME, 2014). Such organizations also comprise divisions and committees dedicated to the practice of testing (e.g., APA's Committee on Psychological Testing and Assessment and AERA's Division D for Measurement and Research Methodology). Importantly, school psychologists have been well represented in all of these test-related professional committees, divisions, and endeavors, as well as the enterprise of test development and publishing.

Test Publication Outlets: Commercial Publishing Houses vs. Public Domain Publishing

Individuals seeking to develop tests have essentially two options for publishing their work: commercial publishing houses or public domain outlets. Generally, the question that directs the author in one direction over the other is whether the proposed test has potential commercial value—that is, can a publisher invest in the development of the author's test, market it, and sell it for a profit? As a president of one large publishing house explained, "I have to ask myself: If I invest in a test that may take three years to bring to market, will I recoup the initial investment *and* make sufficient profit to justify the risk of the initial financial outlay?" Investing in test development is a risky business because many tests fail to sell well enough to defray their developmental costs. The president went on to propose that he could instead invest the same money in a risk-free investment (e.g., a money market account or a certificate of deposit) and be assured a profit three years hence.

I have had the good fortune to have published approximately a dozen commercially produced and distributed tests (e.g., the Bracken Basic Concept Scale, BBCS; Bracken, 1984, 1998, 2006, and the Universal Nonverbal Intelligence Test, UNIT; Bracken & McCallum, 1998, 2016) and several public domain tests as well (e.g., the Children's Ecological Attitude and Knowledge Scale, ChEAKS; Leeming, Dwyer, & Bracken, 1995, and the Test of Critical Thinking, TCT; Bracken et al., 2003). The former tests were deemed to have significant commercial value to warrant the kind of "deep pocket" investment that the corporate president described primarily because the focus of the tests comported with requirements of federal law (i.e., Individuals with Disabilities Education Act; IDEA, 2004) for mandated areas of assessment (i.e., speech/

254 Bruce A. Bracken

language and cognitive functioning), whereas the latter tests met no federal mandates and were developed because of a pressing research need (e.g., grant evaluation). In later sections of this chapter, I will describe how to write a proposal to present a test idea to a commercial publisher, but first I will discuss the inherent value of public domain publications and their possible outlets.

Public Domain Tests

With public domain test publishing, there are essentially three options: self-publishing, agency/institutional publishing, and publishing a test within a book or journal article. The ChEAKS (Leeming et al., 1995), for example, is an attitudinal scale created to serve teachers and researchers interested in changing students' attitudes toward ecology and the environment. There was little perceived commercial value in a scale so limited in its focus, but we deemed that the assessment was worth pursuing for the sake of contributing to the field. We developed ChEAKS and published it as the focus of a journal article, which allowed for its broad dissemination and use. The TCT, on the other hand, was developed as a dependent measure as part of a federal grant. We wanted the instrument to ultimately be more than a "once-use only" scale, so we made it available to researchers and practitioners at no charge. Anyone can obtain the instrument by personal contact with the authors or through the website of the Center for Gifted Education at the College of William and Mary (http://education.wm.edu/centers/cfge/). Despite the limited commercial value of these public domain instruments, we strove for quality construction, and we believe in the potential utility of these tests for use in other research projects.

Self-publishing a public domain test is an option, and the publication process is similar to that of the two aforementioned approaches, but the test author retains copyright of the instrument and controls its use through personal permission and individual dissemination. Whether the test is self-published, agency/institution published, or published as part of an article or chapter in a journal or book, respectively, the instrument should be of sufficient quality to warrant its use. According to a current report by the tracking website ResearchGate, the ChEAKS has received more than 700 reads and 125 citations, which likely attests to its value as a public domain instrument.

Commercial Test Publishing

The remainder of this chapter will address the process of publishing tests with commercial publishers. There are literally hundreds of publishing houses internationally that develop, market, and distribute educational and psychological tests. Some publishers are small, with limited resources that publish only a couple or a few tests; other publishers are among the largest corporate publishing houses in the world (e.g., Pearson). Self-publishing a test as a commercial venture is also an option that some authors have pursued. The primary limitation in self-publishing is cost—the often prohibitive costs associated with development, norming, validation, statistical analyses, materials development, production, marketing, and distribution.

Pros and Cons of Commercial Publishing

The benefits of commercial publishers are many; the cons of publishing with a commercial publisher are also many but less obvious to the first-time test author. The benefits of publishing with a commercial publisher are that the publisher defrays upfront expenses; coordinates the logistics associated with publishing the test; gathers and analyzes normative data; organizes validity and reliability studies; designs, prints, and binds test materials; markets the product through catalog distribution and conference presence (some publishers also possess a national or international sales force); takes and fills orders; stores and replenishes stock as needed; provides and assumes much of the legal responsibilities associated with the venture; and sends detailed royalty statements and payments to authors. The drawbacks associated with publishing with a commercial publishing house include loss of author ownership (i.e., the publisher owns the product henceforth); diminished author control over aspects of test construction, production, marketing, sales support; accepting royalty agreements that reward the publisher disproportionately (appropriately so) for assuming the financial risk for the project and expending the personnel and funds to develop the author's work; compromising one's intellectual concepts and property; loss of control over scheduling and personal responsibilities (e.g., publisher demands for a quick author response to maintain an internal schedule, but the publisher frequently fails to meet contracted publication dates by as many as several years with no repercussions).

One of the greatest misconceptions authors have about publishers, large and small, is that they know what they are doing. Turnover is often high, and expertise within publishing houses is generally equal to that of a recent graduate of a master's or doctoral degree program in education or a practicing field psychologist, which, not surprisingly, represent two of the recruiting pools for test publishers. This personnel limitation is especially common within product development and product marketing and sales divisions in many companies. Many authors are astonished to learn that the marketing director or vice president is not someone with a master's in business administration specializing in marketing. Rather the typical marketing director is a practicing school psychologist, a former textbook salesperson, or someone within the company who has been "promoted" to this new area of functioning based on successes elsewhere. Similarly, the typical project director, the person responsible for shepherding all aspects of the test development process for the publisher, is not a person with a Ph.D. in measurement or research methods but often a practitioner with a Psy.D. or Ed.D. with little to no previous experience developing tests.

As with other industries (e.g., auto manufacturing, breweries, and book publishing), it is common for smaller, privately owned test publishers (and

256   Bruce A. Bracken

sometimes large equity-based publishers) to be bought out in part or purchased entirely by larger companies. Because the publisher owns the author's "work," they may sell any portion of their portfolio at whim to another publisher, including the author's test, without the author's consent. Although the author has no say over such sales and is generally informed by a phone call from one of the selling company's vice presidents or president, the call is a pro forma notification that the sale is finalized and the new owner will notify the author sometime in the future to discuss how his or her test will fit into the existing product line. Fortunately, the contract an author negotiates with the initial publisher remains in effect with the new publisher, so there are no unpleasant contract surprises when one's test is sold to another publisher.

Contacting a Publisher to Pitch a Test Idea

To most consumers, publishing houses are viewed as large, secretive entities. If a consumer has a question about a test or wishes to purchase a test they know enough to contact customer service, but customer service is a dead end for a test author seeking an acquisition editor. Acquisition editors often function in that capacity while possessing another title (e.g., vice president of development or director of marketing), so calling customer service and asking for the "clinical acquisition editor" will likely get you nowhere because the men and women behind the customer service phones generally do not know who is responsible for receiving and reviewing test proposals.

Test authors should peruse the catalogs of the various publishers and determine whether the proposed test "fits" the product line of the publisher *and* whether the publisher already has a test that would compete with the proposed test. A proposal can then be sent directly to the company's postal address, with "acquisition editor" as the addressee, but doing so limits the likelihood of someone actually attending to the proposal. A better strategy is to attend professional conferences and visit the publisher's exhibit booth to make an initial contact. The corporate personnel who attend conferences and staff booths are generally mid-level corporate managers, division heads, and vice presidents. These individuals know in which direction the company is moving, whether they are currently seeking test proposals, what areas of assessment the company is focusing on, and the commercial viability of many test ideas. Importantly, they know who among them is the person or people responsible for reviewing test proposals. Often, a brief meeting can be arranged at a conference with a company representative over a cup of coffee to discuss your test idea. First-time authors often fear that a publisher will steal their idea and leave the author behind. Publishers are quite good about maintaining confidentiality and integrity because to do otherwise would sully their reputation. That being said, I have had an experience where a publisher did in fact "steal" my co-authored test idea and admitted to me that he did so to protect his product line from competition when my co-author and I decided to publish with another company.

Creating and Submitting a Formal Test Proposal

There is no uniform formula or template for creating a test proposal that will ensure acceptance; in fact, publishers do not facilitate the submission process by providing guidelines for proposal submission. The test author should be aware, however, of four things publishers are looking for: (1) publishers seek products that will not be prohibitively expensive to develop, market, and sell; (2) they must be convinced there is a large market for the proposed test; (3) they want to know about the competition for the proposed test; and (4) they want to know that the author has the integrity, knowledge and ability, and commitment to develop the test, write the manual, and support the test through workshops, presentations, and writing. I will elaborate on each of these points in the following section.

Developmental Expense

"Tests" come in many varieties and formats, and each has its own level of expense associated with the variety and format. Self-report or third-party reported attitudinal or symptom scales (e.g., self-concept, motivation, anxiety, depression) are generally easier and less expensive to develop, norm, produce, and distribute than skill-based tests (e.g., cognition, motor, speech/language, development). Within any domain, group administered instruments are generally more easily and less expensively developed and normed than individually administered tests, unless the group tests involve multiple levels, multiple forms, and are normed on enormous samples (e.g., tens of thousands).

Authors who submit proposals for new tests should bear in mind that they should limit proposed expenses where they can: print material is less expensive than manipulatives; black and white print is less expensive than four-color print; group tests are less expensive to norm than individually administered tests; ages or grades represented in the normative sample should match maximum assessment demands; a simple theoretical approach with fewer subtests and scales will be less expensive than representing a complex model; a Level B test (lower examiner qualifications) is generally less expensive to develop than a Level C test (higher examiner qualifications) due to the requisite skills and costs for field coordinators and examiners; and extensive artwork is more expensive than limited artwork. The guiding principle is to propose a test that is reasonable in its anticipated expenses rather than seeking a "pie in the sky" first edition. The first editions of the BBCS (Bracken, 1984) and the UNIT (Bracken and McCallum, 1998) employed no-frill artwork with black and white line drawings. Because both tests were commercially successful, subsequent editions employed more refined four-color artwork.

Accurate Market Projection

Tests with the greatest likelihood of success are those that represent mandated areas of assessment in federal regulations. Tests of intelligence, achievement, speech and language, and some others sell well in part because there is a requirement that they be used in common educational referral-related assessments. Many great tests have limited market share not because of poor quality but because they address optional areas of assessment. The Clinical Assessment of Interpersonal Relations (CAIR; Bracken, 2007) is an example of such a test. Although virtually every diagnostic condition listed in the various *Diagnostic and Statistical Manual of Mental Disorders* (DSM) editions includes impaired interpersonal relations as a diagnostic criterion, interpersonal relations is not a federally mandated area of assessment. The CAIR has had a modest sales history despite its large, nationally representative normative sample, outstanding technical qualities, ubiquitous content representation in the DSM, and ease of use and interpretation, mostly because examiners are not mandated to use it or a comparable measure of relationship quality. Because commercial test publishers have an inherent profit motive, it behooves a test author to be able to convince the publisher that significant sales are likely with the proposed test.

Test Competition

One of the most difficult challenges for a test publisher is to compete with an extant successful test—even when the proposed test is significantly better than the existing test. Having the benefit of being the "first test out" is essential to large-scale adoption and ultimately sales. Sometimes, however, it is not a matter of being first, but first in a long while. The Behavioral Assessment System for Children (BASC; Reynolds & Kamphaus, 1992, 2004, 2015) is a good example of this principle. The original BASC was published at a time when there was abject stagnation in the area of behavioral assessment; existing scales were limited in content, possessed old norms, and lacked the theoretical and psychometric sophistication that newer tests evidenced. Reynolds and Kamphaus seized the opportunity and took advantage of the paucity of quality instruments in this area and had a mega-hit with the BASC. The BASC was not the first behavior rating scale published, but it was the first quality scale to be published in a long while.

Negotiating a Contract

Test publishers have boilerplate contracts that are designed to cover most legal issues and protect their investment and interests. Generally, there is little room for negotiation on many contractual points; however, there are a few areas where the author can negotiate and should be watchful.

- Publishers will sometimes request "first right of refusal" for any future ideas the author might have for new products. Authors should avoid being constrained and eliminate any such "first right of refusal" wording from the agreement.

- To protect their investment publishers will often include a "non-compete" clause in the contract—that is, an author cannot publish a test with another publisher that competes with the test the first publisher is intending to publish. This clause is reasonable in the narrow sense of not competing directly with the proposed test, but contractual wording sometimes is too vague and can be read to include virtually any product that is remotely related to the proposed test in content, age level, title, and so on. An author should be careful to ensure that non-compete wording is not too limiting.
- Because tests are expensive to develop, some publishers propose that the author share in developmental costs—sometimes as much as a 50% cost-sharing for specific portions of test development (e.g., artwork expenses). Author-related expenses are covered upfront by the publisher and are deducted from the author's royalty checks at a given rate (e.g., not to exceed 50% of the royalty amount due in any statement period). Authors should consider this option carefully; it is conceivable that the author who shares such expenses might essentially cut his or her royalty rate in half for the duration of the test's life.
- Royalty rates vary considerably on published works; royalties on my various tests range from a low of 9% on my first test published to 16% on later works. The rationale publishers often use for low royalty rates is that they are investing the money to develop the test, and they are accepting the associated risks. This logic is true, but it does not consider the author's investment or risk. The author is investing several years' effort to bring the test to market and then years more supporting the product through workshops, editing, consulting, and so on. The author, like the publisher, has a lot of investment in the product. To be fair to the publisher and author, I recommend a "risk/profit sharing" royalty approach that employs a graduated royalty rate, with the rate increasing in direct relation to the sales of the test, using specified benchmarks for rate increases.
- Because the author defers payment on his or her work until the first royalty period *after* the test is published—that is, possibly several years after the contract is signed—it is important to negotiate the largest royalty advance possible. Although the amount of the advance will be deducted from future royalties at some negotiated rate (e.g., no more than 50% deducted from what is due during any royalty period), the author benefits from his or her intellectual work upon contract signing.
- Test publishers generally offer two or three complimentary copies of the work to the author as part of a boilerplate contract. I typically request six to ten copies. The rationale for requesting more is to be able to make review and complimentary copies available to important professionals in the field without having to ask the publisher to send a copy to the person and have to justify the relevance or importance of the recipient. The author, however, should always reserve the right to ask the publisher to provide additional complimentary review copies to textbook authors,

260   *Bruce A. Bracken*

journal editors, reviewers, or others who will help make the test better known.

- Authors should insist that the contract include a provision that ensures that should the publisher discontinue development or sale of the product at any time, for any reason, the test's ownership reverts to the author. Even large, well-known, well-respected test publishers have had financial difficulties and leadership failings that required them to sell off portions of their product line, discontinue working on projects they had under contract, and renege on agreements for developing new products. A recent experience I have had is that a large corporate publisher discontinued the scale of my test suite and co-opted the material for a curriculum project. They have denied my request for the return of the entire product, claiming that the contract promises only the return of materials I submitted. Test development is a joint project; returning only author submitted material leaves the author with little of value to take to another publisher. The author must protect his or her interests when a contract is being negotiated against such poor financial or personnel management and insist that the entire project be returned to the author should the publisher discontinue marketing or selling the product.

- Authors should keep in mind that a contract conveys throughout the life of the product. If you settle for a low royalty in the first edition, the fifth edition will have the same low royalty rate. Similarly, if you did not pay any developmental costs on the first edition, you will not pay developmental costs on later editions. I have experienced with some publishers, however, instances in which they wanted to change the nature of the contract before approving a test's revision, trying to gain a more favorable advantage. This kind of heavy-handed leverage by the publisher should be ignored. If the test has sold well throughout its first edition, the revision will be approved under the same contract conditions as the earlier version. As one contract attorney told me, "I'll give you the same advice that the corporate lawyers are giving your publisher: 'Never go backward in a contract.'"

Conclusion

Test publishing is a rewarding professional activity that stirs the passion of many individuals, with the greatest reward being the author's knowledge that he or she has developed a useful tool that will help educators and psychologists better understand their client's current condition. Whether a test is published for public domain consumption or as a commercially sold instrument, the joy of "tinkering" with ideas and words, experimenting with procedures and methods, and developing an instrument with the highest possible technical qualities achievable is a very satisfying way to spend professional time.

References

American Educational Research Association, American Psychological Association, & National Council on Measurement in Education. (2014). *Standards for educational and psychological testing.* Washington, DC: American Educational Research Association.

Bracken, B. A. (1984). *Bracken Basic Concept Scale.* Columbus, OH: Charles Merrell.

Bracken, B. A. (1998). *Bracken Basic Concept Scale—Revised.* San Antonio, TX: Harcourt Assessment.

Bracken, B. A. (2006). *Bracken Basic Concept Scale—Receptive 3rd Edition.* San Antonio, TX: Harcourt Assessment.

Bracken, B. A. (2007). *Clinical Assessment of Interpersonal Relations.* Odessa, FL: Psychological Assessment Resources.

Bracken, B. A., Bai, W., Fithian, E., Lamprecht, M. S., Little, C. A., & Quek, C. (2003). *Test of Critical Thinking.* Williamsburg, VA: The Center for Gifted Education. The College of William and Mary.

Bracken, B. A., & McCallum, R. S. (1998). *Universal Nonverbal Intelligence Test.* Itasca, IL: Riverside Publishing.

Bracken, B. A., & McCallum, R. S. (2016). *Universal Nonverbal Intelligence Test—2nd Edition.* Austin, TX: Pro-Ed.

Individuals with Disabilities Education Act, 20 U.S.C. § 1400 (2004).

International Test Commission. (2005). *International guidelines on test adaptation.* www.intestcom.org

Leeming, F. C., Dwyer, W. O., & Bracken, B. A. (1995). Children's Ecological Attitude and Knowledge Scale. *The Journal of Environmental Education, 26,* 22–31.

Reynolds, C. R., & Kamphaus, R. W. (1992). *Behavioral Assessment System for Children.* Circle Pines, MN: American Guidance Service.

Reynolds, C. R., & Kamphaus, R. W. (2004). *Behavioral Assessment System for Children—Second Edition.* Circle Pines, MN: American Guidance Service.

Reynolds, C. R., & Kamphaus, R. W. (2015). *Behavioral Assessment System for Children—Third Edition.* San Antonio, TX: Pearson.

Thorndike, E. L. (1926). *The measurement of intelligence.* New York, NY: Teacher's College, Columbia University.

Part 5

Writing with Goals in Mind

25 Building Theory and Promoting Basic Science in School Psychology Research

Matthew K. Burns and
Shawna Petersen-Brown

Science is the foundation for school psychology practice and training (Ysseldyke et al., 2006), but school psychology is a new science. School psychology started with Lightner Witmer's psychological and child guidance clinic at the University of Pennsylvania in 1896 (Philips, 1990), but developmental psychology (Thompson, Hogan, & Clark, 2011) and most social sciences trace their roots to the mid-to-late 1700s (Kuper & Kuper, 1996), or even as far back as ancient Greece (Halsey, 2004).

Turner (2004) argued that sociology is a mature science not because of when it was founded, but because it was a complete, self-sufficient, and coherent form of intellectual activity, as evidenced by its set of research methods and clear theoretical implications. Thus, it is a focus on theory that makes a scientific discipline mature and, counterintuitively to most practitioners, most relevant to practice. Theoretical and conceptual frameworks provide a structure to guide practices and solve problems (Tharinger, 2000) and are important for educational innovations to have a lasting impact (Ellis & Bond, 2016). School psychological research has always focused on effectiveness and has recently made great strides on consistency of implementation (e.g., Hagermoser Sanetti & Kratochwill, 2009). Research within school psychology has also become more rigorous than in previous years (Power & Mautone, 2011), all of which will advance the field. However, school psychology is not a mature science because school psychology researchers often do not adequately consider theory (Burns, 2011; Hughes, 2015). Mercer, Idler, and Bartfai (2014) found 94 intervention studies published in school psychology journals between 2007 and 2012, only 48% of which used an explicitly stated or identifiable theoretical framework, and only 37% linked their results to theory.

The purpose of this chapter is to discuss the importance of theoretical implications within school psychological research, discuss what theoretically oriented research would look like, and outline approaches to writing theoretical papers. We will begin by arguing the importance of theory in research.

Does Theory Really Matter?

Theory matters because it provides an underlying conceptual framework from which interventions can be developed. Although many researchers would accept the fundamental role of theory, practitioners are often more skeptical about its role in their work. We agree with Lewin's (1952) famous statement that "There is nothing more practical than a good theory" (p. 169). Take the example of character education, which was widely implemented in K-12 schools during the 2000s. Research on character education resulted in small effects for high-school students ($d = 0.23$) and middle-school students ($d = 0.22$) and was mostly based on behavior and attitude (Hattie, 2009). Perhaps one reason why there were poor effects was because there was a lack of theoretical focus. Many character education programs were based on ideas developed from group consensus that represented various political, racial, religious, and gender groups (Peterson, O'Connor, & Fluke, 2014) with almost no consideration of underlying theories. As a result, there was considerable variability in what was implemented under the auspices of character education because there was no established guiding framework. Later in this chapter, we discuss how theory can be used to understand interventions and to apply them in different settings.

Understanding Interventions

Applying sophisticated conceptual frameworks to intervention research is the best way to advance it (Hughes, 2015) because it allows us to give meaning to data (Tharinger, 2000). Almost everyone reading this chapter will recall a time that they saw a free health screening at a local store, community center, or church. They might have taken advantage of this free service under the idea that early identification of potential health problems is an important first step to effective treatment. Why then did the President of the Minnesota Academy of Family Practice argue against these health screenings? Because the potential patients were better off receiving complete physicals that examined the entire body and considered all risk factors and family history than participating in a "blind search for disease" (Yee, 2009). Health screeners cannot adequately understand risk data without fully considering their context, which is analogous to the role of theory within research in that the data cannot be adequately understood unless they are contextualized within relevant theory (Burns, 2011).

Identifying the theoretical underpinnings of an intervention allows us to better understand critical intervention components and to consider broader implications. Researchers can use theory to hypothesize about which component of the intervention is most closely linked to positive outcomes. The hypotheses are based on theory because (a) theory can provide the framework for which to understand the intervention and to identify components of it, and (b) arbitrarily selecting components to systematically test increases the likelihood of a significant finding due to type 1 error. In other words, a researcher could examine an intervention and assume that there are ten different components, and researching all of them could lead to a significant finding due to sampling error. Researchers could use theory to identify the different components to research which would likely reduce the number of potential components to study and increase the confidence in significant findings. Methodological rigor is needed to assure internal validity of the results, but advancements in theory is how fields truly move forward.

Generalizing Interventions

Once the components of an intervention are tested, some subset of them could be identified as more important than others and adhering to those crucial components allows for different applications of the intervention. For example, previous research with Incremental Rehearsal (IR; Tucker & Burns, 2016), which is a flashcard technique that relies on high repetition of unknown items interspersed among a high percentage of known items, found that IR was highly effective in increasing retention of words, letter sounds, and math facts (Burns, Zaslofsky, Kanive, & Parker, 2012). Research identified opportunities to respond (OTRs) as the most important component of the intervention (Szadokierski & Burns, 2008). Therefore, IR could be used in various different settings such as computer-based applications (Volpe, Burns, DuBois, & Zaslofsky, 2011) or with modified procedures to teach different stimuli to novel groups (e.g., preschoolers (Bunn, Burns, Hoffman, & Newman, 2005) and students with severe disabilities (Burns & Kimosh, 2005)), as long as the approach maintains high OTRs.

Interventions that are implemented in a manner that is inconsistent with the theory from which they are developed are doomed to failure because they often lose the essence of the intervention by focusing on less important components. Unfortunately, it is not unusual for interventionists to drift from intervention protocols over time (Gearing et al., 2011). Modifications to the intervention plan and implementation are acceptable, as long as the most essential components remain intact, but interventionists might deviate from its most fundamental theoretical foundation because they espouse a different theoretical framework. Imagine the Good Behavior Game, which has consistently been shown to be effective in managing student behavior (Flower, McKenna, Bunuan, Muething, & Vega, 2014), if the teacher decided that she disagreed with external rewards and did not provide any while implementing the intervention.

Finally, theory can help practitioners evaluate the novel application of an intervention before research is conducted. Practitioners are frequently presented with newly developed interventions for which the research base is still developing. School psychologists could evaluate the new intervention by examining relevant research (e.g., studies about similar interventions) but could also examine the consistency with theory. Ellis and Bond (2016) identified several interventions that had established effectiveness but were

268   *Matthew K. Burns & Shawna Petersen-Brown*

inconsistent with theory and became educational fads that came and went. Examining how well the intervention aligns with a well-established underlying theory could help practitioners judge if the intervention is worth adopting while effectiveness research is under way. Those new interventions developed with a clear link to an established theory could be attempted, but those without a solid theoretical basis should be avoided (e.g., responsibility-thinking rooms, self-esteem programs, and thinking-skills programs).

Theory and School Psychology Research

Thus far, we have emphasized the importance of theory from a practical perspective, but theory is a fundamental component of research because it provides a systematic way of examining psychological phenomena. Theory can help researchers understand why an intervention is effective, the causal mechanisms for the change in behavior, and the characteristics of the setting or sample for whom the intervention will be most effective (Hughes, 2015). Moreover, considering theoretical implications of school psychology research can help reshape existing theories and even build new ones. Unfortunately, less than half of research published in school psychology journals considers the theoretical underpinnings of the work (Mercer et al., 2014). Below we will discuss research methods and ways to report research that have clear theoretical implications.

Constructing Theoretical Questions

Research questions are the starting point for empirically furthering the field's understanding of the theoretical underpinnings and implications of interventions and other practices. In order to be a mature science, school psychology research has to evolve beyond testing efficacy to move from "did it work?" to "why did it work or not work?" Instead of asking, "What are the effects of Intervention X on outcome Y?" school psychologists could ask questions like "What effect does a specific feature within Intervention X have on outcome Y?" "What effect does pre-intervention skill have on effects of Intervention X on outcome Y?" or "To what extent does a change in Intervention X improve outcome Y among students with learning disabilities?" Below we will discuss questions that address causal mechanisms, moderators, and theory-based modifications for new and existing practices.

Causal Mechanisms

First, we address the example question, "What effect does a specific feature within Intervention X have on outcome Y?" Identifying the causal mechanism for various interventions could more directly link interventions to theory and lead to modifications of interventions and expansions of existing theories—both of which would be a desirable outcome for intervention research.

Mahoney (2002) defined causal mechanisms as the often unobservable entities and processes that actually bring about the desired outcome. Research that examines mediating variables attempts to identify what underlies the relationship between an independent and dependent variable (Baron & Kenny, 1986) and could be helpful in identifying causal mechanisms. However, only 48 studies published in school psychology journals over a 30-year period addressed mediation, and two-thirds of those were published within the last ten years (Fairchild & McQuillin, 2010). The most common approaches used to test mediations were a causal-step approach (Baron & Kenny, 1986) or normal point theory estimation (Sobel, 1982).

School psychologists could also engage in component analyses to better understand causal mechanisms. For example, as mentioned previously, Szadokierski and Burns (2008) used behavioral psychology to examine IR and hypothesized that OTR and percentage of known items were the two components that were most directly related to positive outcomes. They then conducted a 2 x 2 factorial design in which OTR (high and low) and percentage of known items (high and moderate) were directly compared. Students in the High OTR and High Percentage condition rehearsed each new item nine to 53 (M = 35.67) times among 90% known, High OTR and Moderate Percentage rehearsed each 12 to 60 times (M = 34.0) with 50% known, Low OTR and High Percentage rehearsed each item nine times with 90% known, and Low OTR Moderate Percentage rehearsed each new item nine times with 50% known. The High OTR and High Percentage condition led to the best retention of the taught words, but OTR led to a larger effect than did percentage of words known, which suggested that OTR was the more important component. Within this example, identifying OTRs as the more important component provides evidence of the causal mechanism of IR and might suggest future modifications (such as a reduction in the percentage of known items to enhance efficiency).

Identifying Moderator Variables

The second question that we discuss is, "What effect does pre-intervention skill have on effects of Intervention X on outcome Y?" Intervention research has historically only rarely examined moderator variables (McClelland & Judd, 1993), but doing so would foster our understanding of how individual ecology affects intervention effectiveness. Intervention researchers could also more frequently examine individual participants' ecological patterns of development (Hughes, 2015) within the study design. When identifying moderator variables of intervention effects, other theoretical frameworks might be relevant. Theories that address how individuals' unique skill levels interact with intervention methods are especially relevant, such as the theory of automatic information processing (LaBerge & Samuels, 1974) and the instructional hierarchy (Haring & Eaton, 1978). For example, initial skill level moderated the effectiveness of interventions targeting various stages of the instructional hierarchy (acquisition, fluency, generalization, and application) in mathematics (Burns, Codding, Boice, & Lukito, 2010), which provided partial support for students' skill level as a moderator of intervention outcomes.

As with mediators, only 50 studies in school psychology journals over 30 years examined moderators, with most of those occurring within the past ten years (Fairchild & McQuillin, 2010). Most moderating relationships were assessed with the classic regression approach in which the dependent variable was regressed onto the independent variable, the potential moderating variable, and the interaction of the two (Aiken & West, 1991). There are more contemporary approaches to examine moderators, and readers are referred to Fairchild and McQuillin (2010) for detailed discussion of them, but simple regression approaches are a strong first step for researchers interested in studying moderators.

Theoretically Based Intervention Modifications

Finally, we address a third type of research question, "To what extent does a change in Intervention X improve outcome Y among students with learning disabilities?" It might be possible to utilize theory to modify interventions and improve outcomes. For example, maintenance and generalization are important intervention outcomes that are often not integrated into school psychology intervention research. Ensuring maintenance and generalization of learning might enhance the outcomes associated with a wide variety of academic and behavioral interventions. Various theoretical constructs are relevant to the durability and generalizability of learning. For example, cognitive theoretical constructs such as depth of processing theory (Craik & Lockhart, 1972) and the spacing effect (Cepeda, Pashler, Vul, Wixted, & Rohrer, 2006), and principles within behavioral theory such as schedules of reinforcement (Ferster & Skinner, 1957), generalization framework (Stokes & Baer, 1977), and theory of common elements (Thorndike & Woodworth, 1901) might suggest modifications to enhance maintenance and generalization.

Researchers have investigated theoretically based intervention modifications to repeated reading for the purposes of enhancing generalization. Ardoin, Eckert, and Cole (2008) compared repeated reading (reading the same passage repeatedly to increase fluency and comprehension) to using multiple exemplars (based on Stokes and Baer's (1977) generalization framework, reading multiple passages with similar content and high word overlap) to increase generalization. IR has also been modified using cognitive theory to enhance maintenance. Specifically, sight words to be learned were paired with their definitions to facilitate a deeper level of processing, per the depth of processing framework (Petersen-Brown & Burns, 2011). In another investigation, a variation on the spacing effect was utilized in which space between OTRs increased exponentially rather than at a fixed rate (Swehla et al., 2016).

Writing Theoretical Articles

We have argued thus far for designing studies that address conceptual and theoretical underpinnings—to ask "why" rather than just "what." However, research must first examine if something is effective before it can focus on why it is or is not effective. Effectiveness research, and other types of research, can also examine theoretical implications by considering theoretical frameworks that contextualize the study and by discussing the theoretical implications of their work.

Conceptual Frameworks

In this chapter, we have referred to various theories and conceptual frameworks without differentiating between the two. Theory is an often-defined construct for which we assume consistency of understanding. Essentially, most definitions of theory involve collections of scientific observations to most parsimoniously explain and make testable predictions about phenomena. A conceptual framework is a network of "interlinked concepts that together provide a comprehensive understanding of a phenomenon" (Jabareen, 2009, p. 51), and it helps researchers interpret data to better understand the underlying constructs. Both conceptual frameworks and theories can be used to help understand observations and make predictions about behavior, but theories are usually better researched, more parsimonious, and have broader diversity in the phenomena that they explain. For example, behavioral learning theory would predict that the more practice a student has with a skill, the more permanent the skill becomes. The learning hierarchy, a conceptual framework, would predict that students with high accuracy in a skill should receive additional practice for the skill to become more permanent. The latter prediction is much less researched than the former, but it is also much more precise and nuanced.

School psychology researchers could discuss relevant conceptual frameworks when framing their study and use a framework to support their research questions and to justify their operational definitions of their dependent variables. Moreover, researchers could use diagrams and figures to display the theory or conceptual framework and how the study fits within that context. There are many conceptual frameworks that are relevant to school psychology, including the aforementioned learning hierarchy, prevention science (Coie et al., 1993), skill-by-treatment interactions (Burns et al., 2010), and problem-solving (Bransford & Stein, 1984). These conceptual frameworks make testable predictions that are specific to a given behavior, but they do not explain a broad enough behavior and are not researched widely enough yet to be considered a theory. School psychologists who apply conceptual frameworks to their research help better understand the theoretical underpinnings of their findings because they foster better explanations and predictions when the relevant theory is not yet clear.

272 Matthew K. Burns & Shawna Petersen-Brown

Discuss Theoretical Underpinnings

Most researchers know the formulaic approach to writing discussion sections: (a) summarize your results, (b) contextualize the results within previous research, (c) contextualize the results within practice, (d) address limitations, and (e) present directions for future research. When contextualizing results within previous research, researchers should emphasize how this research builds upon the theory or conceptual frameworks introduced previously. Authors should discuss how the results were consistent with a particular theory or conceptual framework or what types of inconsistencies existed. They could also use theory to hypothesize potential causal mechanisms for the findings that can be studied in future research.

Conclusion

We have presented arguments for the importance of theory in research, potential research questions that are theoretical in nature, and approaches to be more theoretical when writing manuscripts. There is one final point to make, which is that theory-driven research happens over time. By definition, a theory is the result of an overwhelmingly consistent finding across a large number of studies. Researchers should understand where each study fits within a larger research agenda and how that agenda could eventually shape current theory. Researchers should engage in a purposeful and well-thought-out research agenda in which each study leads to the next. Doing so will provide a prolific and meaningful research career and will move school psychology to be a more mature science.

References

Aiken, L. S., & West, S. G. (1991). *Multiple regression: Testing and interpreting interactions*. Thousand Oaks, CA: Sage.

Ardoin, S. P., Eckert, T. L., & Cole, C. A. S. (2008). Promoting generalization of reading: A comparison of two fluency-based interventions for improving general education student's oral reading rate. *Journal of Behavioral Education, 17*, 237–252.

Baron, R. M., & Kenny, D. A. (1986). The moderator-mediator variable distinction in social psychological research: Conceptual, strategic, and statistical considerations. *Journal of Personality and Social Psychology, 51*, 1173–1182.

Bransford, J., & Stein, B. (1984). *The ideal problem solver: A guide for improving thinking, learning and creativity*. San Francisco, CA: W. H. Freeman.

Bunn, R., Burns, M. K., Hoffman, H. H., & Newman, C. L. (2005). Using incremental rehearsal to teach letter identification with a preschool-aged child. *Journal of Evidence Based Practice for Schools, 6*, 124–134.

Burns, M. K. (2011). School psychology research: Combining ecological theory and prevention science. *School Psychology Review, 40*, 132–139.

Burns, M. K., Codding, R. S., Boice, C. H., & Lukito, G. (2010). Meta-analysis of acquisition and fluency math interventions with instructional and frustration level skills: Evidence for a skill-by-treatment interaction. *School Psychology Review, 39*, 69–83.

Burns, M. K., & Kimosh, A. (2005). Using incremental rehearsal to teach sight-words to adult students with moderate mental retardation. *Journal of Evidence Based Practices for Schools, 6*, 135–148.

Burns, M. K., Zaslofsky, A. F., Kanive, R., & Parker, D. C. (2012). Meta-analysis of incremental rehearsal using phi coefficients to compare single-case and group designs. *Journal of Behavioral Education, 21*, 185–202.

Cepeda, N. J., Pashler, H., Vul, E., Wixted, J. T., & Rohrer, D. (2006). Distributed practice in verbal recall tasks: A review and quantitative synthesis. *Psychological Bulletin, 132*, 354–380.

Coie, J. D., Watt, N. F., West, S. G., Hawkins, J. D., Asarnow, J. R., Markman, H. J., et al. (1993). The science of prevention: A conceptual framework and some directions for a national research program. *American Psychologist, 48*, 1013–1022.

Craik, F. I. M., & Lockhart, R. S. (1972). Levels of processing: A framework for memory research. *Journal of Verbal Learning and Verbal Behavior, 11*, 671–684.

Ellis, A. K., & Bond, J. B. (2016). *Research on educational innovations* (5th ed.). New York, NY: Routledge.

Fairchild, A. J., & McQuillin, S. D. (2010). Evaluating mediation and moderation effects in school psychology: A presentation of methods and review of current practice. *Journal of School Psychology, 48*, 53–84.

Ferster, C. B., & Skinner, B. F. (1957). *Schedules of reinforcement*. East Norwalk, CT: Appleton-Century-Crofts.

Flower, A., McKenna, J. W., Bunuan, R. L., Muething, C. S., & Vega, R. (2014). Effects of the Good Behavior Game on challenging behaviors in school settings. *Review of Educational Research, 84*, 546–571.

Gearing, R. E., El-Bassel, N., Ghesquiere, A., Baldwin, S., Gillies, J., & Ngeow, E. (2011). Major ingredients of fidelity: A review and scientific guide to improving quality of intervention research implementation. *Clinical Psychology Review, 31*, 79–88.

Hagermoser Sanetti, L. M., & Kratochwill, T. R. (2009). Toward developing a science of treatment integrity: Introduction to the special series. *School Psychology Review, 38*, 445–459.

Halsey, A. H. (2004). *A history of sociology in Britain: Science, literature, and society*. Oxford, UK: Oxford University Press.

Haring, N. G., & Eaton, M. D. (1978). Systematic instructional technology: An instructional hierarchy. In N. G. Haring, T. C. Lovitt, M. D. Eaton, & C. L. Hansen (Eds.), *The fourth R: Research in the classroom* (pp. 23–40). Columbus, OH: Merrill.

Hattie, J. A. C. (2009). *Visible learning: A synthesis of over 800 meta-analyses to achievement*. New York, NY: Routledge.

Hughes, J. N. (2015). Integrating theory and empirical science in school psychology: Progress and remaining challenges. *School Psychology Review, 44*, 262–270.

Jabareen, Y. (2009). Building a conceptual framework: Philosophy, definitions, and procedure. *International Journal of Qualitative Methods, 8*(4), 49–62.

Kuper, A., & Kuper, J. (1996). *The social science encyclopedia*. New York, NY: Routledge.

LaBerge, D., & Samuels, S. J. (1974). Toward a theory of automatic information processing in reading. *Cognitive Psychology, 6*, 293–323.

Lewin, K. (1952). *Field theory in social science: Selected theoretical papers by Kurt Lewin*. London: Tavistock.

Mahoney, J. (2002, August) *Causal mechanisms, correlations, and a power theory of society*. Paper presented at the annual meeting of the American Political Science Association, Boston, Massachusetts. Available online at www.allacademic.com/meta/p66368_index.html

McClelland, G. H., & Judd, C. M. (1993). Statistical difficulties of detecting interactions and moderator effects. *Psychological Bulletin, 114*, 376–390.

Mercer, S. H., Idler, A. M., & Bartfai, J. M. (2014). Theory-driven evaluation in school psychology intervention research: 2007–2012. *School Psychology Review, 43*, 119–131.

Petersen-Brown, S., & Burns, M. K. (2011). Adding a vocabulary component to incremental rehearsal to enhance retention and generalization. *School Psychology Quarterly, 26*, 245–255.

Peterson, R. L., O'Connor, A., & Fluke, S. (2014, October). Character counts! Program brief. Lincoln, NE: Student Engagement Project, University of Nebraska-Lincoln and the Nebraska Department of Education. http://k12engagement.unl.edu/strategy-briefs/Character%20Counts%2010-3--2014.pdf

Philips, B. N. (1990). *School psychology at a turning point: Ensuring a bright future for the profession*. San Francisco, CA: Jossey-Bass.

Power, T. J., & Mautone, J. A. (2011). *School Psychology Review*: Looking back on 2006–2010. *School Psychology Review, 39*, 673–678.

Sobel, M. E. (1982). Asymptotic confidence intervals for indirect effects in structural equation models. *Sociological Methodology, 13*, 290–312.

Stokes, T. F., & Baer, D. M. (1977). An implicit technology of generalization. *Journal of Applied Behavior Analysis, 10*, 349–367.

Swehla, S. E., Burns, M. K., Zaslofsky, A. F., Hall, M. S., Varma, S., & Volpe, R. J. (2016). Examining the use of spacing effect to increase the efficiency of incremental rehearsal. *Psychology in the Schools, 53*, 404–415.

Szadokierski, I., & Burns, M. K. (2008). Analogue evaluation of the effects of opportunities to respond and ratios of known items within drill rehearsal of Esperanto words. *Journal of School Psychology, 46*, 593–609.

Tharinger, D. (2000). The complexity of development and change: The need for the integration of the theory and research findings in psychological practice with children. *Journal of School Psychology, 38*, 383–388.

Thompson, D., Hogan, J. D., & Clark, P. M. (2011). *Developmental psychology in historical perspective*. New York, NY: Wiley.

Thorndike, E. L., & Woodworth, R. S. (1901). The influence of improvement in one mental function upon the efficiency of other functions (I). *Psychological Review, 8*, 247–261.

Tucker, J. A., & Burns, M. K. (2016). Helping students remember what they learn: An intervention for teachers and school psychologists. *NASP Communique, 44*(6), 23.

Turner, S. P. (2004). The maturity of social theory. In C. Camic & H. Joas (Eds.), *The dialogical turn: New roles for sociology in the postdisciplinary age* (pp. 141–170). Oxford, UK: Rowman & Littlefield.

Volpe, R. J., Burns, M. K., DuBois, M., & Zaslofsky, A. F. (2011). Computer-assisted tutoring: Teaching letter sounds to kindergarten students using incremental rehearsal. *Psychology in the Schools, 48*, 332–342.

Yee, C. M. (2009, February 8). Medical tests at churches aren't what docs ordered. *Minneapolis Star Tribune*. Retrieved from www.startribune.com/lifestyle/39266627.html?page=1&c=y

Ysseldyke, J., Burns, M., Dawson, P., Kelley, B., Morrison, D., Ortiz, S., Rosenfield, S., & Telzrow, C. (2006). *School psychology: A blueprint for training and practice III.* Bethesda, MD: National Association of School Psychologists.

26 Writing for Research to Practice

Susan G. Forman and Christina N. Diaz

Although there are many interventions that have research evidence indicating their potential for positive outcomes with a range of child and adolescent problems, the use of these interventions in schools has remained relatively low (Stormont, Reinke, & Herman, 2011). The findings of studies on implementation indicate that several factors influence whether or not a practitioner will implement a practice or program. These include the characteristics of the intervention, characteristics and perceptions of the potential implementer and of other stakeholders, characteristics of the implementation setting, and influences of external systems (Durlak & DuPre, 2008; Forman, 2015). Notably absent from reports of the factors that have been found to influence intervention implementation is practitioners' reading of research literature; in general, practitioners are not looking to the research literature as a major means of guiding practice. Research publications typically have not prompted change in classrooms and schools (Carnine, 2000) or other human service delivery settings (Best & Neuhauser, 2004).

Fixsen, Blase, Duda, Naoom, and van Dyke (2010) described a continuum of approaches that have been and can be taken by researchers to facilitate use of evidence-based approaches. These include the "letting it happen" approach, in which researchers publish their findings and hope practitioners find and use the information; the "helping it happen" approach, in which researchers provide their findings directly to practitioners in the form of manuals, toolkits, and training; and the "making it happen" approach, in which practitioners are provided with support to learn how to use new interventions and with a supportive environment in which to implement these interventions. Many researchers, however, do not have the resources or support from their institutional infrastructure that will allow them to enter the "helping it happen" or "making it happen" arena. This chapter will examine ways in which authors can craft their manuscripts to increase the potential that their research findings will be translated to practice. We will discuss how researchers can design and report intervention studies to increase their potential interest level and usability for practitioners. We will also discuss how case studies, systematic reviews, and research on implementation issues can provide important information not found in randomized controlled trials or quasi-experimental group designs and can make a significant contribution to supporting the movement from research to practice.

General Issues in Writing for Research to Practice

The Research Question

An initial issue for consideration in attempting to write to promote the translation from research to practice is what to focus on. One approach of significance is to focus on questions that are of interest to practitioners. The traditional approach to scholarship is to craft research questions based on the findings of previous literature. While this is certainly important, research questions directly related to the interests or questions of practitioners concerning provision of evidence-based interventions to varying populations in varying settings can be an additional basis of formulating a research question. Such research questions might result from a data-based needs assessment of practitioners regarding how to implement, adapt, and deal with barriers to implementing a specific intervention.

Action research is an approach that focuses on addressing the problems of practitioners by defining a local practice problem, planning and conducting a research study, and implementing the findings to address the local problem. Participatory action research (Ho, 2002) is an approach that builds on this process through full collaboration between researchers and members of an organization in efforts to link theory and research to practice which is both acceptable and effective. Participatory action research views researchers and practitioners as full partners in efforts to frame research questions, design and conduct studies, and utilize outcomes in the design and implementation of interventions. In this process, the full participation of key stakeholders in an organization results in the integration of information about an organization's characteristics in the design of interventions, thereby yielding interventions that are likely to be acceptable and usable (Nastasi, 1998). The development of practice-based evidence (Kratochwill et al., 2012), in which practitioners contribute to the knowledge base by collaborating with researchers in examining adaptations of interventions during the course of providing those interventions in typical practice settings, has also been suggested as a means through which practitioners' ability to deliver high-quality services can be increased.

Defining the Intervention and Its Context

Any published study of an intervention is likely to be of more use to those in practice if the intervention is specifically defined and described so that the nature of the intervention is clear to the practitioner. Programs that are not defined well fare poorly in implementation efforts (Vernez, Karam, Mariano, & DeMartini, 2006). The usability of an intervention is enhanced when it is fully operationalized, or described in observable, measureable ways, so that a potential implementer can easily understand exactly what is supposed to be done. Fixsen, Blase, Metz, and van Dyke (2013) pointed out that when a new practice or program is well operationalized, it is teachable, learnable, doable, observable, and assessable.

A comprehensive description of an intervention will identify the core components of the intervention and exactly what the implementer should do when delivering the intervention. A link to the intervention manual or information on purchasing it will also increase ease of use for the practitioner. In addition, a comprehensive description of an intervention will identify the essential organizational- and systems-level supports for the intervention. These supports include funding; equipment; manuals and other supplies; space requirements; staff and staff skills; training and coaching needed in order to deliver the intervention accurately and with skill; special organizational procedures to deliver the intervention; and information management systems. Specification of these essential supports will allow practitioners to better assess the full cost of the intervention and whether these costs are manageable in their practice settings. Issues related to the social and political context for implementation of the intervention might be important also. Comprehensive intervention descriptions that include this information increase the likelihood that practitioners will be able to successfully implement an intervention described in a publication.

Defining the Population—Which Clients Might Benefit?

Defining the population for which an intervention is effective is essential. Interventions work for specific problems and populations (Chambless & Hollon, 1998), and it is important for the practitioner to understand which clients are likely to experience positive outcomes (APA, 2010). Descriptions of the study might include details about participants in terms of a diagnostic system (American Psychiatric Association, 2013) or special education placement categories. This type of participant description might allow a practitioner to easily compare study participants with their own clients. In addition, cutoff scores on reliable, valid assessment measures can be used in the description of study participants to allow the reader to compare these participants to their client population. The presence of co-morbid conditions is also important to provide. Demographic characteristics, such as age, socioeconomic status, school grade level, and ethnicity, and other dimensions of diversity are important to report as they add to the information that can be helpful to the potential implementer in determining with whom the intervention should be used. Information about how study participants were identified, including recruitment, referral, and outreach strategies, is also needed. This information can help the practitioner develop strategies for reaching and retaining clients.

Outcomes

The nature of outcome measures and the ways in which they are examined in intervention studies also have the potential to enhance the transition from research to practice. For many years, authors have called for reporting clinical and social significance in addition to statistical significance. Early on, Chambless and Hollon (1998) contended: "If a treatment is to be useful to practitioners it is not enough for treatment effects to be statistically significant: they also need to be large enough to be clinically meaningful" (p. 11). Reporting of effect sizes, statistical power, and use of confidence intervals have been recommended as means of providing the reader with information that will help them to determine the clinical significance of findings (Fidler et al., 2005) because they provide information on the magnitude of change and on experimental precision. Kazdin (1999) defined clinical significance as "the practical or applied value or importance of the effect of an intervention—that is, whether the intervention makes a real (e.g., genuine, palpable, practical, noticeable) difference in everyday life to the clients or to others with whom the clients interact" (p. 332). Kazdin further contended that client change can be clinically significant when their symptoms change a lot, or a little, or when symptoms do not change but the client's ability to cope with them is increased. Thus, in addition to using outcome measures of symptom change, outcome measures of everyday functioning, meeting role demands, interpersonal functioning, quality of life, and measures involving subjective judgments of the client and important others in their life can yield information about clinical significance.

The reporting of clinical significance in many journals has been less than optimal. For example, in a review of articles in *Journal of Consulting and Clinical Psychology*, Fidler et al. (2005) found that only 40% considered clinical, and not only statistical, significance and that reporting of effect sizes and confidence intervals was even lower. Social significance or social validity (Foster & Mash, 1999) has been defined as the extent to which an intervention yields outcomes that are important to society, such as reduction of truancy or arrest rates or cost savings or cost benefits of an intervention. Use of measures of social significance has also been suggested as a means of increasing the relevance of research studies to practitioners.

Fidelity

Measurement and discussion of fidelity, or the extent to which an intervention is implemented as planned, is essential to include in publications that aim to enhance the translation of research to practice for several reasons. Without fidelity data, we cannot be sure that clients have received the intervention; we do not know how much of the intervention they received and whether it was implemented skillfully. Fixsen Naoom, Blase, Friedman, and Wallace (2005) suggested reporting on three types of fidelity: (1) context fidelity, which is the degree to which the supports for effective implementation such as staff time, staff training, and materials, are present; (2) compliance fidelity, which is the degree to which core intervention components are used; and (3) competence fidelity, which is the degree to which core intervention components are delivered with skill. Reporting of fidelity data provides the potential practitioner implementer with information about the level of completeness, accuracy, and skill that yields effective outcomes and therefore the types of supports that might be needed for effective outcomes.

Fidelity measurement is important in practice as well as in research because it provides the practitioner information about the quality of service delivery. Fidelity measurement in practice can provide feedback for implementers and program managers so that corrections in the implementation process can be made. Reports of fidelity measurement in intervention studies can provide the practitioner with a model to be used in their own assessments of fidelity.

High levels of fidelity in the practice setting begin with the intervention developer and the nature of their publications about an intervention. The intervention developer who considers the nature and constraints of real-world practice settings in the design of their interventions supports the translation of their intervention research to practice. The intervention developer who (a) identifies core components of the intervention, core implementation strategies, and ways of adapting the intervention for diverse clients and settings and (b) describes them with a high degree of specificity is also providing the support needed for implementation of the intervention in the practice setting. (See www.lifeskillstraining.com for one exemplary program.)

The Discussion Section

The discussion section of a manuscript provides an important vehicle for the manuscript author to increase the likelihood that the practice implications of the manuscript will be put to use. In writing this section, authors should describe the meaning of their results so they will be understandable and useful to a practitioner audience, some of whom might not be familiar with or remember the meaning of some statistical procedures. Explanations of power, effect sizes, and confidence intervals can typically be done in a phrase or a few sentences. Implications for practice should be a significant, central part of this section. Table 26.1 provides a list of important content to include in a subsection on implications for practice. Authors should attempt to answer the following questions: Given the results of the study reported, to what use can the intervention that is the target of the study be put? For which clients and problems can the intervention be used? What are the essential components and organizational supports needed for effective implementation? If procedures or supports were used that might be available to university researchers but not to practitioners (e.g., graduate student support and participant incentives), what were they and how can they be addressed in a practice setting? How can the intervention improve current practice? What unanswered practice questions related to this intervention remain?

Table 26.1 Information Recommended for Inclusion in an Implications for Practice Subsection

How the intervention improves current practice
Clients and problems for which the intervention is appropriate
Potential adaptations for other populations
Settings in which the intervention would be effective
Potential adaptations for other settings
Organizational supports that are necessary for effective implementation
Potential barriers to implementation in a practice setting and possible solutions to barriers
Actions at the policy level that would support implementation
Unanswered questions that remain about the intervention

Special Research Designs and Research Targets

Although randomized controlled trials have been viewed as the gold standard of intervention research, other types of studies can be important vehicles for the translation of research to practice. The following sections provide information on case studies, systematic reviews, and studies that focus directly on implementation issues.

Case Studies

Case studies can be used to test whether interventions that have shown effectiveness in well-controlled outcome studies are effective in service delivery settings and thus can document the effectiveness of interventions in practice (Edwards, Dattilio, & Bromley, 2004). In the past, case studies consisted of narrative accounts of treatment; however, contemporary case study methodology uses data collection and analysis and can be systematic and rigorous. Case studies allow for examination of issues that are not typically addressed in larger scale outcome studies. When case study research is conducted, a large number of observations can be made on each case, allowing for in-depth evaluation of complex processes. Case studies can look at how client change occurs over time and can examine the influence of contextual factors. Case studies do not need to be limited to one student (or unit such as a family or classroom) but can evaluate the outcomes of an intervention with a number of students so that there is a greater degree of confidence for the effects of treatment.

Case studies that use sound methodology, typically called single-case design studies, employ direct measures of client behavior, such as observation, self-monitoring, physiological measures, and permanent product measures, and use assessment repeatedly over the course of an intervention (Kratochwill, 1985; Kratochwill & Levin, 2014). Sound methodology might also assess reports of significant others in the client's social settings, such as teachers and parents, in addition to self-reports of clients. Use of this variety of measures can establish how pervasive intervention effects are. Establishment of a baseline of the target problem is an important means of documenting the existence of the target problem prior to intervention, and continuous assessment (data collection on multiple occasions over time) prior to and during intervention allows for evaluation of the effect of the intervention. Social comparison can also be used to compare the behavior of the target child, before and after intervention, to peers without the target problem in order to establish the clinical significance of client change. Sound case studies also examine generalization (to other settings) and maintenance (over time) of behavior change. As with other types of studies, it is important to use an intervention protocol and conduct fidelity checks when conducting a case study. Otero and Haut (2016) and Miller, Dufrene, Olmi, Tingstrom, and Filce (2015) demonstrated exemplary single-case design case studies worth reviewing.

Formal visual analysis of data, which looks at change over repeated measures in terms of score overlap, variability, and trend can be used. Statistical procedures can also be used with case studies (Shadish, 2014). The investigator can calculate an effect size so that the reader can draw conclusions about the magnitude of client change (Parker et al., 2005). The What Works Clearinghouse (2013) has described methodological design standards that can be used as a way to assess the credibility of results from single-case research. Several rules are used to determine whether design criteria have been met. These include rules related to manipulation of the independent variable, use of an adequate number of data points, use of multiple attempts to demonstrate effect, and reliable inter-assessor agreement. Adherence to these standards enhances the probability of publication of single-case studies and the quality of implications for practice based on those studies.

Pragmatic case studies provide an alternative model for reporting case-based research (Fishman, 2013). These studies employ a mixed methods approach, utilizing both qualitative and quantitative methods, and describe the logic, process, and outcome of professional practice. Pragmatic case studies include a description of the practitioner's guiding conception of therapy as well as how this guiding conception influences client assessment, case formulation, and the intervention plan. Intervention implementation, as well as client monitoring, use of feedback, and client outcomes, including follow-up, are reported. Studies by Clement (2011) and Williams, Carson, Zamora, Harley and Lakatos (2014) are strong examples of pragmatic case studies relevant to school psychology practice.

Systematic Reviews

Systematic reviews can be another means of facilitating the translation of research to practice. A systematic review is a form of literature review that is grounded in objectivity and uses specified systematic methods to identify, select, and evaluate relevant research (Higgins & Green, 2011). The goal of a systematic review is to make sense of the overall findings of a group of research studies that focus on a specific issue. An important feature of a systematic review is that it is carried out in accordance with agreed upon standards and typically uses a protocol to guide the review process. The protocol specifies the procedures used to carry out the review, including how previous research is identified, examined, evaluated, and synthesized. Systematic reviews can be especially useful for the practitioner attempting to translate research to practice because they can integrate a large number of studies, with current technology allowing for comprehensive searches through a variety of research databases. In addition, results of different studies can be compared to examine if findings are consistent, and if not, to hypothesize why. Systematic reviews provide a parsimonious vehicle for the busy practitioner to use in efforts to understand the growing literature on interventions and the conclusions that can be drawn from this literature regarding practice issues. Meta-analysis and narrative synthesis are types of systematic reviews.

Meta-analysis is quantitative and uses statistical techniques to synthesize research studies. It is an analysis of previous research study analyses. Meta-analysis involves a number of steps including formulating the problem or research question, sampling and selecting the studies to be included in the review, conducting and interpreting a data analysis, and reporting (Kavale, 1988; APA Publications and Communications Board Working Group on Journal Article Reporting Standards, 2008). The goal in the sampling phase of meta-analysis is to locate as many primary empirical research studies, on the specified topic of interest, as possible. Data analysis is conducted using the effect size statistic, which quantifies the magnitude of effect for a specific variable. The goal of data analysis is to determine the aggregate effect size across studies and across groups of studies with similar characteristics. Conclusions consider the methodological soundness of individual studies and the studies as a group. Polanin, Espelage, and Pigott (2012) and Schindler et al. (2015) are excellent examples of meta-analyses that have strong implications for the practice of school psychology.

Narrative systematic reviews can also be useful, especially when a meta-analysis is not possible because the number of existing studies is limited, the outcome measures used in existing studies are different, or the authors of these studies have not provided enough information in their results so that the statistical procedures used in a meta-analysis can be performed. A narrative systematic review, like a meta-analysis, involves the systematic identification, appraisal, and synthesis of all relevant studies on a specific topic (Cook, Sackett, & Spitzer, 1995). When a narrative systematic review is reported, tables are typically used to provide a record of information about the studies in the review. A narrative systematic review looks at similarities and differences between existing studies in terms of study participants, interventions, outcomes, and methodology and attempts to bring the results of these studies together in part by quantifying types of outcomes across studies and within groups of studies with similar characteristics. Maggin, Johnson, Chafouleas, Ruberto, and Berggren (2012) and Forman and Barakat (2011) have published strong narrative systematic reviews.

The nature of the systematic review lends itself to facilitating the translation from research to practice because this type of publication aggregates information and draws conclusions from multiple studies. Potential authors of systematic reviews should attend to a number of issues in attempting to maximize the usefulness of their review to practitioners. First, as stated previously, practitioners can be involved in defining the problem and questions addressed by the review in order to increase relevance to practice. In addition, authors should recognize that their review has the potential to influence practice and, to increase this potential, practitioners and policy makers should be recognized as an important part of their target audience. Thus, brief, non-technical explanations of statistical procedures should be included, and implications for practice and policy should be highlighted. Specific implications for practice can target potential users of the information, such as psychologists delivering interventions, administrators, and policy makers at the state and federal levels. Reporting of important take-home points (Harris, Quatman, Manring, Siston, & Flanigan, 2014), such as conclusions and review limitations, should be used to summarize findings. Harris et al. (2014) recommend that in order to be of most use to busy practitioners, the conclusions of a systematic review should answer the following question: "If a reader were to remember one thing about my review, what would it be?" (p. 2767). Petticrew and Roberts (2006) suggest that a systematic review should include brief answers to the questions "What do we already know?" and "What does this article add?" (p. 260).

Implementation Research

It is important to conduct and write about intervention research so that it is likely to be useful to practitioners; in addition, translation of research to practice can be facilitated by research publications that focus directly on the process of implementation. The term *implementation science* refers to empirical research that focuses on the development of new knowledge about implementation. Such research has a number of goals including increasing understanding of barriers of and facilitators to implementation, development of effective implementation strategies, and examination of relationships between an intervention and its impact. Research that focuses on development of implementation strategies has the potential to answer questions about how to effectively deliver core components of an evidence-based intervention in a practice setting, how to adapt an intervention to a local context, and how to increase readiness for implementation (Rabin & Brownson, 2012).

Intervention research and outcomes focus on the effects of an intervention on clients and help practitioners select interventions that are likely to result in positive changes, whereas implementation research and outcomes focus on how and whether an intervention is being delivered and help practitioners understand how to implement evidence-based interventions in practice settings and how to adapt them. Implementation outcomes are important in intervention research because if we do not know what has happened in an implementation effort, we cannot attribute intervention outcomes to the intervention. In addition, implementation outcomes alone are of interest because they have the potential to increase our knowledge about how to deliver interventions effectively and with good outcomes for clients. Types of outcomes typically used in implementation studies include acceptability (perceptions that an intervention is satisfactory); adoption (the initial decision to implement); appropriateness (the perceived fit of the intervention with the setting and problem prior to adoption); feasibility (the perceived fit of the intervention early in implementation); fidelity (the degree to which the intervention was implemented as intended); implementation cost (the expense of implementing the intervention); penetration (the degree of intervention use or integration in a practice setting); and sustainability (the extent to which use of the intervention is maintained; Proctor et al., 2011). Although the literature on implementation and how to translate research to practice has grown in recent years, there is a substantial need for additional knowledge in this area (Forman, 2015).

In a review of existing research on implementation of evidence-based school mental health interventions, Forman (2015) discussed the importance of research with the goal of establishing evidence-based implementation strategies and in which implementation strategies are specified and operationalized. Studies that examine the relative influence of implementation factors, the core components of implementation strategies, and the effectiveness of strategies to develop stakeholder support, implementer competency, and taking interventions to scale will be especially important in providing the information needed by practitioners to yield implementation success. Recent implementation research studies include Long et al. (2016) and Sanetti, Kratochwill, and Long (2013).

Conclusions

In order to facilitate translation of research to practice authors should attend to issues in the design and reporting of intervention studies. Case studies and systematic reviews provide special opportunities to examine the complexity of intervention use and to synthesize large numbers of existing research studies related to an intervention or client problem. Research conducted directly on implementation issues also has the potential to address questions related to how to promote the successful use of evidence-based practices in the context of service delivery. Curran, Bauer, Mittman, Pyne, and Stetler (2012) suggested that researchers use implementation hybrid designs that assess both clinical effectiveness and implementation in one study. They contend that intervention research should explore implementation outcomes as well as intervention outcomes.

Through attention to the manner in which research is targeted, designed, and described, authors can play an active role in providing practitioners with the information-related support necessary for effective implementation of evidence-based practices. Although information alone is not likely to change practitioner behavior and organizational functioning, authors can seek to increase their influence in efforts to translate research to practice through attention to the manner in which new knowledge is developed and reported.

References

American Psychiatric Association. (2013). *Diagnostic and statistical manual of mental disorders: DSM-5*. Washington, DC: American Psychiatric Association.

American Psychological Association. (2010). *Publication manual of the American Psychological Association* (6th ed.). Washington, DC: American Psychological Association.

APA Publications and Communications Board Working Group on Journal Article Reporting Standards (2008). Reporting standards for research in psychology: Why do we need them? What might they be? *American Psychologist, 63*, 839–851. doi: 10.1037/0003-066x.63.9.839

Best, M., & Neuhauser, D. (2004). Ignaz Semmelweis and the birth of infection control. *Quality and Safety in Health Care, 13*, 233–234. doi: 10.1136/qshc.2004.010918

Carnine, D. (2000). *Why education experts resist effective practices (and what it would take to make education more like medicine)*. Thomas B. Fordham Foundation, April 1, 2000. Retrieved September 25, 2017 from www.wrightslaw.com/info/teach. profession.carnine.pdf

Chambless, D. L., & Hollon, S. D. (1998). Defining empirically supported therapies. *Journal of Consulting and Clinical Psychology, 66*, 7–18.

Clement, P. W. (2011). A strengths-based, skill-building, integrative approach to treating conduct problems in a 12-year-old boy: Rafael's story. *Pragmatic Case Studies in Psychotherapy, 7*, 351–398.

Cook, D. J., Sackett, D. L., & Spitzer, W. O. (1995). Methodologic guidelines for systematic reviews of randomized controlled trials in health care from the Potsdam Consultation on Meta-analysis. *Journal of Clinical Epidemiology, 48*, 17–71.

Curran, G. M., Bauer, M., Mittman, B., Pyne, J. M., & Stetler, C. (2012). Effectiveness-implementation hybrid designs: Combining elements of clinical effectiveness and implementation research to enhance public health impact. *Medical Care, 50*, 217–226. doi: 10.1097/MLR.0b013e3182408812

Durlak, J. A., & DuPre, E. P. (2008). Implementation matters: A review of research on the influence of implementation on program outcomes and the factors affecting implementation. *American Journal of Community Psychology, 41*, 327–350. doi: 10.1007/s10464-008-9165-0

Edwards, D. J. A., Dattilio, F. M., & Bromley, D. B. (2004). Developing evidence-based practice: The role of case-based research. *Professional Psychology: Research and Practice, 35*, 589–597.

Fidler, F., Cumming, G., Thomason, N., Pannuzzo, D., Smith, J., Fyffe, P., et al. (2005). Toward improved statistical reporting in the *Journal of Consulting and Clinical Psychology*. *Journal of Consulting and Clinical Psychology, 73*, 136–143.

Fishman, D. B. (2013). The pragmatic case study method for creating rigorous and systematic, practitioner-friendly research. *Pragmatic Case Studies in Psychotherapy, 9*, 403–425.

Fixsen, D. L., Blase, K., Duda, M., Naoom, S., & van Dyke, M. (2010). Implementation of evidence-based treatments for children and adolescents: Research findings and

Writing for Research to Practice 287

their implications for the future. In J. Weisz & A. Kazdin (Eds.), *Implementation and dissemination: Extending treatments to new populations and new settings* (2nd ed., pp. 435–450). New York, NY: Guilford Press.

Fixsen, D. L., Blase, K., Metz, A., & van Dyke, M. (2013). Statewide implementation of evidence-based programs. *Exceptional Children, 79*, 213–230.

Fixsen, D. L., Naoom, S. F., Blase, K. A., Friedman, R. M., & Wallace, F. (2005). *Implementation research: A synthesis of the literature.* Tampa, FL: University of South Florida, Louis de la Parte Florida Mental Health Institute, The National Implementation Research Network (FMHI Publication #231).

Forman, S. G. (2015). *Implementation of mental health programs in schools: A change agent's guide.* Washington, DC: American Psychological Association.

Forman, S. G., & Barakat, N. M. (2011). Cognitive-behavioral therapy in the schools: Bringing research to practice through effective implementation. *Psychology in the Schools, 48*, 283–296.

Foster, S. L., & Mash, E. J. (1999). Assessing social validity in clinical treatment research: Issues and procedures. *Journal of Consulting and Clinical Psychology, 67*, 308–319.

Harris, J., Quatman, C., Manring, M., Siston, R., & Flanigan, D. (2014). How to write a systematic review. *American Journal of Sports Medicine, 42*, 2761–2768.

Higgins, J. P. T., & Green, S. (Eds.). (2011). *Cochrane handbook for systematic reviews of interventions.* Retrieved from the Cochrane Collaboration website: http://handbook.cochrane.org/

Ho, B. S. (2002). Application of participatory action research to family-school intervention. *School Psychology Review, 31*, 106–121.

Kavale, K. A. (1988). Using meta-analysis to answer the question: What are the important, manipulable influences on school learning? *School Psychology Review, 17*, 644–650.

Kazdin, A. E. (1999). The meanings and measurement of clinical significance. *Journal of Consulting and Clinical Psychology, 67*, 332–339. doi: 10.1037/0022-006X.67.3.332

Kratochwill, T. R. (1985). Case study research in school psychology. *School Psychology Review, 14*, 204–215.

Kratochwill, T. R., & Levin, J. R. (2014). *Single-cased intervention research: Methodological and statistical advances.* Washington, DC: American Psychological Association.

Kratochwill, T. R., Hoagwood, K. E., Kazak, A. E., Weisz, J. R., Hood, K., Vargas, L. A., & Banez, G. A. (2012). Practice-based evidence for children and adolescents: Advancing the research agenda in schools. *School Psychology Review, 41*, 215–235.

Long, A. C. J., Sanetti, L. M. H., Collier-Meek, M. A., Gallucci, J., Altschaefl, M., & Kratochwill, T. R. (2016). An exploratory investigation of teachers' intervention planning and perceived implementation barriers. *Journal of School Psychology, 55*, 1–26.

Maggin, D. M., Johnson, A. H., Chafouleas, S. M., Ruberto, L. M., & Berggren, M. (2012). A systematic evidence review of school-based group contingency interventions for students with challenging behavior. *Journal of School Psychology, 50*, 625–654. doi: 10.1016/j.jsp.2012.06.001

Miller, L. M., Dufrene, B. A., Olmi, D. J., Tingstrom, D., & Filce, H. (2015). Self-monitoring as a viable fading option in check-in/check-out. *Journal of School Psychology, 53*, 121–135.

Nastasi, B. K. (1998). A model for mental health programming in school and communities: Introduction to the mini-series. *School Psychology Review, 27,* 165–174.

Otero, T., & Haut, J. (2016). Differential effects of reinforcement on the self-monitoring of on-task behavior. *School Psychology Quarterly, 31,* 91–103. doi: 10.1037/spq0000113

Parker, R. I., Brossart, D. F., Vannest, K. J., Long, J. R., De-Alba, R. G., Baugh, F. G., & Sullivan, J. R. (2005). Effect sizes in single case research: How large is large? *School Psychology Review, 34,* 116–132.

Petticrew, M., & Roberts, H. (2006). *Systematic reviews in the social sciences: A practical guide.* Oxford, UK: Blackwell.

Polanin, J. R., Espelage, D. L., & Pigott, T. D. (2012). A meta-analysis of school-based bullying prevention programs' effects on bystander intervention behavior. *School Psychology Review, 41,* 47–65.

Proctor, E., Silmere, H., Raghavan, R., Hovmand, P., Aarons, G., Bunger, A., et al. (2011). Outcomes for implementation research: Conceptual distinctions, measurement challenges, and research agenda. *Administration and Policy in Mental Health, 38*(2), 65–76. doi: 10.1007/s10488-010-0319-7

Rabin, B. A., & Brownson, R. C. (2012). Developing the terminology for dissemination and implementation research. In R. C. Brownson, G. A. Colditz, & E. K. Proctor (Eds.), *Dissemination and implementation research in health: Translating science to practice* (pp. 23–54). New York, NY: Oxford University Press.

Sanetti, L. M. H., Kratochwill, T. R., & Long, A. C. (2013). Applying adult behavior change theory to support mediator-based intervention implementation. *School Psychology Quarterly, 28,* 47–62.

Schindler, H. S., Kholoptseva, J., Oh, S. S., Yoshikawa, H., Duncan, G. J., Magnuson, K. A., & Shonkoff, J. P. (2015). Maximizing the potential of early childhood education to prevent externalizing behavior problems: A meta-analysis. *Journal of School Psychology, 53,* 243–263.

Shadish, W. R. (2014). Analysis and meta-analysis of single-case designs [Special issue]. *Journal of School Psychology, 52*(2).

Stormont, M., Reinke, W. M., & Herman, K. C. (2011). Teachers' importance ratings for evidence-based behavioral interventions. *Behavioral Disorders, 37,* 19–29.

Vernez, G., Karam, R., Mariano, L. T., & DeMartini, C. (2006). *Evaluating comprehensive school reform models at scale.* Santa Monica, CA: The RAND Corporation.

What Works Clearinghouse. (2013). *Procedures and standards handbook (Version 3.0).* Retrieved September 25, 2017 from https://ies.ed.gov/ncee/wwc/Docs/reference resources/wwc_procedures_v3_0_standards_handbook.pdf

Williams, M. E., Carson, M. C., Zamora, I., Harley, E. K., & Lakatos, P. P. (2014). Child–parent psychotherapy in the context of the developmental disability and medical service systems. *Pragmatic Case Studies in Psychotherapy, 10,* 212–226.

27 Engaging in Advocacy and Affecting Public Policy

Frank C. Worrell, Rena F. Subotnik, and Paula Olszewski-Kubilius

Scholars conduct research and publish theoretical perspectives and empirical findings in journals, books, and reports for other scholars in the field to read and respond to, and they are immensely gratified when their work is taken up and cited by colleagues in subsequent publications. Although there is a substantial amount of basic research in school psychology and related fields, a sizeable percentage of the research in these areas is intended to inform *actual* teaching practice in the classroom. Educational researchers want to increase teachers' efficacy in conveying information to the students in their classrooms and facilitate learning across the full range of the achievement distribution, from students with intellectual disabilities to students classified as gifted and talented. As such, educational researchers want their research to be visible to a wide range of audiences, including teachers, principals, other education professionals and, especially, policy makers, although this last group is often farthest from the minds of researchers when conducting individual studies.

It is not an exaggeration to claim that some of the most important influences on educational practice and schooling over the past century have been court decisions and laws passed by the federal government. Prominent examples include *Brown v. Board of Education* (1954), the Education for All Handicapped Children Act of 1975, the Individuals with Disabilities Education Act of 1990, and the No Child Left Behind Act (2002). Indeed, states and school districts are now beginning to make changes in response to the Every Child Succeeds Act of 2015. For example, although pre-referral intervention has been considered best practice for decades, the inclusion of response to intervention in the Individuals with Disabilities Education Improvement Act of 2004 resulted in schools and school districts taking the idea of pre-referral intervention much more seriously than had been done heretofore. Indeed, it does not matter how efficacious an intervention is if teachers and schools do not use it, as some reading researchers discovered when they could not get teachers to adopt phonics-based reading programs to help struggling students, despite years of supportive empirical evidence.

The goal of this chapter is to discuss publishing as a way to advocate for students and engage in public policy. We begin with a brief discussion of why advocacy and public policy are important considerations for educational

Why Should Educational Researchers Care About Advocacy and Public Policy?

There are several reasons why educational researchers should be concerned with advocacy and public policy. First, educational research can provide answers to questions that are important far beyond the boundaries of individual laboratories. What are the most effective ways to teach reading? What programs in elementary school reduce the probability of students dropping out in middle and high school? What are the best strategies for reducing disruptive behaviors in the classroom? Can the ethnic achievement gap be reduced or eliminated? What educational practices help students at the top of the ability distribution maximize their potential? How do we evaluate teacher effectiveness reliably and fairly? All of these are important questions as their answers have substantial implications for national educational policy. It is not difficult to think of research findings based on long-standing and rigorous programs of research with numerous replications showcasing effective practices that are not being used in classrooms and schools, or of effective programs that are being used in a school or district that are discontinued with the arrival of a new principal or superintendent as these new leaders try to make their mark on the school or district.

To the extent that researchers care about students, teachers, schools, and parents, they must become advocates for changes at the local level and they need to influence policy for changes to occur at the state and national levels. Even as this chapter was being written, the United States was in the middle of another presidential campaign, which serves as a potent reminder that lobbying and convincing individuals with the power to make things happen are integral elements of the system of governance.

Second, beyond wanting research findings to be used, it can be argued that researchers have an ethical responsibility to advocate and lobby. VandenBos (2007, p. 25) defined *advocacy* as "speaking or acting on behalf of an individual or group to uphold their rights" and noted, "in health care, advocates represent consumers to protect their rights to effective treatment." Both Division 16 (School Psychology) of the American Psychological Association (APA) and the National Association of School Psychologists (NASP) contend that helping children and families succeed as learners and become productive citizens are central to what school psychologists should be doing, and the mission of the American Educational Research Association (AERA, n.d.) is "to advance knowledge about education, to encourage scholarly inquiry related to education, and to promote the use of research to improve education and serve the public good."

Considerations when Writing for Advocacy and Public Policy

Gabel and Kamerman (2012) argued that there are five steps involved in this type of writing: knowing the audience, defining the problem, marshaling evidence, proposing policy solutions, and making recommendations. We would add several other considerations. These include choosing the problem to focus on, getting the message in front of the right audience, finding strategic partners, and not giving up if one is not successful the first time. Two additional recommendations come from "Translating Science to Policy" (2015), a document shared with APA's Council of Representatives; these include engaging key internal and external stakeholders early and often and being open to opportunities that arise. All of these principles are presented in Table 27.1 and reviewed briefly below.

Choosing the Problem

The issue of choosing the problem appears to be simple. If I am a reading researcher, then I should choose reading because that is what I know and that is what I write about. However, there are additional considerations. First, areas of research, although focused, are typically still quite broad. Is there a national conversation happening in the area? In other words, is the topic in the news or, in parlance of the internet, is the topic trending? A current example in 2016 is the mental health of veterans and the huge number of suicides that are occurring in this population. In the education arena, the issue of assessing teacher effectiveness has been in the forefront over the past few years in connection with value-added assessments and providing financial incentives to more effective teachers. If yes, what are the concerns being raised, and does your research have a clear connection to the national conversation? If there is no conversation happening more generally, is the topic a "hot" one in the field, and who are the leading researchers in the area? Are there opportunities for strategic partnerships with other researchers, agencies, foundations, or institutions?

Table 27.1 Considerations When Writing to Advocate and Influence Policy

1. Choosing the problem
2. Defining the problem
3. Knowing your audience
4. Finding strategic partners
5. Engaging stakeholders
6. Bringing evidence to bear
7. Proposing policy solutions
8. Making recommendations
9. Getting the message in front of the right audience
10. Trying again if the attempt is not successful
11. Taking advantage of opportunities that arise

292   *Worrell, Subotnik, & Olszewski-Kubilius*

Another important consideration in choosing the problem involves whether there have been recent policy developments in an area. This consideration relates to timing. If a new policy has recently been put in place that runs counter to the policy that you are intending to propose, but has not yet had an opportunity to play out or be evaluated, the probability of effecting change at that point is diminished. It is sometimes appropriate to wait for a more propitious time to propose a new policy than to propose a policy that does not get support. Always remember that, like a research agenda, policy agendas should be thought about in terms of years and not weeks and months.

Defining the Problem

Once you have chosen the problem, you need to frame the problem in a way that it will be received and understood. An article by Conoley, Conoley, Ivey, and Scheel (1991) provided an appropriate analogy for problem definition. In a vignette study, Conoley et al. showed that intervention acceptability could be increased substantially by using rationales that matched teachers' conceptualizations of the problem. Translating this finding to the policy arena means framing the policy so that it is palatable to policy makers and aligns with their agendas and public opinion.

As Plucker (2016) pointed out in a presentation to a group of researchers in gifted education, arguing that students in gifted and talented education programs, who are primarily from the upper end of the income distribution, deserve as much federal dollars as students in special education, many of whom are from low-income and ethnic minority backgrounds, is a losing proposition. If a policy maker has to choose between allocating funds to children who are gifted and children with autism, the latter will almost inevitably prevail. However, the Institute for Education Sciences might be interested in allocating funds to help identify students from low-income backgrounds and children with disabilities for gifted and talented programs, and the National Science Foundation has been funding multiple projects aimed at increasing the number of underrepresented students in the STEM fields.

Knowing the Audience

Knowing the audience is a critical reminder to researchers that policy briefs are not journal articles and should not be treated as such. First, they need to be considerably shorter—usually a few pages—and very accessible, as the primary audience consists of individuals who are not experts in the field and who do not want to become experts. Members of Congress and their aides, who are the ones more likely to read policy briefs, want to know (a) what the issue is, (b) how it fits in with the legislator's priorities, (c) what the policy recommendation is, and (d) the strength of the evidence that can be marshaled in support of the policy recommendation. Development officers and public relations personnel in institutions are sometimes better at providing feedback on these types of documents than faculty colleagues.

Finding Strategic Partners and Engaging Key Stakeholders

Just as projects are often more successful when there are teams of researchers involved, strategic partners and key stakeholders can play an important role in writing papers intended to advocate for and influence public policy. Several votes are always more persuasive than one vote in dealing with elected officials, and partners bring additional networks and resources to a project. Partners can also bring different perspectives that help make the case for the policy stronger. However, it is also important to be careful in choosing a partner, as a strategic partner with a negative reputation can reduce rather than enhance your chances of success. Relatedly, engaging key stakeholders early and often increases the probability that they will become a partner in the enterprise rather than a group trying to get an alternative proposal adopted that is in competition with the one you are working on.

The AERA, the APA, and the NASP often team up to write joint or coordinated statements when there are important policy discussions affecting education and schooling, and these associations can be strategic partners with individual researchers on issues that are of relevance to them. All of these organizations have committees and task forces with particular foci that can be key stakeholders and one way to get an organization involved is to reach out to a specific organizational subgroup (see, e.g., www.aera.net/About-AERA/ Organizational-Structure-and-Governance; http://apa.org/about/governance/ bdcmte/index.aspx). Professional service in organizations is useful in this regard, as individuals who have served on committees related to their research agendas have the advantage of knowing the types of issues the groups address as well as the advantage of being known by members of the organization and committee.

Professional organizations also belong to coalitions that can also become strategic partners if the issue is important and general enough. For example, AERA, APA, and the Society for Research on Child Development are members of the Consortium of Social Science Organizations (COSSA). In addition to the 17 members, COSSA also has several affiliate groups including other professional associations, national centers, and colleges and universities (www.cossa.org/members/). Professional associations also have offices and staff dedicated to advocacy and public policy as well as resources specifically related to advocacy (e.g., www.nasponline.org/research-and-policy/ advocacy-tools-and-resources). Thus, organizational affiliations are extremely useful in the advocacy role.

Marshaling Evidence

Reliable evidence leading to valid inferences should be at the core of every call for a change in policy that researchers make. Thus, advocacy or changes in public policy should not be based on a single study, but on a preponderance of evidence in a field. Although the policy brief or advocacy paper is brief and accessible, it needs to be based on evidence in the extant literature. Table 27.2

294 Worrell, Subotnik, & Olszewski-Kubilius

Table 27.2 Non-Exhaustive List of Journals that Influence Policy in Education and Psychology

Journals Publishing Reviews
   American Psychologist
   Educational Psychologist
   Psychological Bulletin
   Psychological Review
   Review of Educational Research

Journals Publishing Articles with Policy Implications
   American Educational Research Journal
   Analyses of Social Issues and Public Policy
   Educational Evaluation and Policy Analysis
   Educational Researcher
   Journal of Disability Policy Studies
   Journal of Policy and Practice in Intellectual Disabilities
   Journal of Public Health Policy
   Policy Insights in the Behavioral and Brain Sciences
   Psychological Science in the Public Interest
   Psychology, Public Policy, and Law
   Science
   Theory Into Practice

contains a non-exhaustive list of journals in education and psychology that publish policy articles or articles with policy implications. Several of these journals publish review articles, which provide comprehensive summaries of literature and sometimes policy recommendations based on the research summarized. Other journals in the table are ones that publish articles with policy implications. One does not have to be an author of an article to use it in support of a position. However, one useful strategy is to write a research paper with advocacy in mind. Thus, the paper that you write for a traditional journal or book chapter is the first part of a longer-term agenda that includes advocating and influencing policy.

It is also important to recognize that a preponderance of evidence does not mean that all of the available studies are aligned; rather, it means that the field has enough evidence to come to a general consensus (e.g., the use of behavioral interventions for externalizing disorders or teaching phonemic awareness to young children with decoding difficulties). In summarizing the evidence, one should also be able to make some predictions about the impact of the policies, and these decisions should be based on effect sizes and not statistical significance. Hattie (2009) suggested that an effect size of 0.40 signals meaningful differences in educational achievement.

Proposing Policy Solutions

A research conclusion does not necessarily translate into a public policy. Policies are broad-based and intended to affect populations and typically have costs and tradeoffs associated with them. In proposing policy solutions, it is important to articulate the potential costs as well as the potential benefits, and show, ideally, that the benefits will offset the costs fiscally and otherwise. It is also useful to anticipate possible unintended consequences. The legalization of marijuana use for medical and recreational use in several jurisdictions has resulted in the recognition that there is no systematic way to assess the amount of tetrahydrocannabinol (THC) in the system as we do with alcohol, concomitant with a growing concern by critics about the possible increase in individuals driving under the influence.

Making Recommendations

Specific recommendations for action provide the underpinning of the broad-based policy that one wants enacted. Again, consultation provides a useful analogy here. Recommendations should be clear, feasible, and cost-effective in terms of fiscal and other resources, and there should also be recommendations for evaluation metrics to determine if the policy is working. The recommendations should also be framed in terms indicating how they will be operationalized.

Getting the Message in Front of the Right Audience

Once you have your cogent policy brief with appropriate policy implications and specific recommendations, you need to get it in front of the appropriate audiences such as school boards, state legislators, or members of Congress. There are a number of ways in which these messages can be delivered. Ideally, you can have an in-person meeting with a member of your school board or with a legislator. In the case of the latter, you are often more likely to meet with an aide. These meetings can be in the local constituency office or at their state or national offices. It is important to recognize that although the aide might be someone who is a young adult, this person needs to be treated with respect as this aide will decide if your policy brief gets in front of the legislator for whom she is working. Ideally, you want to get your policy recommendation to as many policy makers as you can, and it is at this stage that strategic partners and professional organizations can be of tremendous assistance. If several people and organizations are communicating the same message to multiple legislators at the same time, there is a greater chance that the policy will gain traction and be enacted.

The media—traditional and social—can also play a role here. You can write an OpEd piece for a newspaper, *Education Week*, or the wide variety of online magazines that currently exist, although you have to "pitch" your story and hope that the outlet decides to take it up. Tweeting is another way of getting

296   Worrell, Subotnik, & Olszewski-Kubilius

your message out to a wide variety of audiences and can result in the message being picked up by news outlets and other media. It is important that the key messages are maintained across all of these platforms, so that the outlets intensify rather than dilute the message.

Making Multiple Attempts to Get the Message Out

Much like publishing, there is no guarantee that initial endeavors at getting an advocacy message out will be successful. Legislators might be busy with other priorities and strategic partners and other institutions might be working on other policy agendas that they do not want to displace. Although your policy message could be crucial, it might not yet have enough resonance to gain traction. Getting the message in front of multiple audiences is one way to keep the message alive as you continue to work to get it in front of the right audience. Moreover, even if one succeeds in getting a new policy passed, getting it implemented requires ongoing engagement in the process. Thus, the advocacy process continues (e.g., via strategic engagement with key stakeholders, supporting articles aimed at audiences that the policy is aimed at, and so on).

Taking Advantage of Opportunities that Arise

Many opportunities that come one's way are not planned—they are the result of chance or serendipity—but these opportunities can sometimes provide a springboard for advocacy efforts if they are recognized and taken advantage of. Austin (1978) articulated four types of chance. The third type is chance that your prior preparation allows you to take advantage of, and individuals wanting to have an impact on policy should always be alert to these types of chance encounters.

Some Examples

We now present brief overviews of examples of writing that influenced policy, showcasing some of the recommendations that we have mentioned. It should become clear that there are multiple pathways to having an impact and there is also an element of chance involved in the process.

Facilitating Federal Funding to Gifted and Talented Education

In 2011, Subotnik, Olszewski-Kubilius, and Worrell published a monograph entitled "Rethinking giftedness and gifted education: A proposed direction forward based on psychological science" in *Psychological Science in the Public Interest*. The goal of this monograph was to provide an integrated conceptualization of giftedness and gifted education across multiple domains (e.g., academics, athletics, and the visual and performing arts) and provide guidance for the field and, potentially, policy makers. Some of the key messages in the monograph were that (a) general and domain-specific abilities are important, (b) society should provide opportunities for talent development to all students, (c) individuals need to take advantage of the talent development opportunities that they are given, (d) psychosocial factors (e.g., task commitment and perseverance) play an important role in translating potential into manifest talent, and (e) eminence was the end result of gifted education in fully developed talents. To facilitate getting the main points to multiple audiences, the Subotnik et al. monograph included a two-page summary at the beginning of the piece, a two-page conclusion reiterating the main points, and a three-page set of questions for the researchers in the field to consider.

The authors then created and accepted opportunities to get the message out to a variety of audiences. On the "creation" side, the authors published blog posts and magazine articles aimed at a general audience that highlighted one or more of these messages (e.g., Subotnik et al., 2012b, 2014; Worrell, Olszewski-Kubilius, & Subotnik, 2012b). They also accepted the opportunity offered by the editors of *Gifted Child Quarterly*, the leading journal in the field, to contribute to a 2012 special issue on the monograph guest-edited by two leading scholars (Plucker & Callahan, 2012). The authors wrote a condensed version of the monograph (Subotnik, Olszewski-Kubilius, & Worrell, 2012a) as well as a response (Worrell, Olszewski-Kubilius, & Subotnik, 2012a) to eight commentaries from a variety of perspectives and contexts, including Germany and Australia. Another leading scholar in gifted education wrote a blog commending the article for its substantial contribution to the field of gifted education, but taking issue with the point about eminence (see Borland, 2012), and the authors responded to that blog post (Subotnik, Olszewski-Kubilius, & Worrell, 2012c). The authors also received comments from colleagues about posts and discussions on Facebook—not all of which were positive.

However, the end result was a considerable amount of "buzz" about the piece. In 2014, a call came out from the Institute of Education Sciences for the creation of the National Research Center on Gifted Education with a specific focus on identifying low-income minority students, and the Subotnik et al. (2011) monograph was used as a reference in support of the call for the National Research Center. This multi-million dollar Center, which is now housed at the University of Connecticut, is identifying school districts that are providing quality gifted education opportunities to underserved students. Thus, although the Subotnik et al. monograph did not bring the Center into being, its prominence, magnified by the other articles, resulted in it having an impact on the direction of the call that resulted in the Center's creation.

This outcome showcases many of the points made earlier. The choice of gifted education was timely, given the growing concerns in the gifted education community about No Child Left Behind not serving the educational needs of the most talented learners (Plucker, Burroughs, & Song, 2010; Plucker, Hardesty, & Burroughs, 2013). The Subotnik et al. (2011) monograph both defined the problem and summarized the psychological evidence, including engaging with books on the subject written for general audiences (e.g., Gladwell, 2008). And although the monograph did not make policy recommendations, it raised provocative questions with implications for policy and research, questions which were communicated as part of an advocacy agenda to a number of audiences in shorter, less technical pieces.

It is worth noting that the monograph's messages continue to be sought after and crafted for multiple audiences, including licensed psychologists (Worrell, Subotnik, & Olszewski-Kubilius, 2013), counselors (Olszewski-Kubilius, Subotnik, & Worrell, 2015b), and researchers in other national contexts (e.g., Olszewski-Kubilius, Subotnik, & Worrell, 2015a, 2015c; Subotnik, Olszewski-Kubilius, & Worrell, 2015; Worrell, 2014). After all, the need for educational policies supporting gifted and talented students continues.

Contributing to the Quality of Teacher Training Programs through Strategic Partnership

As the debates were happening about if and how to best evaluate in-service teachers, there was also a re-alignment occurring in the world of teacher education. The two major agencies that accredited teacher training programs—the National Council for Accreditation of Teacher Education and the Teacher Education Accreditation Council—were consolidated into a single unit, the Council for the Accreditation of Educator Preparation (CAEP). One of CAEP's major goals was increasing the effectiveness of teaching candidates at the pre-service stage, and ultimately raising the standards of in-service teachers, thus addressing the calls for greater accountability of teachers. In working toward this goal, CAEP reached out to the Board of Educational Affairs of APA, and a task force was formed, with CAEP's support, to review the ways in which in-service teachers are evaluated and to provide recommendations for how the best of these practices could be translated into the evaluation of pre-service teachers.

The issue of accountability in teacher education is not a trivial one. The fact that very few teacher preparation programs lose their accreditation alongside the increase in alternative teacher education programs such as Teach for America has raised questions about the utility of university-based teacher education: Is teacher education effective or necessary? Thus, this project was quite timely. The fact that policy makers in several states and at the federal level were starting to pay attention to teacher accountability heightened the sense of urgency for the document, as bad policy made in the absence of data and consultation can be worse than no policy at all. Thus, this report answered several explicit recommendations intended for policy-maker consumption: (a) what are the current methods of teacher accountability systems in use, (b) what does the extant literature say about these methods, and (c) under what conditions can and should they be used?

The three methods that were reviewed included value-added assessments, teacher observations, and surveys of teachers, teacher supervisors and

Engaging in Advocacy 299

principals, and students. The initial report (Worrell et al., 2014) was sent to a diverse set of stakeholders in teacher education, including the National Council on Measurement in Education, the National Center for Education Statistics, WestEd, the Southern Regional Education Board, the Carnegie Foundation, the Council of Chief State School Officers, the American Association for Colleges of Teacher Education, and the United States Department of Education, among others, for input and comments. It was also circulated to relevant APA Boards and Committees at APA (e.g., the Board of Educational Affairs and the Committee on Psychological Tests and Assessment) as well as to CAEP's Commission on Standards and Performance Reporting.

Feedback from these groups was incorporated into the final report. As the report was intended for policy makers, the four major sections were short, ranging from two to ten pages. In addition there was a one-page abstract, a two-page executive summary incorporating 13 recommendations, a two-page section on cross-cutting themes, and a more detailed presentation of recommendations with explanatory text consisting of three pages. CAEP accepted the report, and it informed the development of the CAEP standards under which schools are accredited; educator preparation programs are explicitly referred to the report in Standard 4 on Program Impact. Moreover, as timing was essential, the task force also worked to get this project through APA's cumbersome and often lengthy approval process and succeeded in getting the report approved within a year of its completion.

This case exemplifies several of the principles outlined in Table 27.1; some of the most notable in this case include taking advantage of an opportunity (CAEP's request) and involving strategic partners and key stakeholders early in the process, both in the partnership with CAEP and in the solicitation of feedback on the initial draft from a wide number of stakeholders. As part of the process of continuing to build support in the broader education community, (a) presentations were made to CAEP (Worrell, 2013) and at a CAEP conference for teacher education professionals (Worrell, 2015), (b) a short article was written for *Education Week* (Brabeck & Worrell, 2014), and (c) a longer article was recently published in *Theory into Practice* (Brabeck et al., 2016). Also note that different members of the task force took the lead on different dissemination tasks.

Ongoing Efforts

Much of the writing that we do can provide an opportunity for advocacy. Wai and Worrell (2016) were invited to publish an article on gifted education in *Policy Insights in the Behavioral and Brain Sciences*. In addition to writing in user-friendly less-jargon-laced language and limiting article length to eight published pages, that journal, which is distributed to legislators when it comes out, also requires that the authors provide both a tweet to be sent out when the article is published and bullets summarizing the main points and included just after the abstract. This article provided another chance to highlight the

300 *Worrell, Subotnik, & Olszewski-Kubilius*

importance of funding gifted and talented education programs for disadvantaged and underrepresented students. When the article came out online first, the lead author pitched a short piece on the article to an online magazine, *medium.com*, which picked up the piece (Wai & Worrell, 2015). The piece at *medium.com* was then pitched to several other online sources, and versions of it were published by several other outlets, including *The National Review*, *The Huffington Post*, *Quartz*, *The Conversation*, and the University of California's newsroom. Similar efforts are under way with regard to the benefits of competition in schools (see Worrell et al., 2016; Worrell & Subotnik, 2016).

Conclusion

As we have articulated, there are several general principles that increase the probability that one's writing can result in effective advocacy or effecting policy changes. Just as we find a gap in the literature on a topic of interest in advancing our research agenda, we can find gaps in the policy agenda that our research speaks to. Carefully articulating our research findings to important policy challenges, providing cogent and compelling summaries of the literature that speak to those policy challenges, working with partners, and actively promoting our policy agenda with key stakeholders can result in our work moving from the ivory tower into the real world with potential benefits to children, youth, and families. So in the traditions of the science-practitioner or public intellectual, we encourage you to go forth and advocate.

References

American Educational Research Association. (n.d.). About AERA: Our mission. Retrieved from www.aera.net/About-AERA

Austin, J. H. (1978). *Chase, chance, and creativity: The lucky art of novelty*. New York, NY: Columbia University Press.

Borland, J. H. (2012). A landmark monograph in gifted education, and why I disagree with its major conclusion. *The Creativity Post*. Retrieved from www.creativitypost. com/education/a_landmark_monograph_in_gifted_education_and_why_i_ disagree_with_its_major#.T-OjjcRvzWI.twitter

Brabeck, M. M., Dwyer, C. A., Geisinger, K. F., Marx, R. W., Noell, G. H., Pianta, R. C., et al. (2016). Assessing the assessments of teacher preparation. *Theory into Practice*, 55, 160–167. doi: 10.1080/00405841.2015.1036667

Brabeck, M., & Worrell, F. C. (2014, November). Best practices for assessing teacher education programs. *Education Week*, 34(11), 24–25. Retrieved from www.edweek. org/ew/articles/2014/11/05/11brabeck.h34.html

Brown v. Board of Education. 347 U.S. 483 (1954).

Conoley, C. W., Conoley, J. C., Ivey, D. C., & Scheel, M. J. (1991). Enhancing consultation by matching the consultee's perspectives. *Journal of Counseling and Development*, 69, 546–549.

Education for all Handicapped Children Act of 1975, Pub. L. 94-142 (20 U.S.C. and 34 C.F.R.).

Engaging in Advocacy 301

Every Student Succeeds Act of 2015, Pub. L. No. 114-95, C. F. R. Stat. 1802 (2015).

Gabel, S. G., & Kamerman, S. B. (2012). Getting the policy message across to diverse audiences. In W. Green & B. Levy Simon (Eds.), *The Columbia guide to social work writing* (pp. 133–151). New York, NY: Columbia University Press.

Gladwell, M. (2008). *Outliers: The story of success.* New York, NY: Little, Brown, & Company.

Hattie, J. (2009). *Visible learning: A synthesis of over 800 meta-analyses relating to achievement.* New York, NY: Routledge.

Individuals with Disabilities Education Act of 1990, 20 U.S.C. §1400 (1990).

Individuals with Disabilities Education Improvement Act of 2004, 20 U.S.C. § 1400 *et seq.* (2004).

No Child Left Behind (NCLB) Act of 2001, Pub. L. No. 107-110, § 115, Stat. 1425 (2002).

Olszewski-Kubilius, P., Subotnik, R. F., & Worrell, F. C. (2015a). Antecedent and concurrent psychosocial skills that support high levels of achievement within talent domains. *High Ability Studies, 26,* 195–210. doi: 10.1080/13598139.2015.1095077

Olszewski-Kubilius, P., Subotnik, R. F., & Worrell, F. C. (2015b). Conceptualizations of giftedness and the development of talent: Implications for counselors. *Journal of Counseling and Development, 93,* 143–152. doi: 10.1002/j.1556-6676.2015.00190.x

Olszewski-Kubilius, P., Subotnik, R. F., & Worrell, F. C. (2015c). Rethinking giftedness: A developmental approach. *Revista de Educación, 368,* 245–267. doi: 10.4438/1988-592X-RE-2015-368-297

Plucker, J. A. (2016, April). *Blazing new trails: Strengthening policy research in gifted education.* Paper presented at the inaugural European-North American Summit on Talent Development, Washington, DC.

Plucker, J. A., & Callahan, F. C. (2012). Introduction to the special issue. *Gifted Child Quarterly, 56,* 174. doi: 10.1177/0016986212456078

Plucker, J. A., Burroughs, N., & Song, R. (2010). *Mind the (other) gap!* Bloomington: Center for Evaluation and Education Policy, Indiana University.

Plucker, J. A., Hardesty, J., & Burroughs, N. (2013). *Talent on the sidelines: Excellence gaps and America's persistent talent underclass.* Storrs, CT: Center for education Policy Analysis, Neag School of Education, University of Connecticut.

Subotnik, R. F., Olszewski-Kubilius, P., & Worrell, F. C. (2011). Rethinking giftedness and gifted education: A proposed direction forward based on psychological science. *Psychological Science in the Public Interest, 12,* 3–54. doi: 10.1177/1529100611418056

Subotnik, R. F., Olszewski-Kubilius, P., & Worrell, F. C. (2012a). A proposed direction forward for gifted education based on psychological science. *Gifted Child Quarterly, 56,* 176–188. doi: 10.1177/0016986212456079

Subotnik, R. F., Olszewski-Kubilius, P., & Worrell, F. C. (2012b, November/December). Nurturing the young genius. *Scientific American Mind,* 50–57.

Subotnik, R. F., Olszewski-Kubilius, P., & Worrell, F. C. (2012c, July). Response to Borland: In defense of eminence as an outcome of gifted education. *The Creativity Post.* Retrieved from www.creativitypost.com/education/response_to_borland_in_defense_of_eminence_as_an_outcome_of_gifted_educatio

Subotnik, R. F., Olszewski-Kubilius, P., & Worrell, F. C. (2014, August). The talent gap. The U.S. is neglecting its most promising science students. *Scientific American, 13.* Retrieved from www.scientificamerican.com/article/the-u-s-neglects-its-best-science-students/

Subotnik, R. F., Olszewski-Kubilius, P., & Worrell, F. C. (2015). From traditional perspectives on giftedness to embracing talent development: A transition based on scholarship in psychological science. *Psychologia Wychowawcza* [Educational Psychology], 8, 9–19. doi: 10.5604/00332860.1178580

Translating science to policy: Council's work as a strategic policy body. (2015, February). Unpublished manuscript.

VandenBos, G. R. (Ed.). (2007). *APA dictionary of psychology.* Washington, DC: American Psychological Association.

Wai, J., & Worrell, F. C. (2015, October). Why are we supporting everyone except our most talented students? *Medium.com.* Retrieved from https://medium.com/bright/why-are-we-supporting-everyone-except-our-most-talented-students-d122ab08bad4#.neg9m4uo7

Wai, J., & Worrell, F. C. (2016). Helping disadvantaged and spatially talented students fulfill their potential: Related and neglected national resources. *Policy Insights from the Behavioral and Brain Sciences, 3,* 122–128. doi: 10.1177/2372732215621310

Worrell, F. C. (2013, June). *Evaluating teacher education programs using psychological science.* Presentation to the Council for the Accreditation of Education Preparation's (CAEP) Commission on Standards and Performance Reporting, Washington, DC.

Worrell, F. C. (2014, September). *Giftedness and gifted education in the digital age: Continuities and discontinuities.* Invited address presented at the 14th international European Council for High Ability Conference (Rethinking giftedness: Giftedness in the digital age), Ljubljana, Slovenia.

Worrell, F. C. (2015, September). *Assessing and evaluating teacher preparation programs: APA task force report.* Invited session at Council for the Accreditation of Educator Programs Conference (CAEPCON; A Continuous Improvement Mindset), Washington, DC.

Worrell, F. C., Brabeck, M. M., Dwyer, C. A., Geisinger, K. F., Marx, R. W., Noell, G. H., & Pianta, R. C. (2014). *Assessing and evaluating teacher education programs.* Washington, DC: American Psychological Association.

Worrell, F. C., Knotek, S. E., Plucker, J. A., Portenga, S., Simonton, D. K., Olszewski-Kubilius, P., et al. (2016). Competition's role in developing psychological strength and outstanding performance. *Review of General Psychology, 20,* 259–271.

Worrell, F. C., Olszewski-Kubilius, P., & Subotnik, R. F. (2012a). Important issues, some rhetoric, and a few straw men: A response to comments on "Rethinking Giftedness and Gifted Education." *Gifted Child Quarterly, 56,* 224–231. doi: 10.1177/0016986212456080

Worrell, F. C., Olszewski-Kubilius, P., & Subotnik, R. F. (2012b, November). Where are the gifted minorities [Web log message]? Retrieved from http://blogs.scientificamerican.com/streams-of-consciousness/2012/11/02/where-are-the-gifted-minorities/

Worrell, F. C., & Subotnik, R. F. (2016, July 27). Let's re-introduce competition into our classrooms. *The Education Gadfly Weekly, 16*(30). Retrieved from https://edexcellence.net/articles/lets-re-introduce-competition-into-our-classrooms?mc_cid=5050071c01&mc_eid=953c412e24

Worrell, F. C., Subotnik, R. F., & Olszewski-Kubilius, P. (2013, Spring). Giftedness and gifted education: Reconceptualizing the role of professional psychology. *The Register Report, 39,* 14–22.

Index

advocacy 234, 236, 289–300
author note 46, 53, 72–3
authorship credit 47, 70–2

books, publishing: advice 250–1; commercial publishers 246, 247–50; self-publishing 246
books, reference 4, 25–6

copyright law: agreements 75, 77, 258, 260; online posting policies 74–9; SHERPA/RoMEO 75–6, 77–9; violations 64, 74–5

English language: editing services 103, 124–5, 143; writing 30, 89, 94–5, 103, 124–5
ethics: data verification 73; duplicate publications 64; institutional approval 46–7, 63; piecemeal publications 64–6; plagiarism 66–70; publication credit, see authorship credit

impact factors: assessment journals 170–5; behavioral journals 163; clinical journals 204–9; developmental psychology journals 218–22; educational psychology and education journals, 183–6; *Journal of School Psychology* 85; literacy journals 196–200; measurement journals 175–9; metrics 33–43; overview 32–3; pediatric journals 207, 210–11; school psychology journals 37–42; *School Psychology Quarterly* 105; selecting journals 39–43, 183, 186, 196–7, 201, 202, 214–15; special education journals, 191–7
international perspectives: authors 85, 94–5, 102–3, 107, 120, 127–8, 130,

135, 143, 196, 201; *International Journal of School & Educational Psychology* 133–7; International School Psychology Association 229; *School Psychology International* 97–104

journal operations: *Canadian Journal of School Psychology* 122; considering when selecting a journal 30–1; *Contemporary School Psychology* 129; *International Journal of School & Educational Psychology* 135; *Journal of Applied School Psychology* 141; *Journal of School Psychology* 86; *Psychology in the Schools* 93–4; *School Psychology Forum* 148; *School Psychology International* 99; *School Psychology Quarterly* 109; *School Psychology Review* 116; *Trainers' Forum* 154
journals, submitting to: recommendations from editors 87–9, 94–6, 100–4, 110–11, 117–18, 123–5, 130–1, 135–6, 142–3, 149–50, 155–6; special (themed or special topic) issues 29, 87, 92, 98, 99, 108, 115, 121, 123, 128, 134, 149, 150; submission (cover) letter 46, 47, 63, 64, 66, 72, 92, 111, 130, 179, 180; web submission portals 45–6, 120, 124

manuscript formatting: Introduction, Method, Results, and Discussion (IMRAD) 8–10; masking to ensure a blind review 48; supplemental material 47, 102, 121, 145, 146

newsletters: *Communiqué* 117, 150, 229–31, 234–7; *The School Psychologist* 229–34; *World-Go-Round* 229

304 Index

peer review: editorial board composition 31–4; manuscript processing and editorial decisions 49–53, 97, 124–5, 148, 153, 232–3; responding to, see reviewer feedback

plagiarism: definition 66; plagiarism detection programs 68–70; self-plagiarism 48, 67–8

practice, implications for: publication outlets 45, 89, 95, 101, 103, 111, 114, 117, 139, 143–9, 224–5; writing the Discussion section 10, 26, 58, 103, 117, 143, 272, 280–1

public policy 291–6

ResearchGate 74–9

reviewer feedback; coping with 53–4; responding to 54–60

school psychology publications: journals 22–6; newsletters 117, 150, 229–37

scientific perspectives: nature of science 265–8; reporting 268–72

submission (cover) letter 46, 47, 63, 64, 66, 72, 92, 111, 130, 179, 180

test, publishing: commercial publishing 254–60; public domain publishing 254

writing process: proofreading and editing 7–8, 15–17, 60, 95, 103, 124–5, 143, 167; reference management 11–13, 215; stages of writing 5–8

writing resources: books 4, 17, 25–6; checklists 9, 10, 232; Journal Article Reporting Standards (JARS) 9–11, 88, 103, 181, 283; *Publication Manual of the American Psychological Association* 9, 13, 92, 95, 117, 120, 143, 236